SHADES *of* SHEOL

SHADES *of* SHEOL

DEATH AND AFTERLIFE IN THE OLD TESTAMENT

Philip S. Johnston

APOLLOS

IVP

InterVarsity Press
Downers Grove, Illinois 60515

APOLLOS (an imprint of Inter-Varsity Press)
38 De Montfort Street, Leicester LE1 7GP, England
Email: ivp@uccf.org.uk
Website: www.ivpbooks.com

INTERVARSITY PRESS
PO Box 1400, Downers Grove, Illinois 60515, USA
World Wide Web: www.ivpress.com
Email: mail@ivpress.com

First published 2002

British Library Cataloguing in Publication Data
A catalogue record for this book is available from the British Library.

UK ISBN 0-85111-266-8

Library of Congress Cataloguing-in-Publication Data
This data has been requested.

US ISBN 0-8308-2687-4

Set in Adobe Garamond 11/13pt
Typeset in Great Britain by Servis Filmsetting Ltd, Manchester
Printed and bound in Great Britain by Creative Print and Design Group (Wales), Ebbw Vale

Contents

ABBREVIATIONS

Bible versions

AV	*Authorized (King James) Version*
JB	*Jerusalem Bible* (London: DLT, 1966)
JPS	*Tanakh* (Philadelphia: JPS, 1985)
NEB	*New English Bible* (Oxford: OUP, 1970)
NIV	*New International Version* (London: H & S, 1979)
NJB	*New Jerusalem Bible* (London: DLT, 1985)
NRSV	*New Revised Standard Version* (Oxford: OUP, 1989)
REB	*Revised English Bible* (Oxford: OUP, 1989)
RSV	*Revised Standard Version* (London: OUP, 1952)
RV	*Revised Version* (Oxford: OUP, 1885)

General

ABD	D. N. Freedman et al. (eds.), *The Anchor Bible Dictionary* (New York: Doubleday, 1992)
AHw	W. von Soden (ed.), *Akkadisches Handwörterbuch* (Wiesbaden: Otto Harrassowitz, 1965–81)
ANET	J. B. Pritchard (ed.), *Ancient Near Eastern Texts Relating to the Old Testament* (Princeton: Princeton UP, ^{3}1969)
ARM	*Archives Royales de Mari* (Paris: Imprimerie Nationale – Paul Geuthner, 1950–)

ARTU	J. C. de Moor, *An Anthology of Religious Texts from Ugarit* (Leiden: Brill, 1987)
BDB	F. Brown, S. R. Driver and C. A. Briggs, *Hebrew and English Lexicon of the Old Testament* (Oxford: OUP, 1907)
BHS	K. Elliger and W. Rudolf (eds.), *Biblia Hebraica Stuttgartensia* (Stuttgart: Deutsche Bibelgesellschaft, 1983)
CAD	A. L. Oppenheim and E. Reiner (eds.), *The Assyrian Dictionary* (Chicago: Oriental Institute, 1956–)
CARTU	J. C. de Moor and K. Spronk, *A Cuneiform Anthology of Religious Texts from Ugarit* (Leiden: Brill, 1987)
CML	J. C. L. Gibson, *Canaanite Myths and Legends* (Edinburgh: T. & T. Clark, [2]1978 [[1]1956])
DBS	L. Pirot et al. (eds.), *Supplément au Dictionnaire de la Bible* (Paris: Letouzey & Ané, 1928–)
DCH	D. J. A. Clines (ed.), *The Dictionary of Classical Hebrew* (Sheffield: SAP, 1993–)
DDD	K. van der Toorn, B. Becking and P. W. van der Horst (eds.), *Dictionary of Deities and Demons in the Bible* (Leiden: Brill, [2]1999 [[1]1995])
ES	A. Even-Shoshan, *A New Concordance of the Bible* (Jerusalem: Kiryat-Sefer, [2]1989)
GK	W. Gesenius and E. Kautzsch, *Hebrew Grammar* (Oxford: OUP, [2]1910; German original [28]1909)
HAL	W. Baumgartner and J. J. Stamm (eds.), *Hebräisches und aramäisches Lexicon zum Alten Testament* (Leiden: Brill, 1967–90)
ISBE	G. W. Bromiley et al. (eds.), *The International Standard Bible Encyclopedia* (Grand Rapids: Eerdmans, 1979–88)
KAI	H. Donner and W. Rollig, *Kanaanäische und aramäische Inschriften* (Wiesbaden: Otto Harrassowitz, [2]1966–9 [[1]1962–4])
KB	L. Köhler and W. Baumgartner, *Lexicon in Veteris Testamenti Libros* (Leiden: Brill, 1953)
KTU	M. Dietrich, O. Loretz and J. Sanmartín, *Die keilalphabetischen Texte aus Ugarit* (AOAT 24/1, Neukirchen-Vluyn: Neukirchener, 1976)
LXX	The Septuagint
MEE	*Materiali epigrafici di Ebla* (Naples: Instituto Universitario Orientale di Napoli, 1979–82)
NIDNTT	C. Brown (ed.), *New International Dictionary of New Testament Theology* (Exeter: Paternoster, 1975–8)

NIDOTTE	W. A. VanGemeren (ed.), *New International Dictionary of Old Testament Theology and Exegesis* (Carlisle: Paternoster, 1997)
RLA	E. Ebeling, B. Meissner et al. (eds.), *Reallexikon der Assyriologie* (Berlin: de Gruyter, 1927–)
RSP	S. Rummel (ed.), *Ras Shamra Parallels*, 3 (AnOr 51, Rome: PBI, 1981)
TDOT	G. J. Botterweck and H. Ringgren (eds.), *Theological Dictionary of the Old Testament* (Grand Rapids: Eerdmans, 1974–)
THAT	E. Jenni and C. Westermann (eds.), *Theologisches Handwörterbuch zum Alten Testament* (Munich: Chr. Kaiser, 1971–6)
TO	A. Caquot, M. Sznycer and A. Herdner, *Textes Ougaritiques*, Vol. 1 (Paris: Le Cerf, 1974); A. Caquot, J.-M. de Tarragon and J.-L. Cunchillos, *Textes Ougaritiques*, Vol. 2 (Paris: Le Cerf, 1989)
TWAT	G. J. Botterweck and H. Ringgren (eds.), *Theologisches Wörterbuch zum Alten Testament* (Stuttgart: W. Kohlhammer, 1970–)
TWOT	R. L. Harris, G. L. Archer and B. K. Waltke (eds.), *Theological Wordbook of the Old Testament* (Chicago: Moody, 1980)

Note: Abbreviations used in bibliographical details are listed on pages 241–243.

INTRODUCTION

The subject

What on earth is Sheol? What are the 'shades of Sheol'? And why devote a whole book to the subject? Well, for a start, Sheol is not on earth, the phrase 'shades of Sheol' has many connotations, and the topic has important implications for the study of Israelite religion and of biblical theology.

Sheol is the Hebrew name for the underworld, the realm of the dead located deep below the earth. There are many aspects to its shadiness. (i) The usual translation of the rare Hebrew term for the dead is 'shades' – they are the primary 'shades of Sheol'. (ii) The Hebrew Bible gives virtually no description of how the dead continued to exist in the underworld. Sheol itself was very much in the shade! (iii) Different texts suggest various views regarding where Sheol was, what it was like and who went there. So Israelites thought of Sheol in different 'shades'. (iv) Psalmists in distress talked as if they were already experiencing Sheol – it cast a long and sinister shadow over life. (v) And finally, in Christian perspective, 'Christ Jesus . . . abolished death and brought life and immortality to light through the gospel' (2 Tim. 1:10). The obvious inference is that what is now brought to light was previously in the shade. The title *Shades of Sheol* alludes to all these themes, and the book will explore them throughout the Old Testament.

But why study Sheol and its shades at all? For several reasons. First, every serious religious belief merits careful scholarly enquiry in and of itself, and this must be undertaken in relation to the faith's world-view, its cultural context and its development over time. It should be understood empathetically and yet assessed dispassionately. So this study seeks to understand and assess Israelite views on Sheol in relation to their own beliefs, culture and history, and those of neighbouring peoples. At the very least, this study should broaden our religious and historical knowledge.

Secondly, death is a constant of all human societies, whatever their location in time and place, and whatever their language and culture. The study of how the ancient Hebrews understood and responded to death may add to our own understanding of life and response to death, and so contribute directly to contemporary society, especially since much of it developed from a Judeo-Christian world-view.

Thirdly, for Judaism in general and practising Jews in particular, the Hebrew texts remain authoritative and prescriptive to various degrees. However, Judaism has developed beyond its foundational documents, with other early Jewish writing and later tradition containing a much more developed eschatology. Thus it is of inherent interest to examine the treatment of death in the Hebrew Bible itself. And in the Christian Bible these texts are complemented by the New Testament, which has its own distinctive and much richer view of life after death. In most Christian theology, the perspective of the Old Testament is qualified and augmented by that of the New. So the continuity and discontinuity of Israelite with Christian belief deserves study.

However, this leads immediately to a serious problem. The Old and New Testament perspectives on human fate after death are significantly different. Indeed, for many scholars they are not just distinctive but actually contradictory. Thus in the Hebrew Bible the good and the bad alike are destined for Sheol, but in later Jewish texts and Christian Scriptures the righteous and the unrighteous await opposite destinies in heaven and hell. On the one hand, scholars usually explain this difference historically, by the largely intertestamental development of belief in resurrection and in future reward and punishment. But they seldom assess it theologically. On the other hand, traditional Judaism and Christianity have reduced the theological diversity by reading later eschatology back into the earlier Hebrew texts. This resolves the tension, but at the cost of inappropriate exegesis. This study purposely attempts to read and examine the Hebrew Bible in its own cultural and religious setting, without importing later concepts.

And fourthly, there is very little recent detailed study of the topic. Most reference works and many journals carry short articles on 'Death in the Old Testament', and a number of books deal with specific aspects of the topic. These will be noted below in relevant chapters. But there has been little attempt to provide a detailed synthesis since that of Martin-Achard, first published in 1956, nearly half a century ago. Since then there have been enormous developments in the study of the archaeology of Israel and the texts of neighbouring countries, particularly those of Ugarit. The present work seeks to integrate this new material in its re-examination of the age-old topic of death and the afterlife.

By its own records, ancient Israel was a small Semitic group, of no great significance in the fertile crescent numerically or politically (except for the brief period of the Davidic empire). It had many affinities with its neighbours in language, social customs and traditions. For instance, burial in Israel was probably similar to burial in many of the surrounding nations (see Ch. 2.b). So it is vital to set any study of ancient Israel in this wider context, as this study consistently attempts to do. But it also had some marked differences.

Many scholars now suggest that early Israel's religious beliefs were very similar to those of her neighbours throughout much of the Old Testament period, until the development of exclusive, monotheistic Yahwism in the late monarchic and exilic periods. It is certainly true that there were common religious concepts, as with the teraphim in the homes of Laban and David (see further Ch. 8.c.i). Yet the records of early Israel portray a society for which Yahwism was or should have been the norm, unlike her neighbours. This approach therefore assumes that texts dealing with early Israel were written much later, and that they retroject a later orthodoxy back into earlier, more pluralist times, by expunging the unorthodox elements from the early traditions. For example, many scholars now suggest that consulting and venerating the dead were accepted elements of Yahwism until the reforms of Hezekiah and Josiah (see Chs. 7 and 8).

However, there are strong counter-arguments to this approach. In general, the complementary but non-uniform nature of many texts (e.g. Joshua and Judges; Samuel and Kings) suggests that they accurately portray their respective periods, rather than being a product of a later doctrinaire orthodoxy. And the detail seems to confirm this, e.g. the fact that references to unorthodox religious practice were retained (e.g. Saul at Endor; see further Ch. 7.b). So the present study argues that the texts accurately portray the periods they describe, whatever editing they may have received in their transmission.

The study

This book has a simple plan, examining in turn: death in general (Part A), the realm of the dead (Part B), relations between the living and the dead

(Part C), and life after death (Part D). Thus Part A begins with a survey of the literary descriptions and theological interpretations of death in the Old Testament (Ch. 1). It then examines the ancient Israelite customs of mourning and burial, from textual and artifactual evidence (Ch. 2). Part B first explores the Hebrew concept of the underworld, notably the distinctive use of 'Sheol' and its synonyms (Ch. 3). It then questions several assumptions of recent scholarship as to how the underworld was perceived: as the destiny for all without distinction (Ch. 3); as an ominous power invading life (Ch. 4); and as a more pervasive concept than traditionally thought (Ch. 5). Part C studies how the living viewed the dead, in terms of the names used for the dead and their significance (Ch. 6), and the extent of consultation or veneration of the dead and the legitimacy of these practices (Chs. 7 and 8). And finally Part D focuses on texts which may imply post-mortem communion with God (Ch. 9), or more specifically resurrection from the dead (Ch. 10).

Part A is of general interest. It sets the scene, discussing the concept of death in Israel's literature and theology, and the event of death in Israelite experience. These chapters largely survey the relevant evidence, though this sometimes involves discussion of specific texts or concepts (e.g. food for the dead, Ch. 2.b.vi).

Parts 2 and 3 contain detailed interaction with current scholarship, and largely conclude that certain widely held views are ill founded. Thus these chapters argue that the underworld was not viewed neutrally, that psalmists did not fully experience it, that it was not a widespread concern, and that consulting and venerating the ancestors were not acceptable aspects of Yahwism. These conclusions are predominantly negative, and some readers may find that the arguments have too much detail and too little point! However, the detail is necessary to substantiate the case argued here, and this case is important: Israel's religious writers were not particularly concerned with the underworld or with the dead. They related to Yahweh in this life, and were relatively uninterested in the life hereafter.

Part 4 is again of more general interest, as it examines the key texts concerning life after death. The interpretation of these texts has often veered between two poles. On the one hand, the more developed Jewish and Christian eschatologies of later eras have often been read back into these texts. On the other, some scholars have reacted to this by denying that there was any post-mortem individual hope until the Maccabean period. The close examination undertaken here presents a more nuanced picture: a few isolated texts envisage some form of continued communion with God, but only two glimpse a future individual resurrection.

This book has been a long time in gestation. It builds on two research dissertations,[1] which interacted in detail with most of the relevant scholarly views. That interaction is retained here, though the references are considerably pruned and mostly relegated to footnotes.[2] But the present book is also different from the underlying theses in content and style. It aims to be accessible to all readers familiar with the issues of biblical scholarship, from relative beginners in theological study to seasoned scholars. Therefore many of the more technical arguments have been omitted, major new sections and important recent discussions have been added, and the material retained has been entirely rewritten. While the discussion often involves the precise meaning of Hebrew and other terms, these are all transliterated (see below), and they are kept to the minimum necessary. Perhaps most importantly, the book benefits from several years of further reflection on this absorbing topic, in the midst of a demanding schedule of tutorial, pastoral and administrative duties.

Many different biblical texts are studied in the course of this book, and most readers will need to check each text in turn to follow the discussion. For Bible quotations the NRSV is always used here. It is the best modern translation which renders the key Hebrew underworld name *šᵉʾôl* as 'Sheol' (see further Ch. 3.a). However, two small changes have been introduced. God's personal name is changed from 'the LORD' to 'Yahweh', in line with common scholarly practice. (Like most English versions, the NRSV follows Jewish and Christian tradition here.) And the line divisions in poetic sections are not always reproduced, to save space. Chapter and verse references are always given as in English versions, even when the Hebrew text is quoted. (NB: In many psalms and some other passages the Hebrew references differ slightly, and some scholars and commentators follow the Hebrew numeration.)

This study concentrates on the Old Testament and its context, so most dates cited are BCE (Before the Common Era, i.e. BC). Hence these initials will usually be omitted, unless needed for clarification. Later dates are cited as CE (Common Era, i.e. AD).

Inevitably a study of this nature focuses on key words in Hebrew and other Semitic languages. These words are always given in transliteration, to enable all readers to follow the discussion. A few words of explanation may help:

Hebrew: The endings *-îm* and *-ôṯ* normally indicate plurals. Words are

[1] 'The Use and Meaning of Sheol in the Old Testament' (MTh, Belfast, 1988); 'The Underworld and the Dead in the Old Testament' (PhD, Cambridge 1993).

[2] The retained material has mostly been published over the last four decades, in English, and in accessible sources. However, much of the detailed work on non-biblical texts is published in German and/or in less accessible journals.

pronounced more or less as written, except that (i) *š* is pronounced *sh* (hence *š*^{e}*'ôl* is 'Sheol'); (ii) some consonants are softened when preceded by a vowel and then transliterated with an underline or overline (e.g. *b̲*=*v* and *p̄*=*ph*, hence *r*^{e}*p̄ā'îm* is 'Repha'im'); (iii) verb roots are usually written without vowels, but often pronounced with two *a* vowels.

Ugaritic: This Semitic language, spoken at the important trading centre of Ugarit several hundred miles north of Israel, was written without vowels, except that one silent consonant (equivalent to Hebrew aleph) has three forms which indicate the vowels *a*, *i* and *u* respectively. Many scholars add vowels elsewhere according to patterns known in other Semitic languages (e.g. *rpum* as *rapiuma*, *bʿl* as *baʿalu*), but others question these added vowels and prefer simply to 'grunt' the language!

Akkadian: The main languages of Mesopotamia, i.e. Babylonian, Assyrian and their regional variations, are effectively dialects of a single language which scholars call Akkadian (though no-one ever spoke 'Akkadian' as such). These languages have a distinctive and relevant feature. Proper nouns were usually preceded by a sign or 'determinative' to indicate the class of name, e.g. god, country, city. The determinative for a god is transcribed as a raised *d* or 'dingir' before the name.

The support

I am happy to have the opportunity to thank many who have helped me in this study: my various research supervisors in Belfast and Cambridge, especially Robert Gordon for his critical and constructive engagement; colleagues in Wycliffe Hall and Oxford University, especially John Day for his interest and for complementary copies of his work; the Tyndale Fellowship for financial support from the Council and much encouragement from fellow-members; many other scholars for the stimulus of their work, whatever our divergent conclusions; and Philip Duce of IVP for his continued enthusiasm and support during the long process of bringing the shades to light.

Last but certainly not least, I owe an enormous debt to my family for their patience, encouragement and good humour during my many years of grappling with the Hebrew underworld. I gladly dedicate this book to Patricia, from whom I have learnt more about life, love and death than from a whole library of books. As that most excellent song says, 'Love is strong as death' (Song of Songs 8:6).

Part A
DEATH

Chapter 1
Death in the Old Testament

a. Descriptions of death

i. Death and diversity

Death is a profound and complex subject. It is the one universal and undeniable fact of life, irrespective of age, culture, ideology or belief.[1] And yet it evokes a wide variety of human responses, whether emotional, rational, physical or material. This variety can be seen not just across different cultures, but also within any one particular culture. Death is universal, but reactions to it are distinctive.

Many factors shape our attitudes to death: the harshness or ease of life; our own experiences of bereavement; our individual temperament and personality; and our individual and communal religious views. And death arouses a wide range of human emotions: grief at the loss of relationship, anger at the separation, regret of unresolved business or unachieved ambitions, fear of pain and of the process of dying, relief at the end of suffering, fear of the unknown, peace through faith, and many more. Our attitudes to death are very different.

For most people these attitudes are affected at least partly by religious views. Yet even within the same religion quite different beliefs about death can coexist. For instance, self-confessed Christians differ over who will be in heaven: whether all humanity, or all the baptized, or all those with personal faith in Christ. They differ over what occurs between death and judgment:

[1] With the sole exception, in traditional Christian theology, of the generation alive at Christ's return.

whether soul-sleep, or purgatory, or an intermediate state. And they differ over the final fate of those who are excluded from heaven: whether eternal punishment or annihilation. Further, each of the significant terms in the above sentences covers a range of interpretative nuances. Even religious sub-groups can exhibit significant doctrinal diversity, even when the sub-group is defined largely by doctrinal belief. Evangelical Christians, for instance, hold different views on the present state of the dead and the eventual fate of unbelievers.[2]

These differences may be carefully analysed and categorized in theological study, but they are often juxtaposed incoherently in the minds and emotions of many ordinary believers. This can be readily seen in Christian hymns, which have often exerted more influence on general belief than sermons and books. Most collections used by Christian communities include a spectrum of views about death and the future, and different theologies can be sung on the same occasions with little or no regard for their divergent views.[3]

Further, customs regarding death can persist even when they seem to go against religious belief. Christians acknowledge in theory that a corpse no longer constitutes the person who has just died, and yet most think it appropriate to 'show respect for the dead'. Some Christians even express this respect by elaborate and costly care of the body and its burial, in a way which seems to undermine their formal belief. Also, social customs may be observed regardless of their original significance. In many parts of Britain neighbours close their curtains following a death in a nearby house, and Christians often do this too, unaware that it probably once represented an ancient fear of death coming in through the windows (cf. Jer. 9:21).

If, then, beliefs about death and responses to it vary significantly among Christians today, despite high literacy, extensive theological study and some explicit New Testament texts, how much more should this be expected when dealing with ancient Israel, which had none of these characteristics! The Old Testament reflects a time of largely oral instruction (whatever the extent of written documents at any stage), and of acceptance of traditional values and views. It also reflects religious views over many centuries and in various socio-economic, cultural and religious contexts.[4] And most importantly, its theological bedrock is that faith in Yahweh is experienced in this life, not after death: death and the dead lie largely outside the sphere of their religious

[2] For a thorough recent discussion, see ACUTE (2000).

[3] Most hymns on the subject envisage an immediate transfer from earth to heaven, e.g. 'Heaven's morning breaks, and earth's vain shadows flee' (*Abide with me*, Henry Francis Lyte). But a few imply an initial period in graves, e.g. 'Swells the high trump that wakes the dead' (*That day of wrath*, Walter Scott). Cf. Saggs (1958: 157) for other examples.

[4] This view is increasingly contested by scholars who see virtually the whole OT as a post-exilic product. But the variety of language, literature and theology itself suggests a much more extended literary history.

beliefs. So to expect the Old Testament to have a uniform view of death would be quite wrong. And even to expect its perspectives on death to form a recognizable whole may be inappropriate.

Good literature is often evocative, using imagery and metaphor to stimulate the imagination rather than prosaic description to satisfy the intellect. This has the great advantage of enabling the reader to enter creatively into the experience of the author, and more than outweighs the resultant imprecision and possible misunderstanding. But of course imagery by its very nature cannot be pressed too far. Old Testament descriptions of death are often imaginative and evocative rather than prosaic and specific. This allows us to understand the ancient Israelites' attitudes to death more than their beliefs about it. Nevertheless, the imagery and metaphor used inevitably reflect certain beliefs, and it is useful to attempt to trace these.

Further, in all human life, concepts from the cultural background may be taken up and used without acceptance of their underlying ideology. Today people from all walks of life talk of an Achilles' heel, Cupid's arrows, or the fates, or use adjectives like 'titanic' and 'promethean', without believing the Greek mythology which underlies these terms. Christians have often celebrated Halloween as a harmless folk festival, without worrying about its roots.[5] Thus Israel's use of certain terms need not imply acceptance of the mythology associated with them by other peoples. Neighbouring cultures used terms like death, pestilence and plague to represent deities, but the Hebrew usage does not necessarily echo this.

At the same time, the ancient Semitic world had a much greater awareness of the supernatural than does the modern Western world, and the seeming invincibility of pestilence and plague could well have given them an aura of supernatural power, even if they were not recognized as gods. So in interpreting Old Testament texts, we must recognize and allow for their possible metaphorical nature and mythological resonances.

ii. Death as the end of life

Death is often portrayed as the natural end of life. Moses predicts that certain rebels will not 'die a natural death' (Num. 16:29), while a psalmist announces that unjust 'gods' will 'die like mortals' (Ps. 82:7).[6] Both Joshua and David know that they will 'go the way of all the earth' (Josh. 23:14;

[5] However, the recent resurgence of witchcraft in the West has led some Christians to abandon this.

[6] Lit. 'the death of all men' and 'as men' respectively; cf. Aqhat in the Ugaritic epic: 'the death of all men I shall die, even I indeed shall die' (KTU 1.17.vi.38).

1 Kgs. 2:2), and Job knows that God 'will bring [him] to death, and to the house appointed for all the living' (Job 30:23). He also laments poignantly:

> A mortal, born of woman,
> few of days and full of trouble,
> comes up like a flower and withers,
> flees like a shadow and does not last (Job 14:1f.).

Further, a few texts suggest that death is the complete end of existence:

> For now I shall lie in the earth;
> you will seek me, but I shall not be (Job 7:21);

> 'Turn your gaze away from me, that I may smile again,
> before I depart and am no more' (Ps. 39:13).

Nowhere is this more marked than with Qoheleth, the wise man in Ecclesiastes:

> Whatever your hand finds to do, do it with all your might, for there is no work or thought or knowledge or wisdom in Sheol, to which you are going (Eccles. 9:10).[7]

Death is portrayed as a natural and peaceful event when it comes at the end of a long, happy and fulfilled life. This was clearly the case for Abraham, Gideon and David:

> You [Abraham] shall go to your ancestors in peace; you shall be buried in a good old age (Gen. 15:15);

> Abraham breathed his last and died in a good old age, an old man and full of years, and was gathered to his people (Gen. 25:8);

> Then Gideon son of Joash died at a good old age (Judg. 8:32);

> [David] died in a good old age, full of days, riches and honour (1 Chr. 29:28).

On this theme of peaceful death, the book of Job is typically lyrical, and that of Ecclesiastes typically caustic:

> You shall come to your grave in ripe old age,
> as a shock of grain comes up to the threshing floor
> in its season (Job 5:26);

[7] Unlike most scholars, Murphy (1999: 112) suggests that this still implies 'qualified continuation' in Sheol.

> . . . a time to be born, and a time to die (Eccles. 3:2);
>
> Why should you die before your time? (Eccles. 7:17).

Balaam wanted to 'die the death of the upright' (Num. 23:10), i.e. after a life as fulfilled as Jacob's. By contrast, David lamented that Abner had died 'as a fool dies', i.e. in premature and violent death (2 Sam. 3:33). The inter-testamental Wisdom of Solomon confirms the biblical picture of old age as a happy norm in asserting that 'the righteous, though they die early, will [nevertheless] be at rest' (Wisdom 4:7).

However, while old age was normally a blessing in Israel, it was also a time of diminished power preceding death. David grew frail (1 Kgs. 1:1–4) and the elderly need sticks (Zech. 8:4); the undiminished strength of Moses was a noteworthy exception (Deut. 34:7). Qohelet paints a hauntingly beautiful picture of human faculties gradually diminishing, until

> . . . the silver cord is snapped, and the golden bowl is broken, and the pitcher is broken at the fountain, and the wheel broken at the cistern, and the dust returns to the earth as it was . . . (Eccles. 12:6f.)

This fading of human strength reinforces the concept of death as life's natural end.

The Old Testament stresses that humans are merely dust: 'you are dust, and to dust you shall return' (Gen. 3:19; cf. 2:7); 'you turn us back to dust' (Ps. 90:3); 'he remembers that we are dust' (Ps. 103:14b); 'all are from the dust and all turn to dust again' (Eccles. 3:20). Similarly, the transience of life is emphasized:

> You sweep them away, they are like a dream,
>   like grass that is renewed in the morning (Ps. 90:5);
>
> All people are grass,
>   their constancy is like the flower of the field (Is. 40:6).

So death completes the natural cycle of life, and brings it to an end.

iii. Death as a friend

Several texts portray death as rest, inactivity, welcome relief, and sleep:[8]

> Now [if stillborn] I would be lying down and quiet;
>   I would be asleep; then I would be at rest (Job 3:13);

[8] Cf. KTU 1.19.iii.45, where the buried Aqhat is asleep. Similarly, resurrection is 'awaking' (Dan. 12:2).

There the wicked cease from troubling,
  and there the weary are at rest (Job 3:17);

. . . who long for death . . . who rejoice exceedingly . . . (Job 3:21–22.);

so mortals lie down and do not rise again;
  until the heavens are no more, they will not awake
  or be roused out of their sleep (Job 14:12);

Give light to my eyes, or I will sleep the sleep of death (lit. 'lest I sleep the death', Ps. 13:3);[9]

. . . they shall sleep a perpetual sleep and never wake (Jer. 51:39, 57).[10]

Death also provides rest from the inequalities and harshness of life, stripping everyone bare:

There the prisoners are at ease together;
  they do not hear the voice of the taskmaster.
The small and the great are there,
  and the slaves are free from their masters (Job 3:18f.);

'Naked I came from my mother's womb, and naked shall I return there' (Job 1:20).[11]

iv. Death as an enemy

More commonly death is seen as a bitter enemy of life. It is often portrayed in personified terms as a hunter with traps and snares, a marauding shepherd, an insatiable glutton:

the terrors of death have fallen upon me (Ps. 55:4);

. . . more bitter than death . . . (Eccles. 7:26);

The cords of death encompassed me;
  the torrents of perdition assailed me;
the cords of Sheol entangled me;
  the snares of death confronted me (Ps. 18:4f.);

Like sheep they are appointed for Sheol;
  Death shall be their shepherd (Ps. 49:14);[12]

[9] Myers (ISBE 1: 898) sees this as 'a profound sleep simulating death', but the context implies actual death.
[10] Cf. also Sirach 41:2: 'O death, how welcome . . . to one who is . . . worn down by age'.
[11] Also Eccles. 5:15. These are hardly references to naked mourning, so Dhorme (cf. Martin-Achard 1960: 27).
[12] Cf. KTU 1.6.ii.2: 'I [Mot] made him [Baal] like a lamb in my mouth'.

Three things are never satisfied; four never say, 'Enough':
Sheol . . . (Prov. 30:15f.);

They open their throats wide as Sheol;
like Death they never have enough (Hab. 2:5).

A few texts have intriguing parallels with other Semitic literature, and are sometimes thought to echo mythological views of death. In Job 18, Bildad waxes eloquent on the fate of the wicked: their light is extinguished, they are caught in hunting traps, frightened by terrors, consumed by hunger and disease, torn from their tent and thrust into darkness, leaving no descendants.[13] In the midst of this vivid, stylized portrayal come two intriguing phrases:

the firstborn of Death consumes their limbs (v. 13);

they . . . are brought to the king of terrors (v. 14).

The king of terrors is clearly a personification of Death itself, though whether this refers directly to the god Mot (i.e. 'Death', known from Ugaritic texts), or uses ancient mythology without adhering to it, or is just evocative imagery, is impossible to say.[14] Some scholars take the phrase hyperbolically.[15] Others see the firstborn of death as Mot himself,[16] or more plausibly identify him as a demon, possibly one of the 'sons of Resheph/Pestilence' (cf. Job 5:7 lit.).[17] But the references remain elusive and evocative. Bildad is mustering his oratorical skill to present the fate of the wicked as gruesomely as possible, not giving a reasoned exposition of the powers beyond the grave.

Jeremiah 9:21 predicts mourning women teaching their daughters a dirge over Jerusalem:

'Death has come up into our windows,
it has entered our palaces,
to cut off the children from the streets
and the young men from the squares'.

Here death is vividly evoked as an irresistible intruder who captures even the young and vigorous. This probably reflects a popular fear 'that death slips

[13] In v. 13a 'limbs' (*baddê*) is often emended to 'by disease' (*bidway*) and the verb read as passive, see e.g. Clines (1989: 406).

[14] In Mesopotamia, Namtar, the god of plague and vizier of the underworld, was the son (perhaps firstborn) of its queen, Ereshkigal.

[15] E.g. Rowley (1976: 130).

[16] E.g. Habel (1985: 287f.).

[17] Following Sarna (1963); e.g. Burns (1987; 1989), Hartley (1988: 279), Clines (1989: 142, 416–18), Day (2000: 202f.).

through windows to steal away the breath of life'.[18] The language and sentiment are reflected in Akkadian descriptions of the *lamaštu* demon who 'slithers through the window, slips over the wall . . . the young she kills . . . the children she smashes'.[19] There is also a possible parallel with the Ugaritic Baal cycle. At one point Baal wants to build a palace. The craftsman god Kothar-and-Khasis ('Skilful-and-Clever') suggests including a window, but Baal refuses. He then changes his mind and has the window installed, calling it 'a rift in the clouds'.[20] Later Mot captures and kills Baal, and various scholars have suggested that the window allowed Mot access. However, while this window is obviously important in the story, the reason for this is not clear, mainly due to breaks in the text. It would make Baal vulnerable to Yam (Sea) rather than to Mot;[21] certainly there is no link with Baal's ensuing challenge to Mot. So Baal's famous window is probably unconnected to 'death entering windows' in Jeremiah.[22]

Proverbs 16:14 declares that 'a king's wrath is a messenger of death . . .' This could echo a religious background of messengers being supernatural as in the Ugaritic texts, where Gupn-and-Ugar ('Vine-and-Field') takes messages from Baal to Mot and back, and then to El.[23] However, the proverb is more likely to be poetic metaphor, especially since the subject is 'the king's wrath'.

In Song 8:6 one of the lovers asserts:

> . . . love is strong as death, passion fierce as the grave.
> Its flashes are flashes of fire, a raging flame.

This has two possible mythological echoes. The first phrase is reminiscent of the phrase 'Death is strong', which comes in Israelite names (see below) and in texts from Ugarit and Cyprus.[24] The names may reflect a homage to Death in order to allay his attack, similar to the 'covenant with death' disparaged by Isaiah (Is. 28:15, 18). Also, 'flashes' translates the Hebrew *rešep̄*, a term understood in different texts as fire, thunder and plague.[25] But

18 Burns (1989: 32). This may still underlie the custom today of closing curtains when a neighbour has died.
19 Tigay (1986: 70 n. 33).
20 KTU 1.4.v.60–65, vii.13–28.
21 In one Egyptian story a man fears his beautiful wife will be stolen by the sea, cf. Burns (1989: 31).
22 So Carroll (1986: 246), Thompson (1980: 317); some still suggest allusion, e.g. Jones (1992: 168).
23 E.g. KTU 1.3.iii.33, 1.5.i.12. The double name is variously interpreted as one or two messenger-god(s).
24 Cf. KTU 1.6.vi.17–20, threefold repetition of 'Mot was strong, Baal was strong'; fifth-century king of Cyprus called Azbaal (Hill 1904: 10–13), Cypriot deity Baal-Az (Xella 1993); I am endebted to John Day for these references.
25 Cf. NRSV: burning (Deut. 32:24), sparks (Job 5:7), flashing (Ps. 76:3), thunderbolts (Ps. 78:48), plague (Hab. 3:5).

Resheph, or 'Pestilence', was an underworld deity at Ugarit and elsewhere,[26] and a mythological echo is quite possible here.

Several Hebrew names contain the letters *mwt* (vocalised as *māweṯ* or *môṯ*), and this element is often understood as meaning 'death'. They are mainly personal names: *ʾ^{a}ḥîmôṯ*, 'Death is my brother' (?); *ʿazmāweṯ*, 'Death is strong' (?); *m^{e}rēmôṯ* (?); *y^{e}rîmôṯ* (?).[27] There are also a few place-names: *ḥ^{a}zarmāweṯ*, *ʿazmāweṯ*.[28] These names have a similar form to Hebrew personal names which are theophoric (i.e. mention a deity), e.g. Ahijah, Uzziah, Meribaal, Jeriah.[29] Some scholars therefore see them as evidence that Israelites acknowledged Death as a deity and attempted to appease him. However, several factors oblige caution. (i) While some of these names may be theophoric, this remains uncertain for others. (ii) Other motives for including 'death' in a name are easily imaginable, e.g. the death of a previous child or of a family member. (iii) Some names may be used for family reasons, with the original meaning simply vestigial, as in the use today of names compounded with 'Christ' (Christopher, Christine, etc.) by parents with no active Christian faith. (iv) Many of the individuals lived in the post-exilic era, when 'death' may have alluded more obviously to the tragedy of exile than to ancient mythology. So, while some of these names may reflect non-Yahwistic mythology, for both linguistic and theological reasons it is hard to affirm this generally.[30]

As noted above, it is difficult to assess the extent to which ancient mythology colours these various references. On the one hand, in the wider cultural milieu many of the terms were associated with supernatural beings, and this may have influenced the mentality of some Israelites. On the other, poetry by its very nature is evocative, and can use imagery without adopting its inherent assumptions. Further, since these more allusive references are primarily poetic,[31] and since they form a small element in the kaleidoscopic presentation of death, their importance must not be exaggerated.

26 Cf. Fulco (1976), Xella (DDD: 700–703).

27 *ʾ^{a}ḥîmôṯ*, 1 Chr. 6:25; *ʿazmāweṯ*, 1 Chr. 8:36 = 9:42; 11:33 (= 2 Sam. 23:31); 12:3, 27:25; *m^{e}rēmôṯ*, Ezra 8:33; 10:36; Neh. 3:4, 21; 10:5; 12:3; *y^{e}rîmôṯ*, 1 Chr. 7:7, 8; 12:5; 23:23; 24:30; 25:4; 27:19; 2 Chr. 11:18. *m^{e}rēmôṯ* (2x) and *y^{e}rîmôṯ* are also found on Hebrew inscriptions (Tigay 1986: 66).

28 *ḥ^{a}zarmāweṯ*, Gen. 10:26; *ʿazmāweṯ*, Ezra 2:24; Neh. 12:29 (= *bêṯ-ʿazmāweṯ*, Neh. 7:28).

29 *ʾ^{a}ḥîyāh*, *ʿuzzîyāh*, *m^{e}rîbaʿal*, *y^{e}rîyāh*. Cf. also inscriptional evidence (Tigay 1986).

30 Cf. Healey (DDD: 602): 'all are very uncertain'.

31 For Burns (1989: 32), since 'the preponderance of the personifications of Death is found in Wisdom Literature . . . they carry little or no mythological significance'. But this assertion is too strong.

v. Death as separation

Death obviously separates the individual from the community. Indeed to be 'cut off from one's people' was often a sentence of death.[32] Even more importantly, death cut one off from Yahweh:

> For in death there is no remembrance of you;
> in Sheol who can give you praise? (Ps. 6:5);

> [I am] like those forsaken among the dead,
> like the slain that lie in the grave,
> like those whom you remember no more,
> for they are cut off from your hand (Ps. 88:5; cf. 10–12);

> The dead do not praise Yahweh,
> nor do any that go down into silence (Ps. 115:17);

> For Sheol cannot thank you, death cannot praise you;
> those who go down to the Pit cannot hope
> for your faithfulness (Is. 38:18).

This was the ultimate tragedy of death in the devotional Hebrew writings.

Several texts emphasize the irreversibility of death:

> I shall go to him, but he will not return to me (2 Sam. 12:23);

> We must all die; we are like water spilled on the ground, which cannot be gathered up (2 Sam. 14:14);

> As the cloud fades and vanishes,
> so those who go down to Sheol do not come up (Job 7:9);

> . . . before I go never to return . . . (Job 10:21);

> As waters fail from a lake,
> and a river wastes away and dries up,
> so mortals lie down and do not rise again (Job 14:11f.).

Perhaps this is why Qohelet counsels reflection on death:

> . . . the day of death [is better] than the day of birth.
> It is better to go to the house of mourning
> than to go to the house of feasting (Eccles. 7:2f.).

[32] Inflicted by God rather than humans, so Wenham (1979: 241f.). The phrase may also indicate social disgrace or banishment, cf. Hartley (1992: 100).

vi. Death as reunion?

One psalmist consigns the ungodly rich person to Sheol, where he 'will go to the generation of his fathers, who will never again see the light' (lit., Ps. 49:14, 19). And Ezekiel pictures the dead lying inactive in groups in a vast underground cavern (32:22–30). However, in neither text is there any sense of meaningful interaction, let alone of happy reunion, among the dead.

More importantly, two distinctive phrases present death as joining the ancestors: 'gathered to his peoples' and (lit.) 'slept with his fathers'. But these are used in quite specific contexts, and the second developed a different connotation.

'Gathered to his peoples'. In the accounts of Abraham, Ishmael, Isaac and Jacob, each in turn 'breathed his last, died and was gathered to his people' (Gen. 25:8; 25:17; 35:29; 49:33).[33] For Abraham and Isaac, the account of burial immediately follows. The phrase 'gathered to his people' also occurs several times in God's announcement of the deaths of Moses and Aaron, usually with reference to their disobedience (Num. 20:24; 27:13; Deut. 32:50 [x2]), but not always (Num. 31:2). It twice follows the verb 'die' (Deut. 32:50), though it never precedes mention of burial. So this distinctive phrase occurs ten times, and only in the Pentateuch. It is only used of the patriarchs, Moses and Aaron, and only occasionally.

Elsewhere there are a few similar and probably derivative expressions. Joshua's generation was 'gathered to its fathers' (lit., Judg. 2:10). The reformer Josiah would be 'gathered to his fathers . . . to his grave' (lit., 2 Kgs. 22:20 // 2 Chr. 34:28). Occasionally the verb 'gathered' occurs without any further qualification: following the complete phrase (Num. 20:26; 27:13); in parallel with 'perish' (Is. 57:1); and on its own (Ezek. 34:29; Hos. 4:3).[34] Thus 'gathered' without further qualification came to mean 'die'.

In the full phrase, 'people' is literally 'peoples' and refers to the immediate kinship group. (The plural also appears in the formula 'cut off from his peoples',[35] as well as several other texts, again mostly in the Pentateuch.)[36] In a detailed study, Alfrink (1948: 121f.) argues plausibly that the phrase was an ancient stereotyped formula, and concludes (122f.): 'the only

[33] Except that 'he died' is omitted for Jacob; cf. also 49:29.

[34] Also Sirach 8:7 (parallel with 'expire'); 40:28. Lipinski (TWAT 6: 186) sees 'gathered' as a veiled allusion to an ancestor cult conducted in tombs. But the parallel terms hardly allow this.

[35] 12 times, all in the Pentateuch (cf. ES: 889). 'Cut off' also occurs 9 times with 'people' (sg.), and occasionally with other complements. Lev. 17 contains both 'peoples' (v. 9) and 'people' (vv. 4, 10).

[36] Lev. 19:16; 21:1, 4, 15; Ezek. 18:18; Hos. 10:14. Alfrink ignores the last two in his conclusion.

surprising thing is that such expressions from an ancient era reappear exclusively in a particular section of Israelite literature, and were avoided so systematically in the contemporary literature that they do not occur even once.' A plausible explanation is that these Pentateuchal texts reflect genuinely ancient usage.

'Gathered to his people' clearly does not indicate death or burial, since it is mentioned alongside them, and is used of Jacob several months before his actual burial (Gen. 49:33; 50:13). Nor can it mean burial with the ancestors in the family grave, since this did not occur for the burial of Abraham, Aaron and Moses.[37] It may be derived from this practice,[38] but if so its use became divorced from its origin. For Meyers it 'explain[s] the Iron Age innovation of the communal ossuary',[39] but this gives the repository pit an ideological function hardly supported by the jumbles of bones and pottery amassed there. More likely, 'gathered to his peoples' indicates joining one's ancestors in the afterlife.[40] Most scholars assume this reunion takes place in Sheol (as in Ps. 49), even if Sheol is never mentioned in the same context. But whether it is the case for the nation's forefathers is not specified.

'Slept with his fathers'. The narrative accounts of many kings of Israel and Judah conclude that '[he] slept with his fathers and was buried . . .' (lit.). The first phrase does not mean burial, since the account of burial often follows it. Nor does it mean burial in the family tomb,[41] since it occurs for David, Ahaz and Manasseh who were not buried there, and is omitted for Ahaziah and Joash who were. Nor does it indicate rejoining the ancestors,[42] since it is used selectively of some and not others. The phrase simply takes the place of the verb 'he died'. It occurs mostly for the nations' kings (thirty-six times), but also for Jacob and Moses (Gen. 47:30; Deut. 31:16). A similar expression, 'go to his fathers', is used of Abraham (Gen. 15:15). Clearly it is reserved for national leaders.

However, only some kings 'slept with their fathers'. The phrase is not related to their piety or otherwise, since it is omitted for the reformer Josiah but occurs for many who 'did evil'. Rather, with few exceptions it occurs of kings who died peacefully, as has been shown independently by Alfrink (1943) and Driver (1962). Conversely, the stark description 'he died' is used of those who died violently. Driver notes a similar distinction in the Code of

[37] Abraham was of course buried with his wife Sarah (Gen. 25:10), but this does not explain the plural 'peoples'.
[38] So Tromp (1969: 168).
[39] Meyers (1970: 17); see Ch. 2.b.v.
[40] So Alfrink (128), Heidel (1949: 188), Driver (1962: 142), Tromp (1969: 168), Alexander (1986: 45).
[41] Origin of phrase for Pedersen (1940: 480f., implied), Eichrodt (1967: 213).
[42] Origin for Ringgren (TDOT 1: 10).

Hammurabi, where 'went to his fate' and 'died' convey natural and unnatural death respectively, again with rare exception.[43]

There are three exceptions. (i) It is omitted for Jehoram in Chronicles (2 Chr. 21:20). However, the Chronicler possibly interpreted Jehoram's agonizing illness, which is unmentioned in Kings, as a violent death.[44] (ii) Ahab, who was killed in battle, both 'died' and 'slept with his fathers' (1 Kgs. 22:37, 40). This double description is anomalous, so the formula was perhaps mistakenly added later.[45] (iii) A certain king rebuilt Elath after another 'slept with his fathers' (2 Kgs. 14:22 // 2 Chr. 26:2). The texts imply that Amaziah was the king who 'slept with his fathers',[46] but the formula is inappropriate for him since he was assassinated. However, this is the only instance where the phrase occurs outside a regnal summary. Thus arguably the verse is a historical note added (as for Ahab) by someone ignorant of the formula's connotation.[47]

These exceptions imply that the specific use of this formula was later unknown. Otherwise the phrase 'slept with his fathers' occurs only for national leaders who died peacefully,[48] and its use is therefore dissociated from the original meaning of the phrase.

vii. Death by sacrifice

Death by human sacrifice was abhorrent to Israel's faith. Thus the law fiercely condemns the sacrificing of children by fire to the god Molech (or Molek). It profaned God's name (Lev. 18:21), and was religious prostitution which merited death by stoning (Lev. 20:2–5). It was the archetypal Canaanite abomination which summed up the indigenous practices forbidden in Israel (Deut. 12:31) or headed up the full list of such practices (Deut. 18:9–14). Similarly, the historical narratives severely criticize northern

[43] Driver (141). The exceptions are CH 173:46, re the dowry of a woman who 'dies' (Driver–Miles 1955: 66f.), and the phrase 'went to his fate' in a private letter, when unnatural death is suspected (Ungnad 1914: 180f.).

[44] So Alfrink. For the Chronicler, Joram's disease is divinely inflicted, agonizing and fatal (unlike Asa's).

[45] Driver (1962: 140). However, his supporting textual argument is tenuous.

[46] So re Kings: Gray (1970: 614), Jones (1984: 513), Hobbs (1985: 182), Cogan–Tadmor (1988: 158), NRSV. Amaziah rebuilt Elath according to several Greek MSS, followed by some earlier scholars (cf. Montgomery–Gehman 1951: 442f.).

[47] Cf. Montgomery–Gehman (442f.), who see it as a misplaced archival datum. Alfrink suggests that the king who died was Edomite. But there is no immediate reference to this king, and no (other) use of the formula for a foreigner.

[48] So Eichrodt (1967: 213), Ringgren (TDOT 1: 10), McAlpine (1987: 145), Bloch-Smith (ABD 1: 785).

Israelites in general and the southern kings Ahaz and Manasseh in particular for such child sacrifice (2 Kgs. 16:3; 17:17; 21:6). In contrast, they commend Josiah for defiling its cult place, or Topheth, near Jerusalem (2 Kgs. 23:10). Josiah's contemporary Jeremiah goes further by condemning Judeans as well as Israelites for offering their children to Molech (Jer. 32:35).[49] Some of these texts do not mention Molech by name, but the phrase 'make to pass through fire' clearly indicates this or something very similar.[50]

There is considerable evidence that child sacrifice to Molech was widely practised by the Phoenician (or 'Punic') colonies around the Mediterranean, particularly in North Africa and Spain, from the fourth century BCE onwards.[51] So it is often assumed that it was practised in Phoenicia itself and from there spread to Palestine, though the archaeological evidence for this is sparse. Eissfeldt in 1935 and others since have argued that Molech was the name not of a god but of a type of sacrifice, and that the sacrifice involved some form of dedication rather than death. But recent studies by Heider (1985) and Day (1989) have confirmed the traditional view that Molech was seen as a deity, and that sacrifices to him involved the death of the child victims. Neighbouring cultures show much evidence for a deity or deities called *m-l-k*, e.g. divine names at Ugarit and Mari, probably theophoric names at Ebla and Mari, and the *maliku* (shades or chthonic gods) at Mari. There is also some evidence that Molech was seen as an underworld god, e.g. Akkadian texts which associate Malik with Nergal, and the *maliku* with the Anunnaki (underworld spirits).[52] The *m-l-k* names are almost certainly related to the common Semitic root *m-l-k*, 'to be king', with the epithet 'king' becoming a proper name (like *ba'al*, 'master'). But whatever the name's derivation and the associations elsewhere of *m-l-k* deities, in Israel the cult of Molech was roundly condemned.

[49] On sacrificing children, cf. also Jer. 7:31f.; 19:5f. ('to Baal'); Ezek. 16:20f.; 20:26, 31; 23:37–39; Mic. 6:7. The divine initiative in Ezek. 20 is theologically similar to God hardening people's hearts (Exod. 9:12; Is. 6:10; 63:17).

[50] The phrase 'make to pass through fire' occurs in Lev. 18:21 (omitting 'fire'); Deut. 18:10; 2 Kgs. 16:3; 17:17; 21:6; 23:10. The first and last of these also mention Molech, as does Lev. 20:2–5 (x4); Jer. 32:35. Molech also occurs in 1 Kgs. 11:7, but probably erroneously for Milcom, cf. 2 Kgs. 23:10. Some read *melek̲* as 'Molech' in Is. 8:21 (see Ch. 6.b.i); 30:33 (see Ch. 2.b.iii); 57:9 (see Ch. 8.a.vi).

[51] Summarized by Day (1989: 86–91). Kempinski (1995) sees underworld feasting depicted on a funerary monument in Pozo Moro, south-eastern Spain, which dates from c. 500 BCE: a seated animal-headed god is about to devour a child in a bowl. Kempinski suggests the god is Mot, citing KTU 1.5.i.14–22, but the probable Punic origin (though questioned by some) and the child victim suggest instead Molech. Earlier still, on an unpublished eighth-century Phoenician inscription from Turkey, a Cicilian king boasts that his sacrifices to Molech were accepted (Shanks 1996: 13).

[52] See further Heider (1985; DDD: 581–5), Day (1989), and reviews of their work.

Human sacrifice in exceptional circumstances elsewhere is recorded. The outlaw judge Jephthah rashly promised to sacrifice 'as a burnt offering' whoever came out of his house first on his return from defeating the Ammonites, and then fulfilled his vow with his daughter as the victim (Judg. 11:31, 39). A certain Hiel of Bethel laid Jericho's foundations and gates 'on' (*bᵉ*) his oldest and youngest sons, in fulfilment of Joshua's curse (1 Kgs. 16:34; cf. Josh. 6:26). These were possibly 'foundation sacrifices' to ward off evil, with the children then buried in the foundations.[53] When cornered in battle, King Mesha of Moab in desperation sacrificed his heir 'as a burnt offering', with the result that 'great wrath came upon Israel, so they withdrew' (2 Kgs. 3:27). The resultant wrath was probably that of the Moabite god Chemosh, to whom the sacrifice would have been dedicated and whose territory Israel had invaded, or possibly the revulsion of the Israelites at such a horrific act.[54] These last two cases are implicitly censured by the historian.

In light of this consistent abhorrence of child sacrifice, God's command to Abraham to sacrifice Isaac seems incredible (Gen. 22). Why did he ask the patriarch to do what is elsewhere so strongly condemned? And why did Abraham accept without demur? Some scholars see this as an aetiology of Israel's rejection of such sacrifice. However, Sarna (1989: 392) notes that the offering of Abel, the sacrifice of Noah after the flood and the enquiry of Isaac en route to Moriah all imply that animal sacrifice was thought normal from the beginning. He eloquently presents an alternative explanation (392):

> In its present form, the narrative is the product of a religious attitude that is already long conditioned to the notion that Israelite monotheism is incompatible with human sacrifice. An undeniable atmosphere of the singular and the unique pervades the episode. God's request is treated as something utterly extraordinary, something that a person would never think of doing on his own initiative . . . God's request is so clearly shocking and unrepeatable that the reader is informed in advance that God is only testing Abraham and does not want the sacrifice for his own needs . . . Abraham is designated the father of a new nation, a nation that is to be endowed with a unique destiny among the family of nations. He must therefore unequivocally prove his worthiness to be God's elect. The totally disinterested nature of his devotion to God must be established beyond any reasonable doubt.

The incident of Genesis 22 was therefore a unique test of faith, which does not undermine Israel's abhorrence of human sacrifice.

53 For ancient parallels, cf. Jones (1984: 300), DeVries (1985: 205).

54 Elsewhere the noun *qeṣep̄* mostly indicates the wrath of Yahweh, so probably indicates that of Chemosh here.

viii. Death by suicide

Several prominent Old Testament characters apparently wish to die, notably Elijah (1 Kgs. 19:4), Job (7:15) and Jonah (4:3), yet they do not contemplate committing suicide. Elijah is exhausted and Jonah petulant; both suggest that Yahweh should take their life, but show little inclination to do so themselves. Job asserts repeatedly that his life is scarcely worth living, and yet tenaciously clings to it in the hope of vindication. Qohelet maintains a caustic and sceptical attitude to life, which at times verges on despair; yet he still affirms that, for all its faults, life is still better than death:

> whoever is joined with all the living has hope, for a living dog is better than a dead lion (Eccles. 9:4).

Suicide features only rarely in the Old Testament. Abimelek was killed at his own request by his armour-bearer, to avoid the ignominy of being killed by a woman (Judg. 9:53). Samson's last act of defiance killed himself as well as thousands of Philistines (Judg. 16:29f.). The wounded Saul killed himself to avoid the shame of being killed by the Philistines. His terrified armour-bearer then did the same (1 Sam. 31:3f.). Ahitophel, David's advisor who deserted to Absalom, hanged himself when his advice was trumped by Hushai (2 Sam. 17:23). And the rebellious Zimri burnt himself to death when his *coup d'état* failed (1 Kgs. 16:18).

The various narratives make no comment on the nature of these deaths, and a few scholars therefore conclude that 'in ancient Israel the act of suicide was regarded as something natural and perhaps heroic'.[55] However, this overstates the case, for several reasons. (i) All these deaths occur in contexts of war or rebellion, and two of the men involved were already fatally wounded. War is always a dreadful business, and few cultures condemn those who commit suicide rather than face shame, torture and certain death. (ii) Most of the men are portrayed as evil, at least implicitly, so their death is probably seen as a fitting fate. The one exception of Samson (who was always a law unto himself) is a different form of suicide anyway, since he died while killing thousands of Israel's enemies. (iii) The small number of reported suicides in contexts of strife, and their complete absence in other circumstances, suggests rather that suicide was abnormal. (iv) Further cases cited of suicide contemplated but not enacted are scarcely relevant.

All this supports the view that life was of supreme importance to the Israelites, and not to be scorned or taken without good cause. Suicide may

[55] Droge (ABD 6: 228), similarly Droge–Tabor (1992: 58f.). Further discussion in Clines (1989: 98).

have occurred very occasionally and in tragic circumstances, but was hardly normal, natural or generally acceptable.

b. Reflections on death

i. Death and life

Paradoxically, the starting-point for any discussion of death in the Old Testament is life itself. It is not just that death is the end of life, its ultimate and concluding event. Nor that death is the absence of life, the negative defined by the corresponding positive. It is primarily that life is one of the fundamental characteristics of Israel's God and of her faith.[56] Though the Israelites seldom speculated about eternity, one confidently proclaimed: 'from everlasting to everlasting you are God' (Ps. 90:2). The words of Jesus (in discussion of resurrection) aptly summarize the Hebrew understanding of Yahweh: 'He is God not of the dead, but of the living' (Mark 12:27 etc.).

It is widely accepted that the very name 'Yahweh' comes from the verb *h-y-h*, 'to be', even if there remain differences about the precise form and meaning.[57] And even if the name has a different etymology, as some have suggested, it is understood in the Hebrew text as related to 'being', notably in the account of its revelation to Moses: 'I am who I am' (Exod. 3:14). Essentially Yahweh *is* life and Yahweh *gives* life. This is repeatedly stressed in all forms of Old Testament literature, e.g.:

> Now choose life . . . for Yahweh is your life (Deut. 30:19f.);

> In his hand is the life of every living thing
> and the breath of every human being (Job 12:10);

> For with you is the fountain of life;
> in your light we see light (Ps. 36:9).

Other texts assert that Yahweh is the author of both life and death:

> Yahweh kills and brings to life;
> he brings down to Sheol and raises up (1 Sam. 2:6);

> . . . to Yahweh, the Lord, belongs escape from death (Ps. 68:20);

> See, I am setting before you the way of life and the way of death (Jer. 21:8; cf. Deut. 30:15).

[56] Cf. Martin-Achard (1960: 3): 'The Israelite loves life: he meets it with optimism; he sees it as a gift of God.'
[57] Cf. Freedman–O'Connor (TDOT 5: 500–21), Fretheim (NIDOTTE 4: 1295–30).

As a consequence, God knows or predetermines the length of human life:

> . . . their days are determined,
> and the number of their months is known to you (Job 14:5);
>
> In your book were written
> all the days that were formed for me,
> when none of them as yet existed (Ps. 139:16).

The idea of a divine book is often thought to be a late Israelite development, since it occurs mostly in texts of uncertain or late date (though it is also attributed to Moses).[58] But whenever it emerged, it further illustrates the theme that life is fundamental to Yahwism.

ii. Death and creation

The majestic account of creation in Genesis 1 (or more accurately 1:1 – 2:3) does not address human mortality. It asserts that humankind is made in the image of God, though this concept is never explained, here or elsewhere. After the accounts of disobedience and expulsion from Eden, creation in the image of God is still cited as the reason for punishing murder with death (Gen. 9:6). This implies that the image of God was not thought to include immortality (Gen. 9:6; cf. 1 Cor. 11:7; Jas. 3:9).

By contrast, Genesis 2 – 3 does address the theme of mortality, though less straightforwardly than at first sight. God creates a man and places him in Eden with bountiful provision, warning that 'in the day that you eat of [the tree of the knowledge of good and evil] you shall die' (2:17). This might imply that the man is already immortal. However, the very existence of 'the tree of life' alongside the tree of knowledge suggests that its fruit is somehow necessary for perpetual life (2:9). As the story unfolds, God creates a woman, the serpent disputes the prohibition, the woman and the man eat the forbidden fruit, and all three are punished. But the humans do not immediately die; they are sentenced to impaired relationships and to difficulties in bearing children and raising crops. The sentence on man concludes: 'you are dust, and to dust you shall return' (3:19). If this is a simple statement of fact, its conclusion ('to dust you shall return') asserts man's intrinsic mortality.[59] And if it is a statement of divine judgment, its explicit premise ('you are

[58] Also in Exod. 32:32f.; Ps. 69:28; Dan. 12:1; Mal. 3:16. Cf. other registers: Ps. 87:6; Is. 4:3; Ezek. 13:9. See Ch. 9.e.

[59] Cf. Martin-Achard (1960: 19): 'His chastisement changes, not his nature, but his condition . . .'

dust') implies human impermanence. So whether read as statement or as judgment, God's pronouncement in 2:17 implies that man is naturally mortal.

Finally, God expels the man (and the woman) from the garden, since 'he might . . . take also from the tree of life, and eat, and live forever' (3:22). This confirms that the fruit of this tree is necessary for immortality, and without it humans are mortal. Hence the earlier emphatic pronouncement, 'in the day that you eat of it you shall die', is seen in context to mean: 'On the day you eat of it, you will cut yourself off from the tree of life and will therefore eventually die.' So the second creation account portrays human immortality as potential rather than actual, and ends with human death as certain because of human sin. This connection between sin and death is notably unique among ancient literature,[60] and rare even within the Hebrew Bible. But it is explicit here, in this programmatic introduction to the account of God's dealings with humanity.

iii. Death as natural

As noted above, much of the Old Testament presents death as the natural end of human life. And when that life has been long, happy and fulfilled, then death seems to be accepted with equanimity by narrators and their subjects alike. Thus Abraham, Gideon and David all died at 'a good old age' (see Ch. 1.a.ii), and kings who died naturally 'slept with their fathers' (see Ch. 1.a.vi). The impression is given that there is a natural cycle of life, and that death is part of the normal human order. Thus Bailey (1979: 58f.), like others, concludes:

> Death . . . was not an irrational intruding enemy but part of an ordered, controlled harmonious creation. Biological life and death are not separate phenomena, as if the latter intruded to thwart the Creator's design. They are bound together as part of a singular divine will for his creatures.

Bailey contrasts dying in 'good old age' with a 'bad death'. Normally death is natural, but it is bad when premature, or violent, or there is no surviving heir. Certainly such deaths were seen as calamitous and the adjective 'bad' is appropriate, even if it is not used in the biblical text itself (and not further defined by Bailey). But the normality of death in other circumstances can be overstated. As just demonstrated, the Hebrew Bible is prefaced with the pronouncement

[60] By contrast, in the *Epic of Gilgamesh* and in *Adapa* eternal life was stolen or lost through deception. Also, many contemporary prayers, incantations, etc., reveal a fear of death caused by unwitting offences against minor deities.

of death as judgment for human sin. And, as discussed below, it contains occasional further glimpses of this theme, as also of death as defilement and of a future conquest of it. These various concepts are not developed theologically or integrated into a general view of death, as occurred later in the New Testament. But they suggest that, even in normal circumstances, death was not necessarily as natural or harmonious as Bailey concludes.

iv. Death as punishment

Death is often associated with divine punishment elsewhere in the Pentateuch. The enormous antediluvian life-span is reduced to a norm of 120 years as punishment for illicit marriage (whatever the interpretation of these life-spans and marriages, Gen. 6:3). Then the flood itself destroyed nearly all humanity in punishment for its sinfulness (Gen. 6:5–7). Later the death of numerous individuals and communities is presented as judgment for sin: Sodom and Gomorrah (Gen. 19); rebellious Israelites in the wilderness (Exod. 32:28, 35; Lev. 10:2; Num. 11:1, 33f.; 16:31–35; 25:8f.); the entire exodus generation (Num. 14:23); and Canaanites at the conquest (Gen. 15:16). In the same way, disobedience after settlement in the land will bring death and destruction (Lev. 26:22, 25, 30; Deut. 28:21, 26). The rest of the Old Testament paints a similar picture of premature death as punishment for sin in texts too numerous to cite, for Israelites and foreigners, for kings, prophets, priests and ordinary people alike.

The Pentateuch also prescribes the death penalty for certain offences, primarily the taking of human life, as affirmed programmatically after the flood:

> Whoever sheds the blood of a human,
> by a human shall that person's blood be shed;
> for in his own image
> God made humankind (Gen. 9:6).

This is repeated in the Mosaic legislation (Exod. 21:12; Lev. 24:17–21), and applied to premeditated or avoidable murder (Exod. 21:14; Num. 35:16–21, 30f.; Deut. 19:11–13); false witness in capital cases (Deut. 19:16–21); and accidental manslaughter, unless the guilty person flees to a city of refuge (Exod. 21:13; Num. 35:22–28, 32; Deut. 19:4–6).

The death penalty is also prescribed for non-capital offences in several areas: (i) religious offences, including blasphemy (enacted in Lev. 24:14–23), Sabbath breaking (Exod. 31:14f.; 35:2; enacted in Num. 15:32–36), false prophecy (Deut. 13:1–5; 18:20), idolatry (Deut. 13:1–18; 17:2–7), sacrificing children to Molech (Lev. 20:2–5), witchcraft (Exod. 22:18; Lev. 20:27); (ii) kidnapping (Exod. 21:16; Deut. 24:7); (iii) insubordination to parents (Exod. 21:15, 17); (iv) sexual offences, including adultery when married or engaged (Lev. 20:10; Deut. 22:22–24), premarital unchastity (Deut. 22:20f.), rape of an engaged girl (Deut. 22:25), prostitution of a priest's daughter (Lev. 21:9), incestuous relationships (Lev. 20:11f., 14); homosexuality (Lev. 20:13) and bestiality (Exod. 22:19; Lev. 20:15f.). By contrast, death is never prescribed for property offences in Israel, unlike many contemporary and subsequent cultures.

However, in all these cases of narrative and law, it is the immediacy of death rather than the fact of death which is the punishment. It is the specific sin of specific individuals or groups which leads to their death, not the sin of humanity as a whole.

Only very occasionally does the Old Testament associate human sinfulness generally with death, and even then it is somewhat oblique. The majestic Psalm 90 contrasts divine eternity and human mortality, and continues:

> For we are consumed by your anger;
> by your wrath we are overwhelmed.
> You have set our iniquities before you,
> our secret sins in the light of your countenance.
> For all our days pass away under your wrath (Ps. 90:7–9).

Here human sin, divine wrath and human death are clearly associated. Though there is no formal causal connection between sin and death, the wilderness period evoked in the title and reflected in the haunting ruggedness of the psalm was one of repeated rebellion. The psalm's juxtaposition of sin and death, as well as its liturgical appropriation by later generations of Israelites, means that here at least there is a close link between human sinfulness and human death.

v. Death as uncleanness

In the Mosaic laws, all those who touch a corpse, bone or grave, or who even occupy the same tent as a dead body, become unclean for seven days. Open containers in the tent also become unclean. This uncleanness is then addressed in several ways. (i) On the third and seventh days those rendered unclean must wash themselves and their clothes. They must also be sprinkled with 'the water of cleansing', water mixed with the ashes of a red heifer, and those who sprinkle them must also wash their clothes (Num. 19:11–22).[61] Clay pots must be smashed, other vessels washed, and all food and liquid in

[61] See commentaries for further details. Davies (1995: 193) states that elsewhere plain water was sufficient, but the texts he cites have different concerns: Lev. 11:24ff. (dead animals); 22:4ff. (priests touching unclean people).

them destroyed (implicitly from Lev. 11:32–35). (ii) The unclean may undergo temporary exclusion. Those who touch a corpse are excluded from the camp for an unspecified time (Num. 5:2f.), while those who killed the Midianites taken in booty were excluded for seven days (Num. 31:13–24). Since such physical quarantine is not part of the general regulation, it may have been specific to the wilderness setting.[62] (iii) Priests may become unclean only for a death in the immediate family (Lev. 21:1–3), and even this is forbidden to the high priest and to Nazirites (Lev. 21:11; Num. 6:6–12). If it happens unwittingly to a Nazirite, he must completely renew his vow.

No reason is given for the impurity caused by death. Several explanations have been proposed, though as with much of the ritual legislation it is easier to summarize the detail than to discern the underlying theology.

(a) The idea that death causes uncleanness or pollution was common in the ancient East, so Israel's legal codes embodied a widespread attitude.[63] This is certainly true, as far as it goes. However, while the thinking of many ordinary Israelites was doubtless shaped by the wider cultural background, the canonical text is likely to assume a more theological perspective. Further, if these texts represent genuinely ancient traditions of a Mosaic Yahwism, this perspective is an integral part of Israel's inspired faith rather than a later theological gloss on a cultural phenomenon.

(b) Yahwistic priestly writers were combating the cult of the dead by declaring it unwholesome and the source of pollution.[64] This is possible, if the texts reflect a priestly puritanism following the late monarchy reforms and the exile. However, even in this perspective the absence of direct comment suggests that ancestor veneration was hardly the primary concern, especially since other abhorrent practices like necromancy are openly and repeatedly condemned.

(c) Death pollutes because it results from sin. This is seen in a holistic reading of the Pentateuch, as follows: sin and death are linked in the second creation account; the main legislation on death's polluting effect (Num. 19) follows several wilderness rebellions and precedes the deaths of the exodus generation;[65] and in the text itself the water of cleansing 'contains all the ingredients of a sin offering'.[66] However, while this association is clear in the

[62] So Wright (ABD 6: 730). It is not included in the stricter Nazirite laws (Num. 6:6–12).

[63] Gray (1903: 243f.) cites Roman, Greek, Indian and Zoroastrian sources, and tribal customs from North America, Africa and Asia. Recent writers endorse this, e.g. Ashley (1993: 361), Levine (1993: 469).

[64] E.g. Levine (1993: 472): 'the hidden agenda of Numbers 19'.

[65] Ashley (1993: 362).

[66] Wenham (1981: 146), noting that the animal's blood is burnt (here alone in the OT) and contained in the ash. Also Hartley (1992: 347 on Lev. 21). The association of sin and death is further developed in the NT.

wider context, it is not made explicitly in the relevant legislation.

(d) The 'spectrum of sanctity' (holiness–cleanness–uncleanness) purposely mirrored the 'spectrum of life' (Yahweh–living–dead). Yahweh was supremely the God of life; it was the living who could praise him, while the dead were cut off from him (see Ch. 3.a.iii). This is probably the most comprehensive theological explanation for the uncleanness of death, based as it is on the understanding of Yahweh himself.

For some interpreters, the fact that death, like sin, pollutes and defiles means that death is unnatural.[67] However, there are other elements that cause pollution, such as bodily discharges (Lev. 15), which have no moral dimension.[68] So the impurity of death need not relate to morality and hence be a consequence of human sin. As suggested above, it probably relates more to separation from Yahweh.

vi. Death and the future

Several prophetic texts look beyond the immediate contexts of iniquity and judgment, exile and despair, with visions of a new society. Yahweh would be the undisputed Lord, not just of Israel but of the whole world. Nations would flock to pay him homage, all would live in peace and harmony, and even the lion would lie down with the lamb. Whenever these visions emerged, it is noteworthy that the idyllic future portrayed includes old age and implicitly death. Zechariah's vision of prosperous and peaceful restoration includes the elderly sitting with their walking-sticks (Zech. 8:4). And the 'new heavens and new earth' vision which concludes Isaiah envisages everyone living a long and full life, but still assumes their eventual death:

> No more shall there be in [Jerusalem] . . .
>   an old person who does not live out a lifetime;
> for one who dies at a hundred years will be considered
>   a youth . . . (Is. 65:20).

At the same time, a few prophetic texts portray death as an enemy (notably Hos. 13:14) and one proclaims the ultimate disappearance of death itself (Is. 25:7). While this more negative view of death contributed to the development of belief in resurrection (see Ch. 10), it is worth noting that, like the link between sin and death, it is a marginal theme in the Old Testament.

[67] E.g. Alexander (1986: 42). He notes that death is presented negatively, but this can have other explanations.
[68] Frymer-Kensky (1983: 402) gives a full table of causes of pollution.

c. Summary

Like all societies, the Israelites displayed a variety of attitudes to death. In general they accepted it as the natural end of human life. As one of them so elegantly said, 'there is a time to be born, and a time to die' (Eccles. 3:2). But sometimes death threatened the living before they reached their 'time to die'. Occasionally, and for those in great anguish like Job, premature death could be a welcome friend. More commonly, the threat of untimely death was seen as a bitter enemy, and many psalmists prayed earnestly to Yahweh for deliverance from it. The Israelites were not the only people to fear death, and their literature sometimes alludes to widespread Semitic ideas. In a few instances death is portrayed as reunion with ancestors, though the phrase 'gathered to his peoples' is only used of patriarchs and early leaders. (The similar phrase 'slept with his fathers', which is mostly used of royalty, lost this connotation and came to indicate peaceful death.) More generally, death is seen as separation from life, from community, and ultimately from Yahweh. Because of this, suicide was exceptionally rare.

Yahweh was supremely the Lord of life. His very name indicates life, and he is repeatedly celebrated as giver and sustainer of life. In choosing to follow Yahweh, Israel chose life itself. By contrast, the creation accounts narrate early human disobedience, which resulted in exclusion from the garden of Eden with its tree of life, and eventually therefore in death. The association between human sinfulness and death surfaces only rarely in subsequent texts, though death occurs regularly as direct punishment for sin. Contact with death in any form causes uncleanness. While no rationale is given for this, it probably represents the separation from Yahweh which the dead experienced. Old age and death remained part of human expectation, even in prophetic portrayals of the idyllic age to come. Only very rarely is death itself an enemy to be vanquished, but that discordant thread makes its own contribution to the later belief in resurrection from death.

Chapter 2
DEATH IN ANCIENT ISRAEL

a. Reactions of the living

In all societies death elicits a profound response. Often this is articulated in words and gestures. Sometimes it remains unarticulated, yet has a visible effect on the well-being of the living. In ancient Israel, according to the Hebrew Bible, people reacted to death much as elsewhere.

i. Mourning

The account of Sarah's death includes a poignant detail: 'Abraham went in to mourn for Sarah and to weep for her' (Gen. 23:2). Other texts show that grief after death could be deep-seated and long-lasting, e.g. that of Isaac for Sarah, or Jacob for Joseph (Gen. 24:67; 37:35). To mourn was normal, even if many brief accounts of burial do not mention it, e.g. those of Abraham and Isaac. God's instruction to Ezekiel not to mourn the death of his wife (Ezek. 24:16) was as shocking to the prophet's fellow exiles as it is to us, and immediately provoked a demand for explanation.

There are very few Old Testament indications of how long mourning lasted, yet these few record different time periods. The men of Jabesh-Gilead fasted for seven days after burying the bones of Saul and his sons (1 Sam. 31:13). Similarly, Jacob's family and Egyptian officials held 'a very great and sorrowful lamentation' for seven days before burying him (Gen. 50:10f.).[1]

[1] Seven days was normal in the second century BCE, cf. Judith 7:21; Sirach 22:12. The earlier seventy-day period of mourning for Jacob was exceptional, since this occurred in Egypt and he was, after all, the prime minister's father.

On the other hand, the deaths of Aaron and Moses were followed by thirty days of mourning (Num. 20:29; Deut. 34:8). Similarly, a female captive was allowed to mourn the loss of her parents for one month before her enforced marriage (Deut. 21:13). These few examples probably indicate the general custom of a week of intense mourning and a month of social restriction.

Mourning customs are mentioned more frequently.[2] In ancient Israel as elsewhere in the ancient world, mourners would: weep (the most noted custom), tear their clothes, wear sackcloth, uncover and/or dishevel their hair, cover themselves with dust, sit and sleep on the ground, walk barefoot and fast (Gen. 37:34f.; 2 Sam. 1:11f.; 13:31, etc.). They might also cover their lower face, which seems to be the meaning of 'covering the moustache/upper lip' (Ezek. 24:17, 22).[3] They might also wear distinctive clothes, as shown by Joab's accomplice supposedly mourning her son (2 Sam. 14:2, 6f.). Widows' clothes were worn continually (so Tamar, Gen. 38:11, 14). These clothes were probably black, a universal custom probably reflected in Jeremiah's prophecy: 'the earth shall mourn, and the heavens above grow black' (Jer. 4:28).[4]

The law forbade Israelites to trim their hair and mutilate themselves in mourning (Lev. 19:27f.; 21:5; Deut. 14:5). The reason is never specified. It has long been thought that these were Canaanite practices, though there is little direct evidence of this. (Elijah's adversaries cut themselves for other reasons, 1 Kgs. 18:28.) Nevertheless, the practice of shaving one's hair in mourning was common at least in the pre-exilic era, and is presented as normal in several prophetic texts. Even God himself called Israel to 'mourning [and] baldness' (Is. 22:12).[5] Self-mutilation is also noted without censure. After Jerusalem's fall eighty men from the north came to present offerings to Yahweh with their beards shaved and bodies gashed (Jer. 41:5; cf. 16:6). The prophets portray similar customs among neighbouring peoples.[6]

ii. Fasting and feasting

Several texts indicate an early Israelite tradition of fasting following a death. David and his men 'mourned and wept, and fasted until evening for Saul and Jonathan' (2 Sam. 1:12), while the Jabesh-Gileadites who buried their

[2] See further Anderson (1991); Pham (1999:24–35). Also Benjamin–Matthews (1999), though they often go beyond the evidence.

[3] Also done by lepers, Lev. 13:45. The covering of lips in Mic. 3:7 was a reaction of shame.

[4] The young widow's sackcloth in Joel 1:8 may be temporary.

[5] Similarly Jer. 7:29; Ezek. 7:18; Amos 8:10; Mic. 1:16.

[6] Is. 15:2f.; Jer. 47:5; 48:37; Ezek. 27:30–32.

bones then fasted for seven days (1 Sam. 31:13). When Abner was killed in cold blood in the ensuing power struggle, David publicly lamented him and fasted until evening, despite being urged to eat. This public display of grief succeeded in dissociating David from Abner's murder (2 Sam. 3:35–37). When David and Bathsheba's first child died, David had to ask for food to be served, and his servants were perplexed that he did not fast after the death (2 Sam. 12:20f.).

By contrast, several other texts refer in passing to the food of mourners. This implies either that fasting was followed by eating (perhaps with specified food, eaten in a specified way), or that at some stage fasting was replaced by eating. However, the evidence is too sparse to give a clear picture. There is fleeting prophetic reference to 'the bread of mourners' (Hos. 9:4; possibly Ezek. 24:17, 22).[7] Hosea notes that this bread causes defilement. It can only be used to stave off hunger, and cannot be brought to the temple. Similarly, food which has been partially 'eaten in mourning' or 'offered to the dead' cannot then be included in the triennial tithe (Deut. 26:14; see Ch. 8.a.i). Such food is unclean through its association with the dead, and therefore unfit for a religious offering. Jeremiah indicates that bread was given to mourners by others, along with 'the cup of consolation' (Jer. 16:7). Whether this bread was different in composition from normal bread, or simply had a different use, is impossible to tell.

There is also fleeting reference to another custom in God's command to Jeremiah: 'Do not enter a house of mourning, or go to lament or bemoan them' (Jer. 16:5). The word translated 'mourning' (*marzēaḥ*) also appears in Amos 6:7, but there it means 'revelry'.[8] While these are the only Hebrew occurrences, the same stem appears in many other Semitic languages. The evidence when pieced together suggests that the *marzēaḥ* was a widespread social phenomenon of gathering to celebrate, commemorate or simply consume alcohol (see Ch. 8.b). A *marzēaḥ* could have elements of a pub, a drinking club, a London Gentlemen's Club, a Masonic Lodge, an annual fete, and an Irish wake! Texts from Ugarit and Transjordan show that the term *marzēaḥ* could also indicate the property where drinking took place. So the 'house of mourning' in Jeremiah could mean a particular building (like a pub, hall or lodge). However, there is no other textual or archaeological evidence for such public buildings in Judah. Often *marzēaḥ* refers simply to the

[7] Ezek. 24:17, 22 has 'bread of men' (*'ᵃnāšîm*), so Wevers (1969: 143), JB. But given the context many read: 'bread of mourners' (*'ônîm*, as Hos. 9:4; cf. Targum, Vulgate), so Kaufmann (1960: 312), Block (1997: 784), RSV, NIV, NRSV, REB; or 'bread of despair' (posited *'ᵃnušîm*), so Allen (1994: 56, citing Driver and others), NEB.

[8] In Amos 6:7 the construct form (*mirzaḥ*) has an initial *i* vowel, but it is generally accepted as the same stem.

event itself, and this is more likely in Jeremiah. Although this is the only relevant biblical reference, the general prohibition for the prophet suggests that some form of funerary gathering or wake was common in Judah, at least in the immediate pre-exilic period.

iii. Laments and funerals

Jeremiah also gives evidence of the custom of 'mourning women', or 'wise [skilled] women', hired to compose and sing dirges (Jer. 9:17f.). These laments were obviously moving, and their songs provoked much weeping. Mourning women were also common in the ancient world.[9] The custom has continued in the Near East to modern times – women follow the bier and emit high-pitched shrieks. But such mourning wasn't restricted to women. Amos predicts wailing throughout squares, streets and vineyards: 'They shall call the farmers to mourning, and those [men] skilled in lamentation to wailing' (Amos 5:16). The Chronicler refers to 'singing men and singing women . . . in their laments' (2 Chr. 35:25). And Qoheleth's evocative portrayal of death includes: '[male] mourners will go about the streets' (Eccles. 12:5).

Poetic laments could be written after notable deaths, as by David for Saul and Jonathan (2 Sam. 1) and by Jeremiah for Josiah (2 Chr. 35:25). Many ordinary laments start with the interjection *hôy*, as illustrated when Jeremiah prophesies that King Jehoiakim would not receive the standard laments: 'They shall not lament for him saying "Alas, my brother!" or "Alas, my sister!" . . . "Alas, Lord!" or "Alas, his majesty!"' (Jer. 22:18; cf. 34:5; 1 Kgs. 13:30). The onomatopoeic word *hôy* is a sigh of grief and conveys a sense of desolation, as in the usual translations 'Alas!' or 'Ah!'[10]

The Old Testament gives only sparse information on funeral customs. Usually narrative accounts simply note a burial with no further detail, and other literary genres are no more instructive. For instance, the burials of Sarah and Abraham are given as simple factual statements, without elaboration (Gen. 23:19; 25:9). Even for Jacob, the report of lengthy Egyptianized mourning is followed by the simple mention of burial (Gen. 50:13). When Joab's murder of Abner threatened reunification, David pointedly 'followed the bier' to dissociate himself from the murder (2 Sam. 3:31). This indicates a funeral procession, but there is no further detail. There are no references to performing funerary rites, no list of chief mourners, and no mention of

[9] E.g. for Egypt, see NBD (171 and illustration).
[10] Elsewhere *hôy* can express judgment, as 'Woe!', or astonishment, as 'Ho!' (famously in Is. 55:1).

religious ceremonies. This last is perhaps the most surprising absence for modern readers. Whatever the Israelites' customs at death, religious rites either did not occur or were of such minimal importance that they have left no trace in any of the varied literary strands of the Old Testament.

b. Burial of the dead

i. General burial

In most societies, whether ancient or modern, burial of the dead is of great importance. It formally marks the end of the life of the deceased and the change in relationships and status of the living. The ceremony and the form of burial often reflect the dominant religious views of the society, and the remains of the dead are treated with dignity and respect.

Burial was certainly important in Israel, as elsewhere in the ancient Near East. As Ringgren comments (1966: 242): 'Even though the Old Testament tradition never once states in so many words why it is necessary to bury the body, many passages make it unambiguously clear that a burial was considered very important.' This can be seen in several ways.

First, in most cases where the death of a major figure is mentioned, their burial is also recorded. Thus we read of the burial of Abraham, Isaac, Jacob, Joseph, Miriam, Moses, Joshua, Eleazar, eight judges, Samuel, Abner, Joab, Elisha, and most of the kings of Israel and Judah. It is also recorded for several figures whose role in the biblical narrative is minor.

Secondly, several texts testify to the importance of burial in the family tomb. The nomadic Abraham was determined to own a family burial plot (Gen. 23). The elderly Barzillai declines David's offer of hospitality and prefers to return home, 'so that I may die in my own town, near the grave of my father and my mother' (2 Sam. 19:37). A disobedient 'man of God' is told in punishment: 'your body shall not come to your ancestral tomb' (1 Kgs. 13:22).

Thirdly, everyone deserved burial. Indeed, for Qohelet a stillborn child was better off than a man 'who has no burial' (Eccles. 6:3). Even criminals and rebels deserved burial, and on the same day as their execution (Deut. 21:23). Immediate burial was not just a matter of hygiene, though this was obviously a factor in a hot climate where decomposition rapidly follows death. The alternative of cremation was abhorred (see below), and death by burning was reserved for the worst crimes.

However, the importance of burial in ancient Israel can also be exaggerated. The burial of some major figures is not recorded, notably Ishmael,

Aaron, five judges[11] and several kings.[12] There is also no record of burial for several minor figures whose death is specifically mentioned. This is hardly due to their minor role or their impiety, since these criteria are not applied uniformly. Thus burial is recorded for one royal prince (Abijah) but not others (David and Bathsheba's first son, Amnon, Adonijah), for one rebel (Joab) but not others (Abimelech, Sheba, Shimei), for some minor figures (Rebekah's nurse, Asahel, Ahithophel) but not others (Judah's wife, Elimelech and sons, Phinehas's wife, Nabal, Uzzah, Naboth, Athaliah). Thus burial was important, but not so important that it absolutely had to be recorded whenever a death was narrated.

Burial normally occurred in the family burial cave on the family land, as sometimes explicitly mentioned, e.g. Gideon, Samson, Asahel, Ahithophel and Barzillai (Judg. 8:32; 16:31; 2 Sam. 2:32; 17:23; 19:37; cf. also 2 Macc. 12:39), and frequently implied, e.g. Joshua, Eleazar and most judges (Josh. 24:30, 33; Judg. 10:1f.; 12:7–15). Indeed, there are only rare and explicable exceptions. A new family tomb (e.g. Abraham, David) implied a new family line.

Samuel and Joab were each buried 'in his house' (2 Sam. 25:1; 1 Kgs. 2:34). Some scholars take this literally, noting archaeological evidence of house burial under the floor, especially before the Iron Age.[13] Others see this as a reference to the family land, noting that Manasseh was buried, according to Chronicles, 'in his house' (2 Chr. 33:20), but according to Kings, 'in the garden of his house, in the garden of Uzza' (2 Kgs. 21:18).[14] Taking 'house' as 'family land' fits better with other Old Testament burial records.

The account of Abraham's purchase of a burial cave and field (Gen. 23) indicates the importance of ownership of burial land. It is striking that the chapter deals mostly with Abraham's purchase of the cave and only summarily with the burial of Sarah. Many interpret this as Abraham securing a stake in the land promised by Yahweh. But the immediate text makes no such comment, and Abraham did not use his considerable wealth to purchase any other property.[15]

[11] Othniel, Ehud, Shamgar, Deborah and Eli. The deaths of Ehud, Shamgar, and Deborah are not recorded either.

[12] Jeroboam I, Ahab, Jeroboam II, Menahem, Hezekiah (in 2 Kgs.) and Jehoiakim. Each of these kings 'slept with his fathers', but this does not indicate burial; see Ch. 1.a.vi.

[13] Cf. Hertzberg (1964: 199), Baldwin (1988: 146), Gray (1970: 110), Jones (1984: 117). Baldwin comments that this 'would discourage any tendency to venerate [Samuel's] tomb', though the text gives no reason.

[14] E.g. on 2 Sam. 25:1: Klein (1983: 247); on 1 Kgs. 2:34: Noth (1968b: 36f.).

[15] Brichto (1973: 9) posits a link between burial, land ownership and ancestor cult. But Bray (1993: 72) comments tellingly: 'there are no remembrances, no ritual acts, no future hope of an after-life'.

Occasionally burial occurred away from the family tomb, as when death occurred during travel. Rebekah's nurse Deborah was buried 'under the oak' near Bethel (Gen. 35:8), either because trees were associated with religious practice in general and immortality in particular (Gen. 2:9; 21:33), or simply because it was a recognizable landmark. Rachel was buried somewhere between Bethel and Ephrath (= Bethlehem, Gen. 35:19), with a pillar erected to mark the spot.[16] Saul and his sons were initially buried at Jabesh-Gilead, yet reinterred years later in their family tomb (2 Sam. 21:14). There is no record of Israelites ever being 'buried' in rivers or at sea.[17]

By the end of the monarchy, if not before, many ordinary people in Jerusalem were apparently buried in a communal burial ground rather than in family tombs. Two texts refer in passing to 'the grave(s) of the sons of the people': here were thrown the ashes of the Asherah image burned in Josiah's reform (2 Kgs. 23:6) and the body of the murdered prophet Uriah (Jer. 26:23).[18] In the former text the singular 'grave' might suggest a single, common grave,[19] but most scholars take both texts as references to a commoners' burial plot or public cemetery.[20]

Bloch-Smith posits a reason for recording burial locations:

> The Bible records the burial locations of . . . the principal players in Israel's theological history. Following death, these individuals were thought to possess special powers and to maintain intimate contact with Yahweh as they had during their lifetimes. Given the presumed posthumous powers of the dead, it was important for the supplicant to know the location of the burial in order to petition the deceased. (1992a: 111; cf. ABD 1: 786)

However, this interpretation is unsatisfactory. (i) As noted above, burial location is not always recorded, even for some of Israel's 'principal players'. (ii) There is no biblical indication that the dead, famous or otherwise, maintained intimate contact with Yahweh – quite the reverse. (iii) The only recorded consultation of a famous person (Samuel) occurred far away from

[16] Her tomb was also recorded as near Zelzah (1 Sam 10:2, otherwise unknown) and Ramah (Jer. 31:15).

[17] This may have been a Sumerian practice, cf. 'bodies . . . floating on the river' (*Gilgamesh and the Land of the Living*, line 26; ANET: 48), though the passage refers to meteorological disasters. It was not adopted by Semites in Babylon or elsewhere, cf. Saggs (1958: 160).

[18] Bloch-Smith (ABD: 787) suggests that these actions defiled the graves. But Hobbs (1985: 333) comments appropriately that it is rather the graves themselves which cause defilement.

[19] So Hobbs, but he then refers to 'the graves'. The singular may be a collective term.

[20] So Montgomery–Gehman (1951: 530, noting later burial there), Cogan–Tadmor (1988: 279), Thompson (1980: 528), Carroll (1986: 512), Holladay (1986: 110), Jones (1992: 345). However, Holladay (510) and Jones (250) argue that 'sons of the people' in a gate name elsewhere (Jer. 17:19) refers to laity rather than commoners.

his burial place. (iv) There is no biblical evidence of petitioning the dead at their graves, and the only support Bloch-Smith cites is a fourth-century CE rabbi. While Isaiah 65:4 (and possibly 57:6) mentions graveyard activity, this is not specifically petitioning the dead. As Wolff (1974a: 100) comments incisively: 'The dying person has much of importance to say, but his grave has little significance.'

ii. Royal burial

The books of Kings note several royal burial locations: David's descendants down to Ahaz were buried in the City of David; Manasseh and Amon in Uzza's garden (perhaps palace grounds, 2 Kgs. 21:18, 26);[21] and Josiah in his own tomb in Jerusalem. Presumably after Ahaz there was no further space in the City of David's royal tombs. There is no burial record for Hezekiah or Jehoiachim.

2 Chronicles presents a similar picture. For the most part, the same kings are recorded as buried in the City of David (as was also the high priest Jehoiada, 24:16). But there are several minor variations or clarifications: Jehoram and Joash were buried there, but not in the kings' tombs (21:20; 24:25); Amaziah was buried in the 'city of Judah' (25:28, lit.);[22] Uzziah was buried 'with his fathers in the kings' burial field' (26:23); and Ahaz was buried 'in the city, in Jerusalem', but not in the kings' tombs (28:27). Of the kings following Ahaz, Hezekiah was buried 'on the ascent to the tombs of the sons of David' (32:33), Manasseh 'in his house' (33:20), and Josiah 'in the tombs of his fathers' (35:24). There is no burial record for Ahaziah, Amon or Jehoiachim.[23]

For some scholars, the Chronicler's greater detail regarding burial may reflect a theological assessment of the various kings.[24] Bloch-Smith suggests specific reasons why he did not record certain kings as buried in the royal tombs: Asa, Jehoram, Uzziah and Ahaz because of their serious illness; Ahaziah, Joash, Amaziah, Amon and Josiah because they were murdered; and Hezekiah and Manasseh because they committed cultic offences.[25] Of these, the first explanation is stated explicitly for Uzziah ('he is leprous', 26:23), and

[21] Some scholars have identified Uzzah with Uzziah (cf. Gray 1970: 711) or the Uzzah of 2 Sam. 6:8 (cf. Cogan–Tadmor: 270). Many now link Uzzah to an Arabian/Canaanite astral deity *al-uzzā*, e.g. Gray (710), McKay (1973: 24f.), Jones (1984: 660), though in this case its omission from Josiah's reforms is odd (Hobbs 1985: 309).

[22] Some MSS and Versions have 'city of David'; so RSV, NRSV, Williamson (1982: 331).

[23] Chronicles implies that Jehoiachim was taken to Babylon.

[24] So Williamson (1982: 322), Rosenbaum (1979: 29), Bloch-Smith (1992a: 117f.).

[25] By contrast, for Williamson (277), Asa's burial notice indicates approval.

implied for Asa and Jehoram, but there is no record of Ahaz being ill. The second is possible, though it rests on silence regarding Ahaziah and Amon, and it distinguishes unnecessarily between 'City of David' and 'city of Judah/Jerusalem'. But the third is unlikely, since Hezekiah was obviously respected by the Chronicler, and Manasseh was already excluded from his fathers' tombs in the books of Kings, which was one of the Chronicler's sources.

There is some evidence of royal burial practice. Asa was laid out on a bier surrounded by spices, and 'a very great fire' was made. But when his unpopular grandson Jehoram died, 'his people did not make a fire for him like the fire of his fathers' (2 Chr. 16:14; 21:19). Jeremiah tells Judah's last king, Zedekiah: 'like the fires of your fathers, the former kings who preceded you, so they will burn [a fire] for you' (Jer. 34:5).[26] A funerary bonfire was apparently normal for kings, but its significance is never stated. It was most likely a sign of honour,[27] which would explain the 'honour' done for Hezekiah (2 Chr. 32:33). It certainly wasn't cremation (see below). Some scholars suggest wider non-Yahwistic religious motives. For Zwickel (1989) it was an apotropaic rite (to ward off evil spirits), which consisted of burning objects associated with the deceased, and was adopted from Assyria in Manasseh's time. For others it and associated rites involved offerings to the deceased.[28] However, there is no biblical evidence of such apotropaic rites or such offerings. As Spronk comments (1986: 40): 'Everything depends here on whether or not the dead are believed to be powerful.'

iii. Non-burial

Burial should be universal and immediate, and non-burial was a sign of particular opprobrium, in Israel as throughout the ancient world. Even a criminal executed and hung on a tree was to be buried the same day (Deut. 21:22f.). This is actually recorded for various conquered kings (Josh. 8:29; 10:26f.). Non-burial was the terrible fate of soldiers on the battlefield (e.g. Deut. 28:25f.; Jer. 7:33; 16:4, 6),[29] and their exposed corpses were then eaten by birds and animals. In one instance treachery is punished by mutilation as well as exposure: the men who murdered Saul's son Ishbaal, in a vain

[26] Some interpret this as burning spices: RSV, NRSV, Bright (1965: 214), Holladay (1989: 235), cf. de Vaux (1961: 57); but not Thompson (1980: 607), Carroll (1986: 641), Jones (1992: 428).

[27] So Jones (1992: 428).

[28] E.g. Bloch-Smith (1992a: 119) and earlier scholars (cf. Spronk, 1986: 40 n. 2).

[29] Also 1 Kgs. 14:10f. (Jeroboam); 16:4 (Baasha); 2 Kgs. 9:37 (Jezebel); Jer. 22:19 (Jehoiakim: 'the burial of a donkey'); Ezek. 29:6 (Pharaoh); 39:4 (Gog's armies).

attempt to please David, were killed and hung up with their hands and feet cut off (2 Sam. 4:12).

Subsequent disturbance of bodies was equally deplored. Jeremiah predicts exhumation and exposure as punishment for Judah's worshippers of the sun and the moon (Jer. 8:1). Various tomb inscriptions warn of dire consequences for those who disturb the dead, notably on the sarcophagi of two Sidonian kings (see Ch. 6.a.v) and in the 'tomb of the royal steward' near Jerusalem:

> This is the tomb of . . . yahu, who was over the royal household. There is here no silver or gold, only his bones and the bones of his slave-girl with him. Cursed be the person who opens it![30]

Cremation was apparently not practised in Israel. It may have occurred elsewhere: the Moabites were fiercely condemned for burning the king of Edom's bones (Amos 2:1), and a funeral pyre would apparently be fitting punishment for the Assyrian king (Is. 30:33).[31] Josiah also burned human bones, but this was more to desecrate improper altars than to revile those whose bones were used, even if these were probably the improper priests whose living descendants were put to death by Josiah (2 Kgs. 23:16, 20). During the conquest, Achan and family were stoned, and their remains burned and covered with stones (Josh. 7:25). In the law, serious sexual misconduct merited death by burning (Gen. 38:24; Lev. 20:14; 21:9). But these were cases of exemplary capital punishment rather than of normal corpse disposal.[32] The Jabesh-Gileadites burned the corpses of Saul and his sons and then buried their bones (1 Sam. 31:12).[33] But this was respectful and only partial (since the bones remained), and probably necessary for hygiene given the delay following their deaths.

Cremation may possibly be suggested in Amos 6:10. Following the sudden catastrophic death of ten people in a single home, 'his relative and *m^esār^epô* is/are left to remove bodies. The Hebrew stem *s-r-p* is unique here. Some scholars derive it from 'to burn' (*ś-r-p*, despite the different first letter *s/ś*) and so translate it as 'the one who burns (his corpse)',[34] or 'who burns

[30] Text from Smelik (1991: 75, omitting his brackets). This tomb may be that of the royal steward Shebna, condemned in Is. 22:15f.

[31] So Wildberger (1982: 1223). However, many scholars read 'for the king' as 'for Molech' and see this as reference to sacrifice in the Hinnom valley, e.g. Clements (1980: 254).

[32] So, on sexual misconduct: von Rad (1972: 360), Westermann (1986: 54), Noth (1965: 156), Wenham (1979: 291), Gordon (1986: 203); against Hubbard (1989b: 196, 'cremation').

[33] Turner (ISBE 1: 812) calls this an 'ancient practice', but without evidence. Driver (1954: 315) rereads 'anoint with spices', so NEB; but without textual support, and rejected by Stœbe (1973: 522), Klein (1983: 290), REB.

[34] RSV, NIV, NRSV, Heidel (1949: 170), McKeating (1971: 51), Baldwin (1989: 171).

(spices) for him',[35] or even as 'his burnt offering'.[36] However, others see no link with 'burning' and interpret *mᵉsārᵉpô* as another term for a family member, paralleling 'his relative'.[37] Yet others re-read the verb, follow the LXX, or emend the text.[38] Even if the verb does indicate cremation, this is a rare event following a major disaster. There are no other Old Testament references to the burning of corpses.

iv. Place of burial

Archaeological excavation provides a large and ever-increasing amount of evidence about burial in the whole area of the southern Levant, including Palestine. In summary, this shows a dual pattern before and during the time of Israelite occupation. In the hill country, corpses were laid out on rock-cut benches in burial caves. After the flesh had decomposed, the remaining skeleton was removed from the bench to make room for the next corpse. By contrast, in the lowlands, corpses were mostly buried directly in the ground. Occasionally grave goods suggest the ethnicity of those buried, but usually not. Many scholars identify the highland burial pattern with the pre-Israelite inhabitants and the Israelites, and the other patterns with Canaanites and foreign influence.

For the Late Bronze Age (usually dated 1550–1200 BCE), Gonen (1984–5; 1992) studied about 900 burials, and notes two main and distinct types of burial. The first is multiple, successive burials in caves, both natural and man-made. This practice had been more widespread, but during the LBA it became limited to the highlands. Here pottery included the complete range of domestic ware, with no specific funerary items. 'This type of burial . . . must be regarded as a local and long-lived tradition of the indigenous people' (1984–5: 70). The second type is individual burial in the ground (simple or pit graves), or occasionally in stone-lined graves (cist graves), and occurred predominantly in the lowlands. Here pottery was limited to a few large storage jars with small bowls, large bowls with food remains, and juglets. Gonen attributes this type to Egyptian influence, since for them 'the practice of multiple successive burial and the habit of disturbing older bodies when a new one was interred must have been anathema' (1984–5:

[35] JPS, Andersen–Freedman (1989: 572), Bloch-Smith (1992a: 119).

[36] Implicitly Levine (1993: 476) as a form of worshipping the dead, cf. Ugaritic *šrp* and Eblaite *sarapatum* for animal offerings.

[37] Some rabbinic interpretation (cf. Maag 1951: 164–7), Mays (1969: 11), Soggin (1987: 106f.), Stuart (1987: 362), Hubbard (1989b: 197).

[38] Read as 'who anoints him': Driver (1956: 314f.), Paul (1991: 215f.), NEB, REB; follow LXX 'is constrained': Wolff (1977: 280); emend: Rudolph (1971: 221–3).

74). She concludes that burial customs 'prove rather conclusively the gradual development of two population groups in Canaan of the Late Bronze Age' (1992: 148).[39] There are a few other, less common types of burial: 'the foreign groups that did enter Canaan during the Late Bronze Age left only a passing, although sometimes colorful and intriguing, mark on the basic culture of the country' (1992: 148).[40]

Moving to the Iron Age (usually dated 1200–330 BCE), a study by Abercrombie (1979) covered some 670 burials at 36 sites, classifying burials mainly by the types of pottery found in them, and correlating this with burial methods and contexts.[41] Abercrombie notes a difference between highland and lowland practices in this later period as well. There are 'demonstrable patterns in the number and types of selected funerary pottery' (1979: 135), with different pottery types for: coastal and lowland simple graves (Type 1); Transjordan caves (Type 2); central highland caves (Types 3, 4); and the southern coastal plain (Type 5).[42]

More recently, Bloch-Smith (1992a) surveyed Iron Age burials, covering 850 burials at 60 sites. In the coastal and lowland regions burial was normally in simple and cist graves, while in the central highlands burial was in caves and increasingly in bench tombs.[43] Geological conditions were a major factor in burial type, but not decisive. Thus there are occasional instances of pit graves cut right into bedrock, and of bench tombs hewn in soft kurkar stone and needing supporting pillars (19). Bloch-Smith identifies the lowland graves with the Canaanites, and highland bench tombs with the Judahites, concluding: 'the correlation between the distribution patterns of the various burial types and the settlement of different cultural groups known from the Bible, extra-biblical texts and inscriptions is very high' (55). Other burial types were limited to areas of foreign influence.[44] She also notes

[39] Gonen attributes rural burial (both highland and lowland) to nomadic or pastoral groups who adopted the prevailing regional burial pattern. Dever (1999: 300) sees the grave types as merely a function of geology. This may be partially right, but pit or cist graves would be feasible in the highlands. He doesn't comment on the different pottery.

[40] These include: loculi or bench tombs, structural chambers, larnax and jar burials.

[41] Eight burial methods: primary; jar; anthropoid coffin; bathtub and other coffin; massive secondary burial; small secondary burial; pyre; urn. Five burial contexts: cave; grave; cist-grave; pyre; shallow pit with urn(s).

[42] Type 1: 'bowl pattern'; Type 2: 'lamp-1 pattern'; Type 3: 'lamp-2 pattern'; Type 4: 'juglet-1 pattern'; Type 5: 'juglet-2 pattern'. There are also some graves with mixed types (1/2, 1/3, 1/4, 1/5) in coastal and lowland areas.

[43] She distinguishes eight burial types: simple grave; cist grave; jar burial; anthropoid, wooden and stone coffin burials; bathtub coffin burial; cave, chamber and shaft tombs; arcosolia and bench tombs; cremation. Only bench tomb burial underwent significant geographical change, from lowlands to highlands.

[44] Anthropoid coffin (Egyptian), bathtub coffin (Assyrian), jar (Syrian), and cremation (Phoenician).

that surprisingly few burials have been located in the territory of the northern Israelites, and suggests that they probably practised some form of burial largely invisible to archaeologists, e.g. simple graves or a common burial pit. Regarding pottery, Bloch-Smith finds three different assemblages of grave goods in the early Iron Age. The first, typically lamps and bowls, prevailed in highland tombs; the second, typically pyxides, pilgrim flasks and craters, was common in coastal, lowland and Shephelah burials; and the third assemblage characterized sites of Egyptian influence. These were gradually replaced by new, increasingly similar, assemblages, with chalices, store-jars, dipper juglets, plates and cooking pots. She concludes that the range of burial pottery in the highlands and lowlands converged through time, while types of burial remained distinct.

As for the shape of burial caves, Loffreda (1968) notes a development over time. In the twelfth and eleventh centuries, these were mainly trapezoid, with one or two chambers, or roughly circular, with recesses or benches. He describes these as 'the last "floruit" of Late Bronze tomb types . . . in sites controlled by Philistines and Canaanites' (287). About 1000 BCE there was a 'typological gap' (282), which Loffreda explains by the rise of Israelite power under David, and the beginning of rectangular caves, with one or several chambers. Burial caves then displayed 'a homogeneous evolution until the end of the Iron Age' (287), with the main cave or the subsidiary ones being square.[45] Mazar (1990: 521) suggests that the multiple-room rock-cut family tombs resemble a four-room house, and 'such house-like burial caves demonstrate the belief in an afterlife'. But this is unlikely. Multiple-chamber tombs rarely had four chambers, and were far from house-like. Their rationale was probably not theological but practical, to accommodate more burials in one tomb.[46]

Some Iron Age tombs were exceptional. At Silwan, just east of Jerusalem, four monolithic tombs were carved from bedrock: 'the tomb of Pharaoh's daughter', 'the tomb of the royal steward', and two others. Three have inscriptions, including that of the royal steward, who may have been Shebna (condemned for his ostentatious tomb in Is. 22:15f.).[47] They were probably carved for Judahite officials, and have been dated to the later part of the Judean monarchy (late eighth to early sixth centuries). They are unique in Iron Age Israel, without parallel in Jerusalem or elsewhere. A

[45] Bloch-Smith (1992a: 176, 193, 200f., 224f., 288) criticizes Loffreda for circular argument between tomb typology and date at four sites. But at three of these (Abu Ghosh; Beth Shemesh; Jericho) Loffreda (1968: 248 n. 5, 251 n. 28, 257 n. 71) followed the excavators' dating, and at the other (Gezer) Bloch-Smith (176) accepts Loffreda's dating as possible.

[46] Cf. Burger (1992: 112).

[47] Cf. Avigad (1953; 1955), Ussishkin (1970); for text see Ch. 2.b.iii.

burial cave at Khirbet Beit Lei (about five miles east of Lachish) is unusual in containing no grave goods. Naveh (1963: 90) dates the grave's inscriptions to the late eighth century, and attributes it to a conservative levitical group 'who refrained from offerings in accordance with certain religious beliefs'.[48]

In burial caves the corpse was always fully extended, never curled in a foetal position, as Barkay notes: 'In Iron Age II Israelite burial caves, the body was always stretched out and laid on its back on the rock-hewn burial bench, as if in a bed. Not a single case of burial in a knees-to-chin, embryonic position has been found in those tombs' (1988: 49).[49]

The post-exilic period has provided little evidence. In an authoritative study, Stern (1982) surveys twenty-seven sites and finds three main burial types which flourished in different periods: the traditional burial chamber with benches (sixth century), unique to Palestine; cist tombs (late sixth to fifth centuries), which were very similar to Persian and Mesopotamian tombs, and contained both Persian and local artefacts; and shaft tombs (fifth to fourth centuries), mainly in Phoenician coastal settlements and similar to Phoenician and Cypriot tombs.[50] Stern attributes these 'eastern' and 'western' types to Persians and Phoenicians respectively, and concludes: 'It therefore also appears that we have no examples at present of Jewish or Samaritan tombs from the fifth-fourth centuries BC' (1982: 92).[51]

On the other hand, Kennedy (1989: 49) suggests that Stern 'posits a false dichotomy between Jewish and non-Jewish burial modes', and argues instead that their burial practices were indistinguishable. However, this is inappropriate criticism. Stern clearly works from the evidence available, he attributes cist and shaft graves to non-Jewish peoples on the basis of their location and contents, and he notes sites with a possible variety of burial types. Jews may have adopted Persian and Phoenician burial practices, as Kennedy implies, but this conclusion is not inevitable.

To conclude, these studies indicate that in Late Bronze Age and Iron Age Palestine the central highlanders maintained a burial pattern different from those of lowland and coastal dwellers. This pattern came to be distinctively Judahite, particularly during the monarchy period. The post-exilic period is poorly attested.[52]

48 The Qumran community practised similar restraint (cf. de Vaux 1973: 47).

49 Barkay refutes Keel's proposal that the Israelites considered burial as a return to the womb.

50 Pit burials at several sites contained grave goods similar to the third group.

51 However, some may exist at ʿAin ʿArrub, Tell el-Ḥesi, Beit-Lei, Lachish, and Gezer, Naḥshonim and Makmish (Stern 1982: 231, 266 n. 70).

52 For other brief surveys, cf. Mazar (1990), Burger (1992) and, for Jerusalem, Rahmani (1981).

v. Secondary burial

Tombs were habitually re-used. This had several practical and social advantages, as Cooley (1983: 55) notes: it conserved labour in tomb construction, avoided their proliferation, maintained family solidarity, and ensured a monument to an extinct family. Re-use of a tomb meant that for each burial one of the rock-cut benches had to be cleared to make way for the new corpse. This involved gathering up the bones of the skeleton lying there and depositing them in a corner of the cave, sometimes in a repository pit cut into the floor for this very purpose. Non-valuable grave goods were also swept into the pit. (The valuable goods were often retrieved and re-used.) Occasionally skulls were put in a separate pile, but not always.[53] This practice is often called 'secondary burial', but the term is misleading since it suggests an actual burial of the skeletal remains.[54] In fact, the bones were simply removed from the bench with no particular signs of respect, so it is better called 'secondary deposition'.[55] In the late post-exilic period, the practice of collecting bones into a bone box or 'ossuary' became common, but there is no evidence for this before the Hellenistic Age.

Meyers (1970) describes and interprets the practice of secondary burial: 'Perhaps the most outstanding characteristic of Iron Age tombs . . . is the communal ossuary or repository which was adopted to insure the safekeeping of the bones of former burials' (10).[56] However, the usually disordered piles of broken grave goods and bones, sometimes fused together, hardly suggest that the safe-keeping of bones was a paramount concern. He continues: '[bones] represent the full significance of [a] man and it is hard to imagine the callous treatment in a family tomb of the beloved departed whose names were in a very real sense a potent force in the present' (16). However, the displacement of skeletal remains into a tomb corner indicates neither the callous treatment Meyers rejects nor the deferential treatment he deduces, but simply the practical need to place them elsewhere.

Meyers also suggests that 'the bones of a man possess at least a shadow of their strength in life' (15), as indicated by 'numerous' biblical passages (16). But he cites only two, of which only one is relevant, and it refers to the bones

[53] Bloch-Smith (1992a: 37) notes this practice in nine cave, chamber or shaft tombs. Arensburg–Rak (1985: 30) comment: '"selective bone gathering" was traditionally used by the Jews until the late Byzantine period (c. 600 CE).'

[54] This may occasionally have occurred. Abercrombie mentions an incomplete skeleton in Lachish tomb 223 with the skull placed in the pelvis (so Bloch-Smith 1992a: 37, but not 206).

[55] So Bloch-Smith (1992a: 36).

[56] Meyers gives no evidence of communal ossuaries in Iron Age tombs anywhere in the Levant, even among the wealthy Aegeans at Ugarit. (Greek Mycenean tombs elsewhere did have *larnakes*, or bone chests.)

of an exceptional prophet (2 Kgs. 13:21: a hastily buried man revives on touching Elisha's bones). The other (Ezek. 37:1–14) simply cites bones as the visible remains of the dead, which in fact lack any inherent power and need divine power to come to life. Granted, the Old Testament also records the respectful burial of Saul's bones (1 Sam. 31:13), and the removal of Joseph's 'bones' from Egypt (Gen. 46:4; 50:24f.; Exod. 13:19), though interestingly it omits their later interment. But these references to bones are exceptional. Against Meyers, neither archaeological nor textual evidence indicates an Israelite preoccupation with the bones of the dead.

By contrast, Cooley (1983: 52) rightly notes 'a contrast in attitudes . . . between the time of the burial of the body and the eventual destructive treatment of the skeletal remains of the same body after the flesh had decomposed'. The deceased was provided with food and drink for the journey to the underworld, but was deemed to have arrived when the corpse had decomposed. Then no further nourishment was provided, and the bones could be swept aside with impunity. He also notes the lack of ritual, apart from wine libation, associated with the Late Bronze Age tomb which he studied. 'The Dothan practice in regard to objects connected with religion gives no evidence of concern for the spiritual needs of the dead in the afterlife' (52). His comments apply equally to Iron Age bench tomb burial.

vi. Food and burial

In Palestine as throughout the ancient world, food often accompanied a corpse to the grave, hence the presence of jugs and bowls in all types of graves throughout Old Testament times. In highland cave tombs (often identified with the Israelites in the Iron Age), the food could perhaps have been intended for and consumed by mourners, rather than the dead. But in the mainly lowland simple graves, food and drink in buried vessels could only have been intended for the dead.

However, significant difficulties surround the issue of grave food. First, food by its very nature perishes, and very little evidence of the content of these vessels has survived and been identified as food remains by archaeologists. Animal bones in graves may indicate grave food, but these occur only occasionally.[57] Secondly, it is often impossible in re-used caves to know whether food and drink was provided only initially, for the deceased's journey to the underworld (as Cooley describes above), or continuously, for

[57] Horwitz (1987: 251) gives useful criteria for identifying animal bones as food remains: proximity to human remains, narrow range of species, particular body parts, articulated body parts, preference for one side, age-based selection, sex-based selection.

ongoing sustenance there. Replenishment of food and drink could not happen in simple graves, but it could occur in re-used caves.[58] And thirdly, it is often impossible to determine the ethnic origin of the dead, and therefore to know whether provision of food and drink was practised by Israelites as well as non-Israelites.

A few older archaeologists identified food remains in tombs. McCown (1947: 83) concluded that a sticky substance in a beehive-shaped vessel in the ninth-century Tell en-Naṣbeh tomb 5 'suggest[s] that it contained a funerary offering of honey'.[59] Sukenik (1940: 62) interpreted two pits filled with artefacts and animal bones in the eighth-century Samaria tomb 103 as evidence of an Israelite cult of the dead, though others question his interpretation of the remains and his ethnic identification of the tomb.[60] And Mackenzie (1912–13: 67) found sheep bones between two bowls in the seventh-century Beth Shemesh tomb 2.

By contrast, in his comprehensive survey Abercrombie (1979: 189f.) notes a lack of animal bones in most Iron Age burials. Only occasionally do goat, pig or sheep bones occur. There is much evidence of burning oil or spices, since there are numerous lamps and juglets for oil, and most lamps show signs of use.[61] But there is little evidence of food offerings, as bowls and jugs rarely have traces of their former contents.

Bloch-Smith (1992a) interprets the evidence differently. She lists food remains found in several Iron Age sites and in different burial types,[62] and sees this as important evidence of continued nourishment of the dead in pre-exilic Israel. However, she ignores a crucial issue, the location and possible ethnic identity of these sites.[63] In fact, most of the sites listed lie outside the central highlands, and clear evidence of food remains is still lacking for burials which were more probably Israelite. Of possible Israelite sites, Beth Shemesh in the Shephelah had a mixed ethnic background, and the burial customs at Lachish reflect a cosmopolitan city. So the food remains there could have occurred in non-Israelite burials. The only probable Judahite

58 Bloch-Smith (1992a: 105) notes that simple graves show food was intended for the dead, but not that it was only provided initially.

59 McCown thought two classes of juglets here were largely reserved for funeral offerings (cf. Saggs 1958: 162).

60 Questioned by Franken–Franken-Battershil and Lapp (cf. Spronk 1986: 37 n. 2).

61 Bloch-Smith (1992a: 75) agrees that 'lamps predominated in cave and bench tombs'.

62 Bloch-Smith (1992a: 106f.): Iron I: Tell es-Saidiyeh (cist, simple), Tel Kishyon (simple), Kfar Yehoshua (jar), Azor (cremation), Tel Dothan (cave), Gezer (cave); Iron II: Aitun (bench?), Lachish (cave), Akhzib (simple), Tel Bira (simple), Ashdod (intramural), Samaria (cave), Amman (cave), Beth Shemesh (bench).

63 She provides 18 maps in a very useful appendix, but surprisingly no map of sites with food remains, though this is crucial to her conclusions. Cf. reviews by Johnston (1994), Tappy (1995). On the cult of the dead see Ch. 8.

central highland site Bloch-Smith lists is Aitun, but here no food remains were found, and she misinterprets the circumstantial evidence. The excavator Ussishkin (1974: 125) found lamps, jars and arcosolia in Tomb 1 with traces of burning. He surmised that the arcosolia soot was 'probably caused by kindling fires in them' and that this 'may well have some connection with the numerous squat jugs with rounded bases found blackened by soot'.[64] However, Bloch-Smith replaces 'jugs' by 'cooking pots' in her discussion, though Ussishkin (120–22) does not note any soot on these, and she then suggests that 'the ash resulted from cooking food' (107). This is possible, but lacks archaeological evidence.

To conclude, there is some scattered evidence of food remains in burial sites in Iron Age Palestine. Some of these may possibly have been Judahite, but none can be clearly identified as such. Thus there remains no clear archaeological evidence for Israelites regularly providing food for the dead.

c. Summary

In many societies elaborate social customs surround the event of death. This may well have been the case in ancient Israel, but the Old Testament only mentions such customs occasionally and in passing. Mourning certainly occurred, as glimpsed fleetingly, and two specific periods of mourning are recorded, but no general policy is given. Various mourning customs are mentioned more frequently, in both law and narrative, with some inevitable variation over time. In the early monarchy fasting appears to be normative, while later texts mention the food of mourners. This food may have been very basic, though at times there may also have been a celebratory wake. Poetic laments and stylized wailing are also occasionally noted. There is virtually no information on funerary rites, apart from the lavish burning of spices for kings. In particular, there is no reference to religious ceremonies at funerals – burial was simply conducted by the immediate family. Mourning and funerary customs were not apparently invested with religious significance.

Burial is recorded in the Old Testament for most major figures, but not all. Thus its mention was an important but not an indispensable part of Israel's traditions. Burial nearly always occurred on family land, and land ownership was clearly vital for Abraham's burial of Sarah. But no inference is ever drawn from burial locations about consultation or veneration of the dead.

[64] Ussishkin (125 n. 13) also notes similar unblackened jugs in Tomb 1, and similar blackened jugs in other tombs.

Burial was the norm. Exposure, exhumation and cremation of corpses were all abhorrent practices. Archaeological excavation shows a generally consistent pattern of multiple, successive cave burial in the central highlands throughout the Late Bronze and Iron Ages. At each new interment, the skeletal remains of previous burials were simply swept into a corner, and the bones of the dead were not accorded any special reverence.

Burials in caves were accompanied by various pottery assemblages, including bowls and jugs. These may have contained food for the dead at the time of burial, but there is no clear evidence of regular, ongoing nourishment of the dead. Thus, while the act of burial was important, there was no continued reverence for the physical remains or attempt to feed the departed. Despite recent arguments to the contrary, textual and archaeological evidence does not suggest a continued interest in the remains of the dead.

Both the lack of obvious religious rites at burial and the lack of interest in graves confirm that Israelite life and faith were centred on the present life and relating to Yahweh in the here and now. Death was the end of this life, not the start of the next, so religious ceremony was of little significance, and further sustenance was futile. In words attributed to Hezekiah:

> those who go down to the Pit cannot hope
>   for your faithfulness.
> The living, the living, they thank you,
>   as I do this day (Is. 38:18–19).

Part B

THE UNDERWORLD

Chapter 3
THE UNWELCOME UNDERWORLD

People in the ancient world generally believed in a three-tiered universe. The heavens were for the great gods, the earth for humans, and the underworld for the dead and the chthonic deities. Ancient Near Eastern literature dealt at length with all three levels, not least the last. In Mesopotamia several epics discussed it in part or whole, notably *Gilgamesh*, *The Descent of Ishtar*, and *Nergal and Ereshkigal*, while these and other texts testify to a wide variety of names for the underworld.[1] At Ugarit the great *Baal epic* related his temporary consignment to the realm of Mot ('Death').[2] And in Egypt there proliferated books dealing with the afterlife, including the well-known *Book of the Dead*.[3] These portrayed the journey of the deceased through different stages of the underworld until they eventually reached the great hall of judgment where their souls were weighed and their destiny was determined.

In marked contrast, Israel's canonical literature contains no such epics about descent to the underworld or return from it, guided by various deities. By its very definition it could not, since it specifically refused the necessary polytheism. Nor does it have any detailed description of the deceased's journey through the underworld to a place of judgment. Such speculation clearly lay outside the parameters of orthodox Yahwism and was avoided by its authoritative writers. Instead (as already noted), life itself was the starting-

[1] For epics, see Dalley (1989) etc. For names, see Tallqvist (1934), Horowitz (1998).
[2] KTU 1.5, 1.6.
[3] Hornung (1999) provides a richly illustrated summary of some 15 other texts dealing with the dead.

point and the focus for Israel's faith, while death and its aftermath were of little concern. Israelite faith concerned a living relationship with Yahweh in the present, not speculation about the future. This in itself distinguishes Israel's literature significantly from that of her neighbours.

Nevertheless, the Israelites had some notion of what followed death. Even if the afterlife is not a major or a repeated theme in the Hebrew Bible, their attitudes to it can be discerned in the many references to death scattered through its many pages. After all, death is repeatedly reported in narrative accounts, whether of patriarchs, judges, kings or ordinary people. Death is frequently the subject of the psalms, whether the threatened death of the psalmist or the desired death of his enemies. It is predicted in much prophecy, and reflected on in some wisdom writing. So, for the Israelites, what was the underworld like? Who went there? Are there hidden references to it? What emotions did it arouse for the living? This section explores these issues.

Scores of scholarly articles and several detailed studies[4] summarize Israel's view of the underworld. However, most of these adopt a synthetic approach, in which all terms and texts relating to death are studied together without close attention to possible differences in meaning. This gives a comprehensive picture, but does not highlight each term's particular contexts of use and distinctive nuances. Even some of the detailed studies have methodological flaws, e.g. Tromp's (1969) often cited study of underworld terms virtually ignores the main term 'Sheol'. So we will start by examining this key term.

a. Sheol as a place

> Let the wicked be put to shame;
> let them go dumbfounded to Sheol (Ps. 31:17);
>
> For great is your steadfast love toward me;
> you have delivered my soul from the depths of Sheol (Ps. 86:13).

i. Occurrence of the term

The most important Hebrew term for the underworld is clearly *šᵉʾôl* (left untranslated as 'Sheol' in most English versions),[5] for several reasons: (a) It is

[4] E.g. Martin-Achard (1960), Wächter (1967), Tromp (1969).
[5] E.g. RV, RSV, NRSV; JB, NJB; NEB, REB; NASB; but not NIV (see below).

the most frequent, occurring sixty-six times.[6] (b) It always occurs without the definite article ('the'), which implies that it is a proper name.[7] (c) It always means the realm of the dead located deep in the earth, unlike other terms which can mean both 'pit' and 'underworld' (see Ch. 3.c).

The term Sheol occurs as follows:[8]

Literature	*Number*	*Texts*
Psalmodic	21	Psalms (16x): 6:5; 9:17; 16:10; 18:5; 30:3; 31:17; 49:14, 15 (x2); 55:15; 86:13; 88:3; 89:48; 116:3; 139:8; 141:7 Other (5x): 1 Sam. 2:6; 2 Sam. 22:6; Is. 38:10, 18; Jonah 2:2
Reflective	20	Job (8x): 7:9; 11:8; 14:13; 17:13, 16; 21:13; 24:19; 26:6 Proverbs (9x): 1:12; 5:5; 7:27; 9:18; 15:11, 24; 23:14; 27:20; 30:16 Other (3x): Deut. 32:22; Eccles. 9:10; Song 8:6;
Prophetic[9]	17	Is. 5:14; 7:11; 14:9, 11, 15; 28:15, 18; 57:9; Ezek. 31:15–17; 32:21, 27; Hos. 13:14 (x2); Amos 9:2; Hab. 2:5
Narrative	8	Gen. 37:35; 42:38; 44:29, 31; Num. 16:30, 33; 1 Kgs. 2:6, 9

This pattern of occurrence prompts three important observations. First, there is a striking and distinctive pattern regarding the type of literature in which 'Sheol' is used. The term occurs mostly in psalmodic, reflective and prophetic literature,[10] where authors are personally involved in their work. By contrast, it appears only rarely in descriptive narrative, and then almost entirely in direct speech.[11] In particular, 'Sheol' never occurs in the many

[6] 65, in the MT plus Is. 7:11. Here most scholars and modern versions emend the MT *šᵉʾālāh* ('ask') to *šᵉʾôlāh* ('to Sheol'), following early versions (LXX, Aquila, Symmachus, Theodotion, Peshitta).

[7] *šᵉʾôl* is feminine, cf. Ps. 86:13; Is. 5:14. (For related masculine forms in Is. 14:9; Job 26:6; see GK §§144o, 145t.)

[8] Podella (1988) classifies occurrences by literary type as: prayer, 18; prophecy, 11; wisdom (including Gen. 37 – 44), 22; other texts, 7. But he gives no breakdown by book, and his figures do not total 66.

[9] Excluding Is. 38:10, 18 and Jonah 2:2, classed here as psalmodic.

[10] Hence it is sometimes called a poetic term. However, poetry and prose can be indistinct (e.g. Ezek. 31 – 32).

[11] In the sole exception (Num. 16:33), the narrator simply repeats the phraseology already attributed to Moses (v. 30).

narrative accounts of death, whether of patriarchs, kings, prophets, priests or ordinary people, whether of Israelite or foreigner, of righteous or wicked. Also, 'Sheol' is entirely absent from legal material, including the many laws which prescribe capital punishment or proscribe necromancy. This means that 'Sheol' is very clearly a term of personal engagement. It is not a concept to be mentioned casually or dispassionately, in simple report of the past or general legislation for present and future. Rather it indicates personal emotional involvement, in apprehension of one's own destiny or anticipation of one's enemies' fate.

Secondly, the term 'Sheol' was not specific to any one period of Israel's literary endeavour.[12] It occurs in texts from the Pentateuch, the early historical books, and various prophets, psalms and wisdom books. Regardless of the precise dating of these texts, references to Sheol are scattered across the centuries of Israelite writing. Clearly the term did not belong to any one particular period, but remained a constant (if occasional) term for the underworld.

Thirdly, it is remarkable that 'Sheol' occurs so seldom, given the length of the Old Testament and its frequent references to death. Indeed, the stem 'die/death' (*m-w-t*) occurs one thousand times,[13] but there are only about one hundred references to the underworld (using 'Sheol' or a synonym). Some scholars argue that this is the result of a later orthodoxy misreading other underworld allusions, accidentally or deliberately, and that ancient Israel was more preoccupied with the afterlife than the Hebrew Bible implies. Some of this argument is examined term by term and text by text in Chapter 5. But two preliminary points can be made here. First, the way that the existing underworld references are scattered through psalms, prophets and wisdom literature makes it unlikely that a more widespread early usage was pruned by later zealous redactors. And secondly, even if a few further underworld allusions are accepted, this still gives a relatively small total.

This small total is also noteworthy given the numerous references to the underworld in other ancient Near Eastern literature, as noted above. Exact comparison is impossible, since no other body of religious literature became canonical like the Hebrew Bible. However, the contrast is still striking. This indicates that the underworld is not a central feature of the Old Testament in its canonical form. Yahweh has nothing to do with the dead or the world of the dead, and the literature which represents

[12] Some have recently argued that all OT literature comes from the post-exilic period. But its variety in style, theme and language is eloquent testimony against this view, quite apart from issues of the authenticity of the 'earlier' material.
[13] Exactly (cf. THAT 1: 894b; TDOT 8: 191).

Yahwistic faith does not dwell on the underworld at length or with great elaboration. While it is worth studying the Israelite portrayal of the underworld, it is vital to note at the outset that this is a minor Old Testament theme.

ii. Meaning of the word

So far it has been assumed that 'Sheol' means the underworld, the realm of the dead deep below the earth. This is almost universally accepted. It is clearly below ground: to go there one 'descends' (*y-r-d*),[14] and to escape one 'ascends' (*'-l-h*);[15] it is often qualified by adjectives of depth;[16] it is cosmologically opposite to 'heaven' (Job 11:8; Ps. 139:8; Is. 7:11; Amos 9:2; cf. Deut. 32:22); one digs towards Sheol (Amos 9:2); the earth opens its mouth and rebels descend there (Num. 16:30, 33); it is a cavernous communal tomb (Ezek. 32:18–32); and is associated with worms, maggots and dust (Job 17:16; Is. 14:11).

Because Sheol is often associated with the wicked, the term was frequently translated as 'hell' in the Authorized or King James Version.[17] However, the Hebrew Bible never indicates any form of punishment after death, so this translation is inappropriate.

By contrast, because Sheol is sometimes associated with the righteous (see Ch. 3.b), some conservative scholars propose that 'Sheol' does *not* mean the underworld, or at least not always. They argue doctrinally that righteous and wicked would not face the same underworld destiny. Thus Heidel (1949) argues that 'Sheol' often means 'the grave', as shown by references to pomp, worms, maggots and swords (Is. 14:11; Ezek. 32:26f.) or worms and bones (Job 24; Ps. 141; Elephantine papyrus), or by poetic parallels (Ps. 89; Prov. 23) or by the general context (Gen. 37 – 44; 1 Kgs. 2). His argument is also explicitly theological: 'there is no conclusive evidence that the souls of pious persons . . . were believed to descend to *Shĕ'ôl* in the sense of the

[14] 18 times. Other verbs occur rarely: *n-ḥ-t* (Job 17:16; 21:13) and *š-w-b* (Ps. 9:17).

[15] Ps. 30:3. Similarly with synonyms of *šᵉ'ôl*: *'-l-h* (from the pit: Jonah 2:6; Ps. 40:2; the depths of the earth, Ps. 71:20) and *r-w-m* (from the gates of death, Ps. 9:13). Deliverance is also expressed without spatial direction. See Barth (1947: 124–33).

[16] E.g. *taḥtiṯ* etc. ('below') occurs with 'Sheol' (Deut. 32:22; Ps. 86:13), 'pit' (*bôr*, Ps. 88:6; Lam. 3:5) and 'earth' (*'ereṣ*, Ps. 63:9; Ezek. 26:20; 31:14, 16, 18; 32:18, 24); and *'emeq* ('below') with 'Sheol' (Job 11:8; Prov. 9:18; Is. 7:11). Youngblood (TWOT: 969) interprets 'the earth below' in Ezek. 31 – 32 as 'no more than a place below ground where the dead are buried'. But this overlooks Ezek. 32:21, where the mighty chiefs speak 'out of the midst of Sheol'.

[17] AV translates *šᵉ'ôl* as 'hell' 31 times, 'grave' 31 times and 'pit' 3 times (ignoring Is. 7:11).

subterranean spirit world', which means that 'Hezekiah [in Is. 38] uses *Shĕ'ôl* in the sense of "the grave"'.[18]

However, Heidel's argument has several flaws. It ignores the prophetic pictures of Sheol's inhabitants speaking (Is. 14:10; Ezek. 32:21). It posits different meanings of Sheol within the same passage (Is. 14:11–15). It assumes identity between the specific term 'Sheol' and the more general term 'death'.[19] And it arbitrarily determines the meaning of Sheol by theological assessment of the associated individual, which results in the contradiction that the pious go to Sheol (when it means the grave) but not to Sheol (when it means the underworld).[20] Thus Heidel's view is unsatisfactory.

Harris (1961) resolves the apparent problem differently. He argues that Sheol always means the grave, as shown by parallel references to death, the grave, the pit, corruption, worms, dust, etc. In line with this, he interprets references to existence in Sheol as figurative. Thus the powerful evocations of Sheol in Psalm 88 refers only to the tomb: 'There is no declaration here that the afterlife is dark and a place which God forgets.' And the gathering in Sheol in Isaiah 14:9 is at most a figure of speech: 'the prophet only says that the paths of glory lead but to the grave.' As for the expression 'Sheol below', the opposite of 'heaven above', this is 'as far down as the Hebrews could imagine', 'a deep grave'.[21] Harris was a senior member of the NIV translation committee and decisively influenced its translation at this point.[22] So the NIV usually translates *š^e'ôl* as 'grave'.

However, Harris's argument ignores other aspects of the texts he cites; e.g. Psalm 88 also mentions 'the depths of the Pit' (v. 6) and 'the shades' (*r^epā'îm*, v. 10), and Isaiah 14 portrays 'the shades' being roused to greet the fallen tyrant (vv. 9f.).[23] The idea that the Israelites could not imagine anything lower than the grave is naïve, especially given the many biblical references to the depths of the sea. Further, this view cannot be maintained consistently, as the NIV amply illustrates. Occasionally it has to resort to other translations of *š^e'ôl* because the sense of the passage demands it, notably 'depths of the grave' (Amos 9:2), 'realm of death' (Deut. 32:22).

Obviously, the Hebrew term 'Sheol' has different nuances in different

[18] Heidel (1949: 180). He accepts that 'Sheol' sometimes means the underworld (e.g. Is. 14:13–15).
[19] Further, Heidel immediately states that 'death' can mean 'subterranean realm of the dead' (177).
[20] Similarly critiqued by Alexander (1986: 44).
[21] Harris (1961; TWOT: 892f.; quotations from 1961: 132, 133 sic, 130).
[22] This is explicitly acknowledged (Harris, 1987).
[23] Perhaps also in v. 16, so Auvray (1972: 16), Clements (1980: 143). However, most scholars see these as living.

contexts, but these are nuances of the single basic concept of the underworld. Views to the contrary cannot be sustained.

iii. Description of the place

Sheol is at the opposite theological extreme to Yahweh, and the dominant feature for its inhabitants is their separation from him. They cannot remember, praise or thank Yahweh (Ps. 6:6; Is. 38:18; Jonah 2:5). It is characteristically 'the land of forgetfulness' (Ps. 88:12), where they are cut off from him and forgotten (Ps. 88:5). Hence Sheol is a fitting place for the wicked who forget God (Ps. 9:17; 31:17; 55:15), but one which the righteous dread (Ps. 16:10; 30:3; 49:15; 86:13).[24]

At the same time, Sheol is also portrayed as known by and accessible to Yahweh. It provides no escape from him (Amos 9:2; Ps. 139:8), lies open before him (Job 26:5; Prov. 15:11) and does not circumscribe his power (Is. 7:11; Job 11:8).[25] Similar expressions occur in other ancient texts: in the Akkadian *Dialogue of Pessimism* one can reach neither heaven nor the underworld;[26] and in a letter to the Egyptian Pharaoh neither sphere provides escape from his protection.[27] Some scholars take Sheol in these biblical texts as hyperbolic superlative, not meant literally.[28] However, while flight to Sheol was as unachievable as flight to heaven for Amos or flight to the seabed for the psalmist, and while Isaiah's offer of a spectacular sign was declined, their hyperbole reflects the belief that heaven and Sheol were actually within Yahweh's power. Here hyperbole requires literalness; it does not dispense with it.[29] Further, this view does not deal with Sheol as open before Yahweh.[30] Others see Yahweh's omnipotence, even over Sheol, as a late wisdom theme. But Amos 9:2 and Isaiah 7:11 hardly support this.[31] More

24 The rabbis surmised that God created Sheol on the second day, which alone lacks 'it was good' (Bailey 1979: 53).
25 Yahweh's fire reaching Sheol (Deut. 32:22) indicates universal judgment rather than underworld access.
26 Line 85; so Biggs (ANETS: 601), Pope (1973: lxviii). Pfeiffer (ANET: 437f.) translates: '. . . the earth'.
27 El-Amarna letter 264:15–19, cf. Moran (1992: 313).
28 E.g. Maag (1964: 26), Tromp (1969: 200), Hayes (1988: 217).
29 Similarly, the modern curse 'Go to hell!' owes its potency to the belief, however vestigial, in hell's reality.
30 Against Tromp (1969: 201), for whom Job 26:6, 14 corroborates the metaphoric view.
31 E.g. many accept Amos 9:2 as authentic to the prophet: Mays (1969: 12), Wolff (1977: 107), Rudolph (1971: 243), Soggin (1987: 15), Stuart (1987: 287), Andersen–Freedman (1989: 142f.). Some see Amos in the wisdom tradition (Wolff: 340), with cosmological beliefs different from the prophetic tradition (Terrien 1962: 110f.). However, prophets and wise men shared many literary techniques and other theological motifs.

importantly, the contrast between Yahweh's power over Sheol and separation from it is often overstated: that Yahweh has access to Sheol does not imply that its inhabitants have access to him. The themes are complementary rather than contradictory, and are juxtaposed in a single verse (Job 14:13). Here Job longs to be hidden in Sheol from Yahweh's wrath but later to be remembered by him.

Sheol is a place of no return (Job 16:22),[32] a place of captivity with gates (Is. 38:10) and bars (Jonah 2:6).[33] The 'cords of Sheol' may also suggest captivity (Pss. 18:5; 116:3), but more probably evoke hunting. Job's wish to be hidden temporarily in Sheol (14:13; cf. 18–22) initially seems to question this finality, but the wish is hypothetical, an attempt to move beyond his perceived impasse with God, and does not qualify the general picture.

Existence in Sheol is very sketchily drawn. It is a place of darkness (Job 10:21; Ps. 88:6, 12; cf. 143:3; Lam. 3:6; Sirach 22:11), of inactivity and silence (Pss. 94:17; 115:17). Only two prophetic oracles portray any form of activity. In one the denizens of Sheol must be roused to greet a newcomer, and they then describe themselves as weak (Is. 14:9f.). In the other, the long dead declaim that others 'have come down, they lie still' (Ezek. 32:21). These texts simply confirm that inactivity is the norm.

Death, and implicitly Sheol, is the great leveller of all, small or great, slave or free (Job 3:13–19). However, the prophetic texts just noted portray former leaders sitting on thrones or lying with their armies in Sheol. Some scholars suggest that these texts preserve disparate views of the underworld.[34] But the difference is more apparent than real, since enfeebled existence hardly permits meaningful social distinctions, and the prophetic texts actually stress equality in death rather than perpetuation of hierarchy. Isaiah 14 describes the downfall of a mighty king to the level of other deceased rulers, probably including his former vassals. And Ezekiel 32 notes that a similar underworld fate befell several groups who were all uncircumcised, violent and killed in battle.[35] The 'fallen warriors of long ago' in the middle of the list (v. 27) fit this description,[36] and therefore their apparently

[32] Cf. the well-known Akkadian term 'land of no return'.

[33] Cf. 'the gates of death' in Pss. 9:13; 107:18, and notably Job 38:17, which has 'the gates of the shadow of death (*ṣalmāwet*)' in parallel. Cf. also 'gates of Hades' in Wisdom 16:13; 3 Macc. 5:51; Matt. 16:18. Most scholars now reject the translation of *baddê* in Job 17:16 as 'bars': Terrien (1963: 137), Pope (1973: 131), Gordis (1978: 185), Rowley (1976: 126), Andersen (1976: 186 n. 1), Habel (1985: 264), Hartley (1988: 267), Clines (1989: 375).

[34] E.g. Martin-Achard (1960: 39).

[35] The omission of 'uncircumcised' for the Assyrians and 'spread terror' for the Edomites is insignificant.

[36] They were presumably considered pre-Abrahamic and therefore uncircumcised (which the LXX reads instead of 'long ago'). Burial with weapons probably indicates death in battle, not honourable burial.

different status is curious.[37] But with a slight emendation, the fallen warriors meet the same fate as the other reprehensible groups, which gives a more satisfactory reading in context.[38] The oracle then stresses similar notoriety in life and common destiny in death.

These two prophetic passages are sometimes thought to imply different compartments within Sheol, with the king of Babylon consigned to 'the depths of the pit' (Is. 14:15) and the Assyrians to 'the uttermost parts of the Pit' (Ezek. 32:23). But this is not necessarily a worse fate. In the former case the fallen king clearly joins others in Sheol, and in the latter Assyria is 'there' in Sheol like all the other groups (Elam, Meshech and Tubal, Edom, etc.). In later, intertestamental literature Sheol/Hades was divided into separate compartments for the righteous and the wicked, and 1 Enoch 22 specifies three or four separate compartments.[39] However, the Old Testament texts do not assert this.

iv. Origin of the name

The word 'Sheol' occurs almost exclusively in Old Testament Hebrew. Indeed, there is only one certain occurrence elsewhere in the biblical period, in a fifth-century BCE Aramaic text from the Jewish community at Elephantine in southern Egypt, which reads: 'and your bones will not descend to Sheol'.[40] A further Hebrew/Aramaic attestation has been suggested, but is unlikely: Harris reads *š'wl* on a late Second Temple Jerusalem ossuary lid as 'Sheol', but Rahmani notes the adjacent Greek letters 'SAU/LOS' and reads it more probably as the name 'Saul'.[41] Later, of course, Sheol occurs in derivative traditions, as in the Qumran psalms,[42] rabbinic discussion[43] and biblical translations.[44]

For over a century scholars have puzzled over the origin of the Hebrew term *šᵉʾôl*.[45] Derivations have been suggested from a wide variety of terms in

[37] Most scholars accept the MT and envisage them lying separately in Sheol: Taylor (1969: 212), Wevers (1969: 175), Eichrodt (1970: 439), Carley (1974: 217), Zimmerli (1983: 176), Allen (1990: 138).
[38] Omitting the MT's negative (*lôʾ*, v. 27), following LXX, Lucian and Syriac.
[39] Most scholars see four, though the text is ambiguous. Such multiple division is unique (cf. Bauckham 1995), as elsewhere Hades is divided into two.
[40] A. Cowley (1923: 180f., no. 71:15).
[41] Harris (1987: 76), Rahmani (1968: 222; 1982: 113).
[42] 8 times; cf. Kuhn (1960: 214), THAT (2: 844), TWAT (8: 910).
[43] Cf. Levy (1976–89), Jastrow (1903) and Sokoloff (1990) s.v. *šᵉʾôl*.
[44] Syriac, Mandaic, Ethiopic and Tigrean.
[45] For full details see Johnston (1993: 7–14). For selective surveys: THAT, TWAT, Martin-Achard (1960: 37), Eichrodt (1967: 210 n. 2), Stadelmann (1970: 165f.), Wildberger (1978: 548), Rosenberg (1981: 2–12), Spronk (1986: 66f.).

other ancient Semitic and non-Semitic languages.[46] However, none of these is plausible, with one possible exception (see below), and many suggestions were abandoned long ago. *šᵉʾôl* has also been derived from various Hebrew roots. (i) From *š-ʾ-l*, 'ask', giving: 'demand a decision', 'enquiry by necromancy', 'ordeal', 'punishment'. This is the most obvious root phonetically, but it is hard to link the idea of 'asking' with the underworld. (ii) From *š-ʾ-h*, 'be desolate', with epenthetic (additional) *l*, giving 'desolate place' (Köhler). This has gained some scholarly support but remains uncertain. (iii) Various others, all highly improbable.[47] So the etymology of this important term is unknown, and therefore can give no help regarding its meaning.

Until recently, no cognate of Hebrew *šᵉʾôl* had been identified in extant texts in other Semitic languages, whether Akkadian, Ugaritic, Phoenician, Punic or Arabic. Sheol was uniquely a Hebrew term. But the continued discovery of ancient texts at new sites has brought fresh proposals. Dahood sees a link with the place-name *ši-a-la*^{ki} in a text from Ebla.[48] But it is highly tenuous to link a place-name in an administrative list (concerning cereal) written at Ebla in the third millennium with an underworld name in religious texts in Israel in the first millennium. Since *š-ʾ-l* is a common root in Semitic languages,[49] the similarity of name is almost certainly coincidental.

More importantly, Arnaud (1986) identifies the deity ^{d}*šu-wa-la*, mentioned in two *kissu*-festival texts in Akkadian from late second-millennium Emar, as an underworld deity called Sheol. He translates the relevant lines:

Text 385, line	23	The singers enter and sing to Sheol and Nergal.
	26	Thirty . . . of silver are given to Ereshkigal.
Text 388, line	6	On the same day a sheep is sacrificed to Sheol.
	57	The singers [sing to] Sh[eol . . .][50]

This identification, accepted by a few other scholars,[51] would confirm longstanding conjectures that Sheol was originally an underworld deity.[52] De Moor further interprets text 385 as identifying *šu-wa-la* with Ereshkigal, the Akkadian underworld queen and wife of Nergal, and therefore sees

[46] Akkadian: *šuāllu* (?), *šillan* (sunset), *šuʾāra* (home of Tammuz), *šêltu* (sword of death), *šuwala* (deity); Sumerian: *kigal/šiwal* (underworld), *zul/sul/šul* (land of no return); Arabic: *sahâl* (deep); Egyptian: **še-l*; bilingual combination of *š* (Egyptian: sea) and *ʾēl* (Hebrew: God).

[47] *š-ʿ-l*, 'be hollow'; *š-w-l*, 'be wide'; *š-l-ʾ*, 'be quiet'; *š-w-l*, 'be deep'; *š+ʾal*, 'make nothing'.

[48] Text: MEE 1,1027; Dahood (1987: 97).

[49] E.g. Hebrew has the common verb *š-ʾ-l* and two personal names: *šāʾûl* (of four individuals) and *šᵉʾāl*.

[50] My translation from Arnaud's French text.

[51] E.g. de Moor (1990b: 239), Korpel (1990: 348), Lebrun (personal letter, 1992).

[52] E.g. Wood (1916: 268), Gordis (1978: 278).

Hebrew Sheol 'as a remnant of Canaanite religion where she had been a goddess'.[53] The evidence is sparse, and others identify *šu-wa-la* differently, e.g. with the Hurrian god Shuwaliyat, husband of Nabarbi.[54] Nevertheless, the fact that *šu-wa-la* appears alongside other infernal deities does seem to link it to Sheol.

If Sheol was originally an Akkadian name for an underworld deity, several interesting deductions follow. (a) It was at best a minor deity or an uncommon name for Ereshkigal, since it occurs so infrequently in the extant texts (though this may be qualified by future discoveries). (b) The name seems localized in time and place to late second millennium Emar, and does not appear to have been known elsewhere. (c) This obscure Akkadian name of a deity became the principal Hebrew name of a place. (d) In the process, it lost all divine association. In the Old Testament, Sheol is never divinized, and barely even personified. While prophetic texts and epigraphic discoveries reveal the continued appeal of other gods in Israel, the use of the term Sheol suggests that these did not generally include the divinized underworld. Perhaps therefore a practical monotheism was earlier and more widespread than many scholars allow.

The distinctiveness of the term 'Sheol' to Hebrew is frequently noted in discussion of its etymology, but seldom in consideration of its meaning. Since the underworld was a widespread concept in the ancient Near East, it is remarkable that Hebrew has a name for it which is virtually unique.[55] Whether intentional or accidental, this allowed the Israelites and their writers to invest the term with their own religious outlook, without the conceptual baggage that other shared terms might carry. The linguistic distinctiveness permitted a clearer expression of theological distinctiveness.

b. Sheol as a destiny

The term 'Sheol' occurs in different contexts with various connotations. To survey its use it is worth attempting to classify the relevant texts according to their main emphasis. Inevitably, a few texts are more difficult to

[53] De Moor (1990b: 239). During the *kissu*-festival, the goddess Ninkur(ra) is laid flat and sacrifices are made to various deities, including *šu-wa-la*/Ereshkigal. For de Moor, this represents Ninkur's descent to Ereshkigal's realm.

[54] Tsukimoto (1989: 9). Shuwaliyat was the equivalent of Akkadian Ninurta (Laroche 1946–7: 60; 1977: 174), and Hurrian Tashmishu (Güterbock 1961: 1), and appears with the Hittite storm god Telibinu (Laroche 1984: 129).

[55] It is also surprising that this elicits scant scholarly comment. Stähli (1986: 177) notes the name's uniqueness but then suggests that Israel took its underworld concept from surrounding cultures, without seeing the anomaly of this.

classify; nevertheless each occurrence is included below in one category. (Where a text has a significant further connotation, it is mentioned below in parentheses in this further category, but not counted in its number of occurrences.)

Main emphasis		*Number*	*Texts*
1. Cosmological extremity		5	Deut. 32:22; Job 11:8; Ps. 139:8; Is. 7:11 (57:9); Amos 9:2
2. UW*: general term		6	1 Sam. 2:6; Job 17:13, 16; 26:6; Prov. 15:11; Is. 57:9
	place of confinement	4	2 Sam. 22:6 = Ps. 18:6; Job 7:9 (14:13; 17:16); Ps. 116:3
	existence	3	Ps. 6:6; Is. 14:11; 38:18
3. UW* personified		7	Prov. 1:12; 27:20; 30:16; Song 8:6; Hos. 13:14 (x2); Hab. 2:5
4. Escape:	deliverance	5	Pss. 16:10; 30:3; 49:15; 86:13; Jonah 2:2
	avoidance	2	Prov. 15:24; 23:14
5. Destiny:	everyone	2	Ps. 89:48; Eccles. 9:10
	righteous	7	Gen. 37:35; 42:38; 44:29, 31; Job 14:13; Ps. 88:3; Is. 38:10
	ungodly	25	Num. 16:30, 33; 1 Kgs. 2:6, 9; Job 21:13; 24:19; Pss. 9:17; 31:17; 49:14 (x2); 55:15; 141:7; Prov. 5:5; 7:27; 9:18; Is. 5:14; 14:11, 15; 28:15, 18; Ezek. 31:15–17; 32:21, 27

* UW = underworld

This exercise in classification highlights a significant and largely overlooked feature of Sheol in the Old Testament. By far its most frequent use is to indicate human destiny, and predominantly the destiny of the ungodly. This use accounts for half of all occurrences, and is attested across the whole range of Old Testament literature: psalmodic, reflective, prophetic and narrative. For the Hebrew writers this was clearly the most notable aspect of the underworld. By contrast, Sheol occurs relatively infrequently in cosmology, underworld description or personification, and these were not important biblical themes. However, modern scholarship has tended to focus attention on these latter aspects. For instance, in influential works Barth (1947) concentrates on Sheol as a power and Tromp (1969) on its underworld description. Thus the biblical emphasis needs careful consideration.

Scholars often portray Sheol as the destiny of all, without qualification. But the analysis above shows that it is portrayed predominantly as the fate of the wicked. Sometimes it is feared by the righteous in extreme circumstances (though more often they seek deliverance), and very occasionally it is envisaged for everyone. One of the few scholars to note this imbalance is Barr:

> Although Sheol is the abode of the dead, it seems to be spoken of mainly in connection with the persons disapproved, the evildoers . . . or else in connection with quite wrong and disapproved things that happen to good people . . . Though there is no formal demarcation on moral grounds, actual talk of Sheol generally attaches to sinister characters and sinister events. (1992: 29)[56]

First, then, those destined for Sheol are predominantly the ungodly. They are often described in general terms, as wicked (Is. 5:14; Pss. 9:17; 31:17; 141:7; Job 21:13), sinners (Job 24:19), the foolish rich (Ps. 49:14, despite textual difficulties), scoffers (Is. 28:15, 18) and immoral (Prov. 5:5; 7:27; 9:18). A few are specifically named: Korah and company (Num. 16:30, 33), Joab and Shimei (1 Kgs. 2:6, 9). They can also be national enemies: the king of Babylon (Is. 14:11, 15), the Egyptians (Ezek. 31:15–17) and many others (Ezek. 32:18–32). Yet further texts consign the ungodly to the underworld, using other terms for it. Thus identification of the underworld with the wicked is paramount.

Secondly, certain individuals, who are otherwise presumed to be righteous, envisage descent to Sheol, specifically Jacob, Hezekiah, Job and a psalmist (Gen. 37:35 etc.; Is. 38:10; Job 17:13–16; Ps. 88:4). However, they all speak in the context of extreme trial, whether loss, illness, affliction or abandonment; and Hezekiah, Job and the psalmist interpret their circumstances explicitly as divine judgment. Further, the selective use of Sheol in the Joseph narrative is particularly notable. Jacob twice envisages sorrowful descent there, on hearing of Joseph's death and on fearing Benjamin's harm. But, many years later, after his family has been happily reunited, Jacob's death is mentioned repeatedly and in different ways,[57] but 'Sheol is conspicuously absent'.[58] So arguably the righteous only envisage Sheol when they face unhappy and untimely death, which they interpret as

[56] For Haag (1986: 158), Sheol is often linked with Yahweh's justice as the place of punishment for sin, but this view goes beyond the evidence.

[57] 'Die/death' (46:30; 47:29; 48:21; 50:5, 16), 'lie down with my ancestors' (47:30), 'gathered to my/his people' (49:29, 33). Similarly for Joseph: 'die/death' (50:24, 26).

[58] So Rosenberg (1981: 88). This distinctive use is largely unnoticed by commentators. Von Rad (1972: 354) at least notes a contrast: on the earlier occasions Jacob speaks 'with pathos' (mistranslated as 'pathetically' in the first English edition).

divine punishment.[59] By contrast, when they face a contented death at the end of a full and happy life, or where this is narrated, there is no mention of Sheol.

Thirdly, and seemingly at variance with the above, twice Sheol is apparently presented as the destiny for all. These texts merit closer examination.

Psalm 89:48–49 notes that life is brief and created 'for vanity', and asks rhetorically whether anyone can avoid death and Sheol. This follows reference to Yahweh's fiery wrath, in a lengthy and powerful lament of his spurning of king, covenant and city. So this consignment of general humanity to Sheol clearly occurs in a context of widespread divine judgment.

Further, the term translated 'vanity' (*šāw'*) may also point to judgment. Its primary meaning is usually given as 'worthless, (in) vain'.[60] However, Sawyer argues that *šāw'* means primarily 'deceit, evil, falsehood',[61] and his view can be supported by the detailed study of its fifty-two other occurrences. In thirty-one texts the more appropriate rendering is 'deceit', particularly in Ezekiel where it usually parallels 'lying divinations'.[62] In only nine texts, and mostly as an adverb, is it necessarily 'worthless'.[63] In a further thirteen, including the decalogue texts, both ideas could be argued.[64] Scholars often note the conceptual affinity of these meanings, but not the greater frequency of 'deceit, evil'.[65] Mowinckel's proposal that *šāw'* indicates sorcery lacks evidence,[66] but if correct it would support Sawyer's argument, since sorcery was considered evil, not simply worthless.

Thus in Psalm 89 it is humanity as created for falsehood, i.e. sinful and under judgment, which is destined for Sheol.[67] This interpretation is strengthened if the parallelism of the four lines is A B A′ B′, i.e. brevity of

[59] Jacob may also interpret Joseph's untimely death as punishment; cf. Butterworth (1998: 4 n. 3).

[60] E.g. BDB, KB, HAL; cf. the usual LXX rendering *mataios* (31 times).

[61] Sawyer (THAT 2: 882), relating *šāw'* to both *n-š-'*, 'deceive' and *š-'-h*, 'be empty'; cf. TWOT.

[62] Here NRSV translates it as 'false(hood)': Ezek. 12:24; 13:6–9, 23; 21:23, 29; 22:28. Deception is also clear in Exod. 23:1; Deut. 5:20; Job 15:31 (x2); 31:5; Pss. 12:2; 24:4; 144:8–11; Prov. 30:8; Is. 30:28; Lam. 2:14 (x2); Zech. 10:2. General iniquity forms the context in Job 11:11; 35:13; Pss. 26:4; 41:7; 139:20; Is. 5:18; 59:4; Hos. 12:12.

[63] Ps. 127:1(x2), 2; Jer. 2:30; 4:30; 6:29; 46:11. Once *šāw'* occurs as a predicate meaning 'worthless': Mal. 3:14.

[64] Cf. Noth (1962: 163). The meanings merge regarding blasphemy (Exod. 20:7 [x2]; Deut. 5:11 [x2]); other gods (Ps. 31:6; Jer. 18:15; Jonah 2:8) and offerings (Is. 1:13). Either meaning is possible in Job 7:3 (cf. *'āmāl* in parallel); Pss. 60:13 = 108:13; 119:37 (cf. *beṣa'*, 'selfish gain', v. 36); Hos. 10:4 (context of iniquity).

[65] Though cf. Childs (1974: 410) on Exod. 20:7: 'the term almost always carries pejorative overtones'.

[66] Mowinckel (1921: 50–57); cf. van der Toorn (1985: 71).

[67] Against Sawyer, who takes *šāw'* here as 'worthless'. Rosenberg (1981: 239) adds that creation in sinful impotence is a better basis for pleading divine mercy (v. 47) than creation 'in vain'.

life corresponds with death in general (A A′), and falsehood with Sheol (B B′). However, the contextual link is still clear with the more usual parallelism of A A′ B B′:

A	Remember how short my life is –	A
B	for what vanity [falsehood] you have created all mortals!	A′
A′	Who can live and never see death?	B
B′	Who can escape the power of Sheol?	B′

Ecclesiastes 9:7–10 instructs readers to enjoy their life of meaninglessness (*heḇel*) under the sun, since afterwards they will go to Sheol where there is no work, thought, knowledge or wisdom. The seemingly contradictory themes of the absurdity and yet the enjoyment of life dominate Ecclesiastes. But there is also the theme of trust in God, who will judge all deeds (12:14).[68] This implies some form of definitive judgment, however unclear. For many scholars this theme is secondary,[69] but for others it is integral to the book (e.g. Fox), indeed vital to its hidden apologetic (e.g. Eaton). And though less prominent than other themes, it is the final note. That all without distinction go to Sheol is part of Qohelet's reflection on the absurdity of observable life. But it is not the book's final word.

In conclusion, Sheol cannot be identified simply as the Hebrew term for the underworld which awaits all. It is almost exclusively reserved for those under divine judgment, whether the wicked, the afflicted righteous, or all sinners. It seldom occurs of all humanity, and only in contexts which portray human sinfulness and life's absurdity. Thus Sheol is not used indiscriminately to describe human destiny at death.

c. Synonyms

Three Hebrew words for 'pit' can also mean 'underworld'. The first, *bôr*, occurs sixty-nine times. Usually it indicates a well for water, sometimes it means a dry pit for a prison, hideout, animal trap or mass grave, and occasionally it is used metaphorically.[70] *bôr* clearly indicates the underworld

[68] Also, less clearly, Eccles. 3:17; 11:9. These are often attributed to an editor.

[69] Eaton (1983: 40) questions the assumption behind this view: 'It is very odd to imagine an "editor" issuing a work with which he disagrees but adding extensive notes and an epilogue to compensate. Why should an orthodox writer reproduce a sceptical book at all, let alone add orthodox glosses to produce a noticeably mixed bag?'

[70] E.g. well: Deut. 6:11; prison: Gen. 40:15; hideout: 1 Sam. 13:6; trap: Ps. 7:15; grave: Jer. 41:7, 9; metaphor for ancestors: Is. 51:1; for wife: Prov. 5:15. In post-biblical usage *bôr* always means a pit, cf. CD 11:13, 1Q22.2:3.

nineteen times in ten passages, and possibly in three others.[71] Like Sheol, *bôr* as underworld has no definite article. It occurs in similar contexts and literary genres: thanksgiving, lament, mock dirge and wisdom literature. It has fewer descriptive elements, but then it occurs less frequently. The extension of meaning from 'pit' to 'grave' to 'underworld' is obvious and undisputed.[72]

The similar term *bᵉʾēr* (pit) occurs thirty-seven times. Like *bôr*, it usually means a well, but it can indicate a hideout or bitumen pits, or occur metaphorically.[73] It clearly indicates the underworld twice.[74] The texts have familiar themes: one consigns the wicked to the underworld, the other pleads for personal rescue.

The other term for 'pit', *šaḥaṯ*, occurs twenty-three times. Unlike *bôr* and *bᵉʾēr*, it indicates a physical pit only infrequently, some eight times.[75] And two of these contain underworld allusion, since the pit is dug for the deserving wicked.[76] More often *šaḥaṯ* refers to the underworld: fifteen times in eleven passages.[77] Unlike Sheol and *bôr*, it sometimes has the definite article.[78]

Like Sheol, *šaḥaṯ* (pit) usually indicates the fate desired for the wicked. Generally the righteous acknowledge rescue from it, though in his extreme circumstances Job envisages it.[79] By contrast, Psalm 49:7–9 seems to imply that everyone goes to *šaḥaṯ*: no-one can be ransomed to live for ever and not see the pit. However, several factors indicate that this prescription is only partial. (i) The psalmist is clearly discussing the oppressive rich, whose wealth is powerless to redeem them from *šaḥaṯ*. (ii) Elsewhere the verb 'ransom' (*p-d-h*) occurs of life already forfeited.[80] (iii) Most importantly, the psalmist asserts his own redemption from Sheol (v. 16), clearly distinguishing himself from those for whom there is no such redemption. Thus *šaḥaṯ*, like Sheol, is instinctively the destiny of the ungodly rather than the godly.[81]

[71] Pss. 28:1; 30:4; 88:5, 7; 143:7; Prov. 1:12 (sometimes with Sheol); Is. 14:15, 19; 38:18; Ezek. 26:20 (x2); 31:14, 16; 32:18, 23, 24, 25, 29, 30; possibly also Ps. 40:3; Prov. 28:17; Lam. 3:53, 55; see commentaries.

[72] E.g. BDB, HAL, Tromp (except Is. 14:19 and perhaps Lam. 3:53).

[73] Hideout: 2 Sam. 17:18f.; bitumen pits: Gen. 14:10; metaphor for women: Prov. 5:15; 23:27; Song 4:15.

[74] Pss. 55:23; 69:15. This meaning is widely accepted, cf. HAL.

[75] There are also several rare synonyms with no underworld connotations: *šuḥāh*, *šîḥāh*, *šᵉḥîṯ*, *šᵉḥûṯ*.

[76] Pss. 9:15; 94:13.

[77] Job 17:14; 33:18, 22, 24, 28, 30; Pss. 16:10; 30:10; 49:10; 55:24; 103:4; Is. 38:17; 51:14; Ezek. 28:8; Jonah 2:7.

[78] Job 9:31; 17:14; 33:22, 28; Is. 51:14; Ps. 49:9; Ezek. 28:8.

[79] The wicked: Ps. 55:23 (cf. also Pss. 9:15; 94:13); Ezek. 28:8. Job *in extremis*: Job 17:14. The righteous: Job 33 (x5); Pss. 16:10; 30:9; 103:4; Is. 38:17; 51:14; Jonah 2:6.

[80] Especially with 'life' (*nepeš*) and 'price' (*kōper*): Exod. 21:30; Job 33:24, 28 (cf. Prov. 6:35).

[81] On Ps. 49 see further Johnston (1997). BDB (1001) takes 'pit (*šaḥaṯ*) of Sheol' as a distinction within Sheol, but this is unnecessary.

ʾᵃḇaddôn, another underworld term, derives from *ʾ-b-d* (to destroy) and means 'destruction'. It occurs only six times, and clearly refers to the underworld.[82] Of these few occurrences, it is twice paired with Sheol and once with death. This may echo the common contemporary custom of pairing lesser deities together.[83] But if so the echo is more one of phraseology than of theology: 'Sheol and Destruction' are certainly not divinized.

These terms for 'pit' (*bôr, bᵉʾēr, šaḥaṯ*) and 'destruction' (*ʾᵃḇaddôn*) are clearly synonyms of Sheol. They are used in similar contexts, though less frequently, and portray a similar picture of the underworld.

d. Summary

This study of Hebrew terms for the underworld reveals some very interesting conclusions. While Sheol is the most common term, it occurs only infrequently. So the underworld was not a particularly important concept for the Israelite writers. Sheol occurs entirely in 'first person' contexts, and never in simple reportage or general prescription. So it is a term of personal engagement. Whatever the origin of the term, there is no hint of Sheol being a deity. Descriptive details are very sparse, but suggest a somnolent, gloomy existence without meaningful activity or social distinction. There is certainly no elaborate journey through the gates or stages of the underworld, in Mesopotamian or Egyptian style. So there was no great concern with the ongoing fate of the dead.

Instead, in the majority of instances Sheol is used to describe human fate. Sometimes this is a destiny which the righteous wish to avoid, or which in desperate circumstances they see as divine punishment on themselves. More often it is a destiny wished on the ungodly. The occasional synonyms of Sheol portray the same picture. So the underworld in Israel's canonical literature can be summarized as an infrequent theme and an unwelcome fate.

[82] Prov. 15:11; 27:20 (Qere of most MSS), paired with Sheol; Job 28:22, paired with death; Job 26:6, paralleled with Sheol; Ps. 88:11, paralleled with grave; Job 31:12, similar to Deut. 32:22.
[83] So Myers (ISBE 1: 899); e.g. at Ugarit Kothar-and-Khasis, Gupn-and-Ugar; cf. also 'Death and Hades' (Rev. 20:13f.).

Chapter 4
THE THREATENING UNDERWORLD

a. The psalmists and Sheol

i. Figurative language

Many psalmists speak vividly of their rescue by God as deliverance from Sheol itself. They write as if they had actually been in Sheol, and been rescued from its very depths:

> The cords of death encompassed me;
> the torrents of perdition assailed me;
> the cords of Sheol entangled me;
> the snares of death confronted me (Ps. 18:4f.);

> O LORD, you brought up my soul from Sheol,
> restored me to life from among those gone down to the Pit (Ps. 30:3);

> He drew me up from the desolate pit,
> out of the miry bog (Ps. 40:2);

> . . . from the depths of the earth
> you will bring me up again (Ps. 71:20);

> For great is your steadfast love toward me;
> you have delivered my soul from the depths of Sheol (Ps. 86:13);

> You have put me in the depths of the Pit,
> in the regions dark and deep (Ps. 88:6);

> Out of the belly of Sheol I cried,
> and you heard my voice (Jonah 2:2).

How should this language be understood?

Traditionally, most interpreters have understood these expressions as metaphor.[1] The psalmists experienced extreme distress of various forms, and related it in hyperbolic language. Their experiences were certainly terrible and terrifying. But their language does not mean that they actually went to Sheol, any more than the modern idiom 'It was sheer hell' means that its speaker was in hell itself. We all use vivid images, particularly for strongly emotional experiences, without expecting them to be taken literally. The language is evocative, and should be interpreted as such.

Support for this view is seen in the variety of ways in which the underworld is mentioned:

(a) **Simile.** The psalmists sometimes speak of the dead and the underworld to illustrate their own distress. They see themselves '*like* those who go down to the Pit' (Pss. 28:1; 143:7), or *like* the dead (31:12; 143:3). This is clearly comparison, not identity.

(b) **Indirect statement.** Some also use more vivid imagery. They had been entrapped like animals by the cords and snares of death and Sheol, but they cried for help and have been delivered from death (Pss. 18:4–6; 116:3f., 8). They tremble in anguish at death's terrors, but long to flee and pray for help (55:4–8); or they cry from the depths, but expect forgiveness and redemption (130:1–4); or approach Sheol, but cry to Yahweh (88; see further below). Whatever the context, they pray, which implies that are not actually in Sheol.

(c) **Direct statement.** However, others do seem to portray their distress in terms of actually being in the underworld itself: they are in Sheol (Pss. 16:10; 30:3; possibly 49:15), in its depths (Ps. 86:13) or its belly (Jonah 2:2), consigned to its gates (Is. 38:10); they are in the depths of the earth or the Pit (Pss. 71:20; 88:6). Nevertheless, these psalmists can still pray to Yahweh and hope for his deliverance of them, which implies that they are not really dead. Many state explicitly that they are still alive (Pss. 30:8; 86:2; 88:1f., 13; Is. 38:17, 19), so they are clearly not in the underworld, or at least not yet. Further, some of these same psalms affirm that Sheol is a place of no return (Pss. 49:19; 88:12; Is. 38:10; Jonah 2:6), a place permanently separated from Yahweh (Pss. 30:9; 88:5, 10–12; Is. 38:18). This obviously contrasts with their own situation, since they can still appeal for help.

These observations lead many to conclude that the psalmists' use of underworld language is figurative, and not intended to be taken literally. However, several influential scholars have argued otherwise.

[1] E.g. Calvin, Gunkel, Eichrodt, cf. Barth (1947: 14f.; 1997: 13f.). Also some modern writers, see below.

ii. Selective language

Before examining alternative views, it is worth pausing to note how different types of psalm relate these experiences differently. In his pioneering form-critical study, Gunkel noted the varied use of underworld terminology between laments and thanksgivings. In the laments psalmists generally avoid direct reference to the underworld, as if to mention it when in trouble was to tempt fate itself. But in the thanksgivings they are much more open about deliverance from Sheol, now that the immediate danger had receded into the past. Gunkel commented:

> [In laments] the sinister word 'Sheol' is almost always avoided. Rather, the lamenters use suggestive pictures like grave, well or cistern, but even these are rare. They occur more frequently in the related Individual Thanksgiving Gattung.[2]

Barth paints the contrast even more strongly:

> Strikingly, the most obvious term Sheol, frequent in thanksgivings, scarcely occurs in the Laments: the lamenter is at best '*near Sheol*' [Ps. 88:3 . . .].[3]

It is certainly true that the thanksgiving psalms refer relatively frequently to deliverance from death and the underworld. Of the sixteen psalms designated by Gunkel as Individual Thanksgivings,[4] about half have underworld terms.[5] And short thanksgiving sections contained in four laments also refer to the underworld.[6]

At the same time, the contrast between laments and thanksgivings can be drawn too sharply. First, some ten psalms identified by Gunkel as Individual Laments do refer to the underworld. In six (possibly more) the beleaguered psalmists fear it as their own fate,[7] while in four others they desire it as the fate of their enemies.[8] Secondly, as noted, another four laments include

[2] Gunkel (1933: 185f.); my translation. (The 1998 English translation omits 'almost always.') He notes only Ps. 88:3 and (inappropriately) Is. 38:10 as biblical exceptions.

[3] Barth (1947: 111; 1997: 87; emphasis original); my translation throughout this chapter.

[4] Gunkel (1933: 265 n. 2) gives: Pss. 18; 30; 32; 34; 40A; 41; 66; 92; 100; 107; 116; 118; 138; Is. 38:10–20; Jonah 2:2–9; Job 33:26–28; plus four extra-biblical psalms. However, Pss. 100 and 107 seem more communal than individual.

[5] Pss. 18:5; 30:3; 116:3; Is. 38:10, 18; Jonah 2:2 (Sheol); Ps. 40:2; Job 33:28 (pit). Possibly also: Pss. 32:6 (mighty waters); 41:8 (deadly thing); 92:7 (destruction); 107:18 (gates of death); 118:18 (death).

[6] Pss. 71:20 (depths of the earth); 86:13 (Sheol); possibly also: Pss. 22:29 (earth, dust); 56:13 (death).

[7] Pss. 6:5; 88:3 (Sheol); 28:1; 69:15; 143:7 (pit); 130:1 (depths). Possibly also: 7:5 (ground, dust); 13:4 (sleep of death); 22:15 (dust of death, cf. v.29); 55:4 (terrors of death).

[8] Pss. 31:17; 55:15; 141:7 (Sheol); 63:9 (depths of the earth).

thanksgiving sections which mention the underworld. Whatever the origin or form-critical classification of these sections, the (final) authors have placed them in lament psalms. Thirdly, there are many more thanksgiving sections in laments which have no underworld reference, even though the surrounding lament refers or alludes to the underworld.[9] Admittedly, many laments contain no underworld reference or allusion, even when portraying life-threatening situations.[10] However, one can only argue that the psalmists purposely avoid it if such reference is essential to the portrayal of their distress. The great variety of themes and expressions in the laments, despite certain formal similarities, militates against this assumption.

When all the evidence is pieced together, there are still proportionally more underworld references in thanksgivings than in laments, but the contrast is not nearly as dramatic as Gunkel and Barth suggest. Psalmists in danger may have been somewhat more reticent about naming the underworld than psalmists in security. But this probably says more about general human psychology than about specific Israelite theology.

b. The psalmists in Sheol?

i. Pedersen: a present experience

In the early twentieth century the Danish scholar Johannes Pedersen challenged the view outlined above. Strongly influenced by some early anthropology,[11] he argued that ancient thought was inherently concrete. So the Israelites could conceive only of totalities, and could not differentiate between their various aspects, e.g. cause and effect, body and soul, illness and death. Thus he writes:

> The sinner goes to Sheol, but in reality *he is there already* . . . Where there is darkness, there is also the nether world; for the nether world is wherever there is a nether world nature. He who is struck by evil, by unhappiness, disease or other trouble *is* in Sheol, and when he escapes from the misery and 'beholds the light', then he has escaped from Sheol. The thought is so obvious to the Israelite, because he is always governed by the totality. If he has any of the nature of Sheol within him, then he feels it entirely.[12]

[9] E.g. Ps. 69:30–36.

[10] Pss. 3; 25; 26; 27B; 35; 38; 43; 51; 54; 57; 59; 64; 70; 102; 109; 120; 142. In Pss. 43; 51; 120 there is no obvious context for underworld language.

[11] Notably his compatriot Grönbech (1931), to whom Pedersen dedicated his work.

[12] Pedersen (1926: 466, first emphasis added).

However, there are serious flaws in this argument. (i) Pedersen's further comments betray an ambiguity in his thinking, e.g.:

> . . . the man was so ill that he came *near* the grave; but the very disease was a sojourn *in* the grave, from which recovery brings him back.
>
> We have the same duplicity in the sayings here as in the other psalms. His soul is *near* Sheol. He is still partly in the land of the living, but, nevertheless, so strong is the hold which misery has on him that he is *in* Sheol.[13]

Pedersen acknowledges this ambiguity (or 'duplicity'), but never attempts to resolve it by explaining how one can be both *near* and *in* Sheol simultaneously.

(ii) More recent anthropological study has thrown considerable doubt on the earlier view that ancient thought was necessarily concrete. Fieldwork in various places has shown that primitive people today can have logical, abstract thought.[14]

(iii) Old Testament scholarship increasingly rejects Pedersen's description of Israelite thought as 'always governed by the totality'. For Koch, it contains 'too many peculiar fantasies'. For Addinal, it is 'weird and highly improbable', while his approach to language 'ignores the idioms of common speech and assumes that the logic of poetic imagination and expression is the same as the logic of prosaic literal description and inference'.[15]

(iv) Pedersen's underlying principle that language structure reflects thought forms has also been comprehensively critiqued by Barr (1961: 31), and is no longer accepted.

Thus Pedersen's view that Israelites interpreted illness and distress as death itself, because they could only think in terms of totalities, is seriously flawed. Nevertheless, it has been influential in subsequent twentieth-century scholarship, particularly through the work of Barth.

ii. Barth: a powerful experience

Christoph Barth (a son of Karl Barth) developed at length Pedersen's thesis that the psalmists actually experienced Sheol in this life. His study focuses on Individual Laments and Thanksgivings (as classified by Gunkel) on the

13 Pedersen (1926: 467, on Job 33:22–30; 469, on Ps. 88; emphasis added).

14 Cf. Rogerson (1978: 16), Wilson (1979: 176). These and others also caution that one cannot automatically correlate modern primitive peoples, as studied in fieldwork, and ancient Israel.

15 Koch (1968: 263), Addinal (1981a: 83; 1981b: 301). Cf. also Hahn (1956: 72), Porter (1978: 39).

basis that they represent a distinct and uniform sphere of life, their central theme is deliverance from death, and the surrounding cultures provide parallels.

Barth first asserts that life and death are two sides of the same basic issue. Life is characterized by time, freedom of movement, community, sustenance, health, light and water, and death by the lack of these. Any reduction of vitality in life is a form of death, of coming under the power of death. For Barth, Sheol is more a power which invades life than a place to go after life, so he tends to avoid the term 'underworld'. Rather, 'the Totenreich [i.e. Sheol] is wherever death exercises its rulership'.[16]

He then asserts repeatedly that the individual in any form of affliction, whether illness, captivity, enmity, poverty or sinfulness, has a real experience of Sheol: 'When in distress, the individual resides in the Totenreich'; 'In his distress, the individual experiences and suffers the reality of the grave. In his own body – not simply in spirit or imagination – he knows what it means to lie in the grave'; 'Many texts . . . show that the distressed person thinks he is lying in the depths of the underworld.'[17]

However, Barth then qualifies this. He states that, while distress and death are similar in many ways, they are not identical. Distressed psalmists do not feel death's full bitterness. Their experience of death is only partial and limited, and they are not directly identified as dead. Particularly in the laments, they are merely very close to Sheol, merely threatened by death, and can still call to Yahweh for deliverance. 'The distressed person appears to have experienced only the proximity of death, not death itself. But for ancient orientals this proximity was counted as a real experience of death.' Barth stresses throughout that this experience of the proximity of death was sufficient to experience its full reality: 'That death threatened is death already arrived is no poetic fantasy . . . but a true statement on the nature of evil.'[18]

The Laments tend to avoid the term Sheol – the psalmist is at best 'near Sheol' – because of its 'exceedingly graphic ring'. Conversely, the Thanksgivings speak openly of rescue from within the Totenreich itself: 'In hindsight, the psalmist is completely taken up with the reality of death. He knows he has been delivered not just from mortal danger, but from death, from the midst of the Totenreich and from death's control.'[19]

16 Barth (1947: 88; 1997: 70). NB: Barth's work is cited in both original and third editions; the latter is a more accessible reprint, with minor editorial corrections and different pagination.
17 Barth (1947: 111–12; 1997: 87–89). Stamm (1955: 66) describes this as Barth's dominant emphasis.
18 Barth (1947: 116, 145; 1997: 92, 115).
19 Barth (1947: 111, 117; 1997: 88, 93).

Barth concludes by quoting Pedersen, but he then gives a more nuanced appraisal: 'Only by comparison does the distressed person call himself dead; this thought is due to the real but partial identity between distress and death'; 'The complete sinking into the Totenreich was experienced partially.'[20] Others summarize Barth's conclusion similarly: it is 'a real but partial experience of death' (Tromp 1969: 136); 'the experience of death . . . is real, but only partial' (Knibb 1989: 407).

Barth's thesis invites several important criticisms of both substance and detail:

(i) Barth assumes that texts should be taken literally if at all possible. He asserts : 'In principle, a statement should only be understood metaphorically or figuratively if *all* possibilities of a real, direct understanding are examined and their unsuitability adequately established.'[21] But he never attempts to justify this in any way, logically, linguistically or culturally. This is especially surprising since his study focuses on poetry, a medium particularly associated with metaphor. For most other scholars, the biblical text is replete with imagery, particularly the poetic sections. And the religious as well as general use of metaphor has attracted significant recent study.[22] Barth's premise is unsupported by him and inappropriate to the topic.

(ii) Barth regularly personifies death and Sheol as powers active in the world of the living. While he acknowledges that, formally, death is an aspect of divine power,[23] he frequently treats it as a power independent of Yahweh, e.g.: 'the relative independence [of] the powers of death'; 'Here [Ps. 49:15] it is obviously assumed that in death one falls under a power and rulership different from Yahweh . . . So death's power stands opposite Yahweh's'; 'we must remember the property of the Totenreich as a power . . . "Death" and "Totenreich" occur *widely* as personal powers'.[24] Wächter (1967: 50) pertinently criticizes Barth's approach as closer to existentialist philosophy than to Israelite thought.

(iii) Conversely, Barth largely ignores death as an event which ends human life. While he refers to it as crucial and decisive,[25] he does not develop this point and hardly mentions it again.

(iv) Barth also ignores Sheol as a subterranean abode of the departed. Indeed, he argues that it is not localized, and that its apparent localizations

20 Pedersen: 'If he has any . . . entirely'; see quote above (Ch. 4.b.i). Barth (1947: 117; 1997: 93).

21 Barth (1947: 15; 1997: 14; emphasis original).

22 E.g. Soskice (1985). Cf. Krieg's (1988) detailed study of death imagery.

23 Barth (1947: 73; 1997: 57f.).

24 Barth (1947: 75, 68, 89; 1997: 59, 54, 70; 'widely' translates '*promiscue*'; emphasis original).

25 Barth (1947: 53, 67; 1997: 43, 53).

in grave, ocean, desert, south and west merely express the Totenreich's great distance from the world of the living.[26] Tromp (1969: 133) rightly criticizes this, arguing that 'Sheol proper is deep in the earth'.

(v) Barth's language is misleading. He interprets Sheol as 'realm of *death*', which in German should be Todesreich, yet he constantly translates it as 'realm of *the dead*', or Totenreich.[27]

(vi) Like Pedersen, Barth accepts the view of some early anthropologists that primitive people could only think in totalities. But this is now discounted (see above).

(vii) Most importantly, Barth nowhere explains how an experience of death can be real but partial. The term 'partial' poses no difficulty: the separation of psalmists from life, so characteristic of death, was clearly incomplete. But the term 'real' is problematic. If death necessarily entails total deprivation of life and irreversible separation from Yahweh and the community, as Barth argues, then a real experience of death must include these elements. Yet by definition these cannot be experienced by those still alive, however forlorn their situation may appear. The psalmist who can still pray is clearly not dead.[28] Thus a 'real but partial' experience of death is at best ambiguous, at worst a contradiction in terms.

iii. Others: an ambiguous experience

Barth's thesis has been 'widely influential', as Knibb notes in an authoritative summary (1989: 407), and as its recent reissuing demonstrates.[29] Many other scholars have accepted it in principle, despite offering various criticisms of detail. But their work inevitably contains similar ambiguity. Johnson (1949: 94) follows Barth closely: 'just as death in the strictest sense of the term is for the Israelite the weakest form of life, so any weakness in life is a form of death'.[30] Maag is generally more nuanced, and accepts that the

[26] Barth (1947: 85–8; 1997: 67–9). He identifies the Totenreich with: ocean and desert, since both are life-threatening; south, following Jeremias (1906: 396 n. 1); and west, citing 1 Enoch 17:6; 22:1ff. and Egyptian texts. But he gives no OT evidence, and Jeremias is quite speculative.

[27] Tromp also notes this, though adds a dubious distinction (1969: 137): 'the psalmist is in the domain of death, but by no means in the domain of the dead. The latter excludes the possibility of a return, from the former, man can be saved by Yahweh's mighty hand.'

[28] Cf. Maag (1964: 24), Broyles (1989: 88).

[29] Reprinted in 1987; then reissued in 1997, along with three other articles by Barth, plus introduction, brief biography and bibliography by B. Janowski. The latter comments (7): 'Since 1947 there is hardly a publication on the biblical issue of death which has not made detailed reference to Barth's thesis.'

[30] Johnson (1949: 92 n.) refers approvingly to Pedersen and Barth.

distressed psalmist is clearly not dead, yet states (1964: 25): 'When Old Testament man says that Yahweh has placed him in Sheol, killed him, etc., he speaks not metaphorically but of a real situation.' For Keel (1978: 73): 'The realm of the dead was truly and really manifested in these realities [cistern, prison, pit] . . .' Many others follow or echo Barth without further discussion.[31]

Tromp also accepts that 'Barth is fundamentally right' (1969: 136), and gives a similar summary: 'Deadly peril is experienced as real death, diminished life as life finished, partial death as total death . . .' (138). But he does not explain what constitutes 'real death' or 'total death', nor how these experiences can allow the psalmist to continue to hope and pray for deliverance. Moreover, Tromp concludes contradictorily: 'in the case of illness and misery being pictured in terms properly denoting a netherworld situation, we are dealing with a secondary and figurative use of the terms involved' (138). But if the use of Sheol is figurative, the experience of death is hardly real. Later Tromp adds a further qualification: the use of 'netherworld terminology' in laments and thanksgivings, 'though implying a real experience of death', must be considered as 'secondary and technical' (139). But this usually means a use of terminology in other than its primary, normal meaning, and Tromp's description therefore undercuts his argument.

Kraus is initially more nuanced, speaking of the 'relative death' of the one forsaken by God (1986: 165). But he then states that the 'totalistic way of thinking' is foundational to our interpretation, and follows Barth entirely. 'In our way of thinking, we would conclude that the one speaking in Ps. 30:3 has not really died. But he *did really die*![32] For the reality of death struck deep into his life, in the concrete diminution of life that he experienced' (166). However, the third sentence quoted does not prove the second. A person can have a deep experience of the conditions of death, and feel himself to be 'at death's door'; but as long as he can still think, pray and hope, he is alive and not dead.

Barth himself writes more cautiously in a much later student textbook:

> Many scholars think that the reference [to liberation from death] is not to literal death or resurrection. The statements about the grave and Sheol are to be seen as poetic . . . The believer was *almost* dead, and the liberation thus amounted *almost* to a resurrection . . . Another possible explanation is that the victory over death was a real experience, but that death was seen as a two-sided reality: on the one hand as the boundary

[31] E.g. Ringgren (1963: 62f.), Seybold (1990: 169f.).
[32] The original German edition (1979: 209) reads: 'Doch er *ist wirklich gestorben!*'

> of life that God has fixed for each of us, on the other as the power of destruction that menaces us . . . Even though still living, [believers] thus fall into the clutches of death.[33]

Here Barth first mentions the metaphorical view without discounting it. He then presents a qualified form of his earlier argument: he speaks of a real experience of victory over death, not of death itself; it is death, not the realm of the dead, which invades life; and death as the end of human life has equal mention alongside death as a power.

However, not all scholars have followed Pedersen and Barth, and some continue to see the psalmists' language as metaphorical. For instance, Allen (1987: 89) writes of standard images and metaphors of crisis, and of 'the over-reacting characteristic of deep depression'. And others comment similarly on Psalm 88.

iv. Psalm 88: an imminent experience

Psalm 88 merits particular attention, with its pervading sense of gloom and despair. It ends both thematically and literally with 'darkness', and is often called the bleakest of all the psalms.[34] If a psalmist ever really did experience Sheol, then it would be recorded here.

Initially, the author is somewhat guarded. He laments that his life 'draws near to Sheol', and that he is 'counted among those who go down to the Pit'.[35] He has become like those who are helpless, forsaken, forgotten and cut off from Yahweh (vv. 3–5). But then he accuses Yahweh categorically: 'You have put me in the depths of the Pit, in the regions dark and deep' (v. 6). He is in Sheol!

But the psalmist does not stop there. He continues on similar themes: his social isolation and desperate prayer (vv. 8–9); the God-forsakenness of the underworld (vv. 10–12); his fervent but fruitless prayer (vv. 13–14); and his wretchedness, loneliness and darkness (vv. 15–18).

For some scholars v. 6 is not just exaggeration or Near Eastern hyperbole. Kraus comments:

> The sufferer knows that he is already in the 'kingdom of death' . . . He lies there in a mass grave like those killed in battle . . . bereft of Yahweh's

[33] Barth (1991: 277; emphasis original); English condensed by G. W. Bromiley from 7-volume Indonesian original.

[34] Cf. von Rad (1980: 201f.), Haag (1986: 149), Stähli (1986: 185), Tate (1990: 404).

[35] The participle 'going down' could indicate 'those who have already gone down'. But the context implies that it means 'those going down', as it is normally translated.

> attentions . . . He who is destined for death knows that he has been transferred to the 'lowest pit' . . . by Yahweh. (1989: 193)

However, further aspects of Kraus's own exposition undermine this interpretation. (i) On the psalmists' 'imprisonment' (v. 8), he notes that, in Babylonian lament, 'To heal a sick person . . . is tantamount to freeing a person in fetters' (194).[36] But this implies that the imprisonment language is metaphorical of physical illness, in which case the underworld imprisonment of Psalm 88 could also be metaphorical. (ii) The psalmist's rhetorical questions of vv. 10–12 'aim to move Yahweh to intervene . . . God would have to perform a miracle. He would have to raise a dead person to life' (194). But the six rhetorical questions clearly expect a *negative* answer. The psalmist asserts that Yahweh's actions do *not* affect the dead; he does not pray that they will. Further, this psalm of utmost despair is hardly a propitious context for resurrection faith, which Kraus himself describes as 'the extreme limit of the OT'. (iii) Kraus's language is inevitably ambiguous. After noting the exclusion of the dead from Yahweh's actions, he asks: 'Can Yahweh overcome and avert this distress?' (194).[37] The first term, 'overcome', implies a situation already experienced, but the second, 'avert', implies the threatening situation is still only imminent.

In contrast, most other commentators still accept implicitly or explicitly that the psalmist's reference to being in the underworld is metaphorical.[38] Clearly he is still sufficiently alive to pray. His lament contains a three-fold mention of prayer which is repeated day and night (vv. 1, 9, 13).[39] And his opening address to 'Yahweh, God of my salvation' expresses hope of deliverance, at least at that point. In his desperation he approaches Sheol and speaks hyperbolically of already being there. But he still prays for Yahweh to intervene before it is too late, before he goes beyond Yahweh's saving activity. Tate speaks helpfully of his 'variegated metaphorical tapestry' (1990: 401), and concludes:

> The speaker is on the brink of death, but prayer is the lifeline which keeps him/her from the Pit. Even the greatest of those in Sheol cannot rise to praise Yahweh, but the speaker keeps death away by conversation directed to God. (1990: 405)

This interpretation does greater justice to the psalm.

[36] Probably referring to *Ludlul Bel Nemeqi.*

[37] The original (1978: 610) reads: '. . . überwinden und abwenden'.

[38] Weiser (1962: 88f.), Eaton (1967: 217), Anderson (1972: 629), Kidner (1975: 317f.), Rogerson–McKay (1977b: 187), von Rad (1980: 201f.), Brueggemann (1984: 79), Haag (1986: 160f.), Tate (1990: 401–5).

[39] Scholars often note the absence of regular lament features in Ps. 88. NRSV strangely omits 'by day' in v. 1.

c. Summary

Psalmists describe their experiences of distress and despair as an underworld experience, in direct and indirect terms. However, this language can hardly be taken literally, since they are still able to pray to Yahweh and to hope for his deliverance. Even the tormented author of Psalm 88 addresses Yahweh, and calls him his saving God. Clearly he is not *yet* in the underworld.

The biblical psalmists mention the underworld more frequently in thanksgiving, once they are out of danger, than in lament, when still in the midst of it. But the contrast is not absolute, since some laments do refer to the underworld, and in any case the laments contain a great variety of descriptions of distress. Perhaps Israelites (like many others) were somewhat reluctant to name the fate they feared. The underworld was certainly not something they looked forward to!

Pedersen, Barth and others rightly note that life and death are intimately connected. Life means fullness of life, and any illness or misfortune is a partial experience of death's power and of underworld conditions. However, they go too far in asserting that the Israelites could think only in two categories, life and death, so that any restriction of life meant real death. This leads to ambiguity and contradiction in their writing. Barth's seminal presentation in particular is flawed in this respect. Further, the underlying concept of 'totality thought' fails to acknowledge the multitude of intermediate situations in ordinary life. To insist that Israelites were either fully alive or actually experiencing Sheol is to deny the wide range of human experience, or at least to deny Israelite awareness of it. And to insist that reference to the underworld in the laments and thanksgivings cannot be metaphorical or figurative is to impose a constraint out of keeping with their literary context. Psalmists vividly describe their distress as if they were in Sheol, cut off from Yahweh. But they know that they are still alive, and able to pray. While there was life, there was hope.

Chapter 5
THE PERVASIVE UNDERWORLD?

We have already seen that the biblical writers refer only infrequently to the underworld as Sheol, the Pit, and Destruction (Ch. 3). But perhaps there were many more original references to the underworld, showing a greater fascination with the world of the dead than this implies. These many other references were then accidentally misunderstood or purposely hidden by later Jewish scribes, resulting in a false impression of little Israelite interest in the underworld.

Throughout the twentieth century various scholars proposed a few occasional extra underworld references in the Old Testament. Then in the 1960s two in particular, Dahood and Tromp, argued for a much more widespread underworld interest, and reinterpreted a large number of Hebrew terms and texts in this sense. While other scholars have not followed Dahood in his further arguments for a positive afterlife belief in the Old Testament, many have accepted that at least some of these further proposed references are valid, and therefore that there was a greater Israelite interest in the underworld than had previously been thought.

To examine all of these proposals thoroughly would be a complete study in itself, and would take us too far down one specific track. However, it is important to examine at least a few Hebrew terms, to see some of the arguments used and to assess their validity. So the present chapter will examine closely the suggested underworld references in the important terms for earth and water. Inevitably the arguments are more technical and linguistic, but they are worth pursuing, since the outcome is important.

a. Is 'earth' the underworld?

'ereṣ is one of the most common Old Testament words,[1] and normally means 'earth, world, land, country, ground'. However, many scholars have suggested that it can also mean 'underworld', and this view is now accepted by one modern translation (NRSV, Jer. 17:13). There are several obvious reasons for this. (i) The underworld was usually located in the depths of the solid mass of the earth (*'ereṣ*). (ii) At burial the dead are placed in the earth (*'ereṣ*).[2] (iii) Other terms with a primarily physical meaning (e.g. pit, dust) can also indicate the underworld. (iv) Similar terms in cognate languages mean the underworld: Akkadian *erṣetu* is 'clearly the most common and most important . . . name for the underworld and the realm of the dead',[3] and Ugaritic *arṣ* can also mean the underworld.[4]

Nevertheless, despite these apparently strong reasons, this interpretation of *'ereṣ* as 'underworld' is relatively recent. The LXX translates *'ereṣ* mostly with *gē*,[5] meaning simply 'earth, land', and never with an explicitly underworld term. In Sirach 51:9 (a suggested underworld reference) the original Hebrew *'ereṣ* is translated into Greek as *gē* by the author's grandson, who presumably understood the original meaning. The Targumic and Midrashic literature similarly knows no underworld connotation to *'ereṣ*, according to the standard dictionaries.[6]

It was Gunkel in 1895 who first proposed this meaning, initially in eleven texts.[7] Subsequent scholars then suggested various different texts, e.g. BDB three texts, Dhorme two, Baumgartner seven, Barth eight, Cross–Freedman five clear and four probable, and HAL twelve.[8] The texts are given in Table 5.1. Noticeably, they proposed significantly different lists

[1] *'ereṣ* occurs 2,504 times, and the Aramaic equivalent *'ᵃra'* 22 times (cf. THAT 1: 229).

[2] The Aramaic *'rṣh* in two stelae means 'sarcophagus', a natural extension of earth as burial place (KAI 225 and 226), cf. Lewis (2001: 187 n. 58; his critique of my dissertation misreads certain parts, but arrived too late for response).

[3] Tallqvist (1934: 9). Cf. CAD on *erṣetu*, where 'nether world' occupies a quarter of the entry. Also, the name of the chief underworld deity Ereshkigal means 'Mistress of the Great Earth' (de Moor 1990b: 235).

[4] E.g. 'go down to the earth', KTU 1.4.viii:7–9; 1.5.vi:25; 1.6.i:7f.; 'gods of the earth', 1.19.iii:6, 35. However, some other proposed underworld meanings for *arṣ* are questionable.

[5] 2,213 times. Also *chōra* (64 times) and 22 other expressions (all under 10 times; cf. Santos 1973).

[6] Levy (1976–89: 1: 173), Jastrow (1903: 125), Sokoloff (1990: 76f.); against Gunkel (1895: 18 n. 1).

[7] Gunkel (1895). Later he added further texts, e.g. Jonah 2:6 (1904: 240); Pss. 71:20; 143:3 (1926: 97).

[8] Dhorme (1907a: 61f.), Baumgartner (1917), Barth (1947: 84), Cross–Freedman (1955: 247f.), HAL (vol. 1, 1967).

Table 5.1

	Gunkel 1895	BDB 1906	Dhorme 1907	Baumgartner 1917	Barth 1947	Cross–Freedman 1955	HAL 1967
Gen. 2:6						+	
Exod. 15:12	+					+	+
1 Sam. 28:13			+				
Job 10:21–22		+					
Pss. 22:29				+	+		+
44:25					+		
61:2					+		
63:9	+				+		+
71:20				+	+		+
95:4					+		
106:17					+		
139:15	+	+					+
143:3				+			
147:6						+?	
148:7						+?	
Eccles. 3:21	+						
Is. 14:9						+	
14:12	+						
21:9						+?	
26:19			+				
29:4	+					+	
44:23	+	+					+
Jer. 17:13				+			+
Ezek. 26:20	+						+
31:14, 16, 18	(+)						+
32:18, 24	+						+
Obad. 1:3						+?	
Jonah 2:6				+	+	+	+
Sirach 51:9				+			+

of texts, and a glance at their work shows that they did not engage in detailed examination of either their own or other proposals.

Dahood was the first to give a longer list, including 26 texts, and Tromp the first to give some extended discussion of this meaning, examining 31 texts and accepting underworld reference in 22 of them.[9] As a result of their work, many other scholars now accept that *'ereṣ* occasionally means 'underworld'.[10] It is worth noting in passing that, even if all the various proposals were accepted, they amount to under 50 texts, less than 2% of the term's occurrences. So, unlike Akkadian *erṣetu*, this meaning of *'ereṣ* is at best rare.

[9] Dahood (1966: 106), Tromp (1969: 23–46). See ensuing discussion.
[10] E.g. Ottosson (TDOT 1: 399, citing only Is. 26:19), Seybold (1990: 184).

However, closer examination shows that few of these proposals are in fact viable. In many of the texts proposed, *'ereṣ* can easily have a meaning from its usual semantic range, while its interpretation as 'underworld' is strained or involves unlikely reinterpretation of other terms. In some, it is *'ereṣ* with a complement which indicates the underworld, not *'ereṣ* alone. In only a few texts could *'ereṣ* mean the underworld, as the solid earth in which the realm of the dead is located or the ground in which the dead are buried. The texts proposed are discussed below, regrouped according to the more likely meaning of *'ereṣ*.

i. The physical world

Genesis 2:6. A stream rises from the *earth* to water the whole face of the ground. Cross–Freedman see this as a clear reference to 'the primordial river, *'ēd*, flowing up from the underworld', i.e. from the realm of the dead.[11] However, while this river may flow from below ground, nothing here associates it with the realm of the dead. Tromp discounts this view, and most other scholars ignore it.[12]

Job 12:7–8. Job instructs those seeking wisdom to consult animals, birds, *earth* and fish. For Dahood and others these four terms represent earth, heavens, underworld and sea respectively.[13] However, the four sources of knowledge are not given in a typical cosmological order (e.g. heavens, earth, sea, underworld). Also, the other three are animate, while 'earth' alone is inanimate. The Ugaritic text cited by Dahood is different in context and content: it simply mentions the heavens groaning to the earth (*arṣ*) and does not propose any consultation of nature. So Job 12:7f. indicates obvious and accessible sources of knowledge, not the underworld.

Job 38:18. Yahweh asks Job if he comprehends 'the expanse of the *earth*'. Like various terms in the previous verses (sea, deep, v. 16; death, deep darkness, v. 17), this indicates the underworld for Dahood and others.[14] However, while v. 16 may refer to the underworld and v. 17 clearly does, v. 18 could well move on to the related theme of the earth's expansive breadth.[15] This gives a contrast of depth and breadth in vv. 16–18 (cf. light and darkness in v. 19), and v. 18 therefore does not necessarily refer to the underworld.

[11] Cross–Freedman (1955: 247); similarly Hamilton (1990: 150).
[12] Tromp (1969: 25). Cf. von Rad (1972: 76), Westermann (1984: 201f.), Wenham (1987: 58f.).
[13] Dahood (1962: 58, citing KTU 1.3.iii:22–5), Pope (1973: 91), Tromp (1969: 42); against Clines (1989: 279).
[14] Dahood (1966: 111), Tromp (1969: 50, 'exclusively cosmological'), Andersen (1976: 276 n.3), Habel (1985: 541, though he translates *'ereṣ* as 'earth', 517), Hartley (1988: 498).
[15] So Dhorme (1967: 584), Pope (1973: 289), Gordis (1978: 436), Fohrer (1989: 505).

Psalm 18:7. Yahweh's anger shakes the *earth* and 'the foundations of the mountains'. Dahood sees these as synonymous, citing five other texts 'which place the foundations of the mountains in the underworld'.[16] However, this is unconvincing. Three of the texts cited use a different phrase,[17] while another locates 'the roots of the mountains' at the bottom of the sea (Jonah 2:6, cf. v. 5). Only one mentions earth and 'the foundations of the mountains' together (Deut. 32:22), but it actually undermines Dahood's case. Here Yahweh's fire burns Sheol and the foundations of the mountains, but it also 'devours the earth and its increase'. Since 'increase' implies agricultural produce, 'earth' means the physical earth, not the underworld. The foundations of the mountains may rest on the underworld, but they are not synonymous with the earth. So the awesome theophany of Psalm 18:7–15 convulses the physical world, not the underworld.[18]

Psalm 46:2. In ringing confidence, the psalmist will not fear 'though the *earth* be changed' (*bᵉhāmîr 'ereṣ*). Dahood argues that this phrase means instead 'the jaws of the underworld', on the basis that 'to fear' can occasionally take the preposition *bᵉ* before the object, and Hebrew *hmyr* (i.e. the consonants of *hāmîr*) is cognate with Ugaritic *mhmrt*, 'gorge' and *hmry* (Mot's city), so means 'gorge, jaws'.[19] However, this is linguistically and contextually implausible. Hebrew *hmyr* (*hāmîr*) and Ugaritic *hmry* are spelt differently. While *hāmîr* occurs only here, the verse's parallelism implies a verb 'to shake', and the early versions read this.[20] The psalmist proclaims his faith despite a shaking earth, not a gaping underworld.

Psalm 61:2. The psalmist cries for help from 'the end of the *earth*'. Many scholars interpret it as a cry from the underworld.[21] However, this is unlikely. First, this phrase elsewhere always indicates the physical world. Secondly, in the immediate context, the rock (v. 2) contrasts as readily with life's insecurity as with underworld mire; the enemy (v. 3) is as easily human as Death itself; and 'refuge' (v. 4) hardly implies a contrast to the underworld on the basis of a single, debatable occurrence of it in underworld reference (Ps. 139:15). Thus for other scholars 'earth' here means this life, not the next.[22]

16 Dahood (1966: 106). Similarly Anderson (1972a: 157) citing 1QH xvii:13, but this has no direct bearing.

17 They have 'the foundations of the *earth*', not 'of the mountains', as the extremity of the physical world: Is. 24:18 (cf. use of *'ereṣ* in vv. 17, 19, 20); Jer. 31:37; Mic. 6:2.

18 So Craigie (1983: 166), Kraus (1988: 253).

19 Dahood (1959: 167; 1966: 278f.), citing KTU 1.4 viii:8–12, 1.5.i.6–8; see Ch. 5.b.iii below.

20 *mwr* Hiphil: MT, Tromp (1969: 56), Craigie (1983: 342, cf. Ugaritic *mr*); *mwr* Niphal: Driver (1950a: 51), BHS, HAL; emended to *mwg* Niphal: BHS, Loretz (1979: 451).

21 Mowinckel (1921: 123), Barth (1947: 83), Eichrodt (1967: 95 n. 6), Eaton (1967: 157), Dahood (1968: 84), Tromp (1969: 37), Rogerson–McKay (1977b: 58, possibly), Johnson (1979: 353f.).

22 E.g. Weiser (1962: 443), Anderson (1972a: 447), Kraus (1989: 9), Tate (1990: 112).

Psalm 77:18; Jeremiah 10:12. Dahood and Tromp see *'ereṣ* as 'underworld' in a tripartite universe: heaven, world (*tēḇēl*), underworld (*'ereṣ*).[23] However, this is unnecessary and involves further complications. In Jeremiah 10 it implies divine creation of the underworld, something never affirmed elsewhere, as Tromp admits. In Psalm 77 it requires the word translated 'whirlwind' in NRSV (*galgal*) to mean 'vault of heaven', by linking it with 'pitcher' (*galgal*, Eccles. 12:6) and 'skull' (*gulgōleṯ*). But *galgal* means basically 'circle/wheel', not 'dome', and the usual translation 'whirlwind/ storm' makes good sense here. Dahood sees a similar tripartite division in two Ugaritic texts.[24] But in both these texts the 'multitudes of the *arṣ*' parallel 'men' (*nšm*), suggesting a bipartite view of heaven and earth. Thus these biblical texts more probably describe the visible world, with world (*tēḇēl*) and earth (*'ereṣ*) as synonyms.

Psalm 95:4; Proverbs 25:3; Isaiah 44:23. Here the 'depths of the *earth*' (in various Hebrew expressions) are contrasted with the heights of the heavens or of the mountains, and some scholars therefore take 'earth' to mean 'underworld'. However, two of these texts are sketches of the physical world. In Psalm 95:4–5 depths of the earth, mountain heights, sea and dry land are declared to belong to Yahweh; and in Isaiah 44:23 heavens, depths of the earth, mountains, forest and trees are invited to rejoice. The interest of the writers is cosmological rather than anthropological. The other text, Proverbs 25:3, likens 'the heaven for height' and 'the earth for depth' with the unsearchable mind of kings. It focuses on the physical world, not the realm of the dead. Further, to suggest that the dead could praise Yahweh runs completely counter to Israelite thought (see Ch. 1.b.i).

Psalm 141:7. In this difficult and possibly damaged text, bones scattered at the mouth of Sheol are imagined 'like a rock that one breaks apart and shatters on the *land*'. Dahood reinterprets this simile as 'like one rent and riven in the nether world'.[25] However, others see the image of a stone or millstone shattering (on) the earth or a ploughman cleaving the earth.[26] While the section (vv. 5–7) is difficult, the argument that 'earth' means the underworld is not persuasive.

Psalm 148:7. This exuberant psalm first invites celestial hosts to praise Yahweh 'from the heavens' (vv. 1–6), and then the physical world, animals and humans to praise him 'from the *earth*' (vv. 7–12). For Dahood, 'earth' (v. 7) means the underworld, the opposite extreme to heaven. However, 'earth'

23 Dahood (1968: 232), Tromp (1969: 134f., tentatively).

24 KTU 1.3.iii:26–8, 1.4.vii:49–52. Cf. CML (49, 66), ARTU (10, 65), TO (1: 166, 219).

25 Dahood (1970: 313), repointing the participles as passive and paralleling *'ereṣ* with Sheol.

26 (Mill)stone: Tournay (1959: 60), Tromp (1969: 40), Kraus (1989: 526), RSV, JB, NEB, NRSV; ploughman: Anderson (1972b: 921), Allen (1983: 271), NIV, REB.

here clearly includes living human beings who are able to praise Yahweh. For Tromp, 'earth' includes both the underworld of the sea monsters and the deeps (v. 7) and the physical world of humans (vv. 11–12).[27] However, sea monsters inhabit the deeps just as humans the earth (cf. kings of the earth, v. 11), and can hardly praise Yahweh in the underworld. So *'ereṣ* here does not indicate the underworld, nor does it include it.[28]

Jeremiah 10:13. Yahweh 'makes the mist rise from the ends of the *earth*'. For Dahood this actually comes 'from the brink of the nether world'.[29] However, this depends on three dubious interpretations: the tripartite analysis of v. 12, the similar reading of Psalm 61:2, and the concept of water emerging from the underworld (Gen. 2:6, see above). Other scholars see no underworld reference here, nor does Dahood in the identical phrase in Psalm 135:7.[30] More probably the mist comes from the physical world.

ii. The inhabited world

Exodus 1:10. Here Pharaoh fears that the Israelites will 'escape from the *land*'. For Holladay, he fears specifically that they will 'arise from the underworld'.[31] However, this is most unlikely.[32] In Exodus the verb 'go up' normally indicates the journey from Egypt to Canaan (as Holladay admits); the proposal hardly fits the immediate context; and Pharaoh is more likely to fear the loss of slave labour than some unexplained phantom spirits!

Job 15:29. According to Eliphaz, the wicked will not be rich, nor 'strike root in the *earth*'. For several scholars this means that their possessions will not descend to the underworld.[33] This idea accords with 'darkness' in the following verse (often deleted as a gloss), and is stated directly in Psalm 49:17. However, the verb 'strike root' (*n-ṭ-h*) never occurs elsewhere of descent generally, let alone descent to the underworld, unlike 'go down' (*y-r-d*) in Psalm 49. And the context here is the plight of the wicked on earth, not their subsequent fate.

[27] Dahood (1970: 353), Tromp (1969: 41). Ignored by Anderson (1972a: 950), Kraus (1989: 568).
[28] So Hillers (1978: 328), Allen (1983: 313), Tsumura (1988: 265).
[29] Dahood (1968: 84), following the Qere.
[30] E.g. Thompson (1980: 330f.), Carroll (1986: 258f.), Holladay (1986: 335), McKane (1986: 226), Jones (1992: 177); cf. Dahood (1970: 261).
[31] Holladay (1969: 123f.); in deliberate irony, the Egyptians are later swallowed by *'ereṣ* (15:12, see below).
[32] Similarly Rupprecht (1970: 445f.), de Moor (1971: 184), Rosenberg (1981: 29 n. 58). Ignored by Childs (1974: 15), Hyatt (1980: 58), Durham (1987: 8).
[33] Dahood (1962: 60f.; omitted in 1966: 106), Tromp (1969: 42), Pope (1973: 119); against: Clines (1989: 343).

Psalm 41:2. The charitable are called 'happy in the *land*'. Dahood initially read 'land' with the following verb and translated 'do not place him in the underworld'. But later he ignored this, accepting the usual interpretation. Tromp rightly finds his earlier view unconvincing, and others ignore it.[34]

Proverbs 11:31. The righteous are repaid 'on *earth*'. Dahood reinterprets this and the preceding verse as indicating distinctive post-mortem lots for righteous and wicked. This is highly suspect, and rejected or ignored by other scholars. For Driver, Dahood's reading of 'lives' (*nᵉp̄āšôṯ*, v. 30) as 'eternal life' 'strain[s] credulity to breaking point'.[35]

Isaiah 14:9. Sheol beneath rouses 'leaders of the *earth*' to greet the newcomer. For Cross–Freedman, *'ereṣ* as underworld is 'especially clear' here. But they present no argument, and others disagree.[36] The metaphorical use of *'attûḏ* (lit. 'ram') for 'leader' is well attested (cf. Jer. 50:8; Ezek. 34:17; 39:18; Zech. 10:3) and the parallel with 'nations' makes *'ereṣ* more plausibly the inhabited world.

Jeremiah 14:2, 18; 15:7. In 15:7 Yahweh winnows rebellious Israel 'in the gates of the *land*'. For Dahood and Holladay this means at the gates of the underworld.[37] But this is unlikely. Winnowing commonly took place at city gates (cf. 1 Kgs. 22:10), and the phrase here probably means gates throughout the country, or possibly at the borders of the country itself.[38] Dahood sees a Ugaritic parallel, where Anat winnows Mot and scatters his remains, but this differs markedly from winnowing Israel in the underworld. Holladay notes references to 'the gates of Sheol', but they hardly determine the meaning of *'ereṣ* here. Holladay also sees underworld reference in Jeremiah 14, but this is equally unlikely. In 14:2 *'ereṣ* fits the description of a mourning city better as 'earth', and in 14:18 prophets and priests ply their trade more probably in the land than 'all the way to the grave'. Other scholars discern no underworld reference in these texts.[39]

Jeremiah 17:13. The lamenting prophet declares that those who forsake Yahweh will be 'written in the *earth*' (RSV). For many scholars, this means

[34] Dahood (1963b: 297, but not 1966: 248, despite listing it on p. 106); against: Anderson (1972a: 322), Craigie (1983: 320), Kraus (1988: 431).

[35] Dahood (1963a: 25f.); Driver (1965: 112). Also against: Tromp (1969: 43), Scott (1965: 87), McKane (1970: 432f.), Whybray (1972: 70), Murphy (1998: 79).

[36] Cross–Freedman (1955: 247); against: Kaiser (1974: 36), Clements (1980: 142), Wildberger (1978: 549), Watts (1985: 205), Oswalt (1986: 315).

[37] Dahood, citing KTU 1.6.ii:32 (cf. Tromp 1969: 30), Holladay (1986: 442).

[38] Cf. Nah. 3:13 (unless *'ereṣ* means 'city' there) and modern expressions like 'a country with open doors'.

[39] Holladay (429f., 437f.); against: Thompson (1980: 375, 384, 388), Carroll (1986: 309, 316, 322), McKane (1986: 316, 330f., 339), Jones (1992: 206, 212, 217).

rather that they will be 'recorded in the underworld' (NRSV).[40] Dahood notes the phrase 'counted among those who descend to the Pit/earth' (Ps. 88:4; KTU 1.4.vii:8f.), but this is significantly different. He also notes that 'to write' has eschatological connotations elsewhere (Ps. 69:28; Ezek. 13:9), but these and similar texts (all outside Jeremiah) only mention a book of the righteous, never one of apostates.[41] For Holladay, 17:12f. is similar to parts of 14:1 – 15:9 'in which references to Sheol play a prominent part', but the only such references he cites are unconvincing (see above). The book of Jeremiah is notably devoid of underworld terms, and refers nowhere to 'Sheol', 'Pit' or 'Destruction'. Its only clear comments on post-mortem fate concern unburied corpses and disinterred bones (e.g. 7:33; 8:1f.). Thus 17:13 probably indicates a record either in the country or in the dusty ground, echoing the ineradicable writing of Judah's sin on hearts and altars (v. 1).[42] Various other interpretations all take *'ereṣ* as the earth.[43]

iii. The ground

Psalms 7:5; 143:3. The psalmists feel trampled or crushed to the *ground.* Some scholars argue that they actually felt crushed into the underworld.[44] In 7:5 Tromp argues that the enemy is Death, the psalmist puts a curse on himself, and the terms 'lay' and 'dust' indicate the underworld. However, this is unconvincing: the enemy is probably human here as in the rest of the psalm (vv. 1, 4, 6, 9, 14–16); self-imprecation need not imply consignment to Sheol; and the terms cited normally refer to this world, not the next. In 143:3 Tromp similarly notes the 'Arch-enemy' and darkness. But again this need not indicate the underworld: the context implies human enemies (vv. 9, 12); the verb 'crushed' hardly suggests removal to Sheol; and the psalmist prays to avoid the Pit (v. 7). His experience is *like* that of those long dead, not identical to it.[45] Thus *'ereṣ* probably indicates the ground.[46]

[40] Targum (adding 'in Gehenna' here as in other unrelated texts, cf. Is. 66:24; Nah. 1:8), Rashi, Kimḥi (cf. McKane 1986: 407), Baumgartner (1917), Dahood (1959: 164–6), Tromp (1969: 31), Holladay (1986: 501).

[41] Cf. Ps. 139:16; Is. 4:3; Dan. 12:1; Mal. 3:16; see Ch. 9.e.

[42] Cf. Bright (1965: 118), Carroll (1986: 358f., probably), McKane (1986: 407f.), Jones (1992: 246).

[43] Others emend 'written', e.g. 'ashamed' (Ewald et al.), 'cut off' (Targum, Vulgate), 'humbled' (NEB).

[44] Dahood (1966: 43; 1970: 323), Tromp (1969: 32, 40), Anderson (1972a: 95; 1972b: 927f.).

[45] Tromp translates *kᵉ* as 'like', but then accepts its equivalence to *bᵉ*, implying 'among' (n. 96).

[46] So Kraus (1988: 166, 1989: 537), Craigie (1983: 97, 101, with underworld allusion), Allen (1983: 280).

Psalm 44:25. The oppressed faithful 'sink down to the dust' and 'cling to the *ground*'. For Tromp, this suggests the underworld. But the imagery of being crushed in this life is forceful and appropriate enough.[47]

Psalm 147:6. Yahweh casts the wicked not 'to the *ground*' but to the underworld for some scholars.[48] However, the parallelism with the phrase 'Yahweh raises the downtrodden' suggests the reversal of fortunes in this life, and no further significance of *'ereṣ* is necessary.[49]

Ecclesiastes 3:21. Qohelet wonders 'whether the human spirit goes upward and the spirit of animals goes downward to the *earth*'. Some suggest he refers here to the underworld.[50] But this would prove too much, implying that animals go to Sheol, an otherwise alien concept, and that humans do not. Further, the previous verse asserts that all return to dust, echoing Genesis 2:7 rather than alluding to the underworld. Thus *'ereṣ* more likely indicates the ground.[51]

Isaiah 21:9. The images of Babylon's gods 'lie shattered on the *ground*'. This is a probable underworld reference for Cross–Freedman. But images in the underworld would be a unique concept, and a discordant note in the sustained prophetic condemnation of idols as nonentities. More likely *'ereṣ* means 'the ground'.[52]

Isaiah 47:1. The virgin daughter Babylon must come down and sit 'in the dust . . . on the *ground*'. This indicates a descent to the underworld for Franke.[53] However, Babylon's punishment here is clearly disgrace in this world (vv. 1–3), unlike that of the king of Babylon in Isaiah 14 with which Franke sees a parallel. Sitting on the ground was a common sign of mourning, as illustrated even by El on Baal's death in the Ugaritic Baal cycle, and hardly has underworld connotations.

Obadiah 3. Proud Edom scoffs at being brought 'down to the ground', or rather to the underworld for Cross–Freedman. But this is unlikely, despite use of the verb 'go down'. Though Edom has a mountainous home (cf. v. 4) and an exalted self-image, it will be made least among the nations, despised (v. 2) and pillaged (v. 6). This indicates earthly humiliation rather

[47] Tromp (1969: 36); against: Dahood (1966: 268), Anderson (1972a: 345), Craigie (1983: 331), Kraus (1988: 448).

[48] Cross–Freedman (1955: 248), Tromp (1969: 41), Dahood (1970: 345).

[49] Cf. Anderson (1972b: 946), Kraus (1989: 554), Allen (1983: 304).

[50] Gunkel (1895: 18), Tromp (1969: 33), Scott (1965: 222f.).

[51] Explicitly: Hertzberg (Hertzberg–Bardtke 1963: 112), Michel (1989: 117); implicitly: Lauha (1978: 77), Eaton (1983: 87), Crenshaw (1988: 104f.), Ogden (1988: 62), Fox (1989: 196), Whybray (1989: 80), Murphy (1992: 37).

[52] Cross–Freedman (1955); against: Tromp (1969: 28), Kaiser (1974: 128), Wildberger (1978: 784), Clements (1980: 179), Watts (1985: 270), Oswalt (1986: 388). Most read the verb as passive, following 1QIsa[a], etc.

[53] Franke (1993: 254f.). Cf. KTU 1.5.vi.11–12 (CML: 73).

than descent to Sheol, and *'ereṣ* most naturally means the surface of the earth.[54]

iv. The swallowing earth

Exodus 15:12. The Israelites sing triumphantly that Yahweh extended his hand and the *earth* swallowed the Egyptians. Following Gunkel, many see *'ereṣ* here as the underworld. For Tromp, the Egyptians 'were covered by the sea, the waters of chaos, i.e. they were swallowed by the nether world'. So 'the mighty waters' (15:10) and *'ereṣ* both mean the underworld.[55] However, the hymn frequently mentions the water in which the Egyptians drown (vv. 1, 4, 5, 8, 10). Some of its phrases may allude to the underworld, since water imagery often portrays dire circumstances (see section b.iii below), but such allusion is secondary to the description of death. The images of drowning and being swallowed by *'ereṣ* are complementary rather than identical, as is the further image of fire (v. 7). Also, the action of swallowing by *'ereṣ* may indicate the route downwards rather than the underworld itself, as in Numbers 16.

Numbers 16:30–33. Moses declares that Yahweh will be vindicated if the ground opens its mouth and swallows the rebels, and they descend alive to Sheol; the ground then splits apart, the *earth* opens its mouth and swallows them, they descend alive to Sheol and the *earth* closes over them.[56] For Tromp, the 'personification of the ground ("mouth", "swallow up") brings out its affinity with Sheol' and makes it similar to Ugaritic Mot, despite the difference in terms.[57] However, the identification of 'ground' (*'ᵃḏāmāh*) and 'earth' (*'ereṣ*) and the opening and closing of the latter clearly portray *'ereṣ* as the solid earth through which the rebels descend to Sheol, rather than the underworld itself. Further, *'ereṣ* is never divinized, as in Ugaritic mythology, and even its portrayal here as 'personification' may be an overstatement. For others, *'ereṣ* is not the underworld here. Rather, it simply describes the rebels descending into a suddenly appearing chasm or into the mud of a suddenly disintegrating *kewir* (an encrusted mud-flat).[58]

[54] Cross–Freedman (1955); against: Rudolph (1971: 303), Allen (1976: 146), Wolff (1986: 30), Stuart (1987: 410).
[55] Tromp (1969: 25f.).
[56] Num. 16:33 is the only text where a narrator uses the term 'Sheol' (see Ch. 3.a.i).
[57] Tromp (1969: 27).
[58] E.g. Snaith (1967: 260), Noth (1968a: 128f.), Wenham (1981: 137f.). For mud-flat, cf. Hort (1959).

Numbers 26:10; Deuteronomy 11:6; Psalm 106:17. The first two summarize the above story as the earth opening its mouth and swallowing the rebels, and implicitly give *'ereṣ* the same meaning as the former account. The third adds that the earth covered them, making explicit that *'ereṣ* means simply 'the solid earth'.[59]

v. The earth below

Job 10:21–22; Jonah 2:6. Occasionally various complements indicate the nature of the *'ereṣ* mentioned: it is a land of gloom, darkness, chaos (Job 10:21f.) and bars (Jonah 2:7). Here it is the qualifying terms and the context which indicate a reference to the underworld, not *'ereṣ* alone. Further, in both texts *'ereṣ* is used metaphorically as 'land, country'.

Psalms 63:9; 71:20; 139:15. Psalm 63:9 consigns the wicked to 'the depths of the *earth*', and 71:20 anticipates deliverance from there.[60] These expressions echo familiar themes and clearly indicate the underworld. Psalm 139:15 unusually locates individual origin in 'the depths of the *earth*', though whether this is mother earth or the underworld is unclear. However, it is always a compound expression, not *'ereṣ* alone, which is used.

Ezekiel 26:20; 31:14, 16, 18; 32:18, 24. Here '*earth* below' recurs as one of several underworld terms. Again, these verses contain compound expressions, not *'ereṣ* alone. Nowhere in this section does 'below' (*taḥîṯ*, etc.) occur with Sheol or Pit, since these terms indicate the underworld without further qualification. By contrast, *'ereṣ* needs such qualification, so presumably on its own it does not indicate the underworld.

vi. The ground or the underworld

1 Samuel 28:13. The medium at Endor claims to see 'gods' rising from the *earth*, or rather the underworld for many.[61] However, *'ereṣ* could also mean the earth directly underneath the woman.[62]

Psalm 22:29. This difficult verse reads literally: 'All the fat of the *earth*

[59] So Dahood (1970: 71), Kraus (1989: 314), Allen (1983: 45); against Tromp (1969: 39), Anderson (1972b: 741).

[60] Pss. 63:9; 139:15: *taḥtîyôṯ (hā)'āreṣ*; 71:20: *tᵉhômôṯ hā'āreṣ.*

[61] E.g. Dhorme (1907: 61f.), Tromp (1969: 27), McCarter (1980: 421), Lewis (1989: 114).

[62] *'ereṣ* occurs earlier in the same passage with its regular meaning, 'country' (vv. 3, 9). On 1 Sam. 28, see further Ch. 7.b

(*dišnê-'ereṣ*) will eat and bow down before him, and all who go down to the dust will bow . . .' Since the second phrase mentions the dead, many scholars think the first does too, and emend it to 'all who sleep in the earth' (*y^ešēnê-'ereṣ*).[63] For some, this means that the inhabitants of Sheol worship Yahweh.[64] However, this would contradict the many emphatic assertions elsewhere that the dead are isolated from him. For others, the dead worship Yahweh through their living offspring.[65] But this introduces further complications. This leaves a final view, that it is those who are *about to* die who offer worship while they are still alive.[66] In this case, however, 'earth' and 'dust' could refer simply to the ground rather than the underworld, so do not necessarily mean the underworld.

Further, there are no textual variants of *dišnê-'ereṣ*, and not all scholars emend it. Some retain the traditional 'fat of the land'.[67] Others propose alternative meanings. Tournay translates it as 'cinders of the earth'. This would be a unique expression for the dead, but is most unlikely since cremation was abhorred.[68] Lipiński translates the first phrase as 'powerful ones of the earth' and the second as the poor and miserable who 'sink in the dust', so together they mean 'everyone'.[69] But the expression 'those who descend' is not restricted to the poor, so the proposed merism in v. 29 is uncertain. Psalm 22:29–31 is certainly difficult and contains further problems not addressed here. However, the interpretation of *'ereṣ* as 'underworld' is uncertain, and presents its own difficulties.

Isaiah 14:12. The prophet portrays the mighty king of Babylon as fallen from heaven, cut down to the *ground*. For Gunkel and Tromp this indicates the Babylonian king's debasement to the underworld, like v. 15 (in the same oracle) and v. 11 (in the previous one). However, the verb 'cut down' (*g-d-'*) in v. 12 is normally used of trees, etc. (Asherah poles, altar horns, iron bars), felled to the ground, and occasionally by extension of people (e.g. Israel, Lam. 2:3; the wicked, Ps. 75:10). Thus here the king will be felled to the ground like a tree. Further, in Isaiah 14 *'ereṣ* refers often and clearly to this world (vv. 7, 9, 16, 20f., 25f.).

63 E.g. BHS, (NEB), NRSV, REB. Dahood (1966: 143) and Tromp (1969: 34) read 'sleep' without emendation.

64 E.g. Weiser (1962: 226), Dahood, Tromp, Schmid (1971: 135), Stähli (1986: 180), Kraus (1988: 300).

65 E.g. Tournay (1962: 501).

66 So Anderson (1972a: 194), Craigie (1983: 197), Jacquet (1975: 546).

67 So ancient versions, AV, RV, RSV, JB, Kidner (1973: 109).

68 Tournay (1962: 500) noting Jer. 31:40, but the only relationship there of *dešen* to corpses is physical proximity.

69 Lipiński (1969: 160), noting Akkadian *dašnû* and Hebrew *d-š-n* (Piel), 'strengthen'. Similarly Keel-Leu (1970), contrasting their supposedly voluntary homage with the forced homage of those who descend to the dust.

Isaiah 29:4. Fallen Ariel (i.e. Jerusalem) will speak from the *earth* like a ghost (*'ôḇ*) and whisper out of the dust. For many this indicates the underworld,[70] and for some it supports the connotation of 'Ariel' as the underworld or its denizens (cf. the Akkadian underworld name *arallû*).[71] David's proud city will be reduced to the scarcely audible or intelligible mutterings of the spirits, who could only chirp and murmur (cf. Is. 8:19). However, such noises could be thought to emanate from the ground in general rather than the underworld in particular.[72]

Hosea 1:11. The divided nation will reunite, appoint a leader and (lit.) 'go up from the *earth*'. For several scholars this envisages resurrection from the underworld. Holladay sees national resurrection similar to that of 6:2, and Kuhnigk sees an affinity with Ezekiel's vision of resurrected skeletons (Ezek. 37:12f.).[73] However, these other texts have different terms and emphases (see further Ch. 10.a.iii). Hosea 6:2 focuses on national renewal; resurrection is at best implicit, and the underworld is unmentioned. Ezekiel 37 specifically mentions graves being opened in the earth, but does not use the term *'ereṣ*.

While the phrase 'go up from the earth' is hardly likely to mean return from the underworld, its meaning is not immediately obvious. Two interpretations are more plausible. (a) Israel will return from exile.[74] This fits the preceding references to national renewal, though in the prophets (and particularly in Hosea) *'ereṣ* without qualification indicates the land of Israel, not of exile.[75] (b) Israel will sprout from the earth (like a plant).[76] This fits the following declaration that 'great shall be the day of Jezreel', and the surrounding references to Jezreel (meaning 'God plants'; cf. 1:4; 2:22). Other less plausible interpretations of the phrase include: reference to the exodus[77] – but this is unlikely in context; expansion from the central hills to which Israel was reduced in 733 BCE, and repossession of northern and eastern territories[78] – but *'ereṣ* never elsewhere means the reduced territory; military possession of Palestine[79] – but it is doubtful if

[70] Tromp (1969: 29), Scullion (1972: 122), Burns (1979: 8), Wildberger (1982: 1107), Watts (1985: 382).
[71] Albright (1953: 218 n. 86), Exum (1981: 343f.); against Haldar (1945: 130–34, 'oraclers').
[72] So Clements (1980: 236), Oswalt (1986: 524). On *'ôḇ*, see Ch. 7.a.
[73] Holladay (1969: 123f.), Kuhnigk (1974: 8–10). As one of several meanings: Andersen–Freedman (1980: 209), Stuart (1987: 39), Hubbard (1989a: 69).
[74] Jeremias (1983: 35), Stuart (1987: 39, partly), Yee (1987: 75, partly).
[75] Cf. Rudolph (1966: 57), Mays (1969a: 33), Andersen–Freedman (1980: 209).
[76] Cf. same phrase used of plants, Is. 53:2. So Rudolph (1966: 58), Rupprecht (1970: 446), Emmerson (1984: 98), Neef (1987: 133 n. 44), Yee (1987: 75, partly), Davies (1992: 62), REB.
[77] Cf. Exod. 1:10 (see above), so Andersen–Freedman (1980: 209, partial allusion).
[78] So Knight (1960: 49, possibly), Holland (1980: 37).
[79] So KB, Mays (1969: 33), Wolff (1974b: 28), NEB, JPS mg., NRSV.

'go up from' ever means this;[80] pilgrimage within Palestine[81] but this does not fit the context. In both of the plausible interpretations the verse predicts national restoration, but not through a rising from the underworld.

vii. The land of the shades? (Is. 26:19)

This verse is extremely difficult to interpret. It reverses statements of the immediate context (which in any case juxtaposes various motifs), some words are textually uncertain, others occur unusually, and the crucial final phrase is ambiguous.[82] The author has previously asserted that the shades of godless rulers will not rise (v. 14), but now tells Yahweh, 'Your dead will live, my/their corpses will rise',[83] and instructs 'dwellers in the dust' to awake and sing.[84] Next he tells Yahweh, 'Your dew is a dew of light'.[85] Then comes the crucial final phrase, whose three words separately mean: 'and-earth/land', 'shades', 'you/it-will-let/make-fall'. The grammar and meaning are understood very diversely, as follows:

(i) The subject is Yahweh, the implied object is 'dew':
A: *you will let (your dew) fall on the land of the shades.*[86]
(ii) The subject is Yahweh, the object is 'land of the shades':
B: *you will subdue the land of the shades.*[87]
(iii) The subject is 'land of the shades', there is no object:
C: *the land of the ungodly will fall.*[88]
D: *the land of the shades will give birth.*[89]

[80] Cf. Wehmeier (THAT 2: 277), Rudolph (1966: 57), Andersen–Freedman (1980: 208).

[81] So Wolff (1952–53: 95; qualified in 1974b: 28), Östborn (1956: 64, to Jerusalem), Frey (1957: 30), McKeating (1971: 80, to Shechem for coronation and covenant renewal).

[82] Only issues relevant to the meaning of *'ereṣ* are discussed here. For recent study, cf. Millar (1976), Wildberger (1978), Hasel (1980), Spronk (1986), Johnson (1988).

[83] Either 'my corpse' (MT), implying the speaker's identification with Yahweh's people, or 'their corpse' (Syriac, Targum, BHS), referring back to the dead. The singular is generally read as a collective.

[84] Or recounts this in the indicative, cf. 1QIsa^{a}, Syriac, Targum, Aquila, Symmachus and Theodotion.

[85] For Ugaritic parallels, cf. Humbert (1957), etc. For 'dew of herbs' (AV) cf. Margalit (1984: 113; 1987: 393).

[86] RSV, NIV, Young (1969: 222, translation), Millar (1976: 53). For assumed preposition 'on', cf. v. 18.

[87] Peshitta, Vulgate ('land of the giants'), Procksch (1930: 324), Kissane (1960: 284). Cf. also JPS: 'you will make the land of the shades come to life', with note: 'meaning uncertain'.

[88] LXX (reading *rᵉpāʾîm* here as *rᵉšāʿîm*, 'wicked').

[89] JB, Auvray (1972: 236).

(iv) The subject is 'earth', the object is 'shades':
E: *the earth will let/make fall the shades.*[90]
F: *the earth will give birth to the shades.*[91]

Several factors explain these diverse translations. First, the form of the verb means the subject could be either Yahweh or land/earth.[92] Secondly, 'land' could mean 'land of' (if its vowels are ignored), and so be linked to the following word 'shades'. Thirdly and most crucially, the verb *n-p-l*, which in the Causative form normally means 'cause to fall' (as in A, B, C and E above), is given a unique meaning, 'give birth', by many scholars (as in D and F above; also in v. 18) for two reasons. (a) Linguistically, the related noun *nēpel* means 'miscarried/stillborn baby', and both verb and noun occur in later Hebrew and in Aramaic for 'miscarriage'.[93] Similarly, the Greek verb *(kata)piptein*, which normally means 'fall', can also mean 'give birth'.[94] (b) Contextually, this fits the preceding imagery of childbirth. Israel is like a woman in labour, but gives birth (*y-l-d*) only to wind (vv. 17–18a). It has won no victories on earth, and 'no one is born (*n-p-l*) to inhabit the world' (v. 18b, NRSV). In response, the earth will give birth (*n-p-l*) to Yahweh's shades (v. 19), meaning either the physical resurrection of dead individuals or the metaphorical revival of the moribund nation.[95]

However, neither of these arguments is strong. (a) There is little evidence that the Semitic root *n-p-l* ever means 'live birth'.[96] Further, the Greek verb provides meagre support: this meaning is extremely rare in a vast literary corpus, in both texts there are explanatory circumstantial clauses, and Greek is not a Semitic language! (b) Different images are often juxtaposed in the prophets, and particularly in the apocalyptic style which dominates Isaiah 24 – 27. So the childbirth imagery of vv. 17–18a cannot determine the meaning of *n-p-l* in vv. 18b-19. The posited idea of victory gained by repopulation of the world would be novel, and hardly justifies a novel meaning of

[90] Luther, AV, RV, ASV, Young (1969: 229, comment), Watts (1985: 337, translation), Oswalt (1986: 476).

[91] NEB, NJB, NRSV, REB, Fohrer (1966: 27), Tromp (1969: 29), Kaiser (1974: 215), Vermeylen (1974: 27, as 'relecture'), Wildberger (1978: 986), Irwin (1979: 257), Day (1980: 312), Hasel (1980: 271), Watts (1985: 344, excursus), Spronk (1986: 301), Johnson (1988: 107).

[92] In the imperfect, 2nd pers. masc. sg. and 3rd pers. fem. sg. are identical, and *'ereṣ* is feminine.

[93] *nēpel*: Ps. 58:8; Job 3:16; Eccles. 6:3; cf. Levy (1976–89), Jastrow (1903).

[94] Iliad 19:110 (cf. Murray, 1925: 344); Wisdom 7:3. Liddell–Scott (1407) gives no further occurrences. Gray (1912) also cites the Arabic verb *sakaṭa* (fall, miscarry) for 'give birth', but without evidence, and Lane (1863–93) ignores this.

[95] E.g. individuals: Gray, Kaiser, Hasel; nation: Auvray, Kissane, Fohrer, Wildberger. See Ch. 10.a.iv.

[96] HAL notes Arabic *nāpilat*, 'grandson', but this could derive from 'falling down (generations)' and so be unconnected with birth *per se*.

n-p-l. It is more natural to translate the last phrase of v. 18 as 'the inhabitants of the world have not fallen' (RSV), since elsewhere in these chapters 'the inhabitants of the world' are under divine judgment.[97] Israel's victory would bring their downfall – but this has not yet occurred. If, then, *n-p-l* has its usual sense of 'to fall' in v. 18, it is even less likely to have a unique meaning in v. 19. So translations D and F are unlikely.

Of the other translations, B posits a sudden change of emphasis within v. 19 and a peculiar theology of underworld conflict, while C does not give the verb a Causative sense. So both are unlikely. Of the remaining two, A is straightforward in meaning and ties the two halves of the line together. But it has to ignore the vowels of *'ereṣ* to read it as 'land of', so is less likely. E suggests 'the figure of the devourer forced to *drop*, *let fall*, its prey from its mouth', and on balance seems the most likely. The phrase therefore probably means: 'the earth will let go of the shades'.[98]

With A it is not 'land' (*'ereṣ*) alone but 'land of the shades' which indicates the underworld. With E *'ereṣ* could mean the underworld, but it could mean more generally the mass of earth in which the dead were buried and in whose depths the underworld was situated. Other associated terms in the verse (corpses, dust, dew) fit more obviously with *'ereṣ* as 'earth' than as 'underworld'. So it is the earth, as much as the underworld, which gives back the shades.

viii. Summary

'ereṣ, like so many common terms, has a wide range of meanings. As the physical earth, in contrast to the heavens, it stretches far downwards, and contains the underworld in its depths. There are some texts in which *'ereṣ* on its own could mean 'underworld', though these are many fewer than suggested. However, there is none which demands, and therefore proves, this interpretation. Further, no ancient version or tradition testifies to such a meaning. Thus it is wiser to conclude that *'ereṣ* is not a Hebrew term for the underworld.

b. Is water the underworld?

Water is a frequent Old Testament theme. In a land of uncertain rainfall, it is particularly noted as indispensable to life. Its presence brings fertility and

[97] *yôšᵉḇê tēḇēl*, vv. 9,18; *yôšᵉḇê 'ereṣ* (or variants), v. 21; 24:1, 5, 6 (x2), 17.

[98] Oswalt (1986: 476). This view is echoed in 2 Esdras 7:32: 'and the earth shall give up [*reddet*] those who are asleep in it' (Charlesworth 1983: 538). The Latin verb does not mean 'give birth', even though the simile of birth occurs in earlier in 2 Esdras 4:42 in a context which also echoes Is. 26 (birth pangs, return to life, disclosure).

blessing, while its absence results in sterility and curse. But water can also threaten life. Many psalms portray distress and punishment in watery terms, as being submerged, carried away, losing one's foothold or drowning.[99] Further, the waters are occasionally seen as a chaotic power opposed to but subdued by Yahweh. Many scholars have studied the biblical theme of water in general and chaotic water in particular,[100] and several note close associations between water and the underworld. These associations merit examination.

i. Water under the world

In Hebrew cosmology, the earth was often thought to rest on water, as declared in Psalm 24:2:

> for he has founded it on the seas,
> and established it on the rivers [or floods].[101]

The second commandment and other texts refer to water under the earth (Exod. 20:4; Deut. 4:18; 5:8), and the flood story mentions 'the fountains of the great deep' (Gen. 7:11; 8:2). The earth was thought to rest on great pillars, which Jonah called 'the roots of the mountains' (Jonah 2:6). These went down to the bottom of this subterranean ocean, though what they stood on there is never specified.

This interpretation has occasionally been challenged. Sutcliffe (1946: 45f.) argues that the earth was simply higher than the waters, not resting on them, as follows. The earth was too stable to be thought floating on water; unsupported subterranean water would simply flow away; originally water covered the earth (Gen. 1), not vice versa; in Psalm 24:2 'upon' (*'al*) means simply 'higher than' (cf. Deut. 26:19); Sheol was conceived as in the earth, not under it; several Akkadian inscriptions portray the foundations of buildings resting directly on the underworld. McGovern (1959) adds further points. The waters 'under' (*taḥaṯ*) the earth are simply 'lower than' it (cf. *taḥaṯ* in Gen. 35:8; 1 Sam. 7:11; 1 Kgs. 4:12); the fountains of the great deep in the flood story represent a naïve view (Gen. 7:11; 8:2); other texts mention division of the cosmic waters without reference to subterranean water (Ps. 104:5–9; Enuma Elish 4:138–140); Sheol cannot be a place of

[99] Cf. Akkadian prayers: 'Take away your punishment, rescue [your slave] from the morass'; 'Take away, Lord, his guilt . . . Lift him out of the mighty surging waters' (Lambert 1959–60: 59, 64; similarly ANET: 392).

[100] E.g. general: Wensinck (1918), Reymond (1958); chaotic water: May (1955), Kaiser (1959), Habel (1964), Wakeman (1973), Curtis (1978), Day (1985).

[101] Cf. Ps. 136:6. Other proposed readings of *nāhār* as 'flood' are: Pss. 46:4; 72:8; 89:25; 93:3; 104:6; 124:5; Is. 44:27; Jonah 2:3; cf. Dahood (1966: 151), Anderson (1972a: 201), Pope (1973: 183).

both dusty silence and surging, threatening waters; Akkadian texts do not link water to the underworld.[102]

However, these arguments are questionable, even if Hebrew cosmology is varied and imprecise. The earth's observed stability does not disprove a subterranean ocean, and anyway its stability could be attributed to its pillars.[103] The underground ocean was not necessarily thought to be unsupported, and in any case this may not have mattered. The prepositions *'al* and *taḥaṯ* normally indicate 'above' and 'below'; the occasional meanings of 'higher than' and 'lower than' occur in specific contexts and cannot be generalized.[104] Cosmic descriptions which do not mention subterranean waters hardly help us to interpret those which do. Dusty silence and surging water terms could be separate underworld images, conveying different aspects of it and not intended to be juxtaposed. Similarly, various Mesopotamian texts may reflect different conceptions. The 'Babylonian world map', a rare drawing of the cosmos, presents the world separated by water from the seven mountains which touch both heaven and the underworld (*arallu*).[105] Dalley (1989: 132 n. 112) comments: 'There seem to have been two different [Mesopotamian] traditions about the Underworld, with and without a surrounding river.' Thus the grounds for questioning the Hebrew view of subterranean water are unconvincing.

ii. Water as the underworld?

Some texts may suggest that the underworld was itself aqueous.

Job 26:5–6 states:

> 5 The Shades below tremble,
> the waters and their inhabitants.[106]
> 6 Sheol is naked before God,
> and Abaddon [Destruction] has no covering.

There are several ways of identifying these inhabitants of the waters, who tremble before God like the shades.

(a) The shades themselves, for two reasons.[107] (i) This gives underworld references in both halves of v. 5 as in both halves of v. 6. Thus the waters are

[102] Thus the 'waters of death' which Gilgamesh approaches are simply another natural obstacle.
[103] Cf. Johnson (1949: 91f. n. 4).
[104] *'al* is obviously metaphorical in Deut. 26:19, and *taḥaṯ* precedes place-names in the texts listed.
[105] Cf. Keel (1978: 21), Seybold (1990: 178), Horowitz (1998: 32).
[106] Repunctuating the Hebrew, so Rowley (1976), Habel (1985), Gordis (1978). MT: 'The shades tremble, under the waters and their inhabitants.' Dhorme (1967) adds a second verb.
[107] So Terrien (1963: 132), Pope (1973: 183), Rowley (1976: 172), Andersen (1976: 217, implicitly), Habel (1985: 370), Hartley (1988: 365). Rowley suggests that the inhabitants are the ordinary dead, in contrast to the elite shades.

subterranean, and the underworld is located in them. (ii) These verses are really part of Bildad's speech (redefined as 25:2–6; 26:5–14), and the progression in it of heaven–earth–underworld implies that these 'inhabitants' are in the underworld.[108] This interpretation is certainly possible, and the dead are described elsewhere as 'inhabitants' (Is. 26:19). But the posited progression in Bildad's reconstructed speech is uncertain: 25:2–6 contrasts divine power with human unrighteousness, while 26:5–6 portrays the lower regions subjected to God and begins a discussion of divine omnipotence. They are different themes rather than a progression.

(b) Fish and other sea creatures.[109] These are the obvious inhabitants of the waters. The term 'inhabitants' occurs elsewhere of birds (e.g. Job 39:28), so its use of sea creatures is not improbable. Thus v. 5 locates Sheol under the subterranean waters, while v. 6 is a separate element in the description of Yahweh's creation, echoing only the first half-line of v. 5.

(c) Specifically the great sea-monsters Rahab and Leviathan.[110] Later (vv. 12f.) both monsters are mentioned, and Rahab is associated with the sea. Leviathan's realm may comprise both Sheol and the waters.

It is possible that Job 26:5 portrays a watery underworld. However, this would be exceptional in the ancient Near East. The rest of the poem consists mostly of short, single verse units, so vv. 5 and 6 could well be distinct ideas. Thus, while v. 6 focuses on Sheol, v. 5 could well encompass the whole lower region, both underworld and watery depths. In this case the waters are distinct from the underworld itself.

Jonah 2 is often thought to locate Sheol in water, since it portrays drowning at sea (vv. 3, 5), a visit to the underworld, and deliverance from it (vv. 2, 6).[111] However, Sheol is also described as a land with bars and as the pit (v. 6), and this mingling of imagery cautions against its identification simply with water. The writer describes himself as near death and already in the underworld (vv. 2, 6), but is not concerned here with its location.

Other texts associate death and the underworld with life-threatening waters of various forms.[112] But these do not specifically locate Sheol in the sea. (a) Exodus 15:5, 10 describes the Egyptian army drowning in the Sea of Reeds, not in a cosmic subterranean ocean (regardless of whether the hymn

[108] So Dhorme, Terrien. Also Pope, Rowley, Gordis, Habel for Bildad's speech. Against Andersen and Hartley.

[109] So Gordis (1978: 277), Caquot (DBS 10: 347, implicitly), Fohrer (1989: 383).

[110] So Dhorme (1967: 371, noting Ps. 104:25f.), Tur-Sinai (1967: 379f.) and possibly some scholars listed under (b).

[111] The 'belly of Sheol' is a unique expression. Either 'belly' metaphorically means 'centre, heart' (cf. Job 32:18, Prov. 22:18), or Sheol is depicted as a voracious monster (cf. Prov. 1:12; 30:16; Is. 5:14; Hab. 2:5; and Ugaritic Mot).

[112] So Martin-Achard (1960: 44 nn. 39–43), listing 17 texts.

contains mythological language). (b) Many psalms juxtapose death by drowning with other life-threatening situations: entrapment in cords and snares (18:4–5), summer heat (32:4, 8), oppressive enemies (18:16–17; 42:7, 9; cf. 43:2), sinking in mire (69:1, 14–15), being swallowed alive (124:3–5), the sword (144:7–8, 11).[113] This suggests that water is a means of death, but not necessarily the underworld's location. (c) Ezekiel 26:19 prophesies Tyre's sack and submergence under the deep or the great waters. Water is an obvious theme in oracles against this arrogant maritime city: it occurs metaphorically of the relentlessness of her enemies and literally of the destination of her ruins (vv. 3, 12). But water is hardly an aspect of the underworld, which is immediately described as 'the Pit . . . the world below . . . primeval ruins' (v. 20). Finally (d), reference to Sheol in other texts sometimes noted is neither obvious nor likely, e.g. Psalm 77:16, where waters tremble in the context of clouds, skies, thunder and lightning, and Lamentations 2:13, which contains a picturesque metaphor but no hint of the underworld.

Johnson (1951: 171) describes 'the worshipper's fear of death and his vivid sense of already being engulfed by the waters of the Underworld as he descends captive to the realm of the Dead'. However, a brief re-examination of the relevant texts shows that water was primarily an image of distress. It is often presented as being under the earth, and so associated with the underworld, but is not generally seen as identical to it.

iii. Water and the underworld

While various water terms are sometimes associated with chaos, destruction and death, they are not normally seen as underworld names in scholarly study. Thus May regards 'the great waters' as equivalent to 'the deep', the waters which oppose Yahweh and through which one passes to the underworld. Curtis lists passages where life-threatening waters portray adversity, but does not link the various terms to the underworld. Ringgren sees underworld motifs in certain texts, but does not link them specifically to water terms. Similarly, 'waves' and 'breakers' refer figuratively to death and suffering but not specifically to the underworld.[114]

However, other scholars identify water with the underworld. Pedersen was typically categorical: 'the natures of the two worlds [Sheol and the deep] are so related that they merge entirely into one another'; 'he who is in Sheol is also in the ocean, because they both denote the subterraneous, negative

[113] In Ps. 144 both 'mighty waters' and 'cruel sword' parallel deceitful aliens, all potential means of death.

[114] May (1955: 14 nn. 17f., re Pss. 18:16; 32:6); Curtis (1978: 248 n. 1, passim); Ringgren (TDOT 6 s.v. *yām*, re Jonah 2 and Ezek. 26 – 27).

power, the world of death and chaos'. Barth concurs: 'the ocean below figures formally among underworld names', and 'the underworld is manifest in . . . the ocean'. For Reymond, the ocean is also the world of the dead. And Martin-Achard concludes: 'Sheol . . . is in some way present in the Abyss, in the sea, or again in the turbulent waters, in the depths, and even in springs'.[115] Barth lists various texts where 'deep', 'sea', 'waters' and a few other terms mean the underworld. Several of these require closer study.

Sea, waters. For Barth, 'sea' (*yām*) and 'waters' (*mayim*) mean 'underworld' in several texts.[116] However, this is at best exceptional. Job 26:5 possibly pictures the shades in water (see above), which would make it one instance where 'water' means 'underworld'. But the other texts Barth cites are implausible. For instance, in Psalm 46:2 the mountains tremble 'in the heart of the waters', while elsewhere their roots are in the underworld (implied in Deut. 32:22); but these different images need not imply identity between waters and Sheol. Elsewhere ruin is compared to the sea (Lam. 2:13); but the simile ('vast *as* the sea') prevents their direct equation. And in various psalms (18:16; 32:6; 69:1–2, 15; 144:7) water could refer to extreme distress as easily as to Sheol. Clear underworld reference in a psalm hardly implies that the descriptions of distress juxtaposed with it also indicate the underworld.

Attention is also sometimes drawn to Baal's defeat of Yam (Sea) in Ugaritic mythology. This may have echoes in Yahweh's sovereignty over the sea, but Yam is completely different from Mot (Death). While there are obvious conceptual associations between forces of destruction and death, the Ugaritic texts do not support a terminological association between water and the underworld.

Deep/depths. The Hebrew term *t^{e}hôm* occurs thirty-six times.[117] Following Gunkel, most older scholarship derived it from the Akkadian *ti'âmat*, the name of the primordial goddess whose carcass was divided to create the world.[118] More recently, Wakeman still suggests that the biblical term contains depersonalized echoes of the monster myth: 'Tehom, the queen of the netherworld . . . is authorized by God to swallow his enemies'.[119] However, this derivation is less likely than it initially appears,

115 Pedersen (1926: 463), Barth (1947: 85, 91; 1997: 67, 72), Reymond (1958: 158), Martin-Achard (1960: 44).

116 Barth (1947: 85; 1997: 67). May (1955) and Curtis (1978) reach different conclusions.

117 Cf. THAT (2: 1027). Ginsberg adds 2 Sam. 1:21, emending *t^{e}rûmôṯ* to *t^{e}hômôṯ*; cf. McCarter (1984: 70) and Seow (ABD 2:125).

118 Gunkel (1895: 112, 115). The translation by Muenchow both abbreviates and expands.

119 Wakeman (1973: 86–92, quotation from 89). Some of her arguments are weak: *t^{e}hôm rāḇāh* hardly indicates that *t^{e}hôm* was once a monarch; *rbṣ* is not used only of animals (cf. Is. 14:30); and the texts cited are not supportive. Similarly Anderson (1967: 39).

since it should give a middle consonant *aleph* (not *he*), and a feminine ending. Most scholars now accept that the Hebrew does not derive directly from the Akkadian, but that both words derive independently from a common proto-Semitic root *tiham.*[120] In this case the term itself does not have an immediate mythological background.

Barth and Martin-Achard see 'the deep' (*tᵉhôm*) as the underworld in five biblical texts, and Tromp adds another two.[121] However, this view is unlikely in all seven cases. In four texts, other terms in the immediate context suggest that 'the deep' primarily denotes physical water: sea, reed sea, floods, waters, mighty waters (Exod. 15:5, 8); waters, weeds (Jonah 2:6); cataracts, waves, billows (Ps. 42:7); waters, clouds, skies, thunder, whirlwind, lightning, sea (Ps. 77:16). Death may be present (Exod. 15) or feared imminent (Jonah 2), or despair experienced (Ps. 42), and hence underworld descent may be implied (though Pss. 42 – 43 lack obvious underworld reference). But this hardly demonstrates that 'the deep' itself means the underworld. When all nature responds to divine action (Ps. 77), 'the deep' indicates the extremity of the physical world rather than the underworld.

In Psalm 107:26 storm-tossed sailors ascend to the heavens and descend to the depths. For Tromp, *tᵉhôm* here has a double meaning of depths and underworld. However, the psalm uses no underworld terms in its other cameos of distress (desert, prison, illness), and no such double meaning could apply to the parallel term 'heavens'. Tromp's interpretation requires rather than proves that *tᵉhôm* means underworld. In Ezekiel 26:19f. Yahweh will bring 'the deep' over Tyre, cover it with 'the great waters' and consign it to the underworld. Clearly, Tyre's submergence is an image of its fate, but the preposition precludes identifying *tᵉhôm* as the underworld. Finally, in Psalm 71:20 the psalmist celebrates deliverance from 'the depths of the earth'. This could refer to the subterranean waters, either as the underworld or as the route towards it.[122] However, *tᵉhôm* here is usually interpreted as 'depth' without reference to water, and the phrase rendered 'depths of the earth'.[123] Together the terms indicate the underworld, but not as water.[124]

In distinct contrast, Westermann (THAT 2: 1029) shows that 'the deep',

[120] Cf. cognate Eblaite, Ugaritic and Arabic terms; HAL, Heidel (1951: 100), Kitchen (1966: 89f.), Westermann (THAT 2: 1026–31), Day (1985: 50), Tsumura (1989: 51f.). Görg (1993: 6f.) also links it to Egyptian *thm.*

[121] Barth (1947: 85), Martin-Achard (1960: 43f. n. 39), Tromp (1969: 59–61).

[122] NEB and REB (earth's watery depths), Anderson (1972a: 517, underworld); Kraus (1989: 73, route).

[123] RSV, JB, JPS, NRSV, Tate (1990: 208). Neither 'depths' nor 'earth' is itself an underworld name.

[124] Wakeman (1969: 317 n. 18) cites similar expressions (in Pss. 77:16, 18; 95:4; Job 38:16) to argue that 'depth' and 'earth' form a hendiadys. But here they form a construct chain.

like water more generally, is often the source of blessing (e.g. Ps. 78:15). Even if the term had some etymological link with a cosmic enemy, this positive use means that *tᵉhôm* is an unlikely name for the barren underworld.

Interestingly, the equivalent Ugaritic term *thm*, 'ocean' (pl. *thmtm*), has no apparent underworld reference in its various contexts. These are:[125] (i) 'El at the source(s) of the rivers, amid the springs of the two oceans'; (ii) 'sighing of heavens to earth, of oceans to stars'; (iii) 'the oceans the lightning'; (iv) 'without watering by the two oceans'; (v) 'shore of the sea . . . shore of the ocean'; (vi) 'daughter of heaven and ocean'. Whatever the mythological setting of the texts concerned, *thm(tm)* refers to water, not the underworld. Some scholars locate the cosmic mountain of El's residence in the underworld, and hence in 'rivers' (*nhrm*) and 'oceans' (*thmtm*),[126] but this is now generally rejected.[127] Dahood translates *thmtm* in one text as 'nether world', but he is alone in doing so.[128] *thm(tm)* may refer to the water above and below the earth,[129] though the couplet 'heavens and *thm*' (KTU 1.100.i:1) suggests otherwise, or may refer simply to the ocean depths. However, the point remains that Ugaritic *thm* has no direct association with the underworld.

Two other rare Hebrew words for 'depths' can allude to the underworld. One, *maʿᵃmaqqîm*, occurs five times, mostly in the phrase 'depths of the waters/sea'. Twice it indicates physical water (Is. 51:10; Ezek. 27:34). Otherwise it indicates the psalmist's plight, alongside other metaphors (Ps. 69:2, 14) or on its own (Ps. 130:1). These metaphors obviously indicate mortal danger, and hence refer or at least allude to the underworld.[130] The other, *mᵉṣûlāh*, similarly indicates the sea's depths. Occasionally it may refer or allude to the underworld, in contexts of desperate plight (Pss. 69:2, 15; 88:6), or drowning and descent to Sheol (Jonah 2:3; possibly Exod. 15:5, recalled in Neh. 9:11). To these Tromp adds Micah 7:19, but this improbably implies sins being cast into the underworld. He also adds Psalm 68:22, but only by following Dahood's speculative and unnecessary redivision of the Hebrew text.[131]

Mud. Several classical sources portray the underworld as a place of mud

[125] (i) KTU 1.2.iii:4; 1.3.v:7; 1.4.iv:22; 1.5.vi:1[a]; 1.6.i:34; 1.17.vi:46; 1.100.i:3; (ii) 1.1.iii:14; 1.3.iii:25, 1.3.iv:17; 1.7.ii:19; (iii) 1.17.vi:12 (broken text); (iv) 1.19.i:45; (v) 1.23:30; (vi) 1.100.i:1. Cf. further Tsumura (1989: 132–5).

[126] So Pope (1955: 70f.), Kaiser (1959: 54f.).

[127] E.g. Kapelrud (1980: 82), Mullen (1980: 163), Wallace (1985: 98 n. 88).

[128] Dahood (1970: 87): KTU 1.3.iii:25.

[129] De Moor (1969: 182; ARTU: 15 n. 81, 251 n. 178), Tsumura (1989: 151). However, this is neither necessary nor obvious in the texts de Moor cites (KTU 1.19.i:45; 1.100.i:3), and he conjectures 'Upper Flood' in the fragmentary KTU 1.92.i:5.

[130] Possibly also Ezek. 27:34. The stem *ʿmq* occurs with *šᵉʾôl*, as 'depths (of) Sheol' in: Prov. 9:18; Is. 7:11.

[131] Tromp (1969: 56, 57f.), following Dahood (1968: 131, 145f.).

or slime, and by Philo's time some thought that *Mouth* (or Mot) meant 'mud', 'watery putrefaction'.[132] Hebrew terms for 'pit' are sometimes synonyms of Sheol (see Ch. 3.c), and wet pits were inevitably miry, so one might expect mire to be an underworld description. This does occur, at least by association, but only infrequently.

Two psalms may imply that the underworld is miry. In Psalm 40:2 the psalmist rejoices in deliverance 'from the desolate pit, out of the miry bog' (*ṭîṭ hayyāwēn*). In Psalm 69 the author sinks in deep 'mire' (*yāwōn*, v. 2, in parallel with 'waters', 'deep waters' and 'flood'), and pleads for rescue from 'the mire' (*ṭîṭ*, v. 14, in parallel with 'enemies, deep waters', 'flood [of waters]', 'the deep' and 'the Pit'). Dahood and Tromp see all these as poetic terms related to the underworld,[133] though others see the terms more as figurative or illustrative.[134]

The stem *hmr* is also linked to a miry underworld. In biblical Hebrew it occurs only in Psalm 140:10: 'let them be flung into pits (*mah^a^mōrôṯ*), no more to rise!' However, in the Ugaritic Baal cycle, a term with identical consonants occurs first in parallel to Mot's throat, then in description of Mot's city:

> Indeed you must come down into the throat (*npš*) of divine Mot,
> into the miry depths (*mhmrt*) of the hero beloved of El . . .[135]
>
> then indeed they set (their) faces,
> towards divine Mot
> within his city 'Miry' (*hmry*),
> where a pit is the throne on which (he) sits,
> filth the land of his heritage.[136]

It is widely accepted that the Hebrew and Ugaritic terms are cognate, and generally mean 'pit'.[137] But whether there is necessarily an underworld connotation is less clear.

For many scholars, the stem *hmr* means 'pour down', as also in Arabic.[138] Thus Hebrew *mah^a^mōrôṯ* are 'places where the rain is poured down';[139]

[132] Aristophanes, Plato, Cicero, Seneca; cf. Gaster (1944: 35; 1961: 204), Pope (1973: 75).
[133] Dahood (1966: 245; 1968: 60), Tromp (1969: 57, 68); also for Ps. 42: Kraus (1988: 425).
[134] E.g. Kapelrud (TDOT 5: 322). *yāwēn* occurs only here; *ṭîṭ* occurs elsewhere (11 times), but always literally.
[135] KTU 1.5.i:6–8 (CML: 68). Many translate *mhmrt* as 'gullet': Gordon (1955: 259; 1965: 391), Widengren (1954: 99), Driver (1956: 159 n. 16), Gaster (1961: 202), Aistleitner (1963: 91), Pope (1978: 28), de Moor (ARTU: 70).
[136] KTU 1.5.ii:13–16 (CML: 70). Similarly 1.4.viii:10–14 (CML: 66), with slight variation.
[137] E.g. Virolleaud (1934: 309), cf. Cassuto (1962: 81), Pope (1964: 277), Oldenburg (1969: 36 n. 7).
[138] E.g. KB, HAL, Widengren (1954: 98), Gray (1957: 47), Tromp (1969: 54).
[139] Widengren; cf. HAL, Dahood (1970: 305), Allen (1983: 265).

Ugaritic *mhmr* is either Mot's gullet, where food is poured down, or a place of moistness;[140] and *hmry* means 'miry' by extension from watery pits.[141] Since *hmry* describes Mot's city, *mah^a^mōrôṯ* in Psalm 140:10 indicates the underworld.[142]

However, others disagree. Held rejects the link with Arabic, noting that in later Hebrew *mah^a^mōrôṯ* means 'pit/grave' without reference to water, and that Psalm 140:10 lacks further reference to both water and the underworld.[143] Rather, the parallel line reads 'let burning coals fall on them',[144] so the whole verse refers to punishment in this life. Similarly, several scholars take Ugaritic *mhmrt* as 'pit, grave' without reference to water.[145] The posited development of *hmry* from 'pour down' to 'watery pits' to 'mire' remains hypothetical, and the argument from context is equally uncertain. If instead the root *hmr* means 'be deep', then the Ugaritic phrase means 'within his city Deep', and Psalm 140 wants the wicked to be cast into the depths rather than into the mire.

A few scholars find the stem *hmr* in other biblical texts. In Job 17:2 Dahood, Tromp and Pope re-read 'their provocation' (*hamm^e^rôṯām*) as 'miry depths'.[146] But this lacks textual support, and is less likely in the context of mockery.[147] In Psalm 46:2 Dahood re-reads 'the shaking (*hāmîr*) of the earth' as 'the jaws of the nether world', but even Tromp rejects this.[148] So underworld reference in these texts is also unlikely.

iv. Summary

Water obviously has various associations with the underworld. Though a source of life and blessing, it is also a source of death and destruction. It is a force of chaos opposed to Yahweh, and is found under the earth, though its geographical relationship to the underworld is never clearly defined. Various terms for water, depths and mire are images of and metaphors for the under-

140 Gullet: Widengren; moistness: Pope (*Job*, ¹1965: 73; but discussion omitted in later edition, ²1973: 75).

141 Driver (1956: 159 n. 16, 'watery abyss'), Pope (Pope–Röllig 1965: 301).

142 Tromp (1969: 54), Dahood (1970: 305), van Selms (1975: 482).

143 Held (1973: 188), following Ibn Ezra and Qimhi. Cf. Sirach 12:16, 'An enemy . . . plans to throw you into a pit'.

144 Most scholars accept the emendation of BHS; but not Allen (1983: 265, positing an Aramaism), Dahood (1970: 300, 305), van Selms (1975: 482).

145 E.g. Cassuto (1962: 81), Ginsberg (ANET: 138b), Held (1973: 188), Loretz (1979: 450). Ginsberg translates the parallel *npš* as 'tomb', but this is a later meaning (cf. Pope 1978: 28).

146 Dahood (1966: 279), Tromp (1969: 55), Pope (1973: 127), also reading 'mockers' as 'hills (at the underworld's entrance)'.

147 Cf. Habel (1985: 266), Clines (1989: 372f.).

148 Dahood (1959: 167f.; 1966: 277f.); against Tromp (1969: 55f.) Craigie (1983: 342), Loretz (1979: 451).

world, but hardly underworld names. Water, like earth, is associated with the underworld, but is not confused with it.

So, if these two common concepts are not (or hardly ever) names for the underworld, despite their physical association with it, then it is unlikely that other, less common Hebrew terms are references to the underworld which have been accidentally misunderstood or deliberately altered. The underworld truly was a place of little interest to the Hebrew writers. They praised and feared Yahweh in this life and this world alone, and had little interest in the world below.

Part C

The Dead

Chapter 6
Naming the Dead

If the Old Testament has little interest in the underworld in general, does it have any more concern for its inhabitants? If underworld terms are very seldom used to describe the location of Sheol, or conditions there, or the existence of its inhabitants, are there other terms or expressions which reveal more interest in the dead?

The stem 'die, dead, death' (*m-w-t*) occurs 1,000 times, as already noted, and the participle 'dead person' (*mēṯ*) nearly 100 times.[1] However, these terms refer predominantly to the end of this life rather than to existence in the next. And even when they do refer to the afterlife, as in 'The dead do not praise Yahweh' (Ps. 115:17), the stem itself tells us nothing about the underworld. It simply indicates the non-living.

In fact, there are only two significant terms, 'shades' and 'gods' (which between them only occur some ten times), for the underworld's inhabitants – paltry reference indeed, and in themselves hardly worth a whole chapter! Nonetheless, there are intriguing issues associated with both terms which have generated much scholarly discussion. For 'shades' these issues concern primarily the other, very different meanings of the term in Hebrew and in cognate languages, and the way these meanings might relate to each other. For 'gods' they concern the possibility that the Old Testament has several other references to underworld citizens as 'gods', which have been obscured or misunderstood in the course of the text's transmission.

[1] Wigram (1890) lists 94 participles, Gerleman (THAT 1: 894) mentions '72 nominalised participles', ES lists 39 participles of *m-w-t* (nos. 197–235) and 54 occurrences of the noun *mēṯ*. On *m-w-t*, see briefly Ch. 3.a.i.

a. 'Shades'

The Hebrew term *r^e^pā'îm* (pronounced *r^e^-fah-eem*) sometimes means the inhabitants of Sheol. But it also means ancient Canaanites, a valley near Jerusalem, and possibly Philistine ancestors. Interestingly, these meanings were obviously quite distinct for the Hebrew writers, and are not confused in the biblical texts. The stem *rp'm* occurs in similar contexts in other Semitic languages: Ugaritic, Phoenician and Neo-Punic. So the term is well-attested in languages spoken in and around ancient Israel, but with a strange variety of meanings. These meanings will be considered separately below.

i. Dead Rephaim

When the Hebrew term *r^e^pā'îm* indicates underworld inhabitants, it is often rendered as 'shades' in English versions. Whatever its exact meaning, this translation evokes well the shadowy, insubstantial existence which the texts describe. As 'shades', the term *r^e^pā'îm* occurs only eight times, and only in four poetic books (Job, Psalms, Proverbs, Isaiah). So the first and perhaps most important aspect of this word is its rarity. This again underlines the fact that the underworld and its inhabitants are not a major Old Testament concern.

Usually the underworld context is explicit, since *r^e^pā'îm* occurs in the same context as Sheol, the dead and death. Once this context is implicit, in an allusion to the two ways of life or death.[2] The relevant texts are all poetic, and generally dated by scholars as exilic or post-exilic. The Hebrew term *r^e^pā'îm* usually occurs without the definite article, which suggests that it was generally considered a proper noun.[3]

The dead Rephaim are lifeless and flaccid. They tremble before Yahweh (Job 26:5), but cannot praise him (Ps. 88:10; cf. 6:5, etc.). They must be roused to greet a newcomer, and then they note that he has become weak like them (Is. 14:9f.).[4] Here they are clearly deceased kings, but several proverbs state that any foolish person may join them, which suggests that the term applies to all those in Sheol. The Rephaim form an assembly at rest (Prov. 21:16). No text describes them engaging in any activity. One apocalyptic passage envisages their resurrection in reference to Yahweh's people, but precludes it for Israel's enemies (Is. 26:14, 19).

The biblical Rephaim, unlike the Ugaritic *rpum* with whom they are often compared, are never linked with a founder or patron, nor individually

[2] Explicit: Job 26:5; Ps. 88:10; Prov. 2:18; 9:18; Is. 14:9; 26:14, 19. Implicit: Prov. 21:16.
[3] The exception is *hār^e^pā'îm* (Job 26:5, alongside *š^e^'ôl* and *'^a^ḇaddôn* which have no article).
[4] Similarly in Ezek. 32:21, the 'mighty chiefs' welcome newcomers, saying 'They have come down, they lie still . . .'

named. Nor do they have any reported contact with the living: they are never consulted in necromancy, invoked as patrons themselves or invited to feasts. They simply exist in Sheol. It is certainly possible that some Israelites may have held beliefs similar to the Ugaritans – after all, the prophets frequently denounce religious syncretism. However, the Old Testament texts do not reflect any of these Ugaritic concepts.

Some contexts may be thought to imply that the Rephaim are morally reprobate. They are joined by friends of the 'loose woman' or 'adulteress' and by the wilfully ignorant (Prov. 2:18f.;[5] 9:18; 21:16), while the wise pursue paths of life. An anguished psalmist fears joining them (Ps. 88:10). They were formerly oppressive rulers, like the king welcomed by them or the enemy destroyed by Yahweh (Is. 14:9; 26:14).[6] However, scholars usually see no moral assessment in the term. Since the term 'dead' in the same contexts indicates both wicked and righteous (Is. 26:14 and 19 respectively), so too does 'Rephaim'. The fate of the foolish is premature death (cf. Prov. 2:21f.), and joining the Rephaim is simply its consequence. Thus it is the context of *r*^{e}*pā'îm* which indicates moral assessment, not the term itself.

A few scholars suggest that another reference to the Rephaim has now been obscured. King Asa consulted doctors over his foot disease, and is condemned for not seeking Yahweh (2 Chr. 16:12). Some scholars suggest that the Chronicler originally censured him for turning to 'the dead' (*r*^{e}*pā'îm*), and that pious scribes later altered this to 'healers' (*rōp*^{e}*'îm*).[7] However, there is no textual support for this proposal, or reference elsewhere to necromancy as consulting the Rephaim, while there is evidence of post-exilic mistrust of medicine.[8] So the emendation is unlikely.

In the past, many scholars derived the noun *r*^{e}*pā'îm* from the verb *rāpāh*, 'to be weak', despite the different third consonant (*he* . . . instead of *aleph*). Thus the dead were seen as 'weak ones'. But now, given the Ugaritic evidence (see below), most scholars derive *r*^{e}*pā'îm* from *rāpā'*, 'to heal'. Thus the dead were thought to be healers or providers of fertility and life, a view possibly reflected in the occasional LXX translation of *r*^{e}*pā'îm* as 'healers'.[9] This

[5] The link to a Canaanite goddess cult by Boström (1935: 120–23) and others is now largely rejected, e.g. Whybray (1965: 90), McKane (1970: 287), Camp (1985: 25–8), Lang (1986: 168f. n. 21), Murphy (1988: 602).

[6] The LXX translates *r*^{e}*pā'îm* in Is. 26:19 (but only here) as 'ungodly' (*asebes*).

[7] So Rudolph (BHS), de Ward (1977: 6), Smith (1990: 130; ABD 5: 675), Loretz (1994). Ignored by: Myers (1965: 95), Williamson (1982: 277), Dillard (1986: 126). In ancient times, healing may have involved necromancy.

[8] 1 Enoch 8:3f.; 69:8–12 attributes medicine to fallen angels, while Sirach 38:1–15 takes time to defend it.

[9] *iatroi*: Ps. 88:10; Is. 14:9. However, the translators' understanding of *r*^{e}*pā'îm* was uncertain, since they rendered it 'giants' in the other underworld contexts (except Is. 26:19), as also in many of the ethnic contexts.

derivation is quite plausible semantically. However, it is worth noting that no biblical text attributes a healing function to the dead in general or to the Rephaim in particular. Nor indeed is such a function explicit at Ugarit. Whatever the term's etymology, the Rephaim were understood in Israel as 'weak', as shown when they greet the newly arrived king: 'You too have become as weak as we' (cf. Is. 14:10).

ii. Ethnic Rephaim

Exactly the same Hebrew term *rᵉpāʾîm* is used of ancient inhabitants of northern Transjordan (i.e. east of the river Jordan). Chedorlaomer subdued the Rephaim of Ashteroth-Karnaim, along with the Zuzim, Emim and others (Gen. 14:5), and they were one of ten peoples whose land was promised to Abraham's descendants (Gen. 15:20). Later the Israelites described the tall Emim, Zamzummim and Anakim as Rephaim (Deut. 2:11, 20). The Rephaim apparently used to inhabit the whole region of the Argob, but king Og was the last of them (Deut. 3:11,13; Josh. 12:4; 13:12).

Joshua told the cramped tribes of Ephraim and Manasseh to take the forest land of the Perizzites and the Rephaim, despite the iron chariots of the Canaanites in Bethshean and the Jezreel valley (Josh. 17:15–18).[10] Some scholars locate this expansion in Transjordan, since all the other biblical references to the Rephaim place them east of the river, and there was later a 'forest of Ephraim' in Transjordan (2 Sam. 18:6).[11] However, others locate it in Cisjordan (i.e. west of the Jordan), since: the Perizzites are located west of the river;[12] the context refers to opposition from Bethshean and the Jezreel valley, but not to crossing the Jordan; and there are other Cisjordan Rephaim references in the 'Valley of the Rephaim' and possibly the Philistine champions (see below).[13] The immediate context makes this more likely.

Dolmens (large artificial stone structures) have been found throughout Transjordan. For many scholars, the tradition of giant Rephaim is legendary and stems from later Israelites seeing these dolmens.[14] But this is unlikely. (a) While the dolmens are impressive, their construction was

[10] Following Noth (1953: 107), many see vv. 4–15 and 16–18 as parallel accounts. But not Schmitt (1970: 98–9), Woudstra (1981: 268), Butler (1983: 188).

[11] So Noth (1953: 107), Soggin (1972: 183), Caquot (DBS 10: 344).

[12] Gen. 13:7; 34:30, by implication near Bethel and Shechem; Judg. 1:44, in the Judean hills.

[13] So Hertzberg (1959: 104), Woudstra (1981: 268), Butler (1983: 187), Gray (1986: 144).

[14] E.g. Broome (1940: 488), L'Heureux (1979: 222), Boling–Wright (1982: 325), Weinfeld (1991a: 162). For Broome (writing during war, when field study was impossible), Israelites thought dolmens were giants' altars.

hardly extraordinary or superhuman.[15] (b) There are no associated archaeological features suggestive of giants, e.g. unusually large graves or skeletal remains.[16] (c) The dolmens are now dated not to the late Neolithic or early Calcholithic Ages, but to the Bronze Age,[17] i.e. to the relatively recent rather than the mythic past. (d) The biblical text contains several antiquarian notes, including the large iron bed of Og, the last of the Rephaim (Deut. 3:11).[18] But it nowhere links Rephaim to dolmens. Many scholars dismiss Og's iron bed as the confused recollection of a large dolmen or a basalt sarcophagus.[19] However, Millard replies pertinently that the Hebrew words for 'bed' and 'iron' never mean 'sarcophagus' and 'stone', and argues that Og's iron bed (like the Canaanites' iron chariots) accurately reflects the memorable impact of iron on Late Bronze Age society.[20]

Some scholars also see the giant tradition as epic aggrandizement to enhance the Israelite conquest. However, Pentateuchal tradition attributes great height specifically to the Rephaim and the Anakim (Num. 13:33), not indiscriminately to all indigenous groups.[21] Further, the Egyptian letter of Papyrus Anastasi I (late thirteenth century) gives extra-biblical evidence of tall Canaanites: 'Bedouin . . . four or five cubits [from] their noses to the heel'.[22] Similarly, at a later period in Israel's history, giants are noted among the Philistines, but not among Israel's other enemies. These factors suggest rather that the biblical tradition reflects an authentic situation.

Bartlett (1970) argues at length and influentially that most biblical references to Rephaim, including those in Genesis 14 – 15, are Deuteronomistic and secondary: 'The Rephaim and Anakim belong quite clearly to the early southern, Judahite, tradition' (269). The Judahites heard of Og from contact with Transjordan during David's reign, and put him in the same category as the Rephaim of local tradition.[23] However, this view has several difficulties.

15 Cf. Swauger (1966: 108). Cf. also similar large stone structures world-wide (e.g. Stonehenge).

16 Cf. Bahat (1972, north Galilee), Epstein (1972, 1973a, 1973b, Golan), Waterhouse–Ibach (1975, Heshbon), Yassine (1985, Damiyeh). They suggest dolmens were constructed by northern nomadic groups.

17 EB I (Yassine); late EBA or early MBA (Bahat, Epstein, Waterhouse–Ibach).

18 For Rabin (1967: 75*), Og simply means 'man', and was the name adopted by the Rephaim. This may be the root meaning of his name, but the text clearly specifies an individual.

19 Dolmen: Noth (1960: 160 n.1), de Vaux (1978: 567), Braulik (1986: 36). Sarcophagus: Bartlett (1970: 270), Phillips (1973: 27), Thompson (1974: 98), Craigie (1976: 120), Mayes (1979: 144), Weinfeld (1991: 184, tentatively), Christensen (1991: 55); NEB, REB.

20 Millard (1988; 1990). De Moor (1976: 337f.) suggests that this valuable bed was in Rabbah in the Deuteronomist's day, and that the Israelites misinterpreted its inscription.

21 Amos 2:9 generalizes this to the Amorites, 'whose height was like the height of cedars'.

22 ANET (477). This line follows a list of cities concluding with Megiddo, and may locate tall people in that area.

23 Similarly Caquot (DBS 10: 345).

(i) Rephaim were located in northern as well as southern Cisjordan, i.e. not just in Judahite territory. (ii) The Judahite tradition is itself limited, consisting only of the Valley of the Rephaim and one late reference to the Philistine champions (see below). (iii) Deuteronomy applies the name Rephaim not indiscriminately but to specific Transjordanian groups, suggesting knowledgeable comment. (iv) Genesis 14 is seen by others as non-Deuteronomistic.[24] (vi) While Genesis 15 is usually seen as Deuteronomistic, the supporting arguments (e.g. Abram as prophet, covenant terminology) risk circularity. It contains the longest list of Canaan's inhabitants, but whether this indicates its antiquity or its lateness is disputed.[25] Thus there are significant difficulties with Bartlett's thesis that these are late and unhistorical references.

iii. Philistine Rephaim?

The 'Valley of the Rephaim' was somewhere near Jerusalem, on the borders of Judah and Benjamin (Josh. 15:8; 18:16). Here the Philistines camped (2 Sam. 23:13 // 1 Chr. 11:15) and were defeated by David (2 Sam. 5:18, 22 // 1 Chr. 14:9). Its exact location is uncertain,[26] but it was obviously fertile (cf. Is. 17:5). Wildberger (1978: 648) conjectures that the name arose because the remains of giants were found there, but there is no archaeological evidence for this. Alternatively, it may have been linked to the Philistine champions. Whatever its origin, the name was clearly well known, since the book of Isaiah sees no potential confusion with the underworld Rephaim mentioned in chapters 14 and 26.

Goliath and other giant Philistines were associated with the Rephaim in later tradition. In 2 Samuel they are described as descendants of *hārāp̄āh* (21:16, 18, 20, 22), but in the parallel passage in 1 Chronicles this is spelt twice as *hārāp̄āʾ* (20:6, 8) and once as *hārᵉp̄āʾîm* (20:4).[27] The men's great size and the nearby Valley of the Rephaim also support the Chronicler's interpretation of these Philistines as Rephaim.

However, it is unclear how early this link was made. First, in the older Samuel account the final letter of the name is *he*, not *aleph* (though these letters were occasionally interchanged in Hebrew). Secondly, the ancestral

[24] Composite: Emerton (1971), Westermann (1985: 216f.); archaic features: Wenham (1987: 319). Emerton counters Astour's arguments that it is Deuteronomistic.
[25] Antiquity: Lohfink (1967: 65–72), Wenham (1987: 333f.); lateness: Westermann (1985: 230).
[26] For possibilities cf. Hauer (1970: 573 n. 10), Caquot (DBS 10: 345).
[27] These terms are translated as 'the giants' in NRSV; 'the Rephaites' and 'Rapha' in NIV.

name was probably not *rāp̄āh* but *hārāp̄āh*, since the initial *hā-* does not contract when it follows a preposition, as it would if it meant 'the'.[28] So either these giant warriors were another branch of the Rephaim, with the texts preserving an alternative spelling and an unusual grammatical feature; or, perhaps more likely, they were originally a separate group later included by the Chronicler under the better-known term for indigenous giant peoples.[29]

Talmon (1983) argues that these warriors were not Philistines but rather native Canaanite mercenaries, as follows: the men are associated with Gath, Goliath is not initially introduced (in 1 Sam. 17) as a Philistine, and no other biblical tradition presents Philistines as unusually tall. Instead it was the later biblical writers who assimilated diverse traditions.[30] However, his argument is speculative and unsupported. The brief accounts (2 Sam. 21; 1 Chr. 20) clearly identify Israel's opponents as Philistine both indirectly and directly, since Gath was a Philistine town (2 Sam. 21:15, 18, 19f., 22) and Goliath is repeatedly labelled by himself and others as a Philistine (1 Sam. 17:8, 10f., etc.). Further, the texts do not imply that all Philistines were tall, only these exceptional warriors. It is quite possible that the Philistines recruited or forced local Canaanites to fight for them. But the biblical text simply presents these particular warriors as Philistines, whatever their exact ethnic origin.

Other aspects of these texts have attracted scholarly attention. The term translated 'descendant', *yālîḏ*, clearly comes from the verb *y-l-d*, 'be born'. However, Willesen (1958a) notes that the intensive passive form of this verb can also mean 'be adopted' (notably in Ruth 4:17 and Is. 9:6), and argues that in 2 Samuel 21 it indicates an adopted warrior guild.[31] In support of this he argues that *yālîḏ* implies military expertise (also Gen. 14:14; Num. 13:28), and notes that adoption procedures are recorded elsewhere (Exod. 21:5f. // Deut. 15:16f.).[32] But this is unlikely. The intensive form of *y-l-d* usually indicates normal birth.[33] In the supporting texts cited, military expertise is specified by other terms ('trained men', Gen. 14:14; 'great size', Num. 13:32), not by *yālîḏ*. And there is nothing to link the adoption ceremony of slaves with *yālîḏ*.

[28] Cf. *lᵉhārāp̄āh*, 2 Sam. 21:20, 22; *lᵉhārāp̄ā'*, 1 Chr. 20:6, 8. GK (§ 35n) and Caquot (DBS 10: 346) see an exceptional definite article here but the other exceptions cited occur only in late biblical literature (apart from the textually difficult 1 Sam. 13:21): Chronicles (3x), Ezra (2x), Ecclesiastes, Daniel, Nehemiah (once each).

[29] Similarly, 'Canaanite' came to be used for indigenous inhabitants generally.

[30] Followed by Schmidt (1994: 271).

[31] He suggests the Chronicler misunderstood this, and replaced Pual with Niphal.

[32] Followed partially by L'Heureux (1976, 1979, translating 'votaries of Rapha') and Rosenberg (1981: 205).

[33] Elsewhere the Pual occurs 26 times, but means adoption only 3 times (Gen. 50:23; Ruth 4:17; Is. 9:6). The Piel always indicates midwives/midwifery. L'Heureux (1976: 84 n. 7) and Caquot (DBS 10: 346) also reject this point.

Willesen (1958b) argues further that *hārāpāh* has nothing to do with Rephaim, but comes from the Greek *harpe* or *harpa* meaning 'scimitar'. (The Philistines were originally from the Greek Aegean.) He suggests that the scimitar was the patron deity's symbol, and the *yᵉlîdê hārāpāh* were an elite warrior group known as 'the adopted ones of the scimitar'. Willesen is probably correct in seeing the initial *hā-* as part of the name.[34] However, the Greek term would be represented accurately in Hebrew as *harpēh* or *harpāh*, not *hārāpāh*, so his main argument remains tenuous. Goliath and his fellow warriors were more likely descendants of the otherwise unknown *hārāpāh*.

iv. Ugaritic rpum

The term *rpum* occurs in several texts from Ugarit, apparently with similar meanings to the Hebrew term.[35] It has been extensively studied by scholars,[36] and a consensus interpretation has now emerged. Nevertheless, other views are still defended and many uncertainties remain. This is because *rpum* occurs relatively rarely, parallel terms are diversely interpreted, and the potentially most fruitful texts (KTU 1.20–22) are badly damaged, incomplete and lacking in context. Further, while some relationship between Ugaritic *rpum* and Hebrew *rᵉpāʾîm* is generally recognized, 'there has been little consensus about what that relationship is' (Pitard 1992: 33). The relevant texts are as follows.

(a) The lengthy *Baal cycle* (KTU 1.1–6) concludes with a brief hymn to the sun-god, ruling the underworld on her nocturnal passage through it:

Shapash, the shades (*rpum*) are under you;
Shapash, the ghosts (*ilnym*) are under you;
The gods (*ilm*) come to you;
behold! the dead (*mtm*) come to you. (1.6.vi.45–48; translation CML: 81)

Many scholars see the parallelism here as A-B-B-A, i.e. *rpum* parallel 'the dead', and 'the ghosts' parallel 'the gods'.[37] This clearly identifies the *rpum* as 'shades', as translated above.

[34] The suggested pun with the verb 'taunt' (*ḥ-r-p*, 2 Sam. 21:21, cf. 1 Sam. 17:10) is less likely.
[35] *rpum* has the same consonants as Hebrew *rᵉpāʾîm*, since *u* represents one form of the Ugaritic equivalent of Hebrew *aleph* (ʾ). Some scholars vocalize *rpum* as *rapiuma*, though others remain sceptical about vocalizing Ugaritic.
[36] Well summarized by Caquot (DBS 10), Spronk (1986), Dietrich–Loretz (1989).
[37] *ilnym*: 'ghosts' (CML: 81; ARTU: 98), 'deities' (TO 1: 270); *ilm*: 'gods/deities' (CML, ARTU, TO).

(b) The *Keret epic* (KTU 1.14–16) opens with king Keret, a seven-times widower, mourning the absence of an heir. In a dream El tells him how to obtain a new wife, and promises him many children. Keret duly follows the instructions and brings his new wife home. Keret holds a wedding banquet, at which El blesses him with the words:

> Be greatly exalted, Keret, among the *rpum* of the *arṣ*, in the assembly of the gathering of the *dtn*. (lit. *rpi.arṣ . . . qbṣ.dtn*; 1.15.iii.2–4, 13–15)

The immediate context does not specify whether these are gatherings on earth or in the underworld, since *arṣ* can mean both and no one else is mentioned (unlike KTU 1.161, see below).

(c) The *Aqhat epic* (KTU 1.17–19), which also features an heirless king, repeatedly describes its righteous hero Dan'el as 'man of *rpu*' (about twenty times). But there is no explanation of this phrase in terms of this life or the underworld.

(d) The so-called *Rephaim texts* (KTU 1.20–22) are particularly important and yet tantalizingly fragmentary. They seem to mention the *rpum* several times, often in parallel with *ilm/ilnym*, though some of the suggested occurrences involve educated guesswork with damaged texts. These *rpum* apparently perform sacrifice, drink, and move around.[38] They seem to go on a three-day journey by chariot or on horseback to the threshing-floors and orchards, where a seven-day banquet is celebrated.

There are also single references to *rpu.bʿl* and to Dan'el.[39] Some see *rpu.bʿl* as two terms in apposition and equate *rpu* with Baal. Others translate 'the *rpum* of Baal', since the parallel expressions *mhr.bʿl* and *mhr.ʿnt* mean 'the soldier(s) of Baal' and 'the soldier(s) of Anat'.[40]

Pitard (1992: 72f.) explains why 'key parts of these texts are translated in vastly different, mutually exclusive ways'. (i) Of 95 lines, only 22 are complete and 49 are less than half preserved. (ii) Some *rpum* passages on each tablet 'remain intensely obscure'. (iii) It is unclear how the three fragments relate to each other and to the Aqhat epic.[41] (Both mention Dan'el, but there are different scribal hands, and Dan'el, like Gilgamesh, could belong to several legends.) Thus, 'even the most general context of the fragments remains obscure'.

[38] *tdbḥn*, sacrifice, 1.20.i:1(?); *tštyn*, drink, 1.20.i:7(?), 1.22.i:21f., 23f.; *(l)tdd*, move around (?), repeatedly. *(l)tdd* is translated as: 'stand' (L'Heureux), 'flutter' (de Moor, Spronk), 'move' (Dijkstra).

[39] *rpu.bʿl*, 1.22.i:8; *dnil* (*mt rpu*?), 1.20.ii:7, possibly also 1.22.i:12(?), 1.21:8(?).

[40] *rpu* = Baal: de Moor (ARTU: 272), Spronk (1986: 171); 'the *rpum* of Baal': Pope (1977), Horwitz (1979), Pardee (1988: 85).

[41] For possible reconstructions, see de Moor (ARTU: 267), Dijkstra (1988: 36).

(e) KTU 1.82, a series of charms and incantations against illness and demons, includes the phrase 'the voice of the *rpum*' (line 32), but the text is too fragmentary to be clear.[42]

(f) KTU 1.108 is a short text which apparently describes a divine banquet presided over by 'Rpu, king of Eternity' (*rpu.mlk.'lm*), and ends with a blessing on the *rpum* of the *arṣ* (i.e. *rpi.arṣ*):

> To the *rpum* of the *arṣ* may your strength, your protection, your power, your paternal authority, your divine splendour be accorded in the midst of Ugarit . . . (following Ford 1992: 77)

The identity of 'Rpu, king of Eternity' is uncertain,[43] but there seems an obvious link between him and the *rpi.arṣ*. It is not obvious here that the *rpi.arṣ* are the dead, unless 'Eternity' (*'lm*) is a name for the underworld.

The text has another possible link with the underworld: 'El sits on/in *'ṯtrt*, El judges on/in *hdr'y*'. These words are very similar to the town names of Ashtaroth and Edrei, which are associated in the biblical text with Og and the Rephaim (Gen. 14:5; Deut. 1:4; Josh. 12:4; etc.). Many scholars now see a link between the two traditions,[44] though they assess it variously.

(g) KTU 1.161 is a funerary ritual performed during the reign of Ugarit's last king Ammurapi III, either at the death of his father Niqmaddu III or in commemoration of it. The rites last for seven days, as apparently in the Rephaim texts. It opens with an apparent summons of deceased kings and other 'patrons' (?) to a celebratory meal.

The two kings in lines 11–12, usually pronounced as Ammishtamru and Niqmaddu, were historical kings of Ugarit's last dynasty, and clearly dead by the time this liturgy was written. The names in lines 4–7 are usually thought to be legendary former kings, ancestors from the distant past now given the epithet *rpu*. (This was perhaps omitted for the second two because their double names leave no room for it in the short poetic metre.) So here the famous royal dead are summoned to take part in a ritual.

Many scholars interpret this text as a funerary cult or ceremony invoking the dead, similar to the monthly Mesopotamian *kispum* rituals.[45] A few propose instead that it is an actual burial liturgy, i.e. funerary in a primary

[42] De Moor–Spronk (1984) suggest: 'poison by the voice of the Healer[s]!'; Caquot (TO 2: 68f.): 'pity to the voice of the Manes'. The *rpum* are not invoked in other Ugaritic incantations.

[43] Many identify *rpu* as a god: El, Baal, Milik, Reshep, or other; details in Pardee (1988: 84f.), Rouillard (DDD: 694). Rouillard identifies *rpu* as the founder of Ugaritic dynasty.

[44] Following Margulis (1970a: 293f.; 1970b: 344; etc.).

[45] Listed in Bordreuil–Pardee (1989: 163 n. 87). On the *kispum*, cf. Bayliss (1973: 118) and Tsukimoto (1985).

Title	1	Record of the celebration of the 'patrons':[46]
Refrain	2	You are summoned, *rpum* of the *arṣ*
	3	You are convoked, assembly of *ddn*
Legendary Ancestors	4	Summoned is *ulkn* the *rpu*
	5	Summoned is *trmn* the *rpu*
	6	Summoned is *sdn-w-rdn*
	7	Summoned is *ṯr-ʿllmn*
	8	They have summoned the ancient *rpum*
Refrain	9	You are summoned, *rpum* of the *arṣ*
	10	You are convoked, assembly of *ddn*
Historical ancestors	11	Summoned is king *ʿmṯtmr*
	12	Summoned also is king *nqmd*...
	24	... below the ancient *rpum*... (my translation)

rather than secondary sense.[47] The invoking of the *rpum* is not explained, but accords with the general ancient Near Eastern belief that the dead exerted influence over the living.

Lines 18–26 proceed to mention Shapash, a throne, a descent to the *arṣ* (widely interpreted as the underworld), and the same addressees as lines 6–8 and 11–12. It seems that the sun-god again has an underworld role. But scholars disagree as to what or who actually descends to the underworld. Many think it is the throne itself,[48] but others think it is Shapash, a human being, or the *rpum*.[49]

(h) Various administrative texts also contain the element *rpu* in personal names, e.g.: *ʿbdrpu* (= servant of *rpu*), *abrpu* (= father [of] *rpu*), *bn.rpiyn* (= son of the *rpum*), *rpan*.[50] These may be theophoric, i.e. the name refers to a god. But *rpan* at least could suggest a non-divine *rpu*, perhaps a famous ancestor.

Throughout recent decades, some scholars have interpreted the *rpum*

[46] Term unclear: 'patrons': Pitard (1978: 68), Levine–de Tarragon (1984: 651), del Olmo Lete (1986: 92); 'shades': de Moor (1980b: 432; ARTU: 166), Caquot (TO 2: 105), Bordreuil–Pardee (1989: 154–56), Rouillard (DDD: 694); 'deity': Dalley (1986), Tsumura (1993); 'statues': Xella (1979: 838), Dietrich–Loretz (1983: 18), Watson (1983: 18).

[47] Taylor (1988: 154), Bordreuil–Pardee (1989: 163), Dietrich–Loretz (1991: 105).

[48] Cf. Is. 14:9; 47:1; Ezek. 26:16; Healey (1978: 87), Spronk (1986: 192), de Moor (ARTU: 167), Taylor (1988: 156f.), Tropper (1989: 149), Dietrich–Loretz (1991: 105f.)

[49] Shapash: Bordreuil–Pardee (1982: 123), Lewis (1989: 9–46). Niqmaddu: Caquot (TO 2: 109), Bordreuil–Pardee (1989: 155); Ammurapi: L'Heureux (1979: 191); officiant(s): Levine–de Tarragon (1984: 650). *rpum*: Dietrich–Loretz (1983: 21, seeing parallelism with *arṣ*).

[50] *ʿbdrpu*, KTU 4.269:15 (cf. Akkadian equivalent *abdu-rapi*); *abrpu*, RA. 37 S. 27, 10, so Jirku (1965: 82); *bn.rpiyn*, KTU 4.232:8: *rpan*, KTU 4.116:4, 4.204:6, 4.269:13, 4.281:19.

and the *rpi.ars* in at least some of these texts as human groups. In the early period of Ugaritic study Gray suggested that the *rpum* in the Rephaim texts were the king and his immediate associates engaged in a fertility cult. L'Heureux sees the *rpi.arṣ* in these texts as an aristocratic warrior guild, because of their horses and chariots.[51] But Canaanite deities also rode horses, as did the later Spartan *dioscuri* attending *theoxenia*.[52] Heltzer identifies the *rpi.arṣ* in the Keret wedding blessing with the Amorite Rabbean tribe. But evidence for the Rabbeans is scanty and limited to Mari, both geographically and temporally distant from Ugarit.[53] For Margalit, the 'Raphaites of the land' were a warrior aristocracy from Bashan who founded a dynasty at Ugarit, *rpu* was the divinized eponymous ancestor, and the term translated 'man of *rpu*' is simply a place-name. But others question much of the detail of his argument.[54]

More recently, Schmidt (1994: 84–8) argues in general that ancient Near Eastern interest in the dead only emerged with the Assyrians in the eighth century, and in particular that the *rpum* in the earlier Ugaritic texts were living, not dead. For the latter, he reasons as follows. (i) In the Baal cycle, the hymn to the sun-god Shaphash celebrates her power over the living: *rpum* parallels *mtm*, and this means 'men', not 'dead'.[55] More importantly, the sun-god does not go through the underworld, since in Akkadian texts Shamash passes at night through heaven's interior, not the underworld. (ii) In the Rephaim texts the *rpum* whom Baal enlists in his fight against Mot are warriors, not the dead. (iii) The ritual of KTU 1.161 alternately summons the living for benefaction (lines 2–5, 9–10) and lists the dead for commemoration (lines 6–8, 11–12).

However, these arguments are inconclusive. (i) Ugaritic *mt* could mean 'men' in the hymn at the end of the Baal cycle as elsewhere, but this is unlikely in the immediate context. Also the mythology of Akkadian literature is inconsistent, and several texts do give the sun a nocturnal underworld role.[56] (ii) The *rpum* in the Rephaim texts are usually interpreted as the dead, who would be eminently suitable allies against Mot. (iii) Schmidt's distinction

[51] Gray (1949: 138; 1952: 40). L'Heureux (1976; 1979), in distinction to the *rpum* gods.

[52] The *dioscuri* were Jove's sons, and *theoxenia* were games in honour of a god, notably at Pellene (west of Corinth) for Apollo. Several second-century BCE coins depict *dioscuri* on or with horses (Boston Museum: 01.1993; 32.766; 88.383). For mounted deities, cf. Ben-Arieh (1983), Giveon (1986); Nilsson (1940: 69 and fig. 32), Pope (1983: 69).

[53] Heltzer (1978: 16), re KTU 1.15. On Rabbeans, cf. Healey (1989: 42).

[54] Margulis (1970a) = Margalit (1989), critiqued by Dietrich–Loretz (1989), Pardee (1991), Sperling (1991).

[55] Similarly Talmon (1983: 243).

[56] Schmidt cites Heimpel (1986) in support, but ignores the Akkadian inconsistencies which Heimpel notes.

between living and dead in KTU 1.161 is most unlikely: lines 4–7 are identical in grammatical form so their addressees are probably identical in situation. Despite Schmidt, there are strong arguments for an interest in the dead long before the eighth century, and the Ugaritic texts are evidence of this.[57]

By contrast, most scholars argue that *rpum* in the Ugaritic texts are deified ancestors, and that *rpu* is their patron and/or founder.[58] They are subordinate to Shapash, along with *ilnym*, *ilm* and *mtm* (Baal cycle). They are summoned to witness Keret's marriage (Keret epic) and to bless the city of Ugarit (1.161). They are also invited to a banquet, and arrive on horseback (Rephaim texts). The term originally applied to kings and perhaps heroes, but through time it was democratized and applied to all the dead.[59]

For many scholars, the *rpum* provided health, fertility and fecundity.[60] Their name may itself derive from the Ugaritic verb *rpa*, 'heal/restore to strength', which is now attested.[61] De Moor goes further, translating *rpum* as 'Saviours', and describes them as 'the good spirits who were able to neutralise the tricks of their evil counterparts and to heal the victims'.[62] But this goes too far, since no extant Ugaritic text attributes healing to *rpu* or the *rpum*, not even the incantation and ritual texts where healers would naturally be invoked. One possible exorcism appeals to Baal, Hrn, Gllm and El, but not to the *rpum*.[63] Similarly, the incantations against snake-bite are addressed to the major deities, but not to the *rpum*.[64] De Moor's description of the 'Saviours' quoted above relates to KTU 1.82, but this text is fragmentary and the role of the 'voice of the *rpum*' is unclear.

For several scholars, Baal (also called *rpu*) could revivify the dead.[65] There may be evidence for this in the Aqhat epic, when the goddess Anat offers Aqhat immortality in exchange for his bow which she covets (KTU 1.17.vi.26–33):

57 Cf. reviews by Johnston (1996) and Smith (1996).

58 Bordreuil (1990: 15), Caquot (DBS 10: 356), Dietrich–Loretz (1989: 129), Dijkstra (1988), Healey (1978: 88; 1986: 28), Heider (1985: 125), Levine–de Tarragon (1984: 658), de Moor (ARTU: 98; 1990a: 242; 1990b: 243), Pardee (1988: 87), Pope (1977b: 167; 1981: 174), Spronk (1986: 195).

59 A similar democratization is also often argued for the Hebrew Rephaim.

60 Virolleaud, Dussaud, Gray, Xella, Astour (cf. Cooper RSP 3: 464), de Moor–Spronk (1984, 'Healers').

61 KTU 1.114:28 (despite textual uncertainties). Loewenstamm (1969: 77), Pope (1972: 173), Dietrich–Loretz–Sanmartín (1975: 110, 113), Margalit (1979–80: 72, 113), de Moor (1984: 356; ARTU: 136), Caquot (TO 2: 77).

62 De Moor (ARTU: 180 n. 35). Cf. Good (1991: 159f.).

63 RIH 78/20. It exorcizes *dbbm*, translated 'flying demons' by de Moor (1980b: 429f.; ARTU: 183). But Caquot (TO 2: 54) renders *dbbm* as 'words'.

64 KTU 1.100, 1.107. De Moor (1988) acknowledges this.

65 Dahood (1972: 137f.), Marcus (1972: 78–80; 1973: 591 n. 6), Caquot–Sznycer (TO 1: 432), Spronk (1986: 151, 155), de Moor (ARTU: 238 n. 101, ignoring his earlier objection).

Ask life, O hero Aqhat,
ask life and I will give it you,
immortality (*blmt*) and I will bestow it on you;
I will cause you to count the years with Baal,
with the sons of El you shall count the months.
As if he were Baal when he comes alive (*yḥwy*),
when men feast the living one (*ḥwy*), . . .
So will even I give life (*aḥwy*) to the hero Aqhat. (Translation: CML: 109)

But Aqhat accuses Anat of lying when she offers him immortality (i.e. 'counting years with the gods'), and asserts that he would have to die like all mortals.

Interest focuses on the comparison Anat draws with Baal. In the above translation Baal returns to life,[66] and the text may allude to an annual (New Year?) celebration of this.[67] But some now suggest that the text should be translated 'as when Baal *brings* to life', since the same intensive form of the verb is used for Baal's activity (*yḥwy*) as for Anat's offer (*aḥwy*). However, this remains uncertain, for several reasons: an exact comparison would normally be introduced differently;[68] the intensive form of the verb normally has a direct object (as with Anat's offer to Aqhat); and in any case Baal's supposed activity of revivification differed from Anat's offer of immortality. Even if evidence emerges that Baal was believed to revivify the dead annually, this is very different from his granting eternal life to them, and then transferring this ability to the *rpum.*[69]

The same scholars see Baal's revivifying activity in the Rephaim texts, reading one couplet as: 'Then he will heal you, the Shepherd [Baal] will revive you'. But these texts are notoriously difficult, as noted above, and others dismiss this reading as hypothetical and tendentious.[70]

v. Other Semitic rp'm

(a) An Aramaic inscription from the eighth century BCE expresses the wish that the soul of King Panamuwa I of Samal (north of Syria) will eat and

[66] Also de Moor (1971: 217; 1979: 643), Dijkstra–de Moor (1975: 187). Similarly, de Moor (1979: 643; ARTU: 113) translates *ḥwt* in KTU 1.10.ii:20 as passive.
[67] Gaster (1961: 44f.) and Spronk (1986: 155 n. 5) note the widespread belief of the annual (brief) return of the dead. Tropper (1989: 141) sees the annual festival slightly differently, as an occasion for necromancy.
[68] *km . . . kmt,* not *k . . . ap,* so van der Toorn (1991: 46 n. 10).
[69] De Moor (ARTU: 98 n. 478) sees the Shapash hymn (KTU 1.6.vi: 44–52) as a prayer to guide the *rpum* back to earth. But this is not evident, cf. Marcus (1973: 590).
[70] KTU 1.21.ii:5–6. De Moor (1976: 329; ARTU: 266), Spronk (1986: 156; cf. 169); dismissed by van der Toorn (1991: 47), Pitard (1992: 71).

drink with the god Hadad.[71] While this does not have the term *rp'm*, its reference to post-mortem feasting echoes the Ugaritic 'Rephaim texts' and KTU 1.108, as usually interpreted.

(b) The term *rp'm* occurs in two Phoenician inscriptions on the sarcophagi of two Sidonian kings, Tabnit and his son Eshmunazar, of the sixth and fifth centuries BCE. These pronounce curses on tomb robbers in almost identical terms:

> May you have no seed among the living under the sun nor resting place with the *rp'm*.
>
> May they have no resting place with the *rp'm*, nor be buried in a grave, nor have son or seed in their place.[72]

These curses assume that the *rp'm* include ordinary citizens, even potential tomb-robbers.

(c) *rp'm* also occurs in a later inscription in Neo-Punic (a derivative of Phoenician), in a bilingual first-century CE inscription of El Amruni. The inscription reads 'to the divine *rp'm*'.[73] The corresponding Latin is simply the abbreviation '*DMS*', standing for '*Dis Manibus Sacrum*' or 'to the sacred spirits'. This indicates a general correspondence between the Semitic *rp'm* and the Latin *manes*.

All these other Semitic texts clearly identify the *rp'm* as dead, confirming the usage in Hebrew and adding weight to this meaning in Ugaritic.[74]

vi. Summary

The Semitic stem *rp'm* occurs in Hebrew, Ugaritic and Phoenician in reference to the dead, and in Hebrew and perhaps Ugaritic in reference to ancient people. Nearly all scholars now regard the terms and uses as related, despite occasional arguments to the contrary.[75] The Ugaritic *rpum* were initially understood by comparison with the Hebrew *r^epā'îm*. But as study of the texts has advanced, many now think the Ugaritic term sheds light on the Hebrew one.[76] Nevertheless, it is important to note that the few relevant

[71] Cf. KAI 214:21f.
[72] So KAI, texts 13:7f., 14:8f.
[73] *'l[nm] 'r'p'm*, KAI 117:1; cf. Caquot (DBS 10: 348). De Moor (1976: 331) equates Punic *'lnm* with Ugaritic *ilnym*.
[74] Cf. Horn (1982: 55), Talmon (1983: 235).
[75] E.g. initially Virolleaud (1940: 78), more recently van Selms (1970: 367f.).
[76] Cf. Healey (1986: 31): 'we now have a far clearer understanding of the Ugaritic *rp'um* than we have of the Hebrew equivalent'.

texts in each language portray Ugaritic *rpum* and biblical Rephaim quite differently.

The majority scholarly view is that the Semitic *rp'm* were dead ancestors who were seen as semi-divine patrons or protectors; biblical writers in the first millennium were either ignorant of or uncomfortable with this tradition, and historicized the Rephaim as an ancient people similar to the mythic ancient heroes (Gen. 6:4; Ezek. 32:27). Loretz (1994) suggests that the Rephaim were initially historicized to eliminate deities rival to Yahweh; but later, when monotheism was firmly established, the term was accepted for the dead and the possibility of their resurrection was even discussed. However, this posits a radical disjunction between pre-exilic and post-exilic Israelite thought. The minority view is that the Ugaritic and biblical *rp'm* were an ancient people or warrior group, whose name came to be used of the heroic dead, and was later 'democratized' to include all the dead.[77] A few scholars also posit traces of the Ugaritic deity *rpu* in other Hebrew texts, e.g. in the personal name Rephael (1 Chr. 26:7),[78] or the obscure 'Kaiwan' in Amos 5:26, translated as *Raipha* in the LXX (and quoted as *Rompha* in Acts 7:43).[79] But this is speculative.

While the exact relationship between the different languages and uses remains debated, two features in the biblical texts are particularly noteworthy. (a) *r^epā'îm* occurs with distinctly different meanings, without apparent confusion or need for explanation. To the Hebrew writers and editors, this obviously posed no problem. (b) The dead Rephaim are portrayed significantly differently from the Ugaritic *rpum*: they are lifeless and need rousing, they tremble before God, they are not limited to heroes or kings, they are never individually named, they do not travel, participate at banquets or play any role *vis-à-vis* the living as protectors or patrons. Here as so often, the Israelite writers appear to have taken a general Semitic concept and adapted it significantly to fit their particular Yahwistic perspective.

b. 'Gods'

The other term used for the inhabitants of Sheol occurs far more frequently than *r^epā'îm*, but its underworld use is extremely rare. It is *'^elōhîm*, one of

[77] See above. Also Loewenstamm (cf. Cooper RSP 3: 463), Boling–Wright (1982: 325), Boling (1988: 43).

[78] Jirku (1965: 62). Against: Blau–Greenfield (1970: 12 n. 4), Pope (RSP 3: 466).

[79] Pope (1977b: 170), Smith (ABD 5: 676). Against: Rudolph (1971: 207), Wolff (1979: 260), Stuart (1987: 352), Hubbard (1989b: 185). Stieglitz (1990: 86) links Amos 5:26 instead to the Eblaite deity *Kabkab*.

the most common words in the Old Testament.[80] It usually means 'God', i.e. Yahweh, the sole God of the Israelites. In this use, though grammatically plural, it functions as a singular noun (with singular adjectives, verbs, etc.).[81] Sometimes it means other gods, in which case it functions as a plural noun. Occasionally it means household gods, as with Laban's and Jacob's gods,[82] and possibly the god(s) who witness human decisions and oaths.[83] Very occasionally, *'ᵉlōhîm* is used as a superlative,[84] or in figures of speech.[85]

'ᵉlōhîm may also occur occasionally of supernatural beings other than the major deities, as arguably in several psalms:

> . . . you have made them a little lower than *'ᵉlōhîm* . . . (lit., Ps. 8:5)
>
> God has taken his place in the divine council;
> in the midst of *'ᵉlōhîm* he holds judgment . . .
> I say, 'You are, children of the Most High, all of you;
> nevertheless, you shall die like mortals . . .' (lit., Ps. 82:1, 6)

Cognate languages have a similar, flexible use of their terms for 'god'. In Akkadian, *ilu* 'includes virtually all superhuman beings and powers', i.e. city deities, personal deities and demons, and also occurs in personal names of deceased children and ancestors.[86] In Ugaritic, the hymn to Shapash lists *ilm* in parallel with *rpum, ilnym* and *mtm*, all terms for the dead (see above), and in a king list *il* directly precedes the name of each deceased monarch.[87] In a Phoenician inscription from Pyrgi *'lm* may indicate the dead,[88] while in Hittite ritual the dead king is divinized. In Egypt, the dead were commonly

80 It occurs 2,570 times, cf. Ringgren (TDOT 1: 267–84), Fretheim (NIDOTTE 1: 405f.).

81 Traditionally described as a plural of majesty or of intensity, this is better seen as an abstract plural meaning 'deity' (cf. the plurals 'virginity', 'youth', 'old age', etc.) when applied to a single god, cf. GK (§124g). Burnett (2001) cites similar usage of *ilanu* in the Amarna letters, and traces its origin to Phoenicia.

82 Laban's gods (Gen. 31:30, 32, called teraphim in vv. 19, 34, 35), perhaps Jacob's family's gods (Gen. 35:2, 4).

83 Exod. 21:6; 22:8f. Interpreted as: 'judges', so traditionally, also Vannoy (1974), NIV; 'sanctuary God/gods': Cassuto (1967: 267), Childs (1974: 475), Cole (1973: 166), Durham (1987: 321); 'household gods': Noth (1962: 178), Paul (1970: 50), Clements (1972: 133); cf. the Nuzi *ilâni*, see Gordon (1935), Draffkorn (1957).

84 Cf. Thomas (1953), Williams (1967: 19). Note the common English exclamation, 'O God!'

85 Exod. 4:16; 7:1; Ps. 45:6, in metaphor and hyperbole, so not relevant here, despite Niehr (1991: 303).

86 Lambert (RLA 3: 543). Similarly Stamm (1939: 283), Heidel (1949: 153), CAD (7/I–J: 91), Bayliss (1973: 117 n. 19), Bottéro (1980: 28). Against: von Soden (1962: 485: 'An *ilu* "Totengeist" kann ich . . . nicht glauben'), Schmidt (1995: 121f.).

87 KTU 1.6.vi:44–8 and 1.113. Cf. Kitchen (1977), Spronk (1986: 147 n. 4), etc.

88 *bym qbr 'lm*, cf. Knoppers (1992: 114f.). Others see *'lm* as Astarte, Melqart, Adonis or Aphrodite.

called 'gods'.[89] Given this widespread use of terms for 'god' to cover the dead and other supernatural beings, it would be more helpful to translate the Hebrew word *'ᵉlōhîm* with the equally flexible English word 'spirit'.[90] However, since the translation 'god' is so well known, it is better to redefine 'god' to include other super-human beings.

In the Old Testament there are three clear instances and several suggested texts where *'ᵉlōhîm* means 'spirits of the dead'.

i. Clear Old Testament references

Numbers 25:2; Psalm 106:28. At Shittim *en route* to Canaan, Israelite men indulged in sexual immorality with Moabite women, who enticed them to join in 'the sacrifices of their gods (*'ᵉlōhîm*)'. So 'they ate and bowed down to their gods' and 'yoked themselves to the Baal of Peor' (Num. 25.2). No further detail is given in Numbers, and many interpreters have assumed that 'their gods' refers to Chemosh, Astarte and perhaps local Baals like the Baal of Peor.[91]

However, the incident is later interpreted as a cult of the dead. In its review of the wilderness period, Psalm 106:28 comments (lit.): 'they yoked themselves to Baal of Peor, and they ate sacrifices of the dead (*mēṯîm*)'. This clearly refers to the same tradition, since the verb 'yoked' (*z-m-d*, Niphal) only occurs in these two texts,[92] and this Baal Peor apostasy later became infamous (also mentioned in Num. 31:16; Deut. 4:3; Josh. 22:17; Hos. 9:10). A few scholars have interpreted 'the dead' as 'lifeless gods',[93] but this is unlikely since 'the dead' is never used elsewhere of gods. More probably the texts refer to a cult of the ancestors, who are described in Psalm 106 as 'dead' and in Numbers 25 as '*'ᵉlōhîm*'.[94] It is worth noting that in both Numbers

[89] Cf. Hornung (1983: 156).

[90] Modern discussion of polytheism in Israel is skewed by modern terminology, which distinguishes 'gods' as a distinct group among supernatural beings. The evidence presented here shows that *'ᵉlōhîm* and cognates could cover the whole range of supernatural beings.

[91] So Wenham (1981: 184f.). Many see two traditions combined, e.g. Snaith (1967: 302), Noth (1968a: 196), Budd (1984: 276). Some see Baal of Peor as an underworld deity, e.g. Xella, Spronk (1986: 231).

[92] Other shared terms: 'ate', 'sacrifices', 'plague was stopped' (v. 30). Conversely, the psalmist portrays Yahweh's anger and Phinehas's reaction and reward differently (vv. 29–31). Some see dependence: Noth (1968a: 197), Smith (1990: 127); others merely allusion: Budd (1984: 281), Kraus (1989: 320).

[93] E.g. Wächter (1967: 187), Rogerson–McKay (1977c: 47), Allen (1983: 49), Kraus (1989: 320f.).

[94] So on Psalm 106: Weiser (1962: 677), Kidner (1975: 380f.). Both views are possible: Anderson (1972b: 744). Later Jewish tradition interpreted the incident as a funerary *marzēaḥ* (see Ch. 8.b.i).

and Psalms the cult is foreign to Israel, the apostasy is one of many in the wilderness, and no further observance of it is recorded.

1 Samuel 28:13. At a crucial moment in her seance, the medium of Endor declares: 'I see *'ᵉlōhîm* rising up from the earth' (1 Sam. 28:13). There are two important issues here: what does *'elōhîm* mean? and is it singular or plural?

Just before this, Saul has asked the woman to 'bring up Samuel'. And just after this, she sees Samuel, and then Saul converses with him. Therefore it is natural to suppose that *'ᵉlōhîm* here refers to the spirit of the dead Samuel.[95] So for the medium, at least, *'ᵉlōhîm* refers to the spirit of a dead human being, i.e. the dead could be divinized.

Because only one spirit is invoked in the passage, most scholars and translations take *'ᵉlōhîm* here as singular (NRSV: 'a divine being'; NIV 'a spirit'). However, the following verb 'rising up' is plural, so the phrase would more naturally mean 'I see spirit*s* rising . . .' (as in NRSV and NIV footnotes). The traditional Rabbinic and early Christian view saw Samuel accompanied by Moses and perhaps other righteous men,[96] but this is most unlikely in the immediate context. Many modern scholars simply ignore the plural verb,[97] while a few give unconvincing explanations.[98]

Hutter (1983) points in a more fruitful direction. He suggests that the seance's location and ritual reflect Hittite influence, and that the phrase 'gods rising' reflects an ancient Hittite incantation formula for conjuring up the underworld gods, which was used by the pre-Israelite population at En Dor.[99] Necromancy originally involved consulting such gods, which is why it was denounced in Israel. But later the underworld's inhabitants were not seen as divine, so Samuel could be included among the *'ᵉlōhîm* without being identified as a god.[100] The old expression was used simply to affirm the success of necromancy.

[95] Alternative explanations are unlikely. Baldwin (1988: 159) interprets *'ᵉlōhîm* as 'judge'. Dietrich (1987) suggests reference to an underworld god was later deleted, but this doesn't explain either *'ᵉlōhîm* or the plural verb. Tropper suggests an original reference to Saul's 'ancestors', including Samuel as a former leader of Israel, and 'DtrP' corrected this to Samuel by adding v. 14 with singular terms. But certain formal similarities hardly make v. 14 a correction to v. 13, and the proposed redaction was inept in leaving unacceptable plurals in v. 13.

[96] Cf. Smelik (1979: 168).

[97] E.g. Hertzberg (1964), Mauchline (1971), McCarter (1980), Dietrich (1987), Lewis (1989: 115f.), Smith (1990a: 127). Noted without explanation: Gordon (1986: 195f.), Müller (1969: 90 n. 91).

[98] E.g. Smith (1899: 241: agreement is grammatical, not logical); Beuken (1978: 10: shows spirit is from God); Klein (1983: 269: Samuel's appearance was awe-inspiring).

[99] Cf. a ritual text from Hattusha, where the gods are led by a seer (like Samuel). Further arguments: En Dor is near the late Hittite princedoms of Syria; its name reflects the Hurrian *enna durenna*, equivalent to the Hittite primeval gods (so Ebach–Rüterswörden 1977: 59f. n. 14); *'ôḇ* derives from Hittite. On En Dor, see Ch. 7.b.

[100] Schmidt (1995: 126) similarly distinguishes Samuel from the chthonic deities.

The links between En Dor and the Hittites are uncertain, and the proposal that *'ᵉlōhîm* could refer to both forbidden gods and acceptable non-gods seems contradictory. But Hutter's suggestion of a conjuration formula is helpful. Our knowledge of ancient necromantic formulae is still very sparse, even if that of necromantic practice is gradually increasing. So the phrase 'I saw spirits rising' could well be such a formula, and the unusual word order would support this (lit. 'spirits I saw rising'). In time the phrase perhaps came to mean simply 'I see the spirits moving', without reference to their number, and implied 'the consultation is successful'. When the medium uttered this phrase Saul was unaware that she had already seen Samuel, so here it probably means 'I have contacted Samuel'. This then prompted Saul's question 'What is his appearance?' Thus it is better to take 'spirits rising' as a conjuring formula rather than an exact portrayal of events. The phrase refers to many spirits, but in the event only Samuel appeared.

Isaiah 8:19–22. Isaiah 6 – 9 is well known for Isaiah's vision, his confrontation with Ahaz, his apparent withdrawal from public ministry, and the sign-children Emmanuel, Maher-Shalal-Hash-Baz and Wonderful Counsellor (etc.). However, the passage between the prophet's withdrawal (8:16–18) and the new dawn (9:1–7) is more obscure. The general Judean populace apparently rejects Yahweh and his prophet, so will stumble around in distress and hunger, and eventually be thrust into thick darkness (8:19–22).

The people obviously want to continue their popular necromantic practices. But there are several ways of interpreting these verses in general and the term *'ᵉlōhîm* in particular.[101] This is illustrated by the different placing of quotation marks (and other features) in two English versions which are normally very similar:

> RSV: [19]And when they say to you, 'Consult the mediums and the wizards who chirp and mutter,' should not a people consult their God? Should they consult the dead on behalf of the living? [20]To the teaching and the testimony! Surely for this word which they speak there is no dawn.
>
> NRSV: [19]Now if people say to you, 'Consult the ghosts and the familiar spirits that chirp and mutter; should not a people consult their gods, the dead on behalf of the living, [20]for teaching and for instruction?' Surely those who speak like this will have no dawn!

In the traditional view reflected in the RSV, the people's protest is limited to v. 19a (ending with the word 'mutter'). The prophet then replies rhetorically,

[101] See commentaries, also Carroll (1980).

should they not instead consult their God (*'elōhîm*), i.e. Yahweh? should they really be consulting the dead?[102] This maintains the common meaning of *'elōhîm* as 'God'. But it is grammatically difficult. In Hebrew, the question marker is a syllable (*ha*), which is joined to the first word of a question, here the word 'not'. This view takes the question marker as applying to both phrases (consulting God, consulting the dead), but the word 'not' as only applying to the first, which would be most unusual.

Because of this, most scholars now take the view reflected in the NRSV, that the people's protest continues through v. 19, and includes their desire to consult ghosts and spirits, their *'elōhîm* and the dead. In this case, the parallel terms describe the same source, so the *'elōhîm* are the spirits of the dead.[103] This is grammatically more plausible. Verse 19 then indicates that the spirits of the dead were called *'elōhîm*.[104]

The following verses portray people roaming through the land, distressed and hungry, and cursing their king and their *'elōhîm* (v. 21). Here *'elōhîm* presumably has the same meaning as in v. 19, i.e. spirits of the dead. Because of the unusual construction, some scholars translate 'curse *by* their king and their *'elōhîm*'.[105] Others propose 'curse by Molech and their ghosts'.[106] The first of these is possible, the second unlikely, but both allow or accept that *'elōhîm* means 'spirits of the dead'.

ii. Suggested Old Testament references

2 Samuel 12:16. Nathan's rebuke of David following his adultery with Bathsheba includes the divine judgment that the son born from this union would die. The child then became ill, and David pleaded with 'God' (2 Sam. 12:16). Most scholars assume that *'elōhîm* here refers to Yahweh, as the context implies. However, Niehr (1991) argues that *'elōhîm* means the dead

[102] RSV. Also NIV, Eichrodt (1960: 103), Young (1965: 319), Jeppesen (1982: 152), Oswalt (1986: 237). For JB, v. 19b is prophetic but ironic: 'by all means a people must consult its gods' (cf. Standard Edition note).

[103] NEB, REB; Müller (1975: 71; though his parallel with Lachish Ostracon 3:8–12 is inexact), Whitley (1978: 29f.), Clements (1980: 102), Carroll (1980: 129: original meaning, later superseded), Kaiser (1983: 122f.), Heider (1985: 329), Lewis (1989: 131), Wildberger (1991: 373).

[104] A few punctuate v. 19 as NRSV, but interpret *'elōhîm* differently: Fohrer (1966: 135: popular deities); Watts (1985: 125: protester mockingly identifies Isaiah with spiritualists). Schwarz (1974) transposes phrases.

[105] Cf. 1 Sam. 17:43 (also *q-l-l*, Piel, + *b*), so RSV mg., NRSV mg., Whitley (1978: 32f.). Others propose 'rebel/curse against': Ginsberg (1958: 64*), Driver (1967: 49), NEB, REB, JPS.

[106] Heider (1985: 331), Lewis (1989: 132). This discounts the pronoun suffix 'their' on *melek* (king). For Heider, the necromancers will utter their curses in Sheol, but this view is even more difficult.

ancestors, as follows. (i) When someone seeks divine help the verb 'seek/plead (*b-q-š*)' is usually followed by Yahweh, not *'ᵉlōhîm*. (ii) Elsewhere in this passage the divine name is not *'ᵉlōhîm* but Yahweh, so *'ᵉlōhîm* has a different meaning here. (iii) Further evidence of consulting the 'divinized ancestors' (*ilm rbm*) on behalf of a sick child comes from a Ugaritic ritual text.[107]

But Niehr's interpretation is unlikely. (i) The verb 'seek' is followed by many different forms of divine name,[108] so *'ᵉlōhîm* is not problematic here. (ii) Yahweh and *'ᵉlōhîm* frequently occur together in the same narrative in Samuel. (iii) The immediate context assumes that David entreated Yahweh, not the ancestors (v. 22). (iv) The Ugaritic text is not immediately relevant. Thus it is much more likely that David pleaded with God than with the ancestors.

2 Samuel 14:16. In plotting to bring Absalom back to Jerusalem after his vengeance killing of Amnon, Joab sends a 'wise woman' to David with a sad story of family tragedy. Apparently one of her two sons has killed the other, and the avenger now wants to kill the murderer and so cut her and her surviving son off from 'the heritage of God (*'ᵉlōhîm*)' (2 Sam. 14:16). Most interpreters have understood this last phrase as meaning 'inheritance among the people of God', which is threatened when there is no heir. But Lewis (1991) now argues that it means 'estate of the dead ancestors', and that the woman fears no one will be left to venerate the ancestors.

However, there are several major difficulties with this. (i) The woman repeatedly uses *'ᵉlōhîm* to mean 'God': on its own (v. 14), with Yahweh (vv. 11, 17) and in the expressions 'people of God' and 'angel of God' (vv. 13, 17, 20). So this, the only other occurrence of *'ᵉlōhîm* in this section, probably also means 'God'.[109] (ii) While the phrase 'heritage of *'ᵉlōhîm*' occurs only here, the similar phrase 'heritage of Yahweh' also occurs in the books of Samuel, for the nation (1 Sam. 26:19; 2 Sam. 21:3) and for one of its cities (2 Sam. 20:19).[110] Thus 'heritage of *'ᵉlōhîm*' could easily designate the family property as a 'God-given inheritance',[111] without *'ᵉlōhîm* meaning 'ancestors'.

[107] Niehr (1991: 302–4), followed by Loretz (1994: 197 n. 90), citing KTU 1.124.

[108] E.g. Yahweh of hosts: Zech. 8:21; Yahweh *'ᵉlōhîm*: Jer. 50:4; Hos. 3:5; Yahweh *'ᵉlōhîm* of Israel: 2 Chr. 11:16; 15:4; their *'ᵉlōhîm*: Ezra 8:23; face (of Yahweh): 2 Sam. 21:1; Pss. 24:6; 27:8; Hos. 5:15; name: Ps. 83:16.

[109] This is unaffected by placing vv. 15–17 directly after v. 7; so Anderson (1989), McCarter (1984), Lewis (1991). Others maintain the traditional order: Hoftijzer (1970: 438; despite Lewis: 597 n. 1), Gordon (1986: 268).

[110] Lucian, Theodotion and Targum also read 'heritage of Yahweh' in 2 Sam. 14:16. Lewis (1991: 603) notes only Lucian, and sees it as a Greek scribal error.

[111] Anderson (1989: 183). Cf. also 'heritage of the fathers': Num. 27:7, 36:3f., 8; 1 Kgs. 21:3. Despite van der Toorn (1996a: 207), reference to the family estate need not imply a cult of the dead.

Isaiah 19:3. In this oracle of judgment, the Egyptians will become alarmed and consult 'the idols and the spirits of the dead and the ghosts and the familiar spirits'. The LXX reads 'idols' (*'ᵉlîlîm*) as 'gods' (*'ᵉlōhîm*), and some scholars follow this, arguing that *'ᵉlōhîm* here is another synonym for the spirits of the dead.[112] However, it is equally possible that the LXX translators made a mistake (or worked from a different original), and most other scholars accept the Hebrew text as 'idols'.[113] Whether the Egyptians called the dead 'gods' or not, this text does not refer to it.

iii. Summary

Although *'ᵉlōhîm* is one of the most frequent biblical terms, it occurs only very rarely for the spirits of the dead. Further, this usage reflects not mainstream Yahwism but a Moabite cult, an outlawed spiritualist, and a practice condemned by Isaiah. On the evidence available, it is impossible to say how widely *'ᵉlōhîm* was used of ancestors consulted in necromancy. But clearly the Yahwistic biblical authors do not themselves use it for the ancestors. For them, the underworld's inhabitants are occasionally 'shades', very rarely 'gods', and mostly ignored. The dead were of minimal importance.

[112] LXX: *tous theous*; Whitley (1978: 30), Lewis (1989: 133 = 1991: 603). Lewis notes that elsewhere the LXX translates *'ᵉlîlîm* otherwise, including v. 1 here. On *'ᵉlîlîm* cf. Preuss (TDOT 1: 285f.), Wildberger (1991: 109).

[113] Clements (1980: 167f.), Kaiser (1983: 97), Watts (1985: 248), Wildberger (1991: 698).

Chapter 7
CONSULTING THE DEAD

Necromancy, or the consultation of the dead, was widespread among ancient Near Eastern peoples, with the possible exceptions of the Egyptians and the Hittites (for whom clear evidence is lacking). In Mesopotamia it was sufficiently well known for Finkel to conclude his thorough survey: 'it seems possible on present evidence that necromancy is to be listed among those elements of civilised behaviour for which we arc ultimately indebted to Mesopotamia'.[1] Was necromancy equally widespread among the Israelites?

a. Necromancy in Israel

Necromancy is referred to several times in the Old Testament: in several Pentateuchal prohibitions; in the infamous story of Saul at Endor (the only narrative account); in the summary of Manasseh's sin and of Josiah's reform, and twice in Isaiah. The texts are as follows (NRSV):

> Lev. 19:31: 'Do not turn to *mediums* or *wizards* . . .' (also Lev. 20:6, 27);
>
> Deut. 18:10f.: 'No one shall be found among you who makes a son or daughter pass through fire, or who practises divination, or is a soothsayer, or an auger, or a sorcerer, or one who casts spells, or who

[1] Finkel (1983–4: 17, sic). However, his direct evidence is limited to: the 'Lu' professions list, *Gilgamesh* XII, an Old Assyrian letter (Kültepe), a Neo-Assyrian letter (Kuyunjik) and two late (partially duplicate) Babylonian texts.

consults *ghosts* or *spirits* [≠RSV], or who seeks oracles from the dead';

1 Sam. 28: 3, 7–9: 'Saul had expelled the *mediums* and the wizards . . . Seek out for me a woman who is a *medium* . . . There is a *medium* at Endor . . . Consult a *spirit* for me . . . Saul . . . has cut off the *mediums* and the *wizards* . . .' (summarized in 1 Chr. 10:13);

2 Kgs. 21:6: '[Manasseh] made his son pass through the fire; practised soothsaying and augury, and dealt with *mediums* and with *wizards*' (similarly 2 Chr. 33:6);

2 Kgs. 23:24: 'Moreover Josiah put away the *mediums*, wizards, teraphim, idols, and all the abominations . . .';

Is. 8:19: 'Consult the *ghosts* and the *familiar spirits* [≠RSV] that chirp and mutter . . .';

Is. 19:3: 'they will consult the idols and the spirits of the dead and the *ghosts* and the *familiar spirits*' [≠RSV];

Is. 29:4: 'your voice shall come from the ground like the voice of a *ghost*'.

The italicized words above represent the two Hebrew terms *'ôḇ*, translated 'medium' or 'ghost', and *yidd^{e}'ōnî*, translated 'wizard' or 'familiar spirit'. Of these, *'ôḇ* occurs sixteen times, sometimes on its own, while *yidd^{e}'ōnî* occurs elevent times, always in conjunction with *'ôḇ*. These terms are used with several different verbs, which clearly implies that there was no standard technical phrase for necromancy.[2] The less frequent term *yidd^{e}'ōnî* has the more obvious meaning. It clearly derives from the verb 'to know', *y-d-'*, and so means literally 'knowing one'. The more frequent term *'ôḇ* also indicates a sentient being, though its derivation and precise meaning are debated (see section d. below). Both terms occur in singular and plural forms.[3] Since the plurals *'ôḇôṯ* and *yidd^{e}'ōnîm* have endings that usually indicate feminine and masculine gender respectively, they may refer to female and male beings, whether human or spirit.

It is interesting that these two Hebrew words can mean both medium and ghost, i.e. both the human who consults the spirit and the spirit who is consulted. These two aspects of spiritism may seem quite distinct to us, but

[2] *p-n-h*: Lev. 19:31; 20:6; *š-'-l*: Deut. 18:11; 1 Chr. 10:13; *d-r-š*:1 Sam. 28:7; Is. 8:19; 19:3; 1 Chr. 10:13; and *q-s-m* (*b^{e}*): 1 Sam. 28:8. Against Westermann (1960: 23), who sees *d-r-š* as the earlier technical term and *š-'-l* as a later one.

[3] Both plural (x6): Lev. 19:31; 20:16; 1 Sam. 28:3; 2 Kgs. 23:34; Is. 8:19; 19:3. Both singular (x3): Lev. 20:27; Deut. 18:11; 2 Chr. 33:6 (≠ 2 Kgs. 21:6). Mixed (x2): 1 Sam. 28:9 (but cf. early versions); 2 Kgs 21:6. When *'ôḇ* occurs alone it is always singular: 1 Sam. 28:7 (x2), 8; 1 Chr. 19:13; Is. 29:4.

were obviously indistinct to the Israelites. Sometimes the context clarifies the reference, as in the person who is an *'ôḇ* (Lev. 20:27), or the *'ôḇ* speaking from under the ground (Is. 29:4). But sometimes *'ôḇ* can mean either, as illustrated by the fact that the RSV and NRSV occasionally disagree (see above).[4] The word can even be used in both senses in the same passage, as when Saul expels the mediums (*'ôḇôṯ*) and then orders the medium of Endor to consult a spirit (*'ôḇ*; 1 Sam. 28:3, 8). This proves that the Hebrew writers saw no need to differentiate clearly between spirit and medium.

There are a few other suggested occurrences of *'ôḇ* with this meaning. Some see the wilderness camp-site *'ōḇōṯ* (Num. 21:10–11; 33:43–44) as a place of divination.[5] This is possible, if uncertain.[6] In Job 8:8 Bildad intones: 'Inquire now of bygone generations, and consider what their ancestors have found.' Some scholars emend 'their ancestors' (*'ᵃḇôṯām*) to 'their ghosts' (*'ōḇôṯām*).[7] But *'ôḇ* nowhere else has a pronominal suffix, and the usual translation makes good sense.[8] Most now ignore or discount this proposal.[9] There is also one occurrence of *'ôḇ* in a quite distinct sense. In Job 32:19 the long-silent Eliphaz erupts: 'My heart is indeed like wine that has no vent, like new *'ôḇôṯ*, it is ready to burst'. From the context, most scholars see *'ôḇ* here as an unrelated and rare homonym meaning 'wineskin'.[10]

In fact, there are very few references to necromancy in Israel's religious literature. All the Old Testament occurrences of *'ôḇ* are given above. A few other texts which allude to necromancy in other ways will be examined below. But the overall total is small. Prohibition occurs in Deuteronomy (ch. 18) and in the Holiness Code (Lev. 19 – 20), but it is absent from other key legal sections, including the Decalogue, the Covenant Code and the 'Ritual Decalogue' (Exod. 20; 21 – 23; 34).[11] Necromancy is mentioned at the beginning and end of the monarchy, but is unrecorded in other historical

[4] Mediums: Lev. 20:27; 1 Sam. 28:3, 9; 2 Kgs. 21:6 // 2 Chr. 33:6 (*'-ś-h* as 'appoint'); 2 Kgs. 23:24 (*b-'-r* Piel as 'remove'). Spirits: 1 Sam. 28:7 (x2), 8; Is. 19:3; 29:4. Either: Deut. 18:11; Lev. 19:31; 20:6; 1 Chr. 10:13; Is. 8:19.

[5] Ebach–Rüterswörden (1977: 69), Barr (1993: 9).

[6] Tropper (1989: 309) notes other possibilities: a meaning 'ancestors'; a root *'-b-t*; and an Egyptian derivation.

[7] Fitzmyer (so Albright 1968: 124), Albright, Dahood (1969: 78f.), Ebach–Rüterswörden (1977: 69).

[8] Many delete or emend the suffix. But elsewhere 'their ancestors' precede the 'wise' (Job 15:8) and the 'aged' (Sirach 8:9), so here it means the generation before the 'bygone generation'. Cf. Dhorme (1967: 115f.), Tropper (1989: 310).

[9] E.g. Pope (1973: 66), Andersen (1976: 141 n. 3), Gordis (1978: 89), Clines (1989: 199), Tropper (1989: 310).

[10] E.g. Rowley (1976: 210), Pope (1973: 244), Andersen (1976: 247), Gordis (1978: 360), Habel (1985: 442), Hartley (1988: 432).

[11] The Covenant code prohibits sorcery (Exod. 22:18), but not specifically necromancy. Jeffers (1996: 168) speculates that this silence indicates its popularity.

narrative, whether of the wilderness wanderings, the judges period, the bulk of the monarchy, or the exile and after. It is mentioned in only one prophetic book, and only occasionally, and is absent from the whole range of psalmody and wisdom. On this evidence, necromancy was not a major problem in Israel.

There are another fifteen or so references to divination generally, covering a range of books, periods and literature, from Balaam to Zechariah.[12] Some of these may include the specific divination technique of necromancy, since Saul refers to necromancy as a form of divination ('divine for me by a spirit', 1 Sam. 28:8, lit.). But divination usually has a different emphasis. It is often linked to false prophecy and condemned for being misleading, whereas necromancy is a distinct activity which is condemned more strongly for being subversive to Yahwism. Further, in Deuteronomy 18, divination and necromancy are given separately in the list of prohibited practices.[13]

Many scholars suggest that necromancy was more widespread in Israel than the Old Testament record implies, until the great reforms first of Hezekiah in the eighth century and then particularly of Josiah in the seventh.[14] Until then, Israelite religion was much less uniform than the Old Testament implies, and included many practices which were later rejected. The present texts, completed after the reforms, retroject orthodox Yahwism back into a more heterodox period, and so do not accurately portray pre-reformation religion.

It is certainly true that pre-reformation Israelite religion included many unorthodox elements which the reforms addressed. But this does not mean that necromancy itself was widespread, still less that it was an accepted element within Yahwism. First, as already noted, the Old Testament does not contain widespread condemnation of it. Historiographers, prophets, psalmists and sages are more keenly aware of other aspects of religious apostasy, and they devote far more attention to them than to necromancy. So for most Israelite authors, necromancy did not loom large.

Second, the argument that later editors obscured evidence of it is unconvincing. If they had obscured all the evidence, then this argument could be neither proved nor disproved. But they have left some evidence of necromancy, which undermines the argument. (i) It is unlikely that necromancy

[12] *q-s-m* is a proverbial sin (1 Sam. 15:23; 2 Kgs. 17:17), associated with Balaam (Num. 22:7, etc.), Philistines (1 Sam. 6:2), false prophecy (Is. 3:2, etc.), Babylonians (Is. 44:25, etc.) and Ammonites (Ezek. 21:29).

[13] Kuemmerlin-McLean (ABD 4: 468) notes 'the Deuteronomistic tendency to list a general term first'.

[14] E.g., for Dietrich (1987: 28), soothsayers were a pillar of the community until the late eighth century.

was considered so heinous that it was mostly expunged from the records, while many other practices equally condemned by Yahwism were not.[15] (ii) The editors were inconsistent, whether intentionally or not, in leaving several references to necromancy and one detailed account of it. (iii) Certain specific proposals concerning editorial alteration are unconvincing, e.g. that original references to 'worshipping ancestors' (*'āḇôṯ*) were altered to 'consulting spirits' (*'ôḇôṯ*); see further below.

Necromancy and the ancestor cult are obviously related in their preoccupation with the dead, so inevitably some passages are discussed both here and in Chapter 8. Nevertheless, they are distinct practices, and one can occur without the other, as in modern spiritism.[16] Thus it is useful to look at them separately.

b. Necromancy at Endor

The tragic story of Saul consulting the spirit of the dead Samuel is the only Old Testament account of necromancy.[17] Chronologically, the events related in 1 Samuel 28 occur after ch. 30, but the account has been placed here to heighten the tensions of both David's predicament (ch. 27, resolved in 29 – 30) and of Saul's fate (ch. 28, resolved in 31), and to contrast the rival leaders' treatment of the Amalekites and their standing before Yahweh.

The narrative begins by recalling the death of Samuel and his burial at Ramah (v. 3a; cf. 25:1). The ensuing story contains no hint that it was odd to consult the dead prophet at a different location, undermining some scholarly assertions of a link here between burial-place and necromancy (see Ch. 2.b.iv). The introduction continues by noting Saul's previous expulsion of necromancers, the imminent battle, Saul's fear and Yahweh's silence (vv. 3b–7).[18]

Saul asks his servants to find a female medium (v. 7).[19] Some scholars argue from this that necromancers were usually female, or perhaps that Saul

[15] Hutter's (1980: 35) association of necromancy with foreign gods cannot explain editorial alteration, since many other aspects of foreign religions are repeatedly mentioned, and have not been expunged.

[16] Lewis (1989) blurs this distinction by including necromancy in his study of cults of the dead.

[17] Humphreys (1980: 81) asserts: 'Assumptions are made here about the state of the dead that are clearly not found elsewhere . . .' However, the uniqueness lies in the detailed description, not the underlying assumptions.

[18] Cogan (1995) notes several ancient parallels to Saul's desperate search for divine signs.

[19] Hebrew *'ēšeṯ ba'ălaṯ 'ôḇ*. Cogan (1995: 320 n. 6) notes that the double construct can be appositional, i.e. 'woman, mistress of an *'ôḇ*', and need not be a conflation (despite McCarter 1980: 418).

had 'expelled the male representatives of the art'.[20] But the text refers twice to Saul expelling *'ôḇôṯ* and *yidd^{e}ʿōnîm* (vv. 3, 9), which probably implies that they could be either female or male. The woman's ethnic identity is not given. She assumes that Saul's ban on necromancers applies to her, but this does not make her Israelite.[21] Endor has traditionally been located in or near the Jezreel valley,[22] and most if not all of its inhabitants were probably Canaanite (cf. Josh. 17:11f.).[23] The name 'En-Dor' has itself been linked with necromancy, as meaning either (i) 'spring of (former) generations' or (ii) 'spring of the oracular sanctuary'.[24] This is possible, but there is no other evidence that the town was renowned for necromancy. Some scholars think that Saul's servants answered immediately and therefore that Endor's medium was well known,[25] but the text does not state or even imply this.

Both Saul and the medium assume that a specific individual spirit could be consulted (vv. 8–10). Saul names the spirit he requests as Samuel (v. 11), who was clearly not his ancestor (see also Ch. 8.a.ii). The medium then 'sees Samuel', but instead of proceeding with the seance she recognizes her disguised visitor and takes fright, sensing a trap (v. 12). Some commentators find this sequence illogical, and explain it as textual corruption in one of several ways: (i) 'saw Samuel' should read 'saw Saul', as in the LXX; (ii) 'saw Samuel' should read 'heard the name of Samuel';[26] or (iii) some dialogue has dropped out. However, the sequence is not really illogical from the narrator's perspective: Samuel's appearance simply makes Saul's deceit unsustainable. Saul reassures the distraught woman, asks about the spirit, recognizes it as Samuel from her description,[27] and falls down in homage (vv. 13–14).

Samuel then takes the initiative in the dialogue,[28] criticizing Saul for

[20] Emmerson (1989: 376). Old Hittite women were common practitioners of magic (cf. Scurlock ABD 4: 465).

[21] Against Edelman (1991: 243).

[22] Probably Khirbet es-Safsafe, near modern Endûr; so Zori (1952), followed by McCarter (1980: 420), Klein (1983: 271), Gordon (1986: 194). Alternatively, Bar-Deroma (1970: 134) relocates Endor to the south at Khirbet-Duweir and the following battle near Philistine Aphek, but this is unlikely. Brown (1981: 399) equates it with coastal Dor, but Margalith (1985) replies that this is geographically and politically impossible.

[23] Tropper (1989: 216) thinks it Israelite, but his reasons (location, era of flourishing) are weak.

[24] (i) Ebach–Rüterswörden (1977: 59 n. 14); (ii) cf. Ugaritic *dr* in KTU 1.15.iii:17: Margalith (1985: 111), Lewis (1989: 113, tentatively). Other proposals include: spring of dancing (Thomas 1933: 205f.); spring of Douar (Reymond 1958: 106); spring of settlement (Tropper 1989: 216).

[25] E.g. Hertzberg (1964: 218), Ades (1990: 263).

[26] Corrupted by haplography between 'name' (*šēm*) and 'Samuel' (*š^{e}mûʾēl*) and then alteration of the verb.

[27] The robe was probably a prophet's mantle, but this need not indicate burial in it (as Bloch-Smith 1992b: 218).

[28] Only the medium sees the spirit, and only Saul speaks with it. Lang (1988: 148) suggests the medium was the intermediary in the dialogue, but this is not stated.

'disturbing' him (v. 15a). The same verb (*r-g-z*) occurs elsewhere of spirits (*rᵉpā'îm*) being disturbed when a deceased emperor joins them (Is. 14:9) or when robbers desecrate a tomb (Phoenician tomb inscriptions, see Ch. 6.a.v). Greenfield (1971: 258) argues from the Phoenician curse on robbers that Samuel put a curse on Saul, which was fulfilled when Saul was slain in battle, lay unburied, and so found no rest with the Rephaim.[29] But this goes too far: Samuel's message is not a curse, and Saul's remains were eventually buried.

Saul replies by invoking his desperate situation: the Philistines are again attacking, and 'God' has not answered him. (Saul avoids the more intimate name 'Yahweh'.) But Samuel simply repeats the judgment he had delivered when still alive: that Yahweh has abandoned Saul because of his disobedience and has replaced him by David. Samuel then addresses Saul's desire for knowledge by announcing the immediate defeat of Israel and the death of Saul and his family (vv. 15b–19).[30] This prophetic message differs from previous ones only in its precision that the disaster is imminent. Saul's terrified reaction shows he understood that all hope was gone.

In the final scene the frightened and famished Saul eats a meal and then heads off into the night (vv. 20–25). His previous lack of food is usually attributed to his general state of anxiety, though some see it as preparation for the seance or for battle.[31] Some interpret the meal as sacrificial and integral to the necromantic ritual, but here it clearly occurs after the seance has ended. Others see it is a cultic feast of the dead (see Ch. 8.a.ii), but this rewrites the story.[32] Rather, the medium and Saul's servants have to persuade him to eat a meal, and the account of its preparation suggests it was an impromptu dinner (as in Gen. 18:6f.). Simon (1988) favourably contrasts the medium's sensitive generosity with the prophet's stern message. But her motivation was probably as much fright as generosity. More perceptively, Ades (1990: 265f.) notes that the detail of Saul's hunger and nourishment gives perspective to his tragedy 'by embedding it in the simple mundane details of grief and nourishment'.

Most scholars accept 1 Samuel 28 as a substantially pre-Deuteronomistic, authentic account. Some suggest that the original story had an anonymous ghost or underworld god, and that this was changed to Samuel by a

[29] Similarly Hallo (1991:151; 1993: 190).

[30] The middle section (vv. 17–19aa) is often thought a Deuteronomistic addition because of its language, theology and the repetition from 19a to 19b. But repetition can be intentional, to create effect.

[31] Seance: Grintz (1970–71: 89), McCarter (1980: 421); battle: Gunn, Edelman (1991: 249). For Gunn (1980: 109), Saul 'signals for the last time a willingness to sit loose from the constrictions of the sacral world'.

[32] So Beuken (1978: 11).

late-eighth-century northern prophetic writer.[33] A few see the extant story as essentially Deuteronomistic.[34]

For Tropper and others, Saul's expulsion of *'ôḇ(ôṯ)* from the land is a later, Deuteronomistic comment, retrojecting the norms of later orthodoxy back to the early monarchy. However, the illegality of necromancy and its dire punishment is not simply stated. It is thoroughly integrated into the narrative and implied repeatedly, as follows. (a) Saul attempted all other known means of obtaining divine guidance before his recourse to necromancy. (b) He visits the medium secretly and tries to avoid detection by a disguise, a minimal bodyguard and a nocturnal visit. (c) Endor is located behind Philistine lines, which suggests the absence of more accessible mediums. (d) The woman's first words passionately confirm the royal prohibition and the attendant capital punishment. (e) Saul swears forcefully in order to reassure her. (f) When she realizes his identity, her reaction betrays a genuine fear of punishment, and again she requires royal reassurance. (g) Saul excuses his action of disturbing Samuel as a desperate last measure. (h) Finally, in pressing Saul to eat, the woman repeats that she has risked her life. The illegality of necromancy is thus woven into the very warp and woof of the text, and an original story in which it was legitimate would be a pale shadow of the present one.[35] Its illegality is further heightened by the fact that two texts earlier in 1 Samuel already condemn divination: it is associated with the Philistines (6:2), which heightens the irony of Saul's recourse to necromancy, and it is a proverbial sin indicating the awfulness of rebellion (15:23).

The passage reflects its narrator's belief that necromancy worked.[36] Later compilers and editors shared this belief and left the text unaltered, to the puzzlement of some scholars. For Lewis (1989: 117): 'In view of the Deuteronomistic legal material . . . it is extremely odd that the Deuteronomist has preserved a tale about necromancy rather than suppressing it. It is even more surprising that he does not attempt to discredit the efficacy of the practice.' He apparently refrained only because the incident was too well known. But this view makes several crucial assumptions: that the Deuteronomic prohibition of necromancy post-dated the Endor account; that the (seventh-century) Deuteronomist was at liberty to alter earlier traditions; and indeed that he ought to have done so. Each of these assumptions is

33 Ghost: McCarter (1980: 421–3), Ades (1990: 263); god: Dietrich (1987).

34 Caquot (cf. Tropper); Foresti (1984: 132–6), Tropper (1989: 213).

35 McCarter's comment (1980: 422) that the narrative emphasizes the sombre message more than the illicit means takes insufficient account of these details.

36 Baldwin (1988: 159) concludes the contrary from the medium's surprise (v. 12), but this argument is weak. Following early tradition, Heidel (1949: 189) sees it as 'a demonic delusion', but the text gives no hint of this.

open to question. In contrast, this narrative and the various prohibitions suggest that from its earliest period Israel saw necromancy as illegal but also effective.

At the same time, the account presents necromancy as futile: the message Samuel gives Saul simply seals his fate.[37] It also reflects belief in the continued existence of the dead in some somnolent form, though it makes no comment on their post-mortem existence.

c. Necromancy in other texts?

Isaiah 28:7–22 contains a powerful indictment of a rotten society. Priests and prophets stagger in a haze of alcohol, vomit and babble (vv. 7–13), and Jerusalem's cynical rulers (or sages) think Faustus-like that they can make a covenant with death (vv. 14–22). Van der Toorn (1988) argues that this section also contains two echoes of necromancy.[38]

First, he suggests that in vv. 9–10 it is not priests and prophets who mock Isaiah, as most scholars think, but Isaiah who mocks them and their necromantic practices. These enigmatic verses read:

> 9 'Whom will he teach knowledge,
> and to whom will he explain the message?
> Those who are weaned from milk,
> those taken from the breast?
> 10 For it is precept upon precept, precept upon precept
> [*ṣaw lāṣaw, ṣaw lāṣaw*],
> line upon line, line upon line [*qaw lāqaw, qaw lāqaw*],
> here a little, there a little [*zᵉʿêṛ šām, zᵉʿêr šām*]'.

Van der Toorn argues as follows: (i) In v. 9 the one who teaches and explains is the God whom they all claim to represent. (ii) The verb 'teach' (*y-r-h*) alludes to the priestly teaching (*tôrāh*) of v. 7. (iii) The term translated 'message' (*šᵉmûʿāh*) 'belongs to the technical vocabulary of prophetic divination' (205), and indicates 'an oracular message received in a state of semiconsciousness' (214). Here oracles are uttered in an alcoholic haze, while further on (vv. 19–20) the *šᵉmûʿāh* is uttered in sleep. Elsewhere the biblical prophets accept *šᵉmûʿāh* as a means of revelation, and such an oracle sent

[37] Miscall (1986: 172) comments laconically: 'to speak with the dead is to join the dead'.

[38] Most scholars see two sections here, addressed to different groups, e.g. Peterson (1979: 108f.). Van der Toorn argues briefly for unity, on the grounds of common terms (*qaw, šᵉmûʿāh*), common opponents and a common theme of necromancy. But the necromantic element is uncertain, the opponents are apparently different, and the common terms could be the cause of redactional juxtaposition rather than an indication of original unity.

Sennacherib home.[39] (iv) The onomatopoeic terms of v. 10 are phrases spoken in seances, where *ṣaw* and *qaw* reproduce bird-like twitterings and groans. Bird noises are associated with the dead both elsewhere in Isaiah and generally in the ancient world.[40] The aptly named Akkadian 'Birdcall Text' combines onomatopoeic sounds with religious interpretation, so Isaiah 28:10 could also combine bird sounds and message.

However, this is unconvincing. (i) For most scholars, the teacher is more obviously Isaiah than an unmentioned deity. In any case, van der Toorn later argues that many deities were consulted, not just one (v. 15, see below). (ii) Verse 7 does not mention *tôrāh*, so v. 9 can hardly allude to it. (iii) *šᵉmûʿāh* is a common noun meaning 'rumour, message', derived from *š-m-ʿ*, 'to hear', and is mostly unlikely to mean both what is heard and what is spoken. The prophetic texts cited do not support the meaning of 'spoken oracle', for instance vv. 19–20 state that sleep will give no protection from the message of judgment, not that an oracle was received and spoken in sleep. On the contrary, Yahwistic prophets who condemn all divination are hardly likely to use one of its techniques! And the *šᵉmûʿāh* which sent Sennacherib home could be a rumour (as usually translated) as easily as an oracle.[41] (iv) Verse 10 could give bird-like sounds and seance formulae, but the puzzling terms *ṣaw* and *qaw* could have other meanings,[42] and do not obviously indicate necromancy. Further, the phrases recur in what is clearly Yahweh's oracle to the prophet's opponents (v. 13, unmentioned by van der Toorn), and this would hardly contain formulae from an abhorrent practice.

Secondly, van der Toorn sees allusion to necromancy in v. 15. He argues that the covenant with death and Sheol is not figurative language for security from evil or for alliance with Egypt, as others suggest,[43] but rather is a real covenant with the underworld deities Mot and Sheol, 'whose protection had been secured by means of various rites and magical practices' (202). There

[39] Cf. Is. 53:1; Jer. 49:14; Obad. 1; for Sennacherib: Is. 37:7. As a parallel, the Akkadian term *egirrû* can mean both 'rumour' (like *šᵉmûʿāh*) and an oracle uttered in sleep or alcoholic stupor.

[40] Hence the LXX occasionally translates *'ôḇôṯ* as 'ventriloquists' (e.g. Is. 19:3).

[41] Akkadian *egirrû* is not semantically equivalent: CAD 4/E derives it from Sumerian *inim.gar* as 'reputation established by utterances' and does not list 'report' as a meaning. HAL gives no Akkadian equivalent of *šᵉmû'āh*.

[42] Views include: precepts: AV, RSV, NIV, NRSV, Wildberger (1982: 1054), Oswalt (1986: 512), Motyer (1993: 186); alphabet: Fohrer (1966: 53f.), Kaiser (1972: 246), Clements (1980: 228, tentatively), Watts (1985: 363); Assyrian terms: van Selms (1973), Lemaire (1981: 38f.), Roberts (1983: 22); infantile mockery: Lindblom (1962: 201), Melugin (1974: 306); disciples' lessons: Irwin (1977: 22); revellers' din: Driver (1968: 55f.), NEB, REB; filth and vomit: Emmerton (2001, with full review).

[43] Security: Driver (1968: 58), Kaiser (1974: 200), Tropper (1989: 330); alliance: Clements (1980: 229).

may also be references to the deities Chemosh and Milcom disguised in the terms 'lies' and 'falsehood' (*kāzāḇ, šeqer*).

However, this is improbable. Nothing here implies that death and Sheol are deities, and van der Toorn presents no substantial argument for it. Some Israelites may indeed have worshipped underworld deities, but this passage does not indicate it. Further, it is unlikely that *kāzāḇ* and *šeqer* are disguised references to Chemosh and Milcom: other usage of the terms hardly supports it,[44] and the evidence of their cults is irrelevant unless a link is first established. And even if the ungodly Jerusalemites had made a covenant with underworld deities, this is not the same as necromancy.

Given the depravity of prophets, priests and people which Isaiah 28 denounces, it is quite possible that some of them practised necromancy. But necromancy is hardly the target here.

1 Samuel 14:31–35. After battle, Saul's famished troops slaughter animals 'on the ground' (*'arṣāh*) and eat them 'with the blood' (*'al-haddām*, vv. 32, 34). For Grintz (1970–71), following Maimonides, this involves letting the animal blood flow down to the chthonic powers and facilitates divination, and the key terms actually mean 'to the underworld' and 'over the blood'. Similarly, Leviticus 19:26 juxtaposes eating 'with the blood' and divination.[45] However, this is unlikely linguistically and contextually. 'Ground' scarcely means underworld (see Ch. 5.a), and elsewhere the preposition *'al* means 'with' following the verb 'to eat' (*'-k-l*, e.g. Exod. 12:8). Here, Saul is concerned about eating improperly slaughtered animals, not about necromantic ritual. Further, while divination might be appropriate before battle (cf. 1 Sam. 28), it was hardly the priority afterwards.

Isaiah 45:19. Yahweh asserts: 'I did not speak in secret, in a land of darkness'. It is widely agreed that Yahweh's clear declarations are contrasted here with the secretive and confusing oracles obtained by necromancy and perhaps other forbidden magical practices.[46] But this is implied rather than stated.

Isaiah 65:4. Here Yahweh is enraged with a rebellious and provocative people, who engage in private sacrifices and offerings, 'sit inside tombs and spend the night in secret places', and consume unclean food and drink. As elsewhere (e.g. Is. 57; see Ch. 8.a.vi), illicit practices are combined. The Hebrew text gives no reason for passing the night in hidden tombs. The LXX adds the phrase 'through dreams', implying a desire for dream oracles, and

44 Jer. 10:14 (*šeqer*) and Amos 2:4 (*kāzāḇ*, pl.) prove nothing.

45 For Grintz, this predates 1 Sam. 14:31–35. Milgrom (1991: 28) supports Grintz's chthonic interpretation of the Levitical texts (also 17:3–7) but not their wilderness period dating.

46 McKenzie (1968: 82), Tromp (1969: 96f.), Whybray (1975: 111), Watts (1987: 162), Lewis (1989: 142f.).

this likely interpretation is followed by several scholars.[47] This would then be further evidence for necromancy in Israel.

d. Necromantic terms

i. ʾôḇ *as a divination device?*

Ancient tradition explicitly attributes deception to necromancy. The LXX usually translates *ʾôḇ* as 'ventriloquist' (*engastrimuthos*), and the Talmud states that mediums hid air bags in their armpits to produce a hissing sound which was then attributed to the dead. Following Ibn Ezra, some scholars suggest that *ʾôḇ* was originally such an air bag and is onomatopoeic, giving the dull sound ('oov') of a filled wineskin.[48] However, these views do not fit the many texts where *ʾôḇ* indicates a spirit or medium. Other interpretations of *ʾôḇ* as a divination device are equally problematic.[49]

Alternatively, many scholars suggest that *ʾôḇ* means a pit dug specifically for divination. This was first mooted a century ago by van Hoonacker (1898), who cited Greek and Roman oracles from caves, and suggested that the name of the Moabite town Beer-elim (Is. 15:8) means 'pit of the gods'.[50] Building on this, Gadd (1948: 90) noted a parallel with Enkidu's emergence from the underworld through a pit in the *Epic of Gilgamesh* (XII: 79), and tentatively linked Hebrew *ʾôḇ* with Sumerian *ab*. Vieyra (1961) traced the etymology of *ʾôḇ* from Hittite/Hurrian *api* and Akkadian *apu*, which he identified as a ritual pit for communication with the underworld and for offering sacrifices.[51] Hoffner (1967) then argued at length and influentially that Hittite *a-a-bi*, Assyrian *abu* and Ugaritic *(il)ib* are all cognate with Hebrew *ʾôḇ*, and that *ʾôḇ* means 'pit' in 1 Sam. 28:7–8.[52]

However, this view has many difficulties. First, *ʾôḇ* hardly means 'ritual pit' in Hebrew usage, for the following reasons. (i) Its companion term *yiddeʿōnîm* indicates sentient beings, so *ʾôḇ* probably does too. (ii) No biblical text requires the meaning 'pit' for *ʾôḇ*. (iii) On the contrary, the syntax of

47 E.g. Westermann (1969: 401), Whybray (1975: 269), Lewis (1989: 159f.).

48 E.g. Tur-Sinai (1957: 462f. n. 2), Wohlstein (1961: 32). *ʾôḇ* in Job 32:19 would have the same root.

49 Some early scholars saw *ʾôḇ* as the human abdomen from which the spirit allegedly spoke (cf. Tropper 1989: 194), or as a spinning stick (Schmidt 1925: 260).

50 Smith (1894: 198) had previously linked *ʾôḇ* with Greek and Roman chthonic deities.

51 Rabin (1963: 115f.) also suggested the Hittite cognate.

52 Hoffner (also 1969: 47; 1973: 216; TDOT 1: 130–34, except Is. 29:4), Grintz (1970–71: 89), Ebach–Rüterswörden (1977), Gurney (1977: 53), Humphreys (1980: 82, tentatively), Hutter (1983: 33), Dietrich (1987: 29), Podella (1988: 88; similarly *yiddeʿōnîm*), Strauss (1989: 22).

several verses hardly allows it.[53] Thus, if Hebrew *'ôḇ* did develop from a general Semitic term for 'pit', this must have occurred before the biblical texts were written, and the term's meaning must have evolved.[54]

Secondly, the proposed common root is itself uncertain. (i) The link with Sumerian *ab* is now discounted.[55] (ii) The Hittite and Akkadian words both have their second consonant in *p*, not *b*. Ebach–Rüterswörden reply that the basic term is the Hurrian *abi*, and the Hittite can be read this way, but they do not explain the Akkadian terms in *p*.[56] (iii) Hittite *api* does not occur in accounts of necromancy.[57] (iv) In Akkadian, one never consults the *apu*, and the verbal stems used with it are never used in Hebrew with *'ôḇ*.[58] (v) The identity between Ugaritic *ilib* and the Akkadian deity *ᵈa-bi* (see below) clearly dissociates *ilib* from any root meaning 'pit'. (vi) None of these languages uses a form of *ab* for 'spirit'.[59] All this leaves little in the way of supporting evidence.

ii. 'ôḇ *as an ancestor spirit?*

Most scholars now interpret *'ôḇ* as 'spirit of the dead', for different reasons. One early view sees *'ôḇ* as a hostile spirit, derived from Hebrew *'-y-b*, 'to be an enemy'. But this is not an obvious etymology, and does not fit Hebrew usage. Another early view, recently revived, sees *'ôḇ* as a returning spirit (French *revenant*), and derives it from Arabic *'āba*.[60] But most scholars are now cautious about citing Arabic roots (which are very numerous) when there is no supporting evidence. A third early view sees *'ôḇ* as an ancestor spirit, derived from Hebrew *'āḇ*, 'father'. Though not universally accepted, this is now the most common view.[61]

53 Lev. 20:27; Deut. 18:11, and particularly Is. 19:3; 29:4 (your voice . . . like an *'ôḇ*).

54 Lust (1974: 134) argues that the proposed cognates are always singular, unlike *'ôḇ*. However, plurals of Hittite *a-pi* are attested, cf. Vieyra (1961: 50), Hoffner (1967: 390), Friedrich–Kammenhuber (1975: 182).

55 Cf. Hoffner (1967: 385).

56 Hoffner gives *a-a-pi* in transcription of Hittite but *a-a-bi* in translation (cf. Lust). Similarly, the Akkadian word is *abu* for him but *apu* in AHw (62) and CAD (1/A ii: 201). Shaffer (cf. Müller 1975: 69 n. 19) links Akkadian *aptu*, 'window', to this root. Müller notes that Neo-Assyrian *apu* occurs later than 1 Sam. 28.

57 Cf. Podella (1988). Further, the Hittite earth gods were evoked not to reveal the future but to avert underworld pollution.

58 Cf. Cohen (1978: 73 n. 144): 'semantically, the two words have nothing to do with each other'.

59 Cf. Müller (1975: 69).

60 For early scholars, cf. Tropper (1989: 190f.). Also for *revenant*: Eichrodt (1967: 215), Albright (1968: 123 n. 83), Burns (1979: 9), Lewis (1989: 113 n. 36).

61 E.g. Dietrich–Loretz–Sanmartín (1974: 450f.), Lust (1974: 136f.), Müller (1975: 70), Spronk (1986: 253f.).

Tropper (1989: 312–16) presents a recent detailed argument for this, as follows. (i) Both *'ôḇ* and *'āḇ* have a plural in *-ôṯ*, and their consonantal plural forms are identical. (ii) The long *o* vowels in *'ôḇ* and its plural *'ôḇôṯ* are written variously in ordinary and full forms (defective and plene). (iii) Both *'ôḇôṯ* (Lev. 19:31f.) and 'ancestors' (Sirach 8:9) occur in parallel with 'aged' (*śêḇāh*). (iv) Both are sources of wisdom: *'ôḇôṯ* by parallelism with *yidd^e'ōnîm*, and 'ancestors' in Job 8:8, etc. (v) The 'ancestors' also inhabit the underworld, as seen in the phrases 'sleep with / be gathered to the ancestors'. (vi) Hebrew *'ôḇ* plays a role similar to Ugaritic *ilib*. (vii) Each family (*bēṯ-'āḇ*, lit. 'house of the father') was led by its patriarchal father (*'āḇ*), who in times of difficulty prayed to the family ancestor (*'ôḇ*), the guarantor of family continuity. Thus there is no great distinction between *'ôḇôṯ* and *'āḇôṯ*, and the latter must sometimes be rendered 'ancestor spirit'. The choice of term is governed by theological context: *'āḇôṯ* where reference is deemed legitimate and *'ôḇôṯ* where illegitimate.

But Tropper's arguments are all questionable. (i) Similarity of plural form is not decisive. The gender of *'ôḇ* is unknown, but could well be feminine (unlike *'āḇôṯ*),[62] with *'ôḇôṯ* and *yidd^e'ōnîm* indicating female and male spirits/mediums respectively. (ii) These minor variations in spelling are unexceptional.[63] (iii) The supposed parallelism of *'ôḇôṯ* with 'aged' in Leviticus 19 is strained, since they occur in separate, disjunctive verses, while Sirach's observation that 'the aged . . . heard from their fathers' is quite unremarkable. On the contrary, the resort to such an uncertain link (Lev. 19) and a late text (Sirach) demonstrates instead the *lack* of biblical evidence for the supposed parallel use of *'ôḇôṯ* and *'āḇôṯ*. (iv) Wisdom is too general a concept for two sources of it necessarily to be identified together. Further, while *'ôḇôṯ* may have knowledge (by association with the *yidd^e'ōnîm*), they are never attributed wisdom. (v) 'To be gathered to one's people' is used specifically for the patriarchs, Aaron and Moses, and to 'be gathered to one's ancestors [fathers]' of Joshua's generation, while 'to sleep with one's ancestors [fathers]' occurs only of kings who died peacefully (see Ch. 1.a.vi). While there are occasional references to 'ancestors' who have died, the term *'āḇôṯ* never occurs alone in reference to inhabitants of the underworld (unlike *r^ep̄ā'îm*). (vi) The link with Ugaritic *ilib* is uncertain, see below. (vii) There is no evidence that the patriarchal father (*'āḇ*) prayed to the ancestral spirit (*'ôḇ*). It may seem a reasonable hypothesis, but it cannot constitute an argument. Further, the fact that *'ôḇôṯ* are never linked to 'ancestors' weighs against it.

[62] *'ôḇ* ('wineskin') in Job 32:19 is masculine, but this is unrelated, as argued above.

[63] Cf. GK (§8.l): 'scriptio plena in two successive syllables was generally avoided'; similarly Barr (1989: 58–61).

(viii) Tropper cites no text where *'ābôṯ* must be rendered 'ancestor spirit'. Occasionally it indicates people who have died, but never spirits who exercise a role towards the living. (ix) *'āḇ* (father/ancestor) is a very common and general term, while *'ôḇ* is infrequent and specific, which hardly suggests that they were differentiated only on theological grounds. All this leads to the conclusion that *'ôḇ* does not derive from *'āḇ*, and that *'ôḇ* does not refer specifically to an ancestor spirit.

iii. 'ôḇ *and* ilib?

The Ugaritic term *ilib* is now often linked to the Hebrew *'ôḇ*, because of its second syllable and because it occurs in a context of honouring the dead. It has two apparently distinct uses. (a) In many cultic texts *ilib* comes near the head of the list of gods, implying seniority among the gods. In one list which occurs in several texts and two languages, Ugaritic *ilib* is matched by Akkadian ^{d}*a-bi*. Here the prefixed determinative for a god (represented by a raised *d*) shows that it is a divine name. This suggests that *ilib* is one of the high gods.[64] (b) In the Aqhat epic, the duties of a son looking after his father's affairs include 'setting up a stele of his *ilib*'.[65] Here *ilib* takes a personal suffix ('his'). However, suffixes are not normally attached to personal names, which suggests that this *ilib* is not a named deity.

Outside Ugarit there are two probable references to *ilib*. One is *'l'b* on a badly damaged thirteenth-century bowl inscription from Lachish, where it may be part of a name.[66] The other is the name *'bd'l'b*, meaning 'worshipper/servant of *'l'b*', on a seventh-century seal from Philistia.[67] These are marginal to the discussion. There is no Old Testament reference to *ilib*.[68]

The Ugaritic cultic lists show that *ilib* is the name of a god. Most scholars think he is distinct from the 'high god' El, since he is listed separately.[69] Lambert identifies him as the Old Akkadian god Ilaba, who was honoured at

64 Ugaritic: KTU 1.47, 1.118; Akkadian: RS 20.24. For Wyatt (1998: 360), this list appears to be canonical. Other lists: Ugaritic KTU 1.41, 1.46, 1.56, 1.74, 1.87, 1.91, 1.109, 1.148; Akkadian: KTU 4.727, RIH 77/2B; cf. TO 2 and Wyatt (selectively).

65 KTU 1.17.i:27,45, 1.17. ii:16. On *skn* as stele (despite CML), see Ch. 8.a.vii.

66 So van der Toorn (1993: 279). See also Ussishkin (1983), Cross (1984), Puech (1986–87). Cross disagrees with Ussishkin over most letters, including the *aleph*, and reads the two lines in opposite directions.

67 It reads: 'Belonging to *'bd'l'b* son of *šb't*, the servant of *mtt* son of *ṣdqh*'. This *mtt* may be Mitinti, king of Ashkelon, who opposed Ashurbanipal. Cf. Cross (1984: 75 n. 5), Naveh (1985: 9), Lewis (1989: 56).

68 Albright (1968: 123 n. 80) proposes it in Is. 14:19, emending *'el 'aḇnê* ('to the stones of'), but this is unlikely.

69 E.g. Nougayrol (1968: 46).

Mari and hence at Ugarit.[70] In the course of time this *ilib* possibly became a family god.

The Aqhat epic shows that each person or family had their *ilib*. Some scholars have translated the term as 'god of the father', and linked it to similar terms in the patriarchal narratives and other biblical texts.[71] However, most now interpret it as 'deified father' or 'divine ancestor'.[72] This was specific to each family, hence the personal suffixes. This concept is similar to the Hurrian *en atn* and the Roman *manes*.

Van der Toorn (1993) links the two different uses of *ilib* by suggesting that the concept of divinized personal ancestor(s) was even projected onto the gods, like so many other aspects of human life. Thus *ilib* was the individual or collective older god(s), given first place in official lists even if most religious activity related to younger, more active gods.[73] Other ancient Near Eastern cultures also had their 'olden gods'.[74] So *ilib* is the primeval deity or prototypical divine ancestor given pride of place in cultic ceremony but otherwise ignored.[75] This brings together the two otherwise puzzlingly different uses of *ilib*.

For several scholars the meaning 'divine ancestor' links Ugaritic *ilib* with Hebrew *'ôḇ*.[76] The terms occur in the similar contexts of respecting and consulting the dead. They are also similar in form, and perhaps in derivation, if *'ôḇ* comes from *'āḇ*. However the latter is questionable (see above). Some even suggest that *'l'b* was originally used in Israel of the dead, but was later simplified to *'b* and vocalized as *'ôḇ* to conceal its origin.[77] But this is hypothetical, and fails to account for the loss of the first syllable *'l*. So Ugaritic *ilib* may well indicate 'divinized ancestor' and testify to some honouring of the dead at Ugarit, but it remains uncertain how it relates to Hebrew *'ôḇ* or to Old Testament necromancy.

70 Lambert (1981). Many Mari names contain 'Ilabi'. Mari provides a bridge between eastern Mesopotamia and Ugarit. Lambert also identifies *ilib* with El, since deities often have duplicate names.

71 E.g. Gordon (1965: 358, no. 165).

72 E.g. Albright (1953: 203 n. 31), Gray (1957: 75f. n. 7), Laroche (1968: 523), Caquot (1969: 259f.), Greenfield (1973: 48 n. 12), Dietrich–Loretz–Sanmartín (1974: 451), de Moor (1980a: 184 n. 66), de Tarragon (TO 2: 192 n. 152), Tropper (1989: 126), Lewis (1989: 58f.).

73 The Ugaritic order *ilib, il, dgn, b'l* thus parallels the Hurro-Hittite theogony Alalu, Anu, Kumarbi, Teshub.

74 E.g. Mesopotamian: Enlil's ancestor Enmesharra (who 'stands for various archaic and forgotten gods'); Hurro-Hittite: Alalu; Egyptian: the eight primeval gods.

75 Religious practice in Britain provides a modern analogy. In Anglican liturgy, the monarch and other royalty are prayed for by name while the government is simply 'her/his ministers', despite their greater political authority.

76 E.g. van der Toorn (1993). Other suggested links: *ilib* as 'god of the pit', Vieyra (1961: 53); Hoffner (1967: 387; but not TDOT 1: 132); as 'returning spirit': Gaster (1961: 334), Albright (1968: 122).

77 E.g. Dietrich–Loretz–Sanmartín (1974: 451).

e. Summary

Israel's religious literature contains only occasional references to necromancy: in several prohibitions, one narrative account, and a few other references. Clearly necromancy is not an issue which preoccupied its writers. Two terms are commonly used, *'ôḇ*(*ôṯ*) and *yiddeʿōnî*(*m*). But there was no fixed expression for necromancy, as shown by these terms' double meaning of 'spirit' and 'medium', their variation between singular and plural, the occasional use of the first without the second and the variety of associated verbs. Whatever its etymology, *'ôḇ* hardly means divination device or divination pit in Old Testament usage. Further, *'ôḇ* is not obviously cognate with Hebrew *'āḇ* or with Ugaritic *ilib*. Nor are necromancy and ancestor worship associated in the Hebrew Bible, though they may well have coexisted. Isaiah's opponents may have practised necromancy, but Isaiah 28 hardly indicates this. There is only one account of necromancy, 1 Samuel 28, but this furnishes few details of its practice. Nevertheless, this account confirms that it was both highly illegal and highly effective, even if for Saul its effect is to seal his impending fate.

Burns concludes very appropriately:

> The Old Testament, unlike Mesopotamian religious literature, contains no evidence of a highly developed demonology. Nor is it suggested anywhere that the spirits of the dead have power to harm the living. There is none of the dread, so graphically expressed in Babylonian incantations, of the unburied and untended spirit wreaking revenge on the living. In the few verses where *'ōb* does mean unequivocally the spirit of the dead, the usual impression is one of pathetic weakness rather than demonic strength . . . The Old Testament displays little interest in the fate of the dead and certainly no fear of them.[78]

[78] Burns (1979: 11); similarly Bailey (1979: 35).

Chapter 8
HONOURING THE DEAD

In many different cultures today, the dead are honoured in some way by the living. This can take various forms, such as setting up images or pictures, lighting candles, burning incense, addressing in prayer, holding celebratory meals, placing food on graves, and conducting religious rites. Catholic piety includes praying to the saints, saying masses for the dead, and celebrating All Souls Day and All Saints Day, sometimes by visiting graves and leaving flowers and food there. In Buddhism, Confucianism, Shintoism and many other non-Western religions, family ancestors are venerated. Many ancient religions and cultures similarly honoured the dead, particularly family ancestors but also national rulers and heroes. They were given some form of supernatural status, and accorded some ability to affect the living.

Did ancient Israelites honour their ancestors? If so, in what way, and what did it mean to them? Was this an acceptable part of Yahwism, at least in a early period? Was it later rejected, or had it always been abhorrent to orthodox Israelite faith? These are clearly important issues. But there are two immediate problems in studying them. One is that scholars are often imprecise in their use of terms, particularly the common phrase 'cult of the dead' or 'death cult'. This usually means 'any act intended to do good to the dead and to solicit favours from them'. Spronk (1986: 247) defines it as 'a veneration of the dead which can be compared to the veneration of deities'. This is similar, since deities were venerated for their own good and for the benefits they would bestow. However, some scholars also include necromancy in their definition, even though this was undertaken to gain knowledge rather than to secure favours.[1] So the terms used vary in meaning.

The second, more important problem is that evidence for a cult of the dead in ancient Israel is often sparse and unclear, and what there is can be interpreted differently. While there is widespread evidence for such a cult in the ancient Near East,[2] in the Old Testament it is only mentioned three times: once in a prohibition concerning the tithe, and once each in narrative and psalmody concerning a Moabite cult abhorrent to Yahweh. These are the only direct references. The little relevant archaeological evidence of grave food is discussed above (see Ch. 2.b.vi).

In the late nineteenth and early twentieth centuries many scholars saw death rites as widespread in Israel, and as an important key to understanding Israelite religion.[3] In contrast, by the mid twentieth century many scholars denied the influence of an Israelite ancestor cult on Yahwism, and some even discounted its existence.[4]

Now, however, many scholars again think that there was a widespread cult of the dead in pre-exilic Israel. They argue that many more texts originally referred to the cult of the dead, but these were altered by orthodox Yahwistic writers to hide such reference. By extrapolating from surrounding cultures and the few remaining Old Testament references, the original meaning of these altered texts can be recovered. This argument appears plausible, and there is certainly evidence throughout history of religious communities reinterpreting their past, as suggested here. But it has two major difficulties. On the one hand, hypothetical reconstruction without any textual evidence is hazardous, since there are no objective means of assessing its validity. And by definition any reconstruction is purely conjectural, if the undesired references were successfully removed. On the other hand, the fact that a few references do remain implies either that the redactors were inefficient, or that they did not rewrite texts as alleged. If (as it happens) they left one glaring reference to food for the dead, then perhaps they did not see such food in particular or the ancestor cult in general as major issues to be addressed. The relevant texts will be examined below.

[1] Lewis (1989: 2) includes necromancy (even though he accepts that Saul wanted knowledge, not favours), and as a result confuses 'dead spirits' and 'death cult imagery' regarding Is. 29:4.
[2] Cf. Bayliss (1973), Tsukimoto (1985), Spronk (1986: ch. 2), Hallo (1992), van der Toorn (1994).
[3] Cf. Spronk (1986: 28–43), Lewis (1989: 2 n. 9).
[4] Denied influence: Jacob (1958: 306), Martin-Achard (1960: 26, 30f.), von Rad (1962: 275f.), Snaith (1964: 311), Eichrodt (1967: 217f.), Wächter (1967: 192f.), Bailey (1979: 35f.). Discounted existence: Wright (1953: 487), de Vaux (1961: 60), Kaufmann (1960: 312). For other scholars, cf. Spronk (1986: 44 n. 4).

a. The ancestor cult and Old Testament texts

Numbers 25:2 records that Israelite men joined Moabite women in 'the sacrifices of their gods', which Psalm 106:28 calls 'the sacrifices of the dead'. These texts are discussed above (see Ch. 6.b.i). In both texts the cult of the dead is foreign to Israel, the apostasy is one of many in the wilderness, and no further observance of it is recorded. Elsewhere there is one clear reference (Deut. 26:14), one obvious allusion (Is. 57:6) and a few other suggested references of varying probability.

i. Deuteronomy 26

An Israelite presenting the tithe from his produce must declare that none of it has been eaten in mourning, or carried while he was unclean, or given (lit.) 'to/for a dead person (*l*^e^*mēṯ*)'. In other words, he must be ritually clean, especially as regards contact with the dead. The last phrase of the confession is ambiguous, and could indicate either (i) food given to the dead as grave food (also called grave offerings), or (ii) food used in a cult of the dead.[5] A few scholars interpret it as sacrifices to a god called 'the Dead One'.[6] However, the term for 'dead' (*mēṯ*) never elsewhere means a god, and the context of mourning and uncleanness here clearly indicates a dead person.

This law assumes that food was given 'to or for a dead person' in Israel, and does not prohibit it. It merely prohibits any association of such food with the tithe. Many scholars therefore conclude that the offering of food to the dead was a widespread and widely accepted custom. While the reforming seventh-century Deuteronomists strongly disapproved of the practice, they felt unable to prohibit it entirely, so they limited their prohibition to the tithe.[7] However, this argument is weak. Whenever it was written, Deuteronomy has little difficulty in condemning other abhorrent practices such as necromancy (Deut. 18:10–11), and could equally have condemned food for the dead if this was considered inimical to Yahwism. So on the contrary, it is more likely that such food was allowed generally because the custom was not intrinsically opposed to Yahwism. It was only prohibited for the tithe because it caused ritual impurity. In this case, the food would not have involved venerating the dead to gain blessing for the living.

[5] (i) Von Rad (1966: 160), Phillips (1973: 175), Spronk (1986: 248), Lewis (1989: 103). (ii) Brichto (1973: 29), van der Toorn (1996a: 209).
[6] Baal: Cazelles (1948: 67f.), Braulik (1992: 196); Mot: Buis–Leclerq (1963: 169). Possibly a god: Craigie (1976: 323), Thompson (1974: 258), Mayes (1979: 336f.).
[7] E.g. Lewis (1989: 172 n. 2) infers that all offerings to the dead were considered offensive.

Deuteronomy stresses that Yahweh alone gives and sustains life, and it prohibits contact with the dead. Thus the food in question was probably placed in a grave to help the deceased on their journey to the underworld. It was not part of a cult of the dead.

Whether this food was limited to the time of burial or continued regularly for a period is impossible to say. The lack of archaeological evidence for continued food provision inside highland cave tombs implies that it was limited to the time of burial (see Ch. 2.b.vi).[8] Just as importantly, the uniqueness of this reference indicates that food for the dead was not a major concern for the biblical writers.

Some scholars argue that funerary practices and cults were widespread in Israel and attested in its early traditions, but that zealous orthodox redactors expunged many references to them. But this argument is unsafe. The greater their zeal, the less the likelihood of their leaving Deuteronomy 26:14 as a testimony to this supposedly abhorrent practice. That this text has survived indicates rather that food for the dead was considered relatively harmless.

There are later references to grave offerings in several books of the Apocrypha. The pseudonymous Letter of Jeremiah, written sometime in the fourth to second centuries BCE, is a sustained attack on the worthlessness of idols, and includes the comment: 'Gifts are placed before them just as before the dead' (v. 27). The writer explains that it is not the idols but the priests who benefit (by selling 'the sacrifices'), but makes no further comment about the dead. The other two references are in books generally dated to the early second century BCE. The pious Tobit, apparently about to die, instructs his son Tobias: 'Revere the Lord . . . live uprightly . . . give alms . . . Place your bread on the grave of the righteous, but give none to sinners' (Tobit 4:4–7, 17). The writer obviously thought well of grave food. By contrast, the more traditional Jesus ben Sirach thinks it a complete waste of effort: 'Good things poured out upon a mouth that is closed are like offerings of food placed upon a grave' (Sirach 30:18). These texts show that the practice continued but that its value was debated, while the paucity of reference might again suggest that it was not of major importance.

ii. 1 Samuel 28

After Saul's nocturnal seance the medium of Endor offers him food, and he reluctantly accepts. She then kills a fatted calf and cooks a meal, which Saul

[8] Regular offerings inside tombs would also have involved frequent contact with decaying corpses, causing uncleanness (see Ch. 1.b.v).

eats before departing. Tropper (1992: 221f.) argues that the meal was a cultic feast of the dead and that this has been obscured in the present account, as follows. (i) The ancestors, summoned in seance, attended the meal, since the narrative does not record their return to the underworld before it. (ii) The verb 'slaughtered' (*z-b-ḥ*, v. 24) implies a cultic action.[9] (iii) Saul had banned ancestor worship (vv. 3, 9), so contravention of his own ban involved ancestor worship, not simply necromancy. (iv) Saul's prostration before Samuel (v. 14) exhibits the reverence due to divinized ancestors. (v) Killing the fatted calf implies that this was a *marzēaḥ* (see section b. below), since it would be 'quite absurd' simply for three men.

But his argument is unconvincing. (i) There is no mention of the spirit(s) returning to the underworld at any stage, either before or after the meal. In any case, if the text was substantially edited, an argument from silence is hardly conclusive. (ii) The verb 'slaughter' occasionally occurs in non-sacrificial contexts.[10] Anyway, the meal could have been a concluding, cultic part of the seance without the dead being thought present. (iii) According to the text, Saul banished necromancy, not ancestor worship. (iv) There is nothing unlikely in prostration before a revivified prophet. Further, it is irrelevant to the meal.[11] (v) A fatted calf is hardly 'absurd' when one of the guests is the king, who has caught the woman in illegal activity.[12] So Saul's midnight feast is not a veneration of the ancestors.

iii. Psalm 16

The opening verses of Psalm 16 contain several textual difficulties, prompting various emendations and interpretations.[13] In v. 3 the psalmist apparently delights in 'the holy ones (*qᵉḏôšîm*) who are in the earth (*'ereṣ*)'. Some scholars suggest that these are the powerful dead in the underworld, and that the psalm thus indicates a veneration of the dead in Israel. There are several interpretations of 'holy ones'.

(a) **Human saints.** This traditional view, still held by several scholars,[14]

[9] Cf. BDB, Fohrer (1973: 115).
[10] E.g. Deut. 12:15, 21, where purpose, place, type of animal and status of participants distinguish this slaughter from sacrifice; so Weinfeld (1972: 213f.), Mayes (1979: 228), Craigie (1976: 219), Lang (TDOT 4: 11).
[11] This also confuses the two editions Tropper posits, early (ancestors are *'ᵉlōhîm*) and late (Samuel is *'ᵉlōhîm*).
[12] Cf. Edelman (1991: 250): 'a meal befitting the king'.
[13] Comprehensively surveyed by Jacquet (1975: 400–402).
[14] LXX, Targum, Vulgate; Weiser (1962: 174), Kidner (1973: 84), Rogerson–McKay (1977a: 63f., implicitly), Kraus (1988: 236, Levitical priests); also Leveen (1971: 52, with emendation), Lindblom (1974: 191), Beuken (1980: 377f.).

retains an accepted meaning for *q*^e*dôšîm*, which like its Semitic cognates can mean human as well as celestial beings.[15] It fits the earthly situation described in vv. 5–6, and reads v. 3 with least emendation: 'As for the holy ones in the land, they are the noble, in whom is all my delight' (NRSV).[16] Further, *q*^e*dôšîm* never occurs elsewhere to refer to the dead.

(b) **Other deities.** Many scholars interpret the 'holy ones' as local Canaanite deities whose worship is opposed to that of Yahweh.[17] The psalmist supports his declaration of allegiance to Yahweh with a disapproval of foreign cults. This view takes v. 3 as contrastive to v. 2, often with emendation of 'all' (*kôl*) to 'not' (*bal*): 'As for the "holy ones" in the land, the "noble ones", my delight is *not* in them!'[18]

(c) **Powerful dead.** The 'holy ones' are the spirits of the dead who have joined the celestial host and exercise some control over events on earth. The horrified psalmist distances himself from 'the cult of the holy and powerful who are in the earth (i.e. the underworld)', and takes no part in it.[19] Spronk also argues that, since the 'holy ones' are underworld spirits here but lower deities elsewhere (like the Babylonian Anunnaki and the Ugaritic *rpum*), the 'prominent dead could be reckoned among YHWH's host' (1986: 336). He finds this supported by the strophic balance of 'earth' (*'ereṣ*, v. 3) and 'pleasant places' (*n*^e*'imîm*, v. 6), both seen as underworld names. However, this is most unlikely, since Israelite belief rigidly separated celestial and underworld realms.[20] Also, the Babylonian Anunnaki are not parallel, since their role changed over time from celestial and earthly duties to underworld responsibility.[21] Further, Spronk's suggested underworld names and their strophic balance is most unlikely.[22] For van der Toorn (1996a: 211), the inheritance

[15] While use for celestial beings is more common, Hasel (1975: 176–82) takes *q*^e*dôšîm* as 'humans' in Ps. 34:9, and probably also Prov. 9:10; 30:3; Hos. 11:12. He also notes the common description of Israel as 'holy' (*qādôš*).

[16] It changes the Massoretic punctuation, emends 'nobles of' to 'nobles' and deletes 'and' before it.

[17] E.g. Dequeker (1960: 375), Schedl (1964: 171), Brekelmans (1965: 308), Dahood (1966: 87), Anderson (1972a: 142), Mannati (1972: 360), Müller (THAT 2: 601), HAL (998), Craigie (1983: 156), Hubmann (1983: 103f.), Ringgren (TWAT 6: 1199).

[18] Alternatively, Anderson emends 'noble' to 'cursed'; Craigie sees a different, faithless speaker in v. 3.

[19] Zolli (1950). Similarly Reines (1951: 156 n.3; 1954: 87 n.2; citing Midrash Psalms and Rashi for *q*^e*dôšîm* as ancestors), Eaton (1976: 163; ≠ 1967: 58), Pope (*apud* Cooper 1981: 457), Spronk (1986: 334–8), Lang (1988: 148 n. 11), Tropper (1989: 163), Bloch-Smith (1992a: 109), van der Toorn (1996a: 210f.).

[20] Kraus (1988: 323) describes this view as 'conceptually inadequate'.

[21] See Horowitz (1998: 143f.).

[22] On *'ereṣ* for 'underworld', see Ch. 5.a. *n*^e*'imîm* never means 'underworld' in Hebrew (despite Spronk, not Ezek. 32:19; cf. 27:3, 11; 31:2, 7, 9, etc.), despite this meaning for Ugaritic *n'my*. As for strophic balance, the proposed division is not obvious, the strophes have different lengths, and the terms are not in balancing positions within them.

language (portion, lot, boundary lines, heritage, vv. 5–6) 'confirms the intimate link between the possession of the family inheritance and the cult of the family dead'. But this assumes both this unlikely reading of 'holy ones' and a particular purpose of the ancestor cult, which he asserts rather than demonstrates.

While the passage remains difficult, the traditional view remains the most likely both textually and theologically: the psalmist delights in human saints.

iv. Psalm 49

Psalm 49 contrasts the foolhardy rich destined for Sheol with the godly psalmist who will be ransomed from it (see Ch. 9.b.ii). Its description of the former includes: 'though they named lands their own' (v. 11; lit. 'they called by their names over lands'). This is usually thought to indicate their large estates. However, Smith (1993) argues that it alludes instead to invocation of deceased ancestors, for several reasons. (i) The normal idiom for naming land is not 'call by name' (*q-r-' bᵉšēm*) but 'call X by name'. (ii) The commonly attested idiom *q-r-' bᵉšēm* + object is a cultic one, as in the expression 'to call on the name of Yahweh'. (iii) The Ugaritic cognate of *q-r-'* is used of invoking ancestors in KTU 1.161. (iv) Mention of graves in the first line gives the context. Thus v. 11 'refers to the practice of invoking names of deceased ancestors',[23] and presumably means: 'they summoned (ancestors) by their names onto the earth'.

However, this is scarcely convincing. (i) Smith himself notes the wide syntactical variety regarding the naming of land. Thus there is hardly a common idiom, and Psalm 49:11 could well give a further variant. (ii) The fact that *q-r-' bᵉšēm* + the divine name is cultic does not determine other uses of *q-r-' bᵉšēm*, nor does use elsewhere of the very common verb *q-r-'*. (iii) The psalmist is not concerned with illicit religious practice, and does not cite it in condemnation of the foolish rich. Rather, it is their confidence in wealth and power which he criticizes. The traditional interpretation of v. 11 fits this context, whereas Smith's proposal does not. So the rich are castigated for acquiring land, not for invoking ancestors.

v. Isaiah 28

Isaiah 28:7–22 contains a powerful indictment of a rotten society, as discussed above (see Ch. 7.c). For Halpern (1986: 118), 'Isaiah ridicules his

[23] Smith (1993: 107). He does not actually provide a translation.

priestly colleagues . . . as participants in the ancestral cult'. He argues that the passage also mentions tombs, and that the orgy involving drunkenness and excrement implies a *marzēaḥ* like that for the inebriated Ugaritic El, as follows.[24] (i) The words translated 'bed' (*maṣṣāʿ*) and 'covering' (*massēḵāh*) in v. 20 actually mean 'tomb bench' and 'shroud' here, since these roots occur elsewhere in contexts of death and the underworld.[25] (ii) The enigmatic terms translated 'precept' and 'line' (*ṣaw* and *qaw*) in v. 10 are really babyisms for the vomit and excrement of the drunken priests and prophets, echoing the 'filthy excrement' of v. 8 (*qîʾ ṣōʾāh*, normally translated 'filthy vomit'). Isaiah lampoons his opponents for confusing Yahweh's word with such filth. (iii) The ancient belief that excrement was the food of the dead explains the interest in excrement.

However, Halpern's argument is unconvincing. (i) Both 'bed' and 'covering' are general terms. The context might give them a burial or underworld connotation, but the terms themselves do not indicate this.[26] Isaiah may have extrapolated from a covenant with death to refuge in a tomb, but the terms are not evidence for this. (ii) Reference to excrement in this passage is uncertain, since *ṣōʾāh* is also a general term for 'filth'.[27] So the traditional translation of v. 8 as 'filthy vomit' is quite plausible. But even if the cultic officials have defecated on tables, it is hard to imagine Isaiah mocking their lack of control in babyisms, or giving Yahweh's oracle to them in these same terms (v. 13). *ṣaw* and *qaw* form word-plays with other terms in the passage, e.g. 'line' (*qaw*) and 'righteousness' (*ṣᵉḏāqāh*) in v. 17, so they could form similar word-plays with 'filthy vomit/excrement' (*qîʾ ṣōʾāh*, v. 8) without being infantile adaptations of the latter. (iii) The ancient belief that excrement was the food of the dead is uncertain. Xella (1980) traces the belief in Egyptian and Mesopotamian texts, and in the Assyrian commander's prediction that Jerusalemites will 'eat their own dung and drink their own urine' (2 Kgs. 18:27 // Is. 36:12), taken to indicate the underworld. But he cites only one extra-biblical text, which others translate differently.[28] Further, the Assyrians besieging Jerusalem intend to provoke fear, not predict the future, and would do so better by portraying

[24] Cf. Is. 65:4 for illicit cults in tombs, and KTU 1.113 for El's drunken *marzēaḥ*.

[25] Root *y-ṣ-ʿ* in Job 17:13; Ps. 139:8 (*maṣṣāʿ* is a hapax); *massēḵāh* in Is. 25:7.

[26] *massēḵāh* occurs only here and in Is 25:7, where it clearly means 'shroud'. However, it comes from a very common verb 'to cover', so the type of covering depends on the context (cf. *masseḵeṯ*, 'web', Judg. 16:13f.). The parallel term in Is. 25:7, *l-w-t*, is similarly general (e.g. used of Goliath's sword, 1 Sam. 21:9).

[27] Filth: Prov. 30:12; Is. 4:4; Zech. 3:3f.; excrement: Deut. 23:14; 2 Kgs. 18:27 // Is. 36:12; Ezek. 4:12; cf. the English 'dirt', which can refer specifically to excrement (e.g. 'dog's dirt').

[28] *Gilgamesh* XII:145f. (the diet of an unburied person's *eṭemmu*), translated: 'offals of the street' (Speiser ANET: 99), 'abandoned in the streets' (Dalley 1989: 125).

extreme suffering in this life than by predicting misery in the next. But even if Xella's argument about the underworld is correct, its relevance to the disorderly priests of Isaiah 28 is unclear. Isaiah criticizes priests for degenerate behaviour, and rulers for unorthodox beliefs. It is possible that his contemporaries also indulged in ancestor worship, but there is no immediate evidence of this in Isaiah 28.

vi. Isaiah 57

Isaiah 57:3–13 is a stern indictment of fertility rites (vv. 3–5, 7–8), child sacrifice (v. 5) and idolatry in general (v. 13), often using overt sexual imagery. However, some scholars now see it as also a condemnation of the cult of the dead. Indeed, for Lewis, this is the sole aim of the text, and the sexual imagery is 'a stock idea' which is 'merely metaphorical here'.[29] These arguments are plausible for v. 6 and perhaps v. 9.

Verse 6. Scholars have often puzzled over why the prophet's opponents should find their portion among 'the smooth stones' (*ḥᵃlāqôṯ*).[30] Irwin (1967) suggests instead that this term means 'the dead', and that the passage refers to cultic activity at graves (cf. Is. 65:4), reasoning as follows. (i) *ḥᵃlāqôṯ* derives from the posited *ḥ-l-q*, 'to die', and means 'the dead'.[31] (ii) Though this meaning is unique here, rare forms are frequently preserved where there is a play on words, as here with 'your portion' (*ḥelqēḵ*). (iii) These dead are the slaughtered children of v. 5b. (iv) The valley (or wady) was the traditional burial ground.[32] (v) To 'have a portion with' means to share a place or inheritance, so here the people would be numbered with the dead. (vi) Prophetic oracles often envisage slaughter in the valley. And (vii) the food and drink offerings (v. 6b) are part of the child sacrifice ritual. Lewis and Ackerman take this further and interpret the sacrifice as a cult of the dead.

Irwin's interpretation depends on identifying a verb *ḥ-l-q*, 'to die', in Hebrew. Dahood first proposed this meaning in several texts,[33] and a few

29 Lewis (1989: 143–58; quote from 157f.). His book (cited here) repeats exactly his earlier article (1987).

30 Interpreted as: cultic stones: RSV, JB, NJB, McKenzie (1968: 158), Westermann (1969: 321f.), Young (1972: 400), Watts (1987: 252); deceitful (slippery) gods: REB; serpents: NEB, Herbert (1975: 138); smooth ravine walls: Weise (1960: 30f.).

31 As in Ugaritic: KTU 1.5.vi:10, 1.6.i:42, paralleling *mt.* Irwin notes other similarities with Ugaritic texts.

32 2 Kgs. 23:6; Job 21:33. In Is. 57:6 Kennedy (1989: 48f.) reinterprets 'valley' (*naḥal*) as 'tomb', on the basis of Job 28:4 ('mining shaft'), but even there *naḥal* could mean 'river/valley'; cf. Waterman (1952: 169).

33 Dahood (1963c: 548; 1964: 408; 1966: 35, 211): Job 21:17; Pss. 5:9; 12:2f.; 17:14; 35:6; 36:2; 73:18; Jer. 23:12; Lam. 4:16; Hos. 10:2.

scholars now accept it.[34] Cognates exist in other Semitic languages besides Ugaritic, increasing its likelihood in Hebrew.[35] Thus *ḥălāqôṯ* here could well mean 'the dead', not 'smooth stones', and the following reference to drink and grain offerings would then indicate a cult of the dead which the prophet condemns.

Verse 9. A few verses later the idolaters are castigated because they journeyed to 'the king' with oil and perfumes, and sent envoys even to Sheol. Some English translations and many scholars now reread 'the king (*meleḵ*)' as Molech.[36] He was probably an underworld god,[37] and the phrase 'journeyed to Molech' parallels 'sent to Sheol'.[38] Molech received human sacrifices in several neighbouring cultures and occasionally even in Israel.[39] Such sacrifices may be implied here by the oil and perfume, and particularly by the verbs 'journeyed' and 'sent envoys'.[40] (Various other reinterpretations have been proposed for the terms *meleḵ*,[41] 'journeyed',[42] 'envoys',[43] and 'far away',[44] but these are all unlikely.) The horrific practice of human sacrifice to Molech was part of the fascination with the realm of the dead censured by the prophet. This may well have included ancestor worship, but it is not explicit in this verse.

So v. 6 probably criticizes a cult of the dead, and v. 9 may condemn human sacrifice. However, arguments for death cult allusions elsewhere in Isaiah 57 are less plausible.

[34] Accepted in Psalms (except 12:2f.) by Anderson (1972); and in Lam. 4:16 by McDaniel (1968: 48), Hillers (1972: 83); but dismissed in Hos. 10:2 by Andersen–Freedman (1980: 552). Most ignore the proposal.

[35] Akkadian, Ethiopic, Tigrean, possibly Arabic, and at Deir Alla; cf. HAL, Lewis (1989: 148).

[36] E.g. RSV, JB, GNB, NIV, NRSV; Spronk (1986: 233), Healey (1990: 54), Weinfeld (1991b: 828, plausible), Tropper (1992: 235).

[37] Two Mesopotamian texts identify the underworld god Nergal with 'Malik', though other texts identify Nergal with Resheph; cf. Healey (1990: 54). Some scholars identity Ugaritic *mlk* with *rpu* (patron of the *rpum*), e.g. Pope (1977b: 169–72), Heider (1985: 115–23); but others reject this, e.g. Day (1989: 50).

[38] Whybray (1975: 206) sees Sheol as a deity, but it more likely indicates the underworld itself, see Ch. 3.a.

[39] Cf. Lev. 18:21; 20:2–5; 1 Kgs. 11:7; 2 Kgs. 23:10; Jer. 32:35; Heider (1985, ABD 4: 895–8, DDD: 581–5), Day (1989). Day (16) also notes the proximity (though not association) of oil and human sacrifice in Ezek. 16:18–20.

[40] E.g. Heider (1985: 380), Day (1989: 16). Some see necromancy, e.g. Whybray (1975: 206), Lewis (1989: 151), but this is not elsewhere linked with travel.

[41] Thomas (BHS): 'your hair', also reinterpreting 'you journeyed'; cf. NEB, REB. Watts (1987: 255): 'by rubbing', but this verb occurs only in Prov. 6:13, with a completely different connotation. Ackerman (1992: 108): '*mulk*-sacrifice' (cf. Phoenician/Punic term for child sacrifice), but this hardly explains the preceding 'to/for'.

[42] The term is rare, but this meaning is widely accepted. Other views: Driver (1950b: 58f.): 'drenched', cf. LXX, similarly Ackerman (1992: 108 n. 16), Heider (1985: 380 n. 756). Wernberg-Møller (1958: 307f.): 'lavish', cf. LXX of Ezek. 27:25 (but see Day 1989: 52). Watts (1987: 253–55): 'roused yourself (sexually)'.

[43] Tropper (1989: 235): 'balsam'.

[44] Ackerman (1992: 108): 'to a distant throne', cf. Ugaritic *'d*, 'throne' (KTU 1.16.vi:22).

Verses 3–5. In v. 3 the people are first castigated as children of a 'sorceress', which Lewis interprets as 'spirit-raiser, conjurer'. This is possible, but the parallel description, 'offspring of an adulterer and a whore', suggests that sexual misconduct is the primary if not sole emphasis. In v. 4 most translators interpret the facial contortions as mockery, but Lewis sees them as the underworld's anticipation of human food, echoing Ugaritic Mot and Hebrew Sheol.[45] But this is most unlikely, as no change of addressee is signalled and the verbs are plural.

Lewis then completely reinterprets v. 5a, as follows: 'burn with lust' should read 'comforting yourselves', assuming a common verb (*n-ḥ-m*, Niphal) rather than an otherwise unattested one (*ḥ-m-n*); 'oaks' should read 'dead spirits', a preferable interpretation of *'ēlîm* followed by all the versions; and 'under every green tree' should be deleted as a gloss (it usually occurs with 'every high hill'), and replaced with v. 6c, 'Shall I be appeased (comforted) for these things?' However, these arguments are inconclusive. Most other scholars accept that the verb of v. 5a means 'inflame, burn' despite its uniqueness (rarity is not of itself a valid reason for emendation); *'ēlîm* can mean 'oaks', and the versions are not necessarily reliable;[46] the phrase 'under every green tree' can occur without its complement 'every high hill' (Jer. 3:13), though a high hill is mentioned in v. 7 (and again uniqueness need not imply error); there is no textual evidence for the transposition of text; and sexual promiscuity under trees is a common prophetic image. The case for reinterpreting this verse is not strong.

Verses 7–8. In this portrayal of promiscuity, several terms have both sexual and death cult allusions, e.g. 'bed' (*miškāḇ*) can mean 'grave' (as in v. 2), and the word translated 'nakedness' (*yaḏ*, 'hand', here a euphemism for 'penis') can also mean 'mortuary stele' (as in Absalom's stele, 2 Sam. 18:18). However, while these terms are certainly ambiguous, the hilltop setting and the verbs 'set (up)' and 'loved' imply that the reference is primarily sexual rather than funerary.

More speculatively in v. 8, Lewis interprets the difficult second line as 'you tried to discover (oracles) from me (by) bringing up (spirits)'. But this is most unlikely: the first verb (*g-l-h*, Piel) never elsewhere means 'discover oracles'; necromancy was inappropriate for consulting Yahweh; and this translation is as obscure as the usual one. He also interprets the 'bargain' (v. 8b) as one made with the dead ancestors of v. 6. Again this is possible, but the lovers' pact is a common prophetic motif and, as noted, the immediate context is more sexual than funerary.

Verse 13. The prophet ends his condemnation with: 'When you cry out,

[45] KTU 1.5.ii.2–4; Is. 5:14, Hab. 2:5.

[46] 'Oaks' are normally *'êlîm*, but are written defectively as *'ēlîm* in Ezek. 31:14. In Is. 1:29 the LXX translates *'êlîm* as 'idols', when it can only mean 'oaks' (cf. Ackerman 1992: 102).

let your collection of idols (*qibbûṣîm*, lit. 'gathering') deliver you!' Lewis and Ackerman suggest that *qibbûṣîm* refers not to 'idols' but to 'dead ancestors', since in the Ugaritic texts the *qbṣ.ddn* parallel the *rpi.arṣ* (see Ch. 6.a.iv), and in Hebrew *q-b-ṣ* is a synonym of *'-s-p*, 'be gathered', which can mean 'to die' (see Ch. 1.a.vi). However, this is unlikely. In the Ugaritic texts *qbṣ* means 'assembly' (with no semantic connotation of death), and in Hebrew *q-b-ṣ* is never used for death, unlike *'-s-p*.[47]

To conclude, the people condemned in Isaiah 57 are engaged in licentious and illicit cultic activity, which may well be linked to the dead (v. 6) and involve human sacrifice or necromancy (v. 9). But Lewis's assessment that the whole passage focuses on death cults is inappropriate, since much of the suggested evidence for this is tenuous or unlikely. Ackerman is more balanced in seeing the primary focus as fertility cults. Some association in practice between fertility cults, child sacrifice and death cults is likely, though her proposal that they are here addressed twice each (vv. 5a, 5b, 6 and 7f., 9a, 9b respectively) is too schematic. Nevertheless, their popularity in Israel at any stage is impossible to determine. Death cults of some sort may be condemned here, but they are not singled out or highlighted.

vii. Ezekiel 43

Ezekiel's vision of the new temple contrasts future purity with former defilement: 'The house of Israel shall no more defile my holy name, neither they nor their kings, by their whoring and by the *corpses* of their kings at their death . . . Now let them put away their idolatry and the *corpses* of their kings far from me, and I will reside among them forever' (Ezek. 43:7, 9).[48] This defilement could have been caused in different ways, and may have involved ancestor worship, depending on how the Hebrew term *peḡer*, traditionally translated 'corpse', is interpreted.

(a) Corpse. Although elsewhere *peḡer* normally means 'a fresh corpse',[49] here it may refer to the long-decayed corpses of kings who were buried unacceptably close to the temple.[50] There is no other direct evidence for such

[47] Cf. Watson (1984: 433): they are similar, 'except in the specialised meaning of "to die" (of *'sp*)'.
[48] 'At their death' translates *bᵉmôṯām* (so some Hebrew MSS and early versions). The MT has *bāmôṯām*, 'their high places', suggesting a non-Yahwistic shrine in the temple (cf. Tuell 1992: 39). 'High places' and *peḡer* also occur together in Lev. 26:30.
[49] Many texts speak with horror of unburied, decaying bodies (*peḡer*). In narrative: Num. 14:29, 32–33; 1 Sam. 17:46; 2 Kgs. 19:35 // Is. 37:36; 2 Chr. 20:24–25; Jer. 41:9. In eschatology: Is. 14:19; 34:3; 66:24; Jer. 31:40; 33:5; Amos. 8:3; Nah. 3:3. Once of animals: Gen. 15:11.
[50] So RSV, JB, NEB (but not REB), NIV, JPS, NJB, NRSV; Eichrodt (1970: 553), Wevers (1982: 216), Spronk (1986: 150), Bloch-Smith (1992a: 116).

burial, though the historical books note that the early kings were buried 'in the city of David' (see Ch. 2.b.ii). As the palace was adjacent to the temple, the royal burial plot may have abutted the temple complex, and this was later thought to cause defilement. Alternatively, later kings may have been buried within the temple precincts. In both cases the defilement is caused by the corpses, and Ezekiel 43 gives no evidence for ancestor worship.

A Pentateuchal prediction of punishment for disobedience includes: 'I will destroy your high places and cut down your incense altars; I will heap your carcasses (*peḡer*) on the carcasses (*peḡer*) of your idols' (Lev. 26:30,[51] echoed in Ezek. 6:5). The concept of carcasses of idols is rather odd, so some scholars suggest that *peḡer* has a different meaning here, either 'stele' or 'offering', both of which imply ancestor worship. It is certainly possible for a word to have two distinct meanings (or, more accurately, for two terms with different meanings to be spelt identically), especially in Hebrew where there is little variety in word length or vowel pattern. But whether this is the case here is less clear.

(b) Stele. Two stelae found on the 'Dagan temple' site at Ugarit have very similar inscriptions concerning sacrifices. One begins the introduction with *pgr*, the other concludes it:

> A *skn* which A raised up for Dagan (as) a *pgr*: a sheep and a bull for the meal. (KTU 6.13)
>
> A *pgr* which B raised up for Dagan his lord: a sheep and a bull on the altar. (KTU 6.14)[52]

Some scholars take *pgr* to mean 'stele (or monument)', set up here to commemorate the regular sacrifice to Dagan, for several reasons.[53] (i) It occurs in parallel to *skn*, whose meaning of 'stele' now seems confirmed by further evidence.[54] (ii) The sentence structure on these stelae is similar to that of the Phoenician inscriptions of Ahiram (Ethbaal), Yehimilk and Elibaal, which all refer to an '*object* (ark, house, statue) which X made'.[55] Thus Hebrew *peḡer* could mean 'stele'. In this case Leviticus 26:30 predicts Israelite corpses scattered on the *stelae* set up to their idols (with word-play on the

[51] Similarly RSV, JB, NIV, JPS, NJB, NRSV, REB; Porter (1976: 215), Wenham (1979: 332), Harrison (1980: 233), Hartley (1992: 452). NEB's 'rotting logs' is paraphrastic.

[52] A and B are *ṯryl* and *'zn*. The verb 'raised up' could apply to stele or offering.

[53] Aistleitner (1963: 253, 219f.), Lipiński (1973: 200f.), Dijkstra–de Moor (1975: 175), de Tarragon (TO 2: 138), HAL (861).

[54] The Akkadian term *sikkanum* means 'stele' in Emar and Mari texts; see Durand (1985), Arnaud (1986: nos. 125:40, 369:35, 373:23). So Ugaritic *skn*, cf. van der Toorn (1991: 44), de Moor (1995: 9f., cf. *sikkûṯ*, Amos 5:26).

[55] So Neiman (1948).

two meanings of *peḡer*), and Ezekiel 43:7, 9 speaks of *stelae* set up to kings in the temple precincts.[56] This would probably indicate veneration of these kings, or ancestor worship.[57]

(c) **Offering.** However, most scholars now take *pgr* in these inscriptions as '(animal) offering', perhaps a development from 'animal corpse (offering)', for several reasons. (i) The Ugaritic inscriptions are not necessarily parallel, since the second is an abbreviated or variant form of the first. So *pgr* is not the same as *skn.* (ii) The Phoenician texts are irrelevant, since they are not concerned with sacrifice. (iii) In Ugaritic ritual texts, *pgr* apparently means 'offering', with *špš pgr* as 'offering to Shapash'[58] and *yrḫ pgrm* as 'month of sacrifice'. These concur with the 'month of sacrifice' in Akkadian (at Alalah) and in Canaanite-Phoenician (*yrḫ dbḥ*), and with the 'sacrifice to Shamash' in Phoenician (*zbḥšmš*), as evidence of a widespread mid-winter month of sacrifice to the sun god.[59] (iv) The Akkadian texts at Mari repeatedly refer to *pagra'um* '(animal) offering',[60] and occasionally *bēl pagrê* 'lord of the offering' (i.e. Dagan),[61] but never use the stem *pgr* for 'stele'. (Some see the Mari *pagra'um* as a funerary offering because of Dagan's underworld association, but evidence for this is sparse.)[62] This evidence in cognate languages of *pgr* meaning 'offering' suggests that Hebrew *peḡer* in Ezekiel 43 could mean 'offerings (for your dead kings)'. This would then be strong evidence of a royal ancestor cult in pre-exilic Israel.[63]

To conclude, Hebrew *peḡer* is unlikely to mean 'stele', given the lack of supporting evidence. It could mean 'offering', as in cognate languages. In this case, veneration of royal ancestors was one of the defilements of the pre-exilic cult which would have no place in the renewed temple of Ezekiel's vision. Whether this was a long-standing and well accepted practice, and

[56] So generally: Albright (1957: 247), de Vaux (1961: 287), Gordon (1965: 466), Noth (1965: 200). For Ezek. 43: Carley (1974: 286), Zimmerli (1983: 409), Allen (1990: 257), Tuell (1992: 39).

[57] Cf. the stele set up by the dutiful son in the Ugaritic Aqhat epic, KTU 1.17.i.27.

[58] KTU 1.39:12,17, 1.102:12. (KTU 1.102 is a partial copy of 1.39.) For Spronk (1986: 150f.), the *pgr* was a substitute for the offerer, but this lacks corroborative evidence.

[59] So Olivier (1972: 56f.). For Alalah, cf. von Soden (AHw: 809: *pagru(m)* B 4), Greenfield (1973: 48 n. 12).

[60] Linked with animal corpses: ARM XXI 62:1,4,43, 76:2; with money: ARM XXI 147:4, XXIII 561:15; general: ARM II 90:22, XIV 12: rev. 4, XVIII 38:5, XXVI/I 25:38, 233:51; possibly bimonthly: Durand (ARM XXVI/I: 157).

[61] ARM X 63:15. Dagan is also linked to the *pagra'um* rite in ARM II 90:22, XXVI/I 25:38, 233:51.

[62] Jean (ARM II: 165), Malamat (1956: 77; 1989: 97 n. 91), Moran (1969: 43 n. 1, like Akkadian *kispum*). In one text Dagan entrusts the underworld deities to Allatum, cf. Thureau-Dangin (1919: 148f.).

[63] So Ebach (1971), Dietrich–Loretz–Sanmartín (1973), Tropper (1989: 163f.), Malamat (1989: 103 n. 121).

therefore evidence for this cult within an inclusive Yahwism, or a recent innovation of the apostate decades of Manasseh, banned by Josiah but revived by his offspring, is of course another issue, neither addressed nor illuminated by Ezekiel 43. However, the traditional meaning 'corpses' is also still possible, in which case there is no allusion to ancestor worship. So the text may indicate a cult of the dead, but not its popularity or otherwise, and perhaps not at all.

b. The ancestor cult and the *marzēaḥ*

i. The ancient Near Eastern marzēaḥ

In every type of society people meet with friends to celebrate, commiserate, or simply relax together. Ancient societies had various associative groups outside the family, but within the tribe or state. 'These organizations, insofar as they are attested, find their bases in the whole range of human activities . . . The activities may be economic, professional, religious, or cultural, and the organizations devoted to burial, trade, worship, charitable goals, or having fun' (O'Connor 1986: 68). One common West Semitic term for such a social group and/or its gatherings is *mrzḥ*, often pronounced in its Hebrew form as *marzēaḥ*. It occurs in many texts, in different languages and from various eras, including twice in the Old Testament. A few scholars argue strongly that the *marzēaḥ* was primarily a meal associated with the dead, either at the time of burial or in later commemoration. Thus the two biblical references to a *marzēaḥ* would testify to a cult of the dead in Israel.

While evidence for the *marzēaḥ* comes from different countries, languages, texts and centuries, our knowledge of it still remains fragmentary. In each source the term *mrzḥ* occurs in only a few texts, and refers to an apparently well-known institution, so little if any detail is given. Sometimes it denotes a group of people, sometimes a place where they meet. Sometimes it has funerary associations, sometimes not. This evidence can be summarized as follows.[64]

Ebla, late third millennium. Three women receive dresses 'on the day of the banquet (*mar-za-u*) in the month of Man [May]'. This *mar-za-u* may be a *marzēaḥ*.[65]

[64] Cf. further: Porten (1968: 179–86), Bryan (1973), Greenfield (1974), Fabry (TWAT 5: 11–16), Lewis (1989: 80–94), Ackerman (1992: 275–8).

[65] MEE 2.46 rev. I:1–3. Cf. Pettinato (MEE 2: 309), Pope (1981: 179 n. 65), Dahood (1983: 54; 1987: 99), Archi (1988: 103). Dahood also equates *mar-za-u* with *maš-da-u*, 'drinking feast' (MEE 2.2 obv. IV:15–17; cf. Jer. 16:5, 8).

Ugarit, late second millennium. The *marzēaḥ* is mentioned in several Ugaritic lists and legal documents.[66] One document speaks of a named leader of a *marzēaḥ* which meets in his house, who undertakes in the presence of witnesses to pay fifty shekels if he evicts it.[67] Others mention 'son of the *marzēaḥ*' and 'the *marzēaḥ* of [the goddess] Anat', in the context of fields and vineyards.[68] The phrase 'men of the *marzēaḥ*' also occurs in Akkadian documents at Ugarit, in reference to houses and fields, granted with royal authority and legal witnesses.[69] In these texts the *marzēaḥ* was a significant social institution. It received royal sanction, involved substantial finance, required legal documentation, and existed even in minor villages. It had defined membership and leadership, and continued to successive generations. It owned or leased houses and vineyards, so presumably met together to drink, and could have a patron deity. However, these texts mention no generally cultic or specifically funerary aspect of the *marzēaḥ*. Perhaps the nearest modern equivalents are the Masonic Lodges, Rotary Clubs and Gentlemen's Clubs, with their various religious, social and economic elements.

The Ugaritic mythological texts also refer to the *marzēaḥ*. In one, El holds a drinking banquet in/with his *marzēaḥ*, attended by various other deities. Details of the proceedings are unclear, but eventually the inebriated El falls down in his excrement and urine.[70] Here the *marzēaḥ* is the setting for a drunken feast. In the Rephaim texts, the speaker (El or Dan'el) twice invites the *rpum* to 'my *mrz'*... my house ... my palace', with *mrz'* probably a variant spelling of *mrzḥ*.[71] This is the only text from Ugarit which apparently associates the *marzēaḥ* with the dead.

Transjordan, possibly sixth century. A short papyrus document in Moabite assigns 'the *marzēaḥ*, the millstones and the house' to a certain Sara, and orders Yisha to stay away.[72] Here the term '*marzēaḥ*' probably indicates an annexe to the house.

Elephantine, fifth century. An Aramaic ostracon written by Ito asks

[66] Cf. particularly Lewis (1989: 81–8; except for KTU 4.399), McLaughlin (1991).

[67] KTU 3.9, cf. Miller (1971: 37), Fenton (1977: 72), Friedman (1979–80: 197f.), Lewis (1989: 82), McLaughlin (1991: 269f.). Interpreted differently by Dahood (1971: 54), Halpern (1979–80: 131).

[68] KTU 4.399, 4.642.

[69] RS 14.16 (substantial sum, numerous witnesses), 15.88 (grant), 15.70 (transfer), 18.01 (shared *marzēaḥ*). Cf. Virolleaud (1951: 173–79); Nougayrol (1955: 88, 130; 1956: 230).

[70] KTU 1.114:15. The previous line is in parallel but unclear, cf. McLaughlin (1991: 271–3) for survey of views.

[71] KTU 1.21:1–3, 9–11; also 'my *mrz*', line 5. Cf. the various Akkadian spellings *mar-zi-i*, *mar-za-i*, *mar-zi-ḫi*.

[72] Bordreuil–Pardee (1990). They admit having access only to photographs, yet argue for the text's authenticity.

Haggai to collect 'the money for the *marzēaḥ*' from Ashian. The *marzēaḥ* is presumably a banquet, but no indication of its nature is given.[73]

Phoenician territories. A fourth-century bronze bowl inscription in Phoenician dedicates it to 'the *marzēaḥ* of [the sun-god] Shamash'. A late third-century text in Punic from the Phoenician colony at Marseilles refers to 'the *marzēaḥ* of the gods'. A first-century bilingual inscription from the colony at Piraeus describes the honouring of a leading citizen with crown and stele 'on the fourth day of the *marzēaḥ*'. Here the *marzēaḥ* was obviously an important annual festival, but its nature is unspecified.[74]

Nabatea, early centuries CE. One first-century inscription mentions 'the *marzēaḥ* of the god Obodas' (an earlier king). Many scholars see an ancestor cult here, though others suggest that Obodas was honoured as god more than ancestor.[75] Several fragmentary second-century inscriptions on trough-shaped stones, perhaps originally an altar for libations, may also mention '*marzēaḥ*'.[76]

Palmyra, early centuries CE. Four inscriptions mention *marzēaḥ*, three note the leader, and two refer to 'the *marzēaḥ* of the priests of Bel'.[77] The *marzēaḥ* was an important social institution with a leader, about a dozen members, and a banquet lasting several days. Several small 'tokens' (*tesserae*) give a name followed by 'leader of the *marzēaḥ*', and portray a priest or a deity. Some scholars suggest that these were tokens for banquets for the dead, but others note the complete absence of any funerary link.[78]

Jewish tradition. In the Talmud the Moabite sacrifices to Baal-Peor are called '*marzēaḥs*', and in Jewish tradition the site was called 'house of *marzēaḥ*'. A sixth-century CE mosaic map from Madeba (east of the Dead Sea) labels the presumed site of the Baal-Peor apostasy as 'Betomarsea'.[79] Both this map and Midrashic comment associate the *marzēaḥ* with the classical Mayumas festivals, celebrated in Mediterranean coastal cities 'with such licentiousness that Roman rulers felt constrained to ban them' (Pope 1972: 191f.). Like Psalm 106:28, this links the Moabite apostasy with the cult of the dead.

To conclude, this widespread textual evidence associates the *marzēaḥ* only sporadically with the dead. Its primary association is alcoholic

73 Cf. Lewis (1989: 90); against Porten (1968: 184), who presumes it is funerary.
74 Respectively Avigad–Greenfield (1982); KAI 69:16, cf. ANET (503); KAI 60:1.
75 Ancestor: Porten (1968: 181), Miller (1971: 46), Lewis (1989: 91); god: Bryan (1973), L'Heureux (1979: 209).
76 So Negev (1961; 1963) for no. 10; Naveh (1967: 188) for nos. 7b, 8, 9; Starcky (DBS 7, 1966: 919) for no. 9.
77 Altar (dated 29 CE), statue (118 CE), inscriptions (203, 243 CE), cf. Porten (1968: 182f.), O'Connor (1986: 72).
78 Cf. Seyrig (1940: 54), Stucky (1973: 178), Lewis (1989: 91).
79 Talmud: Sifre Num. 131. For map, cf. O'Callaghan (DBS 5: 676f.).

consumption and the varied settings or occasions for it. Funeral feasts were one such occasion, but only one of many, and therefore the term need not imply a funerary feast.[80]

ii. Clear Old Testament references

Amos 6:7. This fierce condemnation of the idle rich (vv. 4–7) concludes (lit.): 'and the *marzēaḥ* of the loungers will pass away', with *marzēaḥ* usually translated as 'revelry' (NRSV) or 'feasting' (NIV).[81] The preceding verses give elements of this *marzēaḥ*: sprawling on ivory beds, feasting on fattened animals, improvising music, drinking wine and using fine oils.[82] Amos castigates lavish self-indulgence and wilful ignorance of Israel's true condition. In the immediate context, this *marzēaḥ* concerns revelry, and has nothing at all to do with the dead.

However, the passage is closely followed by an enigmatic oracle of multiple death and burning (vv. 9–10, see Ch. 2.b.iii). For some scholars the passages are linked, and the *marzēaḥ* is a (somewhat boisterous) funerary cult.[83] But this is most unlikely. Verses 9–10 are quite distinct from vv. 4–7: they are separated both by the clear conclusion to the earlier oracle (v. 7, beginning 'therefore') and by an independent divine oath (v. 8); and they are different both in form (prose rather than poetry) and in content (obscure eventuality rather than vivid description). They are distinct oracles, linked only by the theme of imminent judgment, and the carousing *marzēaḥ* of the former is in no way linked to the death and burial of the latter.

Jeremiah 16:5–9. Here Yahweh instructs Jeremiah not to enter a 'house of *marzēaḥ*' (*bêṯ-marzēaḥ*, usually translated 'house of mourning') or lament the dead, since he has withheld his peace (v. 5). This was a sign of the coming catastrophe, when so many would die that they would lack proper mourning and burial (v. 6). This is the only biblical reference to a 'house of *marzēaḥ*', and clearly links it with mourning and the various funerary rites which presumably took place there, namely 'breaking (bread) for comfort' and 'drinking the cup of consolation' (v. 7).

Yahweh further instructs Jeremiah not to enter a 'house of drinking' (*bêṯ-mišteh*) to eat and drink (v. 8). This is usually seen as a second, different prohibition, explained as a sign that Yahweh would banish the joy of

[80] Similarly Barstad (1984: 139), Smith (1994: 140–44). Lewis (1989: 94) is ambiguous.
[81] Hebrew: *mirzaḥ* (construct). The initial *i* vowel is usually assumed to be a variant spelling.
[82] Cf. Greenfield (1974: 453), King (1988; 1989). The bowls used may imply sacrilege (cf. King 1988: 42).
[83] Greenfield (1974: 453), Hubbard (1989b: 193).

marriage (v. 9).[84] However, some scholars see v. 8 as a conclusion to the first prohibition, and v. 9 as a separate oracle with its own introductory formula.[85] In this case the '*marzēaḥ* house' is the same as the 'drinking house', and funerary ritual includes more general (and perhaps less sober) eating and drinking. This alternative subdivision follows the later Jewish paragraph division, and adequately explains vv. 5–8. But v. 9, whatever its origin, seems to be placed here to explain v. 8, making the traditional division more likely. The *marzēaḥ* house may have been the same as the drinking house, and mourning customs may have included drink (as in many cultures), but the two activities are probably presented separately here.

The 'house of *marzēaḥ*' is mentioned without explanation, so presumably was a well-known custom in seventh-century Judah. It could be an ordinary home in which a *marzēaḥ* (or mourning) took place, as English translations imply. Or it might possibly be a separate '*marzēaḥ* house', as known in surrounding cultures, despite the present lack of archaeological evidence for this in Judah.[86] Visiting a 'house of *marzēaḥ*' was obviously a social norm, and was only forbidden to the prophet (along with marriage and family, v. 2, and attending weddings, v. 8) as a sign of the times.

Some scholars argue from this reference and the wider cultural setting that the *marzēaḥ* was widely practised, and was primarily a meal to commemorate the dead (at burial and at regular intervals) and therefore involved some form of ancestor cult. However, this goes significantly beyond the evidence. (i) This is the only biblical reference to a 'house of *marzēaḥ*'. Its complete absence in other descriptions of mourning hardly suggests a widespread and developed custom of regular commemoration.[87] (ii) If other references were deleted by orthodox editors because of ancestor cult elements, it is most surprising that this reference was left without qualification, and that no disapproval or condemnation is expressed here or elsewhere (unlike necromancy). Thus it is most unlikely that this passage testifies to a widespread funerary phenomenon involving veneration of ancestors.

iii. Suggested Old Testament references

Ezekiel 8:7–12. In his visionary trip to Jerusalem, Ezekiel sees a series of abominations occurring in the temple: an image of jealousy, elders burning

[84] Standard traditional interpretation, cf. still Thompson (1980: 406), Carroll (1986: 340).
[85] E.g. Porten (1968: 181), Pope (1977a: 221), Dahood (1987: 99), Jones (1992: 231). For Lewis (1989: 89), the two prohibitions form an inclusio.
[86] So Ackerman implicitly (1989: 279).
[87] The later Sirach 7:2, 4 has a different term for 'house of mourning' (*bêṯ-'ēḇel*), which it contrasts with 'house of feasting' (*bêṯ-mišteh*) and 'house of mirth' (*bêṯ-śimḥāh*).

incense before murals of unclean animals, women weeping for Tammuz, and men worshipping the sun. Ackerman (1989; 1992: 67–79) argues that the second of these is a *marzēaḥ*, though not necessarily funerary, as follows. (i) Ezekiel sees not murals but a meal, since the first description in v. 10 should be shortened from 'all kinds of creeping things and loathsome (*šeqeṣ*) animals' to 'all abomination (*šeqeṣ*)' following the LXX,[88] and since *šeqeṣ* elsewhere indicates unclean food. (ii) Reference to the wall should be deleted, again following the LXX. (iii) The idols indicate a room reserved for this meal, located somewhere in the temple/palace complex. (iv) It was frequented by leading citizenry. This *marzēaḥ* was an abomination because the elders worshipped an alien god.

However, this is speculative. (i) While the Hebrew text of v. 10 is awkward, the LXX is not a reliable basis for emendation. It describes the loathsome thing(s) as 'foolish' (*mataia*) with no obvious Hebrew equivalent, and it fails to translate 'wall' in adjacent verses.[89] (ii) *šeqeṣ* can refer to unclean animals (Lev. 11 repeatedly; Is. 66:17), but the related verb *š-q-ṣ* (abominate) and noun *šāqûṣ* (abomination) have much wider meanings, and there is insufficient textual basis to restrict *šeqeṣ* to food. (iii) The passage has no other reference to food, tables or eating. Rather, even when emended, v. 10 implies that the *šeqeṣ*, like the idols, surround the idolaters (lit. 'around, around', *sāḇîḇ, sāḇîḇ*), and are therefore on the walls. (iv) The link between these murals and the god supposedly worshipped is unclear. Thus there is little to suggest a *marzēaḥ* here.

Psalm 23:5. Loretz (1993) sees allusion to an ancestor cult in the 'table' and 'cup' of Psalm 23:5. He suggests that the psalm originally recounted a *marzēaḥ* in the temple, to which God invites the king and his friends. After the exile the royal *marzēaḥ* disappeared and the ancestor cult became taboo, so the text was modernized and 'my friends' cleverly changed to 'my enemies' without alteration of the metre. But this is entirely speculative. (i) Apart from v. 5, the psalm contains no possible *marzēaḥ* allusions. (ii) Verses 1–4 are inappropriate to a *marzēaḥ*, and hardly specify the speaker as royal. (iii) There is no evidence that 'my friends' was changed to 'my enemies'. (iv) Verses 5–6 do not locate the meal in the temple. (v) Even if the meal did take place in the temple, this does not link it to an ancestor cult.

Psalm 133. Loretz also suggests that Psalm 133 was originally a 'drinking song' from the cultic *marzēaḥ* or secular tavern, with oil, wine, music and

[88] Similarly Wevers (1969: 69), Carley (1974: 55), Zimmerli (1979: 219), Greenberg (1983: 102), Brownlee (1986: 126f.), Allen (1994: 115); but not Eichrodt (1970: 106), Block (1997: 288).

[89] Ezek. 8:7–8 (x2), 10. It does translate it some 20 other times in the book. Ackerman (1989: 272 n. 12) suggests improbably that 'the Greek translator did not understand the word'.

song. This is preserved only in fragments, and about half the present text has been added later. But this is also completely speculative, and depends entirely on a hypothetical reconstruction. Even with this, there is little to suggest a drinking song and nothing to link it with the *marzēaḥ*.

c. The ancestor cult and other concepts

i. Teraphim

Teraphim (*tᵉrāp̄îm*) are mentioned in several narrative contexts. Before fleeing from her father, Rachel steals his teraphim (NRSV: 'household gods', Gen. 31:19, 34f.), and hides them in her saddlebags. Laban then comes looking for what he calls his 'gods' (*'ᵉlōhîm*, vv. 30, 32). During the anarchy of the judges period, the unsettled Danites steal 'an ephod, teraphim and an idol' (Judg. 18:14, 18, 20), leaving the rightful owner to complain that they have taken his 'gods' (*'ᵉlōhîm*, v. 24).[90] When David flees from Saul, his wife Michal puts the teraphim (NRSV: 'idol') in the bed with a wig and clothes to represent him (1 Sam. 19:13, 16). Much later Josiah destroyed the teraphim as part of his reform (2 Kgs. 23:24).

Teraphim also occur in a few prophetic texts. In their coming subjugation and exile, 'the Israelites [would] remain many days without king or prince, without sacrifice or pillar, without ephod or teraphim' (Hos. 3:4). In seeking guidance, the king of Babylon apparently 'use[s] divination; he shakes the arrows, he consults the teraphim, he inspects the liver' (Ezek. 21:21). And the post-exilic community is leaderless, while 'the teraphim utter nonsense, and the diviners see lies' (Zech. 10:2).

Thus teraphim feature sporadically throughout the Old Testament texts, from patriarchal to post-exilic times, and are associated with ephods, idols and divination. These figures or figurines obviously differed in size, since Laban's teraphim could fit into saddlebags while David's teraphim (one or several together) were near enough life-size. Teraphim have traditionally been interpreted as images of family or local gods, as distinct from the tribal or national gods.[91] Though not authorized within Yahwism and despite occasional prophetic objection, their use continued throughout Israel's history.

Now, however, a number of scholars have revived an older view that these

[90] For van der Toorn (1990), this 'god' (plural of excellence) refers only to the idol, not the teraphim.

[91] E.g. McCarter (ISBE 4: 793), Curtis (ABD 3: 379). Some suggest cultic masks, e.g. von Rad (1962: 216 n. 61), Carroll (1977: 57); but this does not fit Gen. 31 and 1 Sam. 19.

teraphim are ancestor figures, and are therefore evidence of Israelite ancestor worship.[92] In particular, van der Toorn argues: (i) Since *'ᵉlōhîm* in Hebrew can represent divinized ancestors (see Ch. 6.b), so too can *tᵉrāp̄îm.* (ii) Teraphim were consulted in divination and necromancy, and this fits dead ancestors better than local gods. (iii) Josiah destroyed the mediums/spirits and teraphim (2 Kgs. 23:24) in response to the ban on consulting mediums/spirits and the dead (Deut. 18:11), so teraphim represent the dead. (iv) In one passage (1 Sam. 19:13, 16) the LXX renders *tᵉrāp̄îm* as *kenotaphia* ('tomb', cf. English 'cenotaph'), which preserves the original association with the dead. (v) In Assyrian, Nuzi and Emar texts household gods and ancestors together receive veneration.

It is certainly possible that teraphim figures represented dead ancestors. However, van der Toorn's arguments are not decisive. (i) While *'ᵉlōhîm* can mean 'the dead', it normally means 'gods', so this is the more likely meaning of *tᵉrāp̄îm.* (ii) Consultation of *tᵉrāp̄îm* hardly proves that they were ancestors rather than gods. (iii) The supposed parallelism between Josiah's reform and Deuteronomy is deceptive, since both relevant texts include several other terms. (iv) The LXX also translates *tᵉrāp̄îm* with four other terms (though usually transliterates it), so the translation *kenotaphia*, used in only one context, is hardly decisive.[93] (v) All the non-Israelite texts van der Toorn cites mention the patron or household god(s) separately from the *eṭemmu* ('spirits of the dead'; Assyria, Nuzi) or *mētē* ('dead'; Emar). This suggests that they were seen as distinct, and undermines rather than supports this view.

Teraphim were household images of some sort, which may have represented local gods and/or ancestors. Quite possibly the term had different meanings at different times and places. While a few key texts might suggest their pervasiveness (e.g. 2 Kgs. 23:24; Hos. 3:4), their absence from the great bulk of prophetic literature suggests that they were not seen as a major threat to Yahwism.

ii. Pillars

Large commemorative stones were a well-known feature of the ancient Near East (cf. modern war memorials and grave headstones). As well as numerous stelae celebrating the successes of various kings, there were rows of stones set

[92] Wohlstein (1961: 37f.), Lust (1974: 138), Rouillard–Tropper (1987: 351–61), van der Toorn (1990, 1993).

[93] Also *eidola* (3x, Gen. 31), *gluptoi, deloi, apophthengomenoi* (1x each); and transliterated (7x).

up in temples or sanctuary areas just inside city gates, e.g. at Hazor, Ugarit and Byblos, which must have had some cultic function.[94]

Jacob erected pillars (or standing stones) on several occasions:[95] on leaving Bethel, when confronted by Laban, and again at Bethel (Gen. 28:18; 31:52; 35:14). He anointed those at Bethel with oil, and made a drink offering at the second. The Israelites set up twelve pillars when the law was given on Mt Sinai (Exod. 24:4). Absalom set up a pillar, since he had no children (2 Sam. 18:18). And an Isaianic vision of universal Yahwism envisages a 'pillar to Yahweh' on the Egyptian border (Is. 19:19). In other references, Israelites were to demolish pillars associated with Canaanite religious practices, and avoid erecting their own, though historical and prophetic texts show they habitually failed to do this.[96]

In various neighbouring cultures, such stones apparently commemorated both deities and the divinized dead. These groups merged into each other, without clear demarcation, so the stones testify to ancestor worship.[97] The best known example of ancestral veneration is in the Ugarit Aqhat epic, where the dutiful son sets up a stele or pillar (*skn*) for his 'divine ancestor' (*ilib*).[98] Hence de Moor (1995) argues that they fulfilled the same role in Israel. In particular, Hosea 3:4 links these pillars with royalty, sacrifice, ephod and teraphim, and implies a generally accepted royal ancestor cult.

Ancestor worship was certainly widespread in the ancient world, as noted above, and there is growing evidence that at least some stone pillars or stelae were set up to commemorate them.[99] The biblical evidence suggests that pillars were intrinsically neutral, and could have positive as well as negative religious value. However the repeated Pentateuchal prohibition and the historical record show that they were usually non-Yahwistic and deplored by the biblical writers. But the reason for this could be their association with Baal(s) and Asherah(s) as much as with ancestors. Further, Hosea 3:4 contains several distinct couplets, which may be independent of each other. In this case, pillars are associated with sacrifice, but not necessary with royalty or teraphim. They are condemned by Hosea (cf. 10:1f.), but their association with ancestor worship is uncertain.

[94] Cf. Mettinger (1995), de Moor (1995: 13). There is also Hittite and Emarite textual evidence.

[95] Usually *maṣṣēḇāh*; variant *maṣṣeḇeṯ* in Gen. 35:14; 1 Sam. 18:18. For Jacob's pillars, cf. Pagolu (1998).

[96] E.g. Exod. 23:24; 34:13; 1 Kgs. 14:23; 2 Kgs. 3:2 (pillar of Baal); 23:14; Hos. 3:4; Mic. 5:13.

[97] De Moor (1995) cites evidence from Ebla, possibly Mari, Hittite texts, Egypt, Emar and Ugarit.

[98] KTU 1.17.i.27,45; see Boda (1993), Husser (1995) and many others. On *ilib*, see Ch. 7.d.iii.

[99] However, the Emar stelae apparently commemorate the high gods, as de Moor notes (1995: 14).

iii. Kinship names

In the ancient Near East, many personal names were 'theophoric', i.e. they made reference to a god worshipped by the name's bearer. (For instance, Hebrew names beginning or ending with *el* refer to God, while those beginning with *ho* or *jeho* or ending with *iah* refer to Yahweh.) Many other personal names contain kinship terms, particularly 'father' (*'āḇ*), 'brother' (*'āḥ*), 'clan/people' (*'amm*), e.g. Absalom, Ahab, Amminadab.[100] Traditionally, these have been taken as references to living relatives. Noth (1928) suggested that these names were theophoric, and that 'father', 'brother' etc. referred to the anonymous tribal god. Others have argued subsequently that the kinship terms could refer to major, named deities, and that in personal devotion people referred to their gods in kinship terms.[101]

Van der Toorn (1996b) now suggests that these kinship terms refer instead to deceased and deified family members, and are further evidence of ancestor worship. The names reveal that the cult was only addressed to male ancestors, and that these were worshipped as gods and regarded as benevolent.[102] While such names could be simply a vestigial relic of ancient religion, they corroborate other evidence for an ancestor cult in Israel throughout the Iron Age (i.e. much of the first millennium BCE).

This is a stronger argument than many of the others examined in this chapter, and may indeed indicate that the veneration of ancestors was widespread. However, several factors still encourage caution. (i) Only a minority of Hebrew names have kinship terms. (ii) Other explanations for these terms are still feasible. (iii) Even if they do formally refer to divinized ancestors, this need not indicate ongoing veneration. After all, many modern parents still give their children names like Christine and Christopher, even if they have little or no active faith in Christ.

iv. Family life

The fifth commandment enjoins respect for parents. For Brichto (1973), this applies particularly to performing rites for them after their death, as

[100] For Mari Amorite names, Huffmon (1965) also notes: paternal uncle (*dād*), maternal uncle (*ḫāl*), people (*lim*).

[101] E.g. Albertz (1994: 97f.), following Stamm (1939) on Akkadian kinship names. Stamm also argued that some were 'substitute names'.

[102] E.g for *'āḇ* and *'āḥ*, cf. Abida ('knows'), Abiezer/Ahiezer ('helps'), Abishua ('rescues'), Ahisamach ('supports'), Abidan ('judges [kindly]'), Abiasaph ('adds [children]'), possibly Abinadab/Ahinadab ('gives freely').

illustrated elsewhere. The rebellious son would fail to do this, so should be executed as a warning to others (Deut. 21:18–21). David's grief over Absalom's death was due to losing 'another assurance of his comfortable immortality' (43; re 2 Sam. 18:33). Various wisdom texts suggest that a son disrespectful of his parents in their afterlife would himself be denied repose there (Job 18:5f.; 14–17; Prov. 20:20; 24:20; 30:11). However, none of this is obvious, and it is asserted by Brichto more than argued. By contrast, it is inherently unlikely that a son upon whom parents depended for their afterlife would be executed, as Brichto admits, which robs this particular law of its supposed cautionary value.

In the winsome story of Ruth, Boaz becomes the destitute women's 'kinsman-redeemer' (*gō'ēl*), marrying Ruth and redeeming Elimelech's property, which the unnamed 'nearer kinsman' was unwilling to do. But at the end of the book, it is Ruth's first child Obed who is declared to be Naomi's *gō'ēl* (Ruth 4:14f.).[103] For Brichto, this is because Obed would guarantee her afterlife by performing the appropriate rites. However, Brichto offers no supporting argument, and the use of *gō'ēl* also for the nearer kinsman and for Boaz (and its use elsewhere in the Old Testament) hardly indicates the descendant who secures one's afterlife.

In one of his rare moments of remorse, Saul asked David to swear not to cut off his descendants and destroy his name (1 Sam. 24:22). For Malamat (1989: 104), 'Saul was begging David to leave his family line intact, so that there would be someone to commemorate his name'. This is possible, but is certainly not explicit.

Later Absalom erected a pillar saying, 'I have no son to keep my name in remembrance' (2 Sam. 18:18). Some argue that this is indirect evidence of the ancestor cult, which was the normal setting for remembering the dead.[104] Normally the son erected a pillar for his father, as in the Aqhat epic, but Absalom had to do this for himself. However, such a cult involved at least 'invoking' the name of the deceased, and probably also nourishing and feasting with them. It is hard to see how erecting a pillar could substitute for this. If the cult was as important as is claimed, Absalom could have adopted a son or commissioned a priest to conduct it, as happened frequently in Egypt. To erect a monument might suggest on the contrary that ongoing veneration was not thought necessary.

[103] Morris (Cundall–Morris: 1968: 313); Leggett (1974: 257f.), Sasson (1979: 163f.), Zenger (1986: 96f.), Hubbard (1988: 271), Gow (1992: 110), Bush (1996: 253). A few see the *gō'ēl* as Boaz, e.g. Gray (1986: 402).

[104] Lewis (1989: 119), Bloch-Smith (1992a: 113), van der Toorn (1996a: 208). Cf. a similar phrase in the Hadad inscription, KAI no. 214 (see Ch. 6.a.v).

v. Sacrifice and cult

Elkanah went to offer the 'yearly sacrifice' at Shiloh (1 Sam. 1:21; 2:19). When Saul was looking for his father's donkeys, he met Samuel at a clan sacrifice at Ramah, and witnessed various religious activities the next day (1 Sam. 9:12; 10:2–6). David's excuse for missing Saul's new moon banquet was to attend the family's 'yearly sacrifice' at Bethlehem (1 Sam. 20:5f.). Some scholars interpret these various sacrifices as occasions of ancestor worship, either monthly like the Akkadian *kispum* festival, or annually at any new moon.[105] Malamat suggests that 'yearly sacrifice' (lit. 'sacrifice of days') really means 'sacrifice of yore', i.e. for past generations. Bloch-Smith also notes the LXX[B] addition (to 1 Sam. 1:21) that Elkanah paid a tithe, and interprets this as food for the dead. This view is unlikely regarding Elkanah, since the central shrine is an unlikely venue for venerating and feeding one's ancestors, and the textual basis for his tithe is slender.[106] The proposal is possible for Samuel's sacrifice at Ramah, though its association with the new moon and subsequently with ancestor worship remains tenuous.[107] It is also possible for David's family, and this would testify to regular commemoration of the ancestors. However, there is no direct evidence for it in the text.

The high places (*bāmôṯ*, better translated as 'cultic places') were primarily burial sites and centres for the cult of the dead, according to Albright.[108] But other scholars have discounted his archaeological, etymological and textual evidence and emphatically rejected any such connection, and this view is not now accepted.[109]

Some prophetic texts criticize 'new moon and sabbath' cultic assemblies. For Hallo (1992: 386), this was because assemblies on new moon and full moon (his suggested original meaning of 'sabbath') involved ancestor worship. But this is unlikely. (i) Such condemnation occurs only twice, within criticism of the complete cultic system as practised (Is. 1:13f.) and within prophecy of its removal (Hos. 2:13). Further, prophets mention new moon and sabbath elsewhere without comment (Amos 8:5) and envisage their future celebration (Is. 66:23; Ezek. 45:17; 46:3), while the post-exilic community both recorded

[105] E.g. Malamat (1968: 173 n. 29; 1989: 105), Bloch-Smith (1992a: 122–4), van der Toorn (1996a: 211–18).

[106] His sacrifice was clearly annual, cf. distance travelled, new coat at each visit, 'year by year' (lit. 'from days to days', 1:3, 2:19, used elsewhere of annual commemoration: Exod. 13:10; Judg. 11:40).

[107] Despite van der Toorn (1996a: 215), not all the following activity is necessarily ritual, e.g. reference to Rachel's tomb may be geographical.

[108] Albright (1957; cf. 1968: 177f.), followed by Dahood (1970: 74).

[109] Vaughan (1974), Barrick (1975); followed by: Haran (1978: 22), Dotan (1981: 80 n. 22), Fowler (1982: 205f.), Lewis (1989: 140f.), etc. Albright's four texts all require emendation and/or reading *bāmôṯ* as *b^eḇāmôṯ*.

earlier custom approvingly (1 Chr. 23:31; 2 Chr. 2:3; 8:13; 31:3) and revived it enthusiastically (Ezra 3:5; Neh. 10:33). New moon and Sabbath were also occasions for consulting prophets (2 Kgs. 4:23).[110] None of this suggests disapproval of new moon and sabbath cultic practices *per se.* (ii) While Hebrew *šabbāṯ* may well be related semantically to Akkadian *šab/pattu*, this does not imply that it originally meant 'full moon festival'.[111] Both terms could refer to a rest day (like the Hebrew verb *š-b-t*), which was determined differently in Mesopotamia and Israel. Further, as Hallo himself noted earlier (1977: 3f.), the Mesopotamian cultic calendar was mainly lunar, while the Israelite one was only minimally so.

vi. Burial and bones

After Jezebel's death, Jehu orders: 'See to that accursed woman and bury her' (2 Kgs. 9:34). Lewis (1989: 121) suggests that 'see to' (*p-q-d*) indicates 'fulfilling the customary funerary rites including the essential services of the cult of the dead', since the same stem occurs in Akkadian of the 'caretaker' (*pāqidu*) in the ancestor cult. The further phrase 'for she is a king's daughter' implies ritual appropriate to Jezebel's royal (Canaanite) lineage. However, this is just as unlikely as suggesting that the verb 'undertake' in English always implies funerary provision! The stem *p-q-d* has a wide range of meaning in both Hebrew and Akkadian and, as Lewis admits, there is no other West Semitic occurrence of it for a funerary cult.[112] Thus 'see to' here means simply 'attend to'. Anyway, even an elaborate royal funerary ritual (which is unlikely here) hardly indicates a cult of the dead.

When marauding Moabites interrupt a funeral and the corpse is abandoned in Elisha's grave, the dead man returns to life (2 Kgs. 13:20f.). For Lewis (1989: 123), this story is 'more at home in the arena of death cult rituals'. But even if bones were attributed curative powers in Mesopotamia, the posited link with death cults is most unclear.

d. Summary

The Israelites may have been tempted to venerate their dead as other ancient peoples did. But the arguments examined here that many Old Testament

[110] These are all the relevant texts. It is possible that a custom of consulting the dead was later recorded by Yahwists as consulting the prophets, but this remains hypothetical.
[111] Cf. Hasel ('Sabbath', ABD 5: 849–56), Stolz (THAT 2: 863), HAL, etc., against Fishbane (1985: 149f.).
[112] On *p-q-d* cf. THAT (2: 466–86); on *pāqidu* cf. AHw (824–6).

texts contain traces of this as an acceptable Israelite practice are mostly unconvincing.

One narrative records the apostasy of the wilderness generation with the Moabites (Num. 25:2), and a psalm describes this as their eating 'sacrifices of the dead' (Ps. 106:28). But neither text elaborates further on the nature of the cult, and both describe Yahweh's punishment of Israel for their participation in it. This is the only biblical reference to such sacrifices.

Other posited references to such a cult are mostly unlikely. The interpretation of Saul's meal at Endor as part of a death cult (1 Sam. 28:20–25) involves unsupported assumptions concerning the original story, and unconvincing arguments for substantial Deuteronomistic rewriting of it. Neither the 'holy ones' of Psalm 16:3 nor the 'calling by names' of Psalm 49:11 are likely to indicate venerated ancestors. The people criticized in Isaiah 28 and 57 may have practised death cults, but only the latter text is likely to allude to it. In Ezekiel 43 the '*peḡer* of kings' could indicate either the corpses of dead kings or offerings made to them, and here the latter meaning would imply a royal ancestor cult. The arguments for veiled references to the ancestor cult in various other texts are unconvincing.

Amos (6:7) describes a *marzēaḥ* as an extravagant feast of the pampered rich, which will soon be swept aside in judgment, but gives no hint of a funerary aspect to it. By contrast, the restriction on Jeremiah's mourning (16:5–9) does link *marzēaḥ* with the dead. These texts accord with extra-biblical evidence for the *marzēaḥ* as a widespread term for social gatherings usually linked with drinking and feasting, but only occasionally with the dead. The term itself is too general to indicate a cult of the dead. Other suggested Old Testament references to a *marzēaḥ* (funerary or otherwise) are unconvincing.

The interpretation of *tᵉrāp̄îm* as ancestor images is possible but not essential, and in any case they are of minimal importance in the prophetic critique of religious malpractice. Pillars feature more frequently, but are also of unclear usage. Kinship names may refer to ancestors and imply their veneration, but these names are a minority in Israel, and such reference may be vestigial. There is insufficient evidence to link respect for parents, levirate marriage, annual sacrifice or other cultic practice with the cult of the dead.

Certainly some associations with death and the dead were condemned by the prophets, and some practice of giving food to or for the dead was deemed inappropriate for the tithe (Deut. 26:14). But the complete lack of wider censure of such grave offerings suggests that they were not inimical to Yahwism, and therefore that they did not involve veneration of or communion with the dead. Further, the fact that there is so little censure of death cults, by writers who have no qualms against lambasting illegitimate practices, strongly suggests that that they were not a major Israelite preoccupation. Thus the Hebrew Bible does not substantiate the scholarly view that veneration of the ancestors was widespread in Israel and that evidence of it was later suppressed. On the contrary, it suggests that, while it may have occurred, it was of marginal importance. For all their faults, Israelites seem to have been more concerned with the living than the dead.

Part D
THE AFTERLIFE

Chapter 9
Communion Beyond Death

Was Sheol the only fate ever envisaged in Israel? If it is predominantly associated with the wicked in the Hebrew Bible (see Ch. 3.b), what about those who protested their innocence and saw themselves as godly? What did they think would happen to them?

In fact, and perhaps strangely so to modern readers, there is no clearly articulated alternative to Sheol, no other destiny whose location is named, no other fate whose situation is described, however briefly. So the majority of Israelites may well have envisaged no alternative. And yet there seem to be some exceptions, a few texts which hint at or hope for some form of continued communion with God beyond death. Or do they? These texts will be examined below.

a. Enoch and Elijah

In notable contrast to its general tenor, the Old Testament reports that two individuals escaped death. Embedded in the pre-flood genealogy is the laconic statement: 'Enoch walked with God; then he was no more, for God took him' (Gen. 5:24). This clearly diverges from the regular genealogical pattern, where every other paragraph ends with the phrase 'and he died', except of course the final one regarding Noah. Enoch's fate was clearly acknowledged as different, though no further detail is added to this tantalizingly brief statement. Scholarly interest tends to focus on ancient parallels,[1]

[1] E.g. Adapa, Utuabzu (Mesopotamia); Aeneas, Heracles (Greece); cf. Wenham (1987: 128), Hess (ABD 2:508). Day (1996: 237) notes parallels between Enoch and the Mesopotamian Enmerduranki, but not regarding ascension.

and the date of composition or redaction. But what often escapes notice is that Enoch's fate does not occasion later theological comment or devotional fervour in Israel's religious literature. Nowhere in the Hebrew Bible is there an explanation of its significance, or a prayer for a similar destiny.[2] Enoch's mysterious experience remained singular in Israel's story and unassimilated in her theology. From the second century BCE onwards, Enoch was the inspiration of much Jewish literature, with at least three Books of Enoch, all composite. But none of this elaboration of an Enochic tradition occurs in the Old Testament itself.

The other character to escape death was the prophet Elijah. As he walked with Elisha (who refused to be deterred), a fiery chariot and horses separated them and 'Elijah ascended in a whirlwind into heaven' (2 Kgs. 2:11). While the passage focuses on prophetic succession, Elijah's permanent departure is implied by the 'double inheritance' of his spirit, and is confirmed by the inability of the disbelieving prophets to find his body. But here again Elijah's fate remains a singular event, which does not become a model for Elisha or other prophets, and which receives almost no theological reflection. The only later acknowledgment of it in the Old Testament occurs in the penultimate verse of the prophetic corpus, with its concluding prediction that God will send 'the prophet Elijah before the great and terrible day of Yahweh comes' (Mal. 4:5).

It is hard to know what ancient Israelites thought to be the fate of these two men, if indeed they knew these traditions and reflected on them. The silence on Enoch implies ignorance of or unconcern with his non-death, and the sole reference to Elijah suggests that it was only much later, well into the post-exilic period, that he was seen as a potential heavenly messenger. Even the great Moses was said to have died, despite ignorance of his burial location.[3] Nowhere is the fate of Enoch and Elijah presented as a paradigm for the righteous: not in narrative of impending death, nor in prophetic aspiration, nor in wisdom musing, nor – most strikingly – in the numerous psalms which grapple with the inequity and reality of death. Thus the experience of Enoch and Elijah remained entirely marginal for Israel's religious writers.

b. Psalms

Many psalms imply that this life is the only forum for relationship with Yahweh, and a few state this explicitly, e.g. 'Turn your gaze away from me,

[2] On the suggested echo of the verb *l-q-ḥ* in Pss. 49:15; 73:24, see section b. below.

[3] There are some parallels between Elijah and Moses, suggesting variously Elijah's death (Schmitt 1973: 109–11) or Moses' ascension (noted by Josephus, *Antiquities* 4.8.48 §326, cf. Matt. 17:3, etc.); see Day (1996: 239) for references.

that I may smile again, before I depart and am no more' (39:13); 'My enemies wonder in malice when I will die, and my name perish' (41:5). As already noted, in Sheol one can no longer praise Yahweh (6:5; 115:17), which explains why many psalmists plead to be saved from their enemies. The rupture in relationship caused by death even effects Yahweh, as one writer boldly asserts: 'The death of the devout costs Yahweh dear' (116:15, JB).[4] However, within this general framework, a few psalms seem to glimpse a different perspective.

i. Psalm 16

This psalmist begins with a plea for protection,[5] an avowal of allegiance to Yahweh and a repudiation of alternative cults (vv. 1–4).[6] He continues with a strong declaration of present assurance: he has a delightful inheritance (vv. 5–6) and his relationship with God is continuous and secure (vv. 7–9). He concludes by expressing his unshakeable hope directly to Yahweh (vv. 10–11):

> [10]For you do not give me up to Sheol,
> or let your faithful one see the Pit.
> [11]You show me the path of life.
> In your presence there is fullness of joy;
> in your right hand are pleasures forevermore.

For most scholars, the psalmist implies in v. 10 that he is in immediate danger of death (cf. v. 1). But he is confident of imminent deliverance, and looks forward to further joyful life on earth in relationship to Yahweh, enriched by this very deliverance. The avoidance of Sheol is certainly real, but temporary and provisional, and the psalmist will eventually go there like everyone else.

However, the psalm invites a different interpretation. The danger alluded to in v. 1 may well have made him fear untimely death. But if he felt instinctively that Sheol was not a fitting fate for Yahweh's 'faithful one', then he could be affirming an equally instinctive confidence in deliverance from it, and a personal if undefined hope for some form of continued communion with Yahweh beyond death. After all, as he says in v. 11, he is on the path of life, not death, sated with divine joy and endless pleasure. The form of this

[4] For this meaning, see also Kidner (1975: 410f.).
[5] Hence this is an Individual Lament for Gunkel (1926: 51). For others it is a Psalm of Confidence (possibly a derivative *Gattung*), e.g. Anderson (1972a: 140), Craigie (1983: 155). On Ps. 16 see further Johnston (1995).
[6] For the translation of vv. 2–4, see Ch. 8.a.iii.

continued communion with God remains tantalizingly vague; no spatial location is indicated, no name (contrasting with the name Sheol) is mentioned, no fellow beneficiaries are acknowledged – in fact no details are given at all. Only Yahweh's presence and blessing are clear. Caught in the tension between an underworld associated predominantly with the ungodly (see Ch. 3.b) and the lack of a clear alternative for the faithful, the psalmist affirms that some alternative is eminently appropriate.

It is perhaps this very tension which constitutes the psalm's forward-looking, prophetic perspective. By affirming something which partly fitted received views on human destiny but also partly transcended them, the psalm sets up a tension which awaits resolution. This resolution is sketched at the margins of the Old Testament, in resurrection and post-mortem distinction between righteous and wicked (Is. 26:19; Dan. 12:2; see Ch. 10.a.iv). And it is fully realized in Christian theology when Christ's resurrection from the grave opens up eternal life in God's presence as the true alternative to Sheol. In this perspective the psalmist points forward to the one who would resolve this tension (cf. Acts 2:27; 13:35).

ii. Psalm 49

The psalm opens in typical wisdom style: its address in vv. 1–2 is universal, to all peoples of the world, and explicitly inclusive, to low and high,[7] rich and poor. This address is followed by a profusion of wisdom terms in vv. 3–4: wisdom, meditation, understanding, proverb and riddle (*ḥîḏāh*). It is a riddle which the psalmist sets and then solves, to his own satisfaction at least.[8]

This riddle is then presented in vv. 5–6: it is the age-old problem of an apparently pious person in trouble and suffering oppression. Two responses are given to this. The first, and longer by far, is enunciated in vv. 7–9: no human can pay a ransom to avoid the underworld and live for ever. The Hebrew text of vv. 7a and 8a reads: 'no man can ever ransom a brother . . . the ransom of their life is costly'. The concept of ransom obviously comes from the legal world, and the Hebrew text might reflect the scenario where a wealthy individual pays to redeem an impecunious relative or, somewhat differently, where a victim's family allows a guilty party to pay a ransom instead of incurring the death penalty.[9] However, the text is usually emended to '*surely* no man can ransom *himself* . . . the ransom of *his* life is

[7] Lit. 'sons of *'āḏām* and sons of *'îš*'; contrast Bratsiotis (TDOT 1: 224).
[8] Perdue (1974) locates the riddle primarily in vv. 12 and 20, but this focuses on verbal parallels in an apparently refrain-like comment, at the expense of the bulk of the psalm.
[9] Cf. Exod. 21.30: the owner of a lethally goring ox is spared death 'if a ransom is laid on him'.

costly'.[10] While the two readings have different emphases, both stress that human wealth is powerless to prolong life and to ransom people from the pit, i.e. the underworld.

This first response is further developed in vv. 10–14. It opens with the observation that all die, whether foolish like the unwelcome oppressors, or wise like (presumably) the psalmist, and remain permanently in their graves, v. 10.[11] However, while acknowledging that death comes to all, the psalmist seems to have in view his wealthy opponents, since he adds that they leave to others their wealth, the object of their former trust (v. 6),[12] and he apparently contrasts their future lowly homes with their former landed estates, v. 11. Death makes a mockery of self-importance, v. 12. While the following verses, 13–14, are the most textually difficult of the psalm,[13] their overall sense is largely undisputed: the destiny of the foolishly self-confident is Sheol. Here the psalmist clearly concentrates on the ungodly, and stresses that their fate is the underworld.

The psalmist's second response to his riddle is presented succinctly in v. 15. God will ransom him from Sheol and will 'take' or 'receive' him. What humans are powerless to do, God will do for his faithful follower: God will provide for him an alternative destiny to the underworld. Here, more explicitly than anywhere else in the Hebrew Bible, the consignment of the ungodly to Sheol is contrasted with the ransom of the godly from Sheol.[14]

Some scholars interpret v. 15 as immediate rescue from imminent death without reference to permanent fate. For instance, Barth argues that the psalmists generally rejoiced in immediate deliverance from the power of Sheol but did not deny eventual consignment to the underworld.[15] However, this fails to do justice to Psalm 49 generally and to v. 15 specifically. Here the problem is not so much temporary oppression as an unjust order, and the final phrase of v. 15 implies more than preservation in

[10] Changing *'āḥ*, 'brother', to *'aḵ*, 'surely' (cf. v. 15), and reading *p-d-h*, 'ransom', as reflexive (niphal); so e.g. Anderson (1972), Craigie (1983), Kraus (1988). The idea that one person might want to ransom another from death is often discounted as unintelligible. By contrast, Goulder (1982) retains the MT.

[11] So LXX, Syriac, Vulgate, reading *qiḇrām* for MT's *qirbām*.

[12] BHS and others relocate v. 10b to follow v. 11b, but this does not affect the interpretation.

[13] In v. 14b Kraus abandons translation. The MT indicates vindication for the godly 'in the morning', the time of God's salvation (cf. Barth TDOT 2: 226–8), but many scholars emend the whole phrase, cf. NRSV etc.

[14] Ransom from Sheol also occurs in Hos. 13:14. But its usefulness as an interpretative key to Ps. 49 is limited by its national application, pervasive metaphorical language and versional variants.

[15] Barth (1947: 158–61; 1997: 125–7). Similarly Pleins (1996), though his posited chiastic structure actually suggests the contrary, since the corresponding v. 9 describes a permanent destiny.

life. While the same verb 'receive/take' occurs in Psalm 18:16 of immediate rescue, there physical rescue from immediate danger is explicit in the parallel lines. The context of Psalm 49 is quite different.

Craigie reads v. 15 not as the fervent faith of the psalmist but as the foolish hope of the self-confident, who think that their privilege in life will also give them privilege in death. But this is unlikely.[16] There is no textual hint that this is a false statement, and it would give little comfort to the righteous to know that they would share the same fate as their foes.

The final verses of the psalm, vv. 16–20, return to the theme that the wealthy cannot take their riches with them on death. Rather, they rejoin their ancestors, never again to see the light, v. 19.[17] Out of context, this verse might seem to imply that everyone, regardless of piety, goes to Sheol. But in the context here the psalmist probably refers to his enemies, whose predecessors he presumes to have been equally ungodly. Thus v. 19 fits the interpretation of differentiated destinies.[18]

iii. Psalm 73

Psalm 73 is another wisdom psalm which ponders the prosperity of the wicked. The psalmist is openly envious of them (vv. 1–14), but he then enters 'the sanctuary', where he perceives the ruinous end of these wicked people (vv. 15–20). Castigating himself for bestial stupidity, he asserts that continued communion with God forms the essence of his very existence. The sanctuary experience of v. 17, whatever its exact nature, is widely acknowledged as the psalm's turning-point.[19] And the ringing affirmation of v. 24, however imprecise, is the psalm's high-point:

> You guide me with your counsel,
> and afterward you will receive me with honour.

Unfortunately, the second half of this climactic line is ambiguous. In the Hebrew it consists of three words, meaning respectively 'after', 'honour' and 'you will receive me'. The first term, *'aḥar*, is normally taken adverbially as 'afterward', in an absolute sense, linking with the first half of the line to give: 'after you have guided me with your counsel'. Alternatively it could be a preposition before the following term, *kāḇôḏ*, giving 'after honour', but this is less likely, since the psalm does not otherwise suggest an initial honour

16 Cf. Alexander (1987: 9).
17 For the similar phrases 'gathered to his people' and 'slept with his fathers', see Ch. 1.a.vi.
18 For further views on Ps. 49 and discussion of its date, see Johnston (1997).
19 This is generally understood as a temple experience, and the impulse for reorientation described variously as visionary, prophetic, cultic, or even mystic.

which is then superseded. The second term, *kāḇôḏ*, has often been translated 'glory' (as in RSV and other traditional versions).[20] But this common Hebrew term means 'honour' or 'dignity', and is never elsewhere a synonym for the afterlife, unlike 'glory' in Christian theology. Unless it is read as *'aḥar kāḇôḏ*, with the difficulty just mentioned, the term *kāḇôḏ* stands on its own, with a preposition assumed (a common feature of Hebrew poetry). Thus it is usually translated as '*with* honour'. The third term, the verb *l-q-ḥ* ('take' or 'receive'), occurs elsewhere of Enoch (see above), and is often thought to be a conscious echo of Genesis 5:24. But *l-q-ḥ* is as common in Hebrew as is the verb 'to take' in English, with just as wide a semantic field, so it is hard to prove that the use here necessarily echoes Genesis 5:24.

Scholars are divided over whether the psalmist envisages 'honour' in the present life or in some unspecified future existence.[21] Both views can be argued from the immediate context. In support of a this-worldly interpretation: there is no reference to the psalmist's death; he concludes his poem by celebrating his nearness to God and declaring all God's works, presumably to a human audience; and this fits with the general view of the psalms and the Hebrew Scriptures. In support of post-mortem hope: there is no obvious reference point for an adverbial *'aḥar* other than 'after death'; v. 25 denies that the psalmist has any other concern 'in heaven [or] upon earth'; and v. 26 contrasts his failing 'flesh and heart' with God as his portion 'forever' (*'ôlām*).[22]

Martin-Achard (1960: 165) has helpfully proposed an alternative approach:

> It is possible, but not certain, that [the psalmist] envisages being received, before or after his death, into the presence of God; but for him the heart of the matter remains, not this unprecedented occurrence, but the actual and, as it were, definitive presence of Yahweh in his daily life.
>
> Wherever the Living God is accepted, death is effaced, its power is blunted, and it is rendered irrelevant; in the psalm this truth is understood rather than expressed; the psalmist has no intention of proclaiming a universal abstract law, he is confessing a living personal experience.

This refocuses the issue from the time-frame of the psalmist's hope to its nature. Nevertheless, the stronger the Israelite writer's sense of divine

[20] Cf. recently Magonet (1994: 166): 'in glory'.

[21] In the mid-twentieth century Martin-Achard (1960: 163; original in 1956) estimated that the majority opted for hope beyond death. This is less likely now.

[22] Similarly Weiser (1962: 514), Crenshaw (1984: 108: 'divine presence now and forever'), Kraus (1989: 91); and more tentatively Anderson (1972: 535), Westermann (1989:141f.), Tate (1990: 236f.).

presence in this life, the more likely the development of a concept of hope that transcending death.[23]

Psalm 73 (like Psalm 49) is often described as a post-exilic or late psalm, for various reasons. Its content indicates a wisdom psalm, wrestling with the prosperous wicked and hinting at continued communion with God.[24] And its language has several Aramaisms, abstract plurals and other features more common in late biblical literature. Though not conclusive, these arguments are certainly suggestive.[25] Neither form-critical nor cult-functional study add significantly to our understanding of the psalm, since wisdom psalms are categorized more by content and style than by structure, and contain little or no cultic reference. However, redactional study may add insights. Brueggemann (1991) and others have argued that Psalm 73 is strategically placed at the psalter's midpoint, between obedience (Ps. 1) and praise (Ps. 150). This implies that its positioning was among the final elements of the book's composition. If so, then the redactors perhaps chose it for their mid-point as the supreme example of hope available to them, which may point to its being understood by them (even if not by an earlier author) as pointing beyond death.[26]

iv. Other psalms

Psalm 17:15b asserts: 'when I awake, I shall be satisfied, beholding your likeness'.[27] The Hebrew verb 'awake' (*q-y-ṣ*) refers primarily to waking from ordinary sleep, but sometimes to waking from the sleep of death, notably in the two resurrection texts (see Ch. 10.a.iv).[28] Hence traditional Christian interpretation has taken Psalm 17:15b as an expectation of seeing God after death.[29] However, though he is surrounded by threatening enemies, the psalmist makes no reference to death. On the other hand, he does mention being tested at night (v. 3), so this is more likely the

[23] In his frequently cited essay, Buber (1983: 116) is equivocal: while this is not immortality, 'the "pure in heart" have in the end a direct experience of the Being of God'. Similarly Terrien (1978: 316–20).

[24] However, Murphy (1963) and others argue that it is a thanksgiving song.

[25] Some wisdom writings could be earlier, as perhaps some of Proverbs and Ps. 49. Schmitt (1973) presents the linguistic evidence, seeing it as indicative but not conclusive.

[26] Mitchell (1997) argues similarly that various psalms have been reinterpreted in an eschatological redaction.

[27] Lit.: 'I will be satisfied in awaking (with) your likeness.' Of the ancient versions, Targum, Aquila and Symmachus translate literally, while LXX, Syriac and Theodotion have 'appear' instead of 'awake'. None mentions death.

[28] E.g. sleep: Pss. 3:5; 73:20; death: 2 Kgs. 4:31; Job 14:12; Jer. 51:39, 51.

[29] Cf. Dahood (1966), Kidner (1973: 90; this 'abundantly answers the prayer of verse 7').

prayer of someone too worried to sleep,[30] rather than of someone looking beyond death.

Psalm 139:18b also refers to awaking, if translated 'When I awake, I am still with you' (NIV, RSV). This has also been taken as awaking from the sleep of death.[31] However, the psalm has no reference to sleep (the darkness of vv. 11–12 is simply another arena where one cannot hide from Yahweh), let alone to death, so 'awaking' has no immediate context and seems incongruous. Instead, some translations and scholars derive the opening verb (*hᵉqîṣōṯî*) from the noun 'end' (*qēṣ*), giving: 'I come to the end' (NRSV).[32] This would be a suitable response to the vastness of God's thoughts in the previous verse.

The later, more developed interpretations of these verses are not necessarily wrong. Craigie's comment on Psalm 17 is apposite:

> The psalm, in its current usage, may provide both hope for the immediate crisis, as for the psalmist of old, but beyond that a deeper hope for ultimate deliverance from a more dangerous and insidious enemy, a hope that reaches beyond the sleep of death itself. (1983: 165)

However, this 'deeper hope' is unlikely to have been the original focus of these psalms.

c. Proverbs

Proverbs 15:24; 23:14. These sayings suggest that Sheol is not for the wise and disciplined, though whether they imply an alternative is unclear:

> For the wise the path of life leads upward,
> in order to avoid Sheol below (15:24; cf. 13:14);
>
> If you beat them with a rod,
> you will save their lives from Sheol (23:14).

In 15:24 the path of life, a common wisdom motif, leads upward. For some scholars, 'upward' simply refers to the present life, balancing 'Sheol below'.[33] This is certainly possible, though interestingly in 5:5–6 'the path of life' contrasts with 'down to Sheol', without the addition of 'up'. This might

[30] He may have been in the temple (Anderson 1972), undergoing an ordeal, though this lacks evidence.
[31] So the later Jewish interpretations of Targum and Symmachus.
[32] Also Allen (1983: 253), who describes the afterlife interpretation as 'both contextually inappropriate . . . and probably theologically anachronistic.'
[33] E.g. Murphy (1998: 114). Robert (1940: 167) sees a strong parallel with Deut. 28:13f.

suggest that 'upward' in 15:24 is more significant, though the discreteness of individual proverbs makes such comparison uncertain. The LXX of 15:24 avoids spatial terms,[34] and McKane argues from this that the Hebrew terms 'upward' and 'below' truly represent afterlife bliss and punishment, but are a later (Hebrew) reinterpretation of an originally this-worldly proverb (preserved in the LXX). Again this is possible, but the different LXX reading may be due to a different Hebrew text or to the translator's adaptation,[35] and need not imply that the canonical Hebrew text is a later version.

23:14 is the strongest of several references to the fate of the undisciplined son, though 19:18 talks similarly of 'his death'.[36] This picks up the life–death antithesis which pervades chapters 1 – 9 and occurs elsewhere (e.g. 15:24). However, the alternative to death and Sheol is implicitly the present life, and these proverbs neither suggest nor imply a blissful afterlife.

Proverbs 12:28 is another potential after-life text:

> In the path of righteousness there is life,
> in walking its path there is no death.

But the second half has several difficulties: 'walking its path' is literally 'way of path', with unnecessary repetition; the expression 'no death' (*'al-māweṯ*) is both unique and awkward, since the negative *'al* normally precedes verbs, not nouns;[37] the ancient versions render the line differently, and they (plus many Hebrew manuscripts) end with '*to* death' (*'el-māweṯ*); as it stands 12:28 does not have antithetical parallelism, unlike the proverbs immediately before and after it,[38] whereas the other 'life-death' proverbs are antithetical. Hence many scholars reasonably propose 'but the way of abomination/folly leads to death',[39] and some suggest that the extant text reflects a later, more developed eschatology. This removes the immediate reference to immortality, though in the first half the general reference to 'life' remains.

Proverbs 14:32, as it stands in Hebrew, implies that death may be welcome:

> The wicked is overthrown through his evil-doing, but the righteous finds refuge in his death. (lit.)

[34] 'The thoughts of an intelligent man are ways of life . . .'

[35] Puech (1985) discusses the relationship of LXX Vorlage and proto-MT, though is uncertain of priority.

[36] Thomas (1955: 288) compares English idioms like 'I will thrash you to death', but these are exaggerations.

[37] Elsewhere *'al* before a noun is an interjection ('No!'), or assumes a jussive verb ('let there be' or similar), e.g. 1 Sam. 1:21; Ps. 83:1; Is. 62:6. Cf. GK (§152g), Driver (1965: 112); against Dahood (1960).

[38] A rare exception in the two immediate chapters is 12:14.

[39] Replacing *nᵉtîḇāh* with *tôʿēḇāh*, e.g. JB, Puech (1985), Murphy (1998: 88), or with *pᵉtî ḇāʾ*, e.g. Tournay (1962), McKane (1970: 451). Cf. also Lucas (1997: 282).

However, the LXX and Syriac versions read the final word as 'in his integrity'. This assumes the interchange of two Hebrew letters (in an unpointed text), and gives a more appropriate reading. The idea of finding refuge in death would be anomalous in the Old Testament. Thus the Hebrew text either represents a later eschatology (cf. Wisdom 4:7–17), or conveys a simple copyist's mistake retained because it fitted later eschatology.

To conclude, there are very few proverbs which suggest a positive life after death. These few suggestions are conceptually unclear and textually uncertain, and they may reflect the later emendation or re-reading of misunderstood texts. So at best they testify to an afterlife belief which was becoming more widespread during the period of the text's transmission and translation.

d. Job 19

In popular Christian devotion, bolstered by Handel's magnificent aria 'I know that my Redeemer liveth', Job 19:25–27 is often thought to assert Job's faith that after death he would see his redeemer Messiah on earth. This of course reads a fuller New Testament understanding back into the Old Testament. But does Job even envisage a post-mortem experience? Or does he affirm that he will be vindicated in this life? Unfortunately the relevant text is difficult to interpret because of its unusual theme, poetic form, and awkward Hebrew. The early versions also found the text difficult, and give a variety of renderings.[40] It merits close consideration.

First, we must note the general context of chapter 19. Job has met unprecedented calamity. Although he refuses to curse God, he curses his birth and longs for the peace of stillbirth and death. He rails against the advice of his friends to confess sin, repeatedly protesting his innocence and his desire to present his case directly to God. Thus he laments the lack of court (*mišpāṭ*, 9:32) and mediator/umpire (*môḵîaḥ*, 9:33), which would give him the chance to speak. His ultimate wish is to present his case (*mišpāṭ*), in confidence of vindication (*z-d-q*, 13:18). While acknowledging that death is irreversible (14:12), he nevertheless sees a temporary sojourn in Sheol as a possible solution to his dilemma: 'Oh that you would hide me in Sheol . . . until your wrath is past, that you would appoint me a set time and remember me!' (14:13). He refuses to relinquish hope of a heavenly go-between: 'Even now . . . my witness is in heaven, and he who vouches for me

[40] See commentaries for full discussion of text and versions. Scholars are divided on many issues, notably whether Job envisages vindication in this life (Hartley, Clines) or after death (Gordis, Rowley, Andersen, Habel).

[NIV: my advocate] is on high' (16:19).[41] And having lost all his own possessions, he wants someone else to provide the legal pledge or surety (forfeited by the party which loses the case, 17:3). Throughout these chapters, Job's primary interest is to clear his name before God. Whether this takes place in this life or not is of secondary importance.

Job's friends also mention heavenly assistants. In the very first friend's speech Eliphaz asks dismissively: 'To which of the holy ones will you turn?' (5:1). And after Job and his friends have finished, Elihu paints an inviting picture of a mediating angel delivering the upright from the pit with a ransom (33:23–28). Their emphases are different to Job's, but they reinforce the concept of intercession taking place in the unseen world.

After chapter 19 there are fewer relevant texts, perhaps partly because Job has already made his case, partly because the third cycle of speeches seems to have suffered in transmission. But Job still continues the legal argument: he wants to find God, lay out his case, be acquitted forever by his judge, be tested and come out like gold (23:3, 4, 7, 10). And his defiant concluding speech is a summary of his defence: 'let me be weighed in a just balance . . . Oh, that I had one to hear me!' (31:6, 35). There is no suggestion from either Job or his respondents that in chapter 19 he had reached a new insight which altered the course of subsequent discussion. Nor does the 'knowledge' which Job asserts there feature in the closing chapters of the book, with the speeches by Yahweh, the responses by Job and the denouement of chapter 42.

Secondly, we must examine the immediate context. The relevant verses come near the end of Job's second speech in the second cycle, in response to Bildad.[42] Job starts by lambasting his friends as tormentors (19:1–4), but turns quickly to rehearse the heart of his dilemma, that God has 'closed his net' around him, stripping him of all dignity so that he is repulsive to his wife, abhorred by his friends and despised by his children and servants (vv. 5–22). At this point 'Oh that . . .' introduces another momentous wish.[43] Job longs for a permanent record of his 'words', engraved on a rock forever (vv. 23–24).[44] Finally, after his key declaration (vv. 25–27), Job turns to warn his friends that in persecuting him they risk punishment themselves (vv. 28–29).

These verses preceding and following Job's declaration could fit either main interpretation of it. The permanent record Job desires could be his

[41] Some emend the next phrase to 'my intercessor is my friend' (v. 20; e.g. NIV).

[42] This is the middle speech in the middle cycle, which might seem structurally important. However, in the speech cycles there is no apparent chiasm or other literary feature which would highlight this speech.

[43] Cf. 6:8; (11:5); 13:5; 14:13; 23:3; 31:35.

[44] In the ancient world, inscribed stones were the standard form of permanent record.

general protest of innocence or his specific declaration of vv. 25–27. Both possible records would fit the expectation of earthly vindication. Both would also fit a post-mortem vision of God, though the latter would clearly underline its startling nature. Job wants the record to outlive him. This could imply that he expects vindication only after death and, since this would not be witnessed by his contemporaries, he needs an earthly record of his innocence.[45] Equally it could mean that he wants a permanent record dated to the time of his protest, so that when eventually vindicated in his lifetime he can prove that he maintained his innocence throughout. The final warning to friends of their judgment is couched in this-worldly terms ('punishment of the sword') though this could be metaphoric of future judgment.

Thirdly the relevant verses must be examined in detail. NRSV translates:

> 25For I know that my Redeemer lives,
> and that at the last he will stand upon the earth;
> 26and after my skin has been thus destroyed,
> then in my flesh I shall see God,
> 27whom I shall see on my side,
> and my eyes shall behold, and not another.
> My heart faints within me!

This is accompanied by five footnotes, four with alternative translations and one noting that v. 26 is unclear! Even the translation given suggests ambiguities and difficulties. What is meant by 'at the last', or 'thus', or 'on my side', or 'another'? And why is v. 27 longer? A literal translation would be something like this:[46]

> 25And I, I know my *gō'ēl* living, and last upon dust he will stand.
> 26And after my skin [masc.] this [fem.] is flayed, and from my flesh I will see God.
> 27Which I, I will see to/for me, and my eyes will see and not a stranger, my kidneys are consumed in my bosom.

Verse 25 begins with Job mentioning his *gō'ēl* (translated variously as redeemer, vindicator or champion).[47] Elsewhere this is the next-of-kin who redeems a family member from slavery, unmortgages property, marries a

45 So Habel (1985: 303). He also sees the plural 'words' as indicating a legal case, as in 13:17; 32:14. However, he also cites 32:11, which is hardly legal and shows that the plural in itself does not necessarily indicate a legal context.

46 While the term 'literal' can mask important issues of meaning and translation, it is used here as a shorthand to help unpack some of the textual problems.

47 'Redeemer' is potentially misleading, because of the danger of importing later Christian connotations.

childless widow and avenges a death.[48] No legislative or narrative text describes the *go'el* acting in a human court, but legal imagery in other contexts suggests that his role was to plead a cause on behalf of his accused next-of-kin.[49] The *gō'ēl* whom Job affirms is presumably the same as the witness/advocate of 16:19, a heavenly being who will plead his cause to God. Several scholars argue that the *gō'ēl* is God himself, since: God is Israel's redeemer elsewhere in Israelite tradition; Job is monotheistic; and the following verses stress his seeing God.[50] However, none of these points is decisive: national traditions are not relevant in Job; the book assumes the existence of heavenly beings (1:6); and the role of Job's *gō'ēl* is precisely to break the impasse and enable Job to see God. In the context of Job's previous longings, it is much more likely that he sees the *gō'ēl* as an independent heavenly being.[51] Job declares that his heavenly *gō'ēl* is alive,[52] i.e. he truly exists, a clear advance on what earlier had been merely a hope.

Job then asserts that (lit.) 'at the end/last upon dust he will stand/rise up'. While each word is debatable, NRSV gives the likely, consensus interpretation. 'At the end/last', in the context of Job, means after the present calamity, without specifying exactly when.[53] 'Dust' here must mean the earth, as usually translated and as frequently elsewhere.[54] While 'dust' is an occasional term for the underworld,[55] and while the book of Job explores the frontiers of Israelite theodicy, it still reflects standard cosmology, and the concept of God appearing in Sheol is most unlikely. 'Stand' (*q-w-m*) occurs in legal contexts for taking one's place in court,[56] which is the obvious connotation here. It can mean 'rise from the earth (in resurrection)', but it is hardly appropriate here for a spokesperson in heaven to rise up from below ground.

[48] Cf. Lev. 25:25, 48; Num. 35:19; Deut. 19:6, 12; Josh. 20:5; Ruth 3:12; 4:1; 2 Sam. 14:11; Jer. 32:7, etc.

[49] E.g. Yahweh should 'plead a cause (*r-y-b rîḇāh*)' in Ps. 119:154; Prov. 23:11; Jer. 50:34; Lam. 3:58.

[50] E.g. Gordis (1965: 264), Rowley (1976: 138), Andersen (1976: 194), Hartley (1988: 292), Atkinson (1991: 94).

[51] So cogently Habel (1985: 305–307). Clines' view that it is Job's personified cry or witness is unconvincing.

[52] *ḥay*, 'living', is a very common term. Here it could possibly be the rare homonym *ḥay*, 'kinsman' (1 Sam. 18:18 only), reinforcing *gō'ēl* but removing the note of existence (though this is implicit anyway).

[53] *'aḥ^a^rôn*, 'last', is normally an adjective or noun. Hence some translate 'he the last' (e.g. NRSV note, Rowley), i.e. the *gō'ēl* is the final friend. Elsewhere the longer form *'aḥ^a^rônāh* occasionally functions as an adverb, always with a preposition (*b*, *l*, *k*). However at Qumran the shorter *'aḥ^a^rôn* occurs 5 times adverbially and without a preposition (cf. DCH). So given poetry's more flexible grammar, *'aḥ^a^rôn* here could be adverbial, meaning 'lastly'.

[54] Cf. the identical Job 41:33 ('upon the earth'); also 8:19; 28:2 (both 'out of the earth'); 30:6 ('in the ground'). Hartley (294) identifies the dust as Job's ash heap (2:8).

[55] E.g. Job 17:16, in parallel to Sheol.

[56] E.g. Deut. 19:15f.; Job 30:28; 31:14; Pss. 27:12; 35:11; Is. 54:17; Mic. 6:1.

Further, the concept of human resurrection is not only totally absent from Job, it would undermine the book's final outcome.

Verses 26–27 are much more difficult, with issues of translation and meaning inseparable. To start with what is clearer, Job affirms repeatedly that he himself will see God: in 26b (stated), 27a (restated with an emphatic 'I'), and 27b (further amplified by 'my eyes'). This dominant theme suggests that the two ambiguous terms 'to/for me' and 'not a stranger' are further ways of underlining the message: I will see God 'for myself', I and 'not someone else'. The anticipation is so vivid that it has a strong physical effect. This final phrase lengthens the verse, but makes good sense and is appropriate here.[57]

When and how will this occur? 'After my skin is destroyed' could refer to post-mortem experience, perhaps echoing the wish to be hidden in Sheol (14:13).[58] But then 'from my flesh' would have to mean 'beyond my fleshly existence', which is possible if somewhat strained, and 'my eyes' would imply physical sight in a future state similar to the present one. Further, the earlier wish to be hidden (temporarily and hypothetically) in Sheol gave no indication of a changed status. It was simply a vain hope of some relief from divine oppression. In the present context, 'destroyed skin' could easily indicate Job's current 'loathsome sores' (cf. 3:7), resulting in repulsive breath (19:17, if taken literally) and in his becoming 'skin and bones' (19:20). The destruction may not have been total, but it was certainly real. So 'from his flesh', whatever is still left, Job will see God. It is worth adding that at the conclusion of the book Job asserts that he has seen God with his own eyes (42:5). In the end he has not needed an intermediary – God has appeared to him directly. And Job's ultimate vindication by God takes place in this life, not in the next.

So in beleaguered yet defiant faith, Job asserts that he will have a defender who will stand on earth and support him, and that after all his suffering he will get the one thing that matters most, an opportunity to present his case to God. This interpretation makes most sense in the book of Job, even if it removes both the resurrectional and the messianic elements.[59] It is just possible that he envisages some form of vindication after death, though without any indication of physical change or continued communion with God.

[57] While most verses in Job have two stichs (usually 'half-lines'), there are enough irregular verses to suggest that at least some of these come from the final author/editor, and not from textual corruption.
[58] Many take 'this' as adverbial, 'in this way' (e.g. NRSV, Clines). There is no Hebrew basis for AV's 'worms', which is clearly interpretative.
[59] For the opposing arguments, see Hartley (1988: 294ff., this life) and Andersen (1976: 194, after death).

Christians may wish to re-use Job's words and invest them with Christian meaning, as in Handel's *Messiah*, but they should realize that this was hardly Job's understanding.

e. Heavenly books

There are a few intriguing Old Testament references to heavenly books. These occur with different wording in a variety of contexts, and may well imply different underlying ideas. Some scholars trace the Israelite concept of heavenly books back to the Babylonian 'tablets of destiny' or to Persian civilian registers,[60] but at most these show religious and administrative parallels, and they may have no relevance at all.

One book apparently records the name of Yahweh's people. After the golden calf idolatry Moses prays, 'blot me out of the book that you have written'. But Yahweh replies, 'Whoever has sinned against me I will blot out of my book' (Exod. 32:32f.). A psalmist denounces his enemies: 'Let them be blotted out of the book of the living; let them not be enrolled among the righteous' (Ps. 69:28).[61] In a prophetic vision, the restored community 'will be holy, everyone who has been recorded for life in Jerusalem' (Is. 4:3). The last prophetic book offers an alternative to the prevalent religious cynicism: 'a book of remembrance was written before him of those who revered Yahweh and thought on his name' (Mal. 3:16). And Daniel's final apocalyptic vision concludes: 'But at that time your people shall be delivered, everyone who is found written in the book' (Dan. 12:1).[62]

Other books seem to record events, as in several psalms: 'Here I am; in the scroll of the book it is written of me' (Ps. 40:7, in the context of obedience); 'are [my tears] not in your record?' (Ps. 56:8); 'In your book were written all the days that were formed for me, when none of them as yet existed' (Ps. 139:16). Daniel's terrifying vision featuring the Ancient of Days includes heavenly assizes: 'The court sat in judgment and the books were opened' (Dan. 7:10). And the events detailed in his lengthy final vision are recorded in a 'book of truth' (Dan. 10:21).[63]

The book of life also appears in extra-biblical Jewish literature. In 1 Enoch 'the names [of wrongdoers] will be erased from the books of the holy ones' (108:3). Jubilees notes that names are recorded in or erased from 'the

[60] Cf. Ezra 2:62; Neh. 7:5, 64; 12:22 (also Jer. 22:30; Ezek. 13:9); Clements (1980: 54), Wildberger (1991: 169f.).

[61] The only OT occurrence of the phrase 'book of the living' or 'book of life', *sēp̄er ḥayyîm.*

[62] Cf. also 1 Sam. 25:29 ('the bundle of the living'); Pss. 87:6; 109:13.

[63] Cf. also Neh. 13:14; Ps. 51:1.

heavenly tablets', 'the book of life', and the variously described book of destruction (30:20, 22; 36:10). Books of deeds also recur. 1 Enoch states 'the books of the living were opened' (47:3, conflating the different books of Daniel), and 'all the sealed books [were] opened' (90:20). Several texts note sins recorded in books (Jubilees 39:6; 2 Baruch 24:1; 2 Esdras 6:20). And the Rabbinic Pirqe Aboth warns: 'Know what is above you . . . all your deeds written in a book' (2:1).[64]

The New Testament further appropriates these themes, with names of believers 'written in heaven' (Luke 10:20) or 'in the book of life' (Phil. 4:3) and 'the firstborn . . . enrolled in heaven' (Heb. 12:23). In Revelation the book of life ('of the Lamb that was slaughtered', 13:8) appears repeatedly, with names 'not blotted out' (3:5), 'written' (21:27) or 'not written' (13:8; 17:8; 20:15), and the book of life is finally opened along with the books of deeds (20:12). This last text clearly shows two sets of heavenly records, one with names and the other with deeds.[65]

Inter-testamental and New Testament writers understood 'the book of life' as referring to post-mortem fate, and this interpretation has often been read back into the Old Testament. This approach takes the few Old Testament references as glimpses of future hope, like the verses in Psalms 16, 49 and 73 discussed above. However, there is no other indication that Moses envisaged a personal afterlife, and the texts can all be interpreted otherwise. Since life in its full sense meant life lived under Yahweh's blessing (see Ch. 1.b.i), to be blotted out of the book of life probably meant to receive a premature death.[66] Thus Yahweh's reply to Moses continues: 'when the day comes for punishment, I will punish [the people] for their sin' (Exod. 32:34). The psalmist who wants his enemies' names erased also wants them ruined, banished and condemned (Ps. 69:22–27). The record for life in Jerusalem (Is. 4:3) applies to the current life on earth, not a later one. Yahweh says of those recorded in Malachi's book of remembrance: 'They shall be mine . . . on the day when I act, and I will spare them' (Mal. 3:17). This suggests preservation during judgment rather than life after death. Even the book of names in Daniel's final vision (12:1), though mentioned just before resurrection, concerns 'your people [who] shall be delivered', i.e. who will survive the unprecedented 'anguish' and presumably remain alive on earth. Similarly, the books of events or deeds mentioned in several psalms need imply no more than Yahweh's careful concern and provision for his people.

[64] Quotations from Sparks (1984), Allen (1983: 262).
[65] For later Christian references, see E. W. Smith (ISBE 1: 534).
[66] Cf. Wildberger (1991: 169).

In Daniel's earlier vision, the opening of books in the heavenly court (Dan. 7:10) leads to the destruction of the fourth beast and the subjugation of the other three, followed by the coming of 'one like a human being' who receives an eternal kingdom along with his holy ones. In the perspective of the book of Daniel, this is divine judgment on current ungodly oppression, a vital prerequisite to the 'heavenly human' and his earthly people receiving God's kingdom. The opening of the heavenly books leads here to judgment on the four beasts, not on all humanity. This is a slightly different function to that ascribed it in later eschatology, though the development is natural. The New Testament recasts the various elements of Daniel's visions to describe the parousia of Christ and the resurrection and final judgment of all humanity. The books opened in Daniel's heavenly court are one significant element in this, and the strongest Old Testament link between heavenly books and the afterlife.

f. Summary

Two Old Testament characters apparently escaped death, in different ways. Enoch simply 'was no more, for God took him', and Elijah 'ascended in a whirlwind into heaven'. However, neither becomes a paradigm for the righteous in any form; their fate is never invoked by psalmists or others as they face the trauma of impending and often unwelcome death. These two may have escaped death, but this had no obvious relevance to Israelite beliefs or aspirations.

Several proverbs juxtapose wise and foolish, life and death, upward and below, and may therefore imply differentiated post-mortem fates. But proverbs are by definition pithy sayings, without immediate context and easily misunderstood. The difficulties in the Hebrew text and the emendations in the ancient versions suggest that the earliest readers puzzled over their meaning, and make it hazardous to conclude that they are necessarily eschatological. As in Job 19, these textual difficulties may reflect a growing belief in resurrection during the finalization and early transmission of the Hebrew text and its translation into Greek, and the desire of some scribes and translators to emend their text accordingly.

Job 19, while it is now popularly linked with resurrection, is a notoriously difficult text, as the notes in some translations and the discussion in all commentaries indicate. In the book as a whole, Job repeatedly longs for a spokesperson to present his case to God, and his friends confirm a general belief in spiritual intermediaries. In 19:25–27 Job's faith that he has such an advocate and that he will see God could apply to this life or the next. But the references to skin, flesh and eyes suggest the former, as does the book's eventual denouement in which his wish is fulfilled, as he confesses 'now my eye sees you' (42:5). Further, a belief in resurrection would undermine the book's conclusion, with its vindication of Job in his present life. So Job is vindicated and sees God, but before rather than after death.

Several isolated texts refer to heavenly books in which the names of God's people are recorded. Later writers understood these books as recording names for the afterlife, and this theme may be implicit in some of the Old Testament texts. At the same time, most if not all the references can be read in an immediate time perspective: to be recorded in Yahweh's book was to be numbered among his people, as part of his chosen community. Even the book in Daniel's final vision records those who will be delivered from times of anguish on earth. So while the concept lends itself to a post-mortem eschatology, it need not originally have included it.

Finally, and more positively, a few psalms seem to affirm a continued communion with God after death. Psalm 16 builds on the delight of present experience, and projects it into the future. Psalm 49 wrestles with the issue of unjust reward in this life and asserts that it will be reversed at death: the rich and foolish will be consigned to Sheol; while the oppressed psalmist will be ransomed from it. And Psalm 73 combines the themes of continued communion with God and rectification of present injustice to affirm that 'afterward' God will receive him. These psalms give no elaboration of how, when or where this communion will take place. They simply affirm it in faith. For most Israelites, hope remained firmly anchored in the present life. But a few seem to glimpse some form of continued communion with God beyond it.

Chapter 10
RESURRECTION FROM DEATH

As we noted at the outset, death is a complex subject which elicits a wide variety of responses. And the Hebrew Bible reflects Israel's religious views over many centuries, in many different social and political contexts. Given these two major impulses towards diversity, it is hardly surprising that a belief in resurrection should emerge in some places. What is surprising is rather the opposite, that it emerges so little!

What are the relevant Hebrew texts, and what exactly do they mean? This chapter examines those texts which have been taken to imply a belief in individual resurrection from the dead, sets Israel's beliefs in their wider cultural context, and traces the underlying theology which led to the emergence of belief in resurrection.

a. Resurrection in Israelite literature

i. Divine potential (Deut. 32; 1 Sam. 2)

Two isolated Old Testament texts affirm Yahweh's power to raise the dead:

> See now that I, even I, am he;
> there is no god beside me.
> I kill and I make alive;
> I wound and I heal;
> and no one can deliver from my hand (Deut. 32:39);

Yahweh kills and brings to life;
he brings down to Sheol and raises up (1 Sam. 2:6).

The first comes towards the end of the 'song of Moses', a hymn of praise to Yahweh, where his power to renew life is cited as yet further evidence of his incomparability. The second occurs in the 'song of Hannah', following the birth of Samuel, where Yahweh's power to raise from Sheol is another sign of his reversing the polarities of this life (mighty–feeble, full–hungry, barren–mother of many, poor–rich, etc.).[1] Both statements are categorical. They flow from an absolute confidence in Israel's god as all-powerful, and are the straightforward theological development of this faith.

Yet there are also several intriguing elements in both texts. First, neither comes as the climax of their song, the final clinching argument or the grand finale. While the first comes near the end of the song of Moses, the song actually concludes with Yahweh taking vengeance on his enemies; this is further evidence of his incomparability, the motive for a final invitation to praise (Deut. 32:40–43). And the second comes in the middle of Hannah's song, between God's making the barren fertile and the poor rich. So in both songs the reversal of death is subordinate to the main theme, national vindication and personal blessing respectively. (The national theme in the former may in any case imply national rather than personal return to life.) Secondly, God's power to raise to life is asserted without fanfare. The authors seem to slip their momentous assertion in almost casually, without drawing attention to it or implying that it is anything extraordinary. It is simply a corollary of Yahweh's greatness that he can 'make alive'. The point needs no other introduction. Thirdly, the assertion is made without further comment, explanation or development. Who the recipients of this power are, in what circumstances, and with what consequences, is all left unsaid. The details are unimportant; perhaps they have never even been considered. And fourthly, there are no instances recorded in the immediate contexts of Yahweh actually raising individuals to life. So in their historiographical contexts, the songs proclaim something beyond personal Israelite experience. All this suggests that Yahweh's power to 'raise up from Sheol' is a potentiality which is affirmed rather than an actuality which has been witnessed. As supreme god, Yahweh obviously can 'make alive', even though there is no recorded occurrence of this happening in the Mosaic or early monarchic tradition. This is who Yahweh is, not what he has done.

Of course, it could be argued that the verses are due to Deuteronomists of the late monarchy, writing when the stories of Elijah's and Elisha's miracles (see below) were well known. But this in turn raises its own problems. For

[1] Bailey (1979: 40) therefore interprets v. 6 as simply a metaphor for reversal in this life.

one thing, the relevant resuscitations clearly occurred through physical contact with the prophets themselves (or their bones), yet the songs contain no hint of prophetic mediation. For another, the Elijah-Elisha material sits rather loose in the books of Kings, with only occasional integration into the national history, minimal 'Deuteronomistic' editing and little incorporation of its motifs elsewhere in Israel's literature.[2] It would be odd for this one theme to be lifted from the middle prophetic section of Kings and reproduced in two isolated texts elsewhere, when the prophetic chapters are themselves more of an interlude in Israelite historiography. Further, the 'Yahweh makes alive' motif shows no obvious dependence on the ninth-century prophetic traditions, whatever the date of writing of the two songs.[3] This supports the conclusion above, that these songs extrapolate from the writers' understanding of Yahweh to affirm his power over life and death, rather than testify to known instances of return from the dead.

ii. Occasional resuscitation (Elijah and Elisha)

The Old Testament records three instances where the newly dead return to life, all through contact with the prophets Elijah and Elisha. In his temporary exile from Israel, Elijah stays with a widow in the Sidonian town of Zarephath, and ensures her survival through the famine with unfailing grain and oil (1 Kgs. 17). But her son dies, and she blames the Israelite prophet for exposing her sin. He carries the boy's body to his roof room, prays and stretches out three times on it.[4] The child's life returns, and Elijah takes him down to his relieved and now believing mother. The story is recorded simply and without elaboration, though the text makes clear that mother (v. 18), prophet (v. 20) and narrator (v. 22) all thought the boy was indeed dead.[5]

A similar incident occurs with Elisha, when tragedy strikes his Shunamite hostess (2 Kgs. 4). Her precious only child, given as a reward for her hospitality, dies (v. 20), and the anguished mother blames the absent prophet. Elisha first sends his servant Gehezi to place his staff on the boy's face. He then arrives, prays and prostrates himself on the 'still warm' body, face to face

[2] For summary of recent redactional study, cf. Jones (1984: 64–73).

[3] Moses' song is dated early by some (e.g. Craigie 1976: 374, following Albright, Eissfeldt, etc.), but late and archaizing by others (e.g. Mayes 1979: 381f., following Robertson, Fohrer, etc.). Hannah's song is widely seen as an independent psalm of the monarchy period (e.g. Klein 1983: 14f.), inserted in 1 Sam. 2 for obvious thematic reasons.

[4] Cf. Jones (1984: 308) for references to Babylonian parallels.

[5] Montgomery–Gehman (1951: 296) suggest that death in the ancient world 'was not certain until after a certain delay', and follow Josephus in seeing this as 'apparent death'. Similarly DeVries (1985: 221f.), seeing v. 20 as secondary.

and hands to hands (v. 34). The child sneezes, opens his eyes, and is returned to his mother.

The third story is the most laconic. An invading band of Moabites forces mourners to abandon in Elisha's grave the corpse they were intending to bury, presumably before they had reached the appropriate family grave. On touching Elisha's bones, the dead man returns to life (2 Kgs. 13:20f.).[6]

These stories are told in a simple matter-of-fact style, with minimal detail and no theological interpretation. Only in the first incident is there any recorded verbal response, when the widow proclaims, 'Now I know that you are a man of God, and that the word of Yahweh in your mouth is truth' (1 Kgs. 17:24). In the second the response is shown physically in the mother's prostration before the prophet. In the third there is no response recorded at all.

The similarities between the first two stories has often been noticed. Overholt (1996: 30f.) also notes their similarities with resuscitation and healing accounts from shamanistic societies, and the more general similarities between the roles of Elijah and Elisha and of shamans in many other cultures. These parallels are acutely observed. But here as elsewhere the biblical accounts are unashamedly monotheistic in attributing the prophets' power to Yahweh. And that power is shown in three isolated incidents involving the newly dead, not the dead in general.

iii. National restoration (Hos. 6; Ezek. 37)

Two prophetic texts use the concept of renewal of life as a metaphor for national restoration.

Hosea 6:1–2. In the third quarter of the tumultuous eighth century, Hosea proclaims to his Israelite audience poignant messages of punishment (e.g. 1:4f.; 3:4) and revival (e.g. 1:10f.; 3:5). Exile is imminent: Yahweh himself will carry off and destroy (5:14; 13:9), and the people will end up in Egypt or Assyria (8:13; 9:3; 11:3); but return and restoration is also glimpsed (11:11). The nation's eventual repentance is graphically portrayed in 6:1–2:

> [1]Come, let us return to Yahweh; for it is he who has torn, and he will heal us; he has struck down, and he will bind us up. [2]After two days he will revive us; on the third day he will raise us up, that we may live before him.

In the preceding verses Ephraim was sick and Judah wounded, but Assyria's king could not heal them. Yahweh himself would tear and carry off like a

[6] Overholt (1996: 61 n. 12) observes that this episode 'strengthens the idea that touching is a key element in curing'.

lion (5:13f.). Now, when the people return to Yahweh, he will heal, bind up, revive and raise up after a few days.[7] The context and the language suggest healing and restoration from physical wounds and sickness. The reference to 'three days' supports this, since it occurs in similar contexts elsewhere, e.g. Hezekiah's healing and Mesopotamian medical texts.[8]

Some scholars see a death-and-resurrection motif here. Hubbard suggests that 'the wounding is unto death (v. 2)', and notes that the verbs 'revive' (*ḥ-y-h*, Piel) and 'raise up' (*q-w-m*, Hiphil) occur in resurrection contexts (1 Sam. 2:6; Is. 26:19). However, the text does not specify that the wounding is fatal, and both verbs occur frequently and in many different contexts.[9] Day notes references to death in the wider context (5:14; 6:5). But prophetic texts in general and Hosea in particular juxtapose diverse images; so the immediate context of a phrase is more decisive for its meaning than the wider one. Day further notes various parallels between chapters 5 – 6 and 13 – 14 as well as the theme of death in chapters 13 – 14, and therefore concludes that chapters 5 – 6 are also about death (and resurrection). But Hosea's profuse images appear throughout his book, giving several themes within each chapter and numerous parallels across different chapters. Death is *a* theme in chapters 5 – 6 and 13 – 14, as elsewhere, but this does not determine the meaning of 6:2. Nevertheless, there is perhaps a more profound link between wounding and death, healing and resurrection. Hosea grapples in anguish with the message of God's punishment and destruction of the nation, while still clinging to the hope of healing and restoration. Inevitably the images he uses may fuse together, so that healing from grievous (or fatal) wounds and resurrection from the dead are alternate images for the renewal of a moribund nation.

Some Christian interpreters, following Tertullian, see 'third day' as indicative of resurrection (cf. also Jonah 1:17), and the text as predictive of Christ. But this goes beyond the evidence. Three days may be characteristic of healing generally and therefore of return to life specifically, but in context the text clearly refers to Israel, not to a future individual deliverer.

It is possible that Hosea and his audience may have been aware of death-and-resurrection motifs, from whatever source. But they are not necessarily evident here.

Ezekiel 37:1–14. In this stupendous vision, easily the best known passage of the book, Ezekiel is taken by the hand/spirit of Yahweh to see a valley lit-

[7] The verbs 'tear' and 'heal' in 6:1 are repeated from 5:13–14.

[8] So Wolff (1974b: 117), Rudolph (1966: 135), Mays (1969: 95), Davies (1992: 161).

[9] Hubbard (1989a: 125). For Day (1996: 246, 1997: 126) the word pair indicates resurrection, as in Is. 26:14, 19; Job 14:12, 14. But in Job 14 the terms are not a word pair, and the remaining evidence is too slim for such conclusion.

tered with dry and dusty bones.[10] 'Can these bones live?' he is asked. Surely not! But the wise prophet replies cautiously: 'O Lord Yahweh, you know' (v. 3). On Yahweh's command he then prophesies to the bones, which promptly regroup as skeletons and grow sinews, muscles and skin. But they lack breath. Again he prophesies as commanded, 'and the breath came into them, and they lived, and stood on their feet, a vast multitude' (v. 10). There the vision ends, and is immediately explained: 'these bones are the whole house of Israel' (v. 11). They feel dried up and cut off. But Yahweh will open their graves, bring them back to their land, put his spirit within them, and they will live. Then they will truly know him.

This vision comes in the second, more hopeful half of Ezekiel. By their own dating, the first twenty-four chapters were uttered in Babylon in that twilight period of false hope between the Babylonians' first and second captures of Jerusalem (597 and 587 respectively). Many Judeans thought that the nation's problems were superficial, and hoped that relief would be swift. But in chapter after unremitting chapter, in violent language and bizarre drama, Ezekiel proclaims that God's judgment would fall, resulting in death, destruction and exile. The second siege of Jerusalem finally occurs, revealed immediately to Ezekiel (24:1) and reported later by an exiled survivor (33:21, following the literary interlude of chs. 25 – 32, the oracles against other nations). Only then, when judgment has fallen, can Ezekiel proclaim directly that beyond it there lies the hope of restoration.[11] And part of that message, to an uprooted and traumatised people, is the vision of chapter 37.

The vision of reconstituted and revivified bodies clearly indicates a reconstituted, revivified and restored people, as interpreted to the prophet in vv. 11–14. It is a dazzling parable of return from exile.[12] But it says nothing about personal resurrection, even if it was later interpreted in that way.[13] The language of 'opening graves' and 'bringing up from graves' in vv. 12f. may seem to imply the latter, but it must be taken in context. Israelites normally buried their dead in rock-cut tombs (see Ch. 2.b.iv) or, for the poor, in shallow pits, so the equivalent for them of a valleyful of bones coming to life would be hundreds of bodies emerging from such graves. In applying his

[10] Presumably the remains of soldiers, cf. the term 'slain' (v.9) and the curse of non-burial (Deut. 28:25f.; Jer. 34:19f.). An Assyrian curse reads 'May Ninurta . . . fill the plain with your corpses' (ANET: 538).

[11] There are, of course, a few isolated glimpses of hope in the early chapters, e.g. 11:16–20; 12:16; 18:31f.

[12] Its visionary nature is confirmed by similar introductory language in Ezekiel's other visions, cf. 1:3; 3:14; 8:1–3; 11:1.

[13] E.g. a parchment with Ezek. 37 was found buried under a synagogue floor at Masada. 'Perhaps Ezekiel's vision was the last text one of the rebels read before committing suicide . . .' (Lang 1986b: 308). Some rabbis took the event as literal and debated the later history of those 'resurrected', cf. Block (1998: 388).

vision to Israel, Ezekiel first translates the imagery into a culturally relevant equivalent before giving its meaning.

Whether Ezekiel or his contemporaries thought in terms of personal resurrection or not is irrelevant. It is neither affirmed nor denied by this passage, though the prophet's cautious reply to Yahweh's opening question makes it doubtful. It is possible that it was part of the religious backdrop, but the vision would make just as much sense without it. Ezekiel was proclaiming and pondering God's message of restoration after destruction, of resettlement after banishment, of national life after death. So the imagery of physical bodies being reconstituted would be a perfect illustration. Its use does not imply a prior belief in resurrection, any more than our understanding of science fiction implies a prior knowledge of or belief in any of its imaginative worlds. So Ezekiel's vision contains physical reconstitution as an image of national restoration, but says nothing about individual resurrection.

iv. Individual resurrection (Is. 26; Dan. 12)

Two other Old Testament texts go further.

Isaiah 26:19. Isaiah 24 – 27 are clearly set apart from the preceding and following chapters by their focus, language, imagery and theology, and are widely described as apocalyptic or at least proto-apocalyptic. After the oracles against the nations (chs. 13 – 23) and before the messages addressed to Judah (chs. 28 – 35) comes this panoramic vision of world-wide cataclysm and threatened national annihilation, yet ultimate vindication. Death and life themes abound, with the utter devastation of the earth and its inhabitants (e.g. 24:1–13) but the preservation of those who trust in Yahweh (e.g. 25:1–5). In this bewilderingly bright kaleidoscope of vivid images and momentous themes, there are also glimpses of triumph over death, most notably in 25:6–10: 'he will swallow up death forever' (v. 8).[14]

Following this, chapter 26 juxtaposes the nation's present plight with its future vindication. Thus it confesses:

> 13Yahweh our God,
> other lords besides you have ruled over us,
> but we acknowledge your name alone.
> 14The dead do not live;
> shades do not rise –
> because you have punished and destroyed them,
> and wiped out all memory of them.

[14] This is the reverse of Ugaritic mythology, where Mot (Death) swallows Baal (Lord); KTU 1.5.i.33–35, 1.6.ii.22f. (NRSV wrongly attributes to v. 7 this first phrase of v. 8.)

But a few verses later, after lamenting the nation's impotence, it boldly asserts:

[19]Your dead shall live, their corpses shall rise . . .[15]

The context is one of national revival and restoration. The nation is already portrayed in personal imagery, as a woman in labour but unable to give birth. So the imagery of resurrection also applies to the nation.[16]

But there is probably more than national restoration here. Both v. 14 and v. 19 refer specifically to 'the shades' and 'the dead', i.e. to deceased individuals. In the former verse they emphatically do not rise; in the immediate context this presumably refers to the shades of the 'other lords' who have ruled God's people. By contrast, in the latter verse 'your dead [addressing Yahweh] shall live, their corpses shall rise', the dust-dwellers will awake and sing, Yahweh's life-giving dew will fall and the earth will disclose the shades.[17] The imagery clearly envisages the personal resurrection from death of at least some Israelites. Foreign oppressors will definitely not rise, but God's people clearly will. The application may be national, but the imagery presupposes a concept of individual resurrection.[18]

Daniel 12:2. Finally, one text speaks unmistakably and unambiguously of personal resurrection. In Daniel's final vision (chs. 10 – 12) a heavenly being reveals to him in increasing detail events which unfolded in the fourth to second centuries and perhaps beyond,[19] culminating in the rise of the arrogant 'king of the north' and the desecration of the temple, and 'at the time of the end' the invasion of 'the beautiful land' and the end of the king. The focus then immediately switches to 'your people' (12:1, twice). Despite the supernatural protection of 'Michael, the great prince', there will be a time of unprecedented anguish.

> [1]. . . But at that time your people shall be delivered, everyone who is found written in the book. [2]Many of those who sleep in the dust of the earth shall awake, some to everlasting life, and some to shame and everlasting contempt. [3]Those who are wise shall shine . . . like the stars forever and ever. [4]But you, Daniel, keep the words secret and the book sealed until the time of the end. Many shall be running back and forth, and evil shall increase.

[15] NRSV and others translate the verse's last line as also indicating resurrection, but this is uncertain; see Ch. 5.a.vii.

[16] So e.g. Wildberger (1978: 995), Clements (1980: 216).

[17] For translation see Ch. 5. a. viii.

[18] So e.g. Martin-Achard (1960: 137f.), Hasel (1980: 272–76), Puech (1993: 1.71).

[19] 11:5–13: third century BCE. 11:14–39: second century to 167 BCE. 11:40–45: for most scholars, inaccurate prediction; for some, events still to occur; for Gurney (1980), first-century struggles between Egypt ('south'), Syria, Rome (now 'north') and Parthia ('east').

This is clearly personal, individual resurrection 'at the time of the end'. It is also resurrection of both righteous and wicked, to eternal life and eternal contempt respectively.[20] So here (at last) in the Old Testament there is a developed concept of resurrection.

However, this may still be limited. First, as noted, the focus of these verses is Daniel's people. They will suffer great distress, and those among them who are 'written in the book' will be delivered. This implies that there are some among them whose names are not recorded, and who will therefore not be delivered. Similarly, the following verses refer both to the wise who 'lead many to righteousness' and to those who scurry around in evil times. During the previously recounted persecution some would be godly and wise, but others insincere (11:32–34).[21] So the resurrection announced in this context probably also focuses on Daniel's people. This does not preclude a wider, universal resurrection, but nor does it envisage it.

Secondly, the phrase 'many of . . .' probably means 'many, but not all', rather than 'the many', 'the multitudes' (as NIV). Thus it is exclusive of some, rather than inclusive of all.[22] Thus even within Daniel's people, it is only some who will rise. In context, they are probably those who die in or after the final period of persecution and anguish, some to be rewarded for their resistance, others to be shamed for their collaboration. So the resurrection envisaged is not a general one of all humans, but focuses on the Jewish people, and possibly only one generation among them.

The two texts just discussed are dated by nearly all scholars much later than the times of their putative canonical authors. Thus the Isaianic Apocalypse is often seen as one of the latest, post-exilic sections of the book, and Daniel is generally assigned to the period of the Maccabean revolt in 167–164 BCE. While the form-critical, historical and theological arguments are too complex to explore here, it is worth noting that the theme of overcoming death forms an important part of the argument, since it is thought to be a very late post-exilic development. In particular, resurrection in Daniel (as in 2 Maccabees) is seen as a theological response to the crisis of the Antiochene persecution and of the martyrdom of faithful Jews. Thus

[20] Alfrink (1959) argues from the context and the use of 'some . . . some' elsewhere (5x) that 'many' only includes the righteous and that the wicked remain dead. But neither point is convincing.

[21] The former were obviously the Maccabeans resisting Antiochus IV, the latter their uncertain followers.

[22] The phrase here (*rabbîm min*) also occurs in Ezra 3:12: 'Many of the priests and Levites . . . wept', and Est. 8:17: 'many of the people of the country professed to be Jews'; and a similar phrase (*rabbaṯ min*) in 2 Chr. 30:18: 'many of them from Ephraim . . .' Of these, Est. 8:17 and 2 Chr. 30:18 are clearly exclusive, and Ezra 3:12 probably so. For fuller discussion see Hasel (1980: 277–9).

resurrection belief emerges at the very end of the Old Testament period, too late to influence other writers or to appear in other books.

At the same time, a few other scholars have argued for an earlier, pre-exilic date for Isaiah 24 – 27.[23] And conservative scholars have continued to argue for the unity of Isaiah and Daniel and for their ascription to the eighth-century Jerusalem prophet and the sixth-century exilic sage respectively.[24] In this case, however, it must be accepted that the potentially revolutionary belief in personal resurrection remained theologically unassimilated into Israelite faith. Though apparently glimpsed by Isaiah and envisaged more fully by Daniel, the theme remained unexplored by these writers in other sections of their books. It was also ignored by successive prophets, psalmists, sages and historians of the seventh, sixth and fifth centuries. To them the concept of resurrection was unknown or incomprehensible, and their works maintain the traditional Israelite view of the unwelcome underworld.[25] Thus resurrection remained marginal to Old Testament belief, whether chronologically or theologically.

v. Other Old Testament texts

Psalm 1 contrasts the worthless wicked with the Torah-centred righteous, concluding:

> Therefore the wicked will not stand in the judgment,
> nor sinners in the congregation of the righteous (Ps. 1:5).

Does this refer to experience in the present or in the afterlife? Scholars mostly interpret the original reference as to the present life, with 'judgment' indicating some civil or more probably religious procedure, and 'congregation' meaning the worshipping community. There are many reasons for this. The psalms elsewhere contain no obvious reference to resurrection or post-mortem judgment, but they do refer regularly to the worshipping community (e.g. Pss. 74:2; 111:1) and occasionally to the personal integrity required to join it (e.g. Pss. 15; 24:1–6). Psalm 1 itself has a present-life perspective, both in the opening description (vv. 1–3) and crucially in the verse which follows the reference to judgment (v. 6).

Nevertheless, early Jewish and Christian commentators often read the passage eschatologically, because of its reference to judgment and the use of 'stand up' (*q-w-m*) elsewhere for rising from the dead (Job 14:12; Is. 26:14, 19). Sawyer (1973: 232) also notes the themes of fruitfulness in paradise (v.

[23] Notably Johnson (1988).
[24] E.g. Isaiah: Oswalt (1986), Motyer (1993, 1999), Webb (1996); Daniel: Baldwin (1978), Gurney (1980).
[25] With the possible exception of a few texts discussed above in Ch. 9.

3, cf. Ezek. 47:12), chaff scattered on Yahweh's Day of Wrath (v. 4, cf. Is. 17:13; Zeph. 2:2), and the happy fate of the righteous (v. 6). He concludes: 'In the universe of discourse described above, the meaning of this passage can hardly be in doubt.' It is also widely accepted that Psalm 1, with its theme of meditation on the law, is post-exilic, and that it was placed at the head of the Psalter in the book's last redactional stage. Thus it may have been composed at a time when resurrection belief was already emerging.

However, this reads too much into the psalm. While it may be among the latest to be written, neither the psalm itself nor the psalter as a whole suggest a belief in resurrection. And *q-w-m*, one of the most common verbs in the Hebrew Bible, generally refers to ordinary physical movement. Sawyer's further points are all tenuous and inconclusive in themselves: fruitfulness also applies to present faith (Jer. 17:8, a clear parallel to Ps. 1:3); comparison of the wicked to chaff implies current demise rather than eschatological judgment (cf. Job 21:18; Hos. 13:3); and Yahweh's protection of the righteous (v. 6) applies more naturally to the present than the future. Clearly, Psalm 1 was later read in eschatological terms. But this was more a rereading than the original intent.

Isaiah 53. The famous fourth servant song paints a harrowing picture of Yahweh's enigmatic servant, who is despised, wounded, oppressed, 'cut off from the land of the living' and buried.[26] Nevertheless, the final strophe affirms (vv. 10–12, lit.):

> . . . he shall see offspring and prolong days . . . out of his anguish he shall see[27] and be satisfied . . . Therefore I will allot him a portion with the great . . . because he poured out himself to death . . .

This clearly implies that after the servant's death Yahweh rewards him with renewed life. There is no mention of resurrection. But the few descriptions of the new life are strongly reminiscent of earthly existence: offspring, days, seeing, allotted portion. The text therefore portrays the servant returning to life in some unspecified form.

However, unlike Psalm 1, the canonical book in which this text is located gives an interpretative key, in the explicit resurrectional language of Isaiah 26. Whenever the book of Isaiah was finalized, and whoever completed it, 53:10–12 could then be understood as a post-resurrection life of the suffering servant.

[26] Whybray (1978: 79–106) argues strongly but unconvincingly that the servant did not actually die.

[27] LXX and the two main Isaiah scrolls at Qumran (1QIsa[a], 4QIsa[b]) add 'light'.

vi. Other Jewish writings

From the second century BCE on, the concept of resurrection began to take vivid hold in Jewish belief and writing. It is frequently cited in 2 Maccabees as a spur to faith, by the martyred family of seven brothers and their mother (2 Macc. 7:9, 11, 14, 23, 29), and by the brave Razis (14:46). It is also the basis for an offering 'to make atonement for the dead' (12:43–45). However, for the tyrant Antiochus 'there will be no resurrection to life' (7:14). Resurrection occurs implicitly in the older parts of the composite 1 Enoch (22:13; 90:33), and explicitly in the later 'Similitudes' (51:1; 61:5; 62:15). It provides hope in the pre-Christian Psalms of Solomon (3:16) and Testaments of the Twelve Patriarchs (T. Judah 25:1f.; T. Zebulon 10:2). The latter affirms a total resurrection: first the patriarchs will rise to God's right hand in gladness, then 'all men will rise, some to glory and some to disgrace' (T. Benjamin 10:6–8). And in the late first century CE resurrection occurs in the Apocalypses of Baruch (42:8; 50:2; 51:3) and 2 Esdras (7:32, 97). This material goes beyond the parameters of this book, and is well summarized elsewhere.[28] It is sufficient here to note its regular occurrence in this diverse literature.

It has often been thought that the Qumran community had little or no interest in resurrection. For one thing, their sectarian writings did not mention it. For another, their radical isolationism downplayed its role. As Nickelsburg explains (ABD 5:687):

> The world outside . . . is described as Sheol. Entrance into the community is construed as resurrection into the realm of eternal life and the presence of the angels. What 'traditional' eschatology ascribes to the end time is said to be the present possession of the member of the sect.

The dominant imagery of the two ways implies that at death one passes directly to eternal life.

However, this view is now seriously challenged. First, it has long been known that the graves at Qumran were all aligned north to south, with the head to the south. This might suggest an expectation of rising up together to face north. Secondly, texts have now been discovered which mention resurrection, notably the 'Messianic Apocalypse' (4Q521), which says of the Messiah (line 12):

> For he will heal the wounded, and revive the dead and bring good news to the poor. (Vermes 1995: 245)

[28] E.g. Nickelsburg (1972; ABD 5: 686f.), Cavallin (1974), Brown (NIDNTT: 269–74), Bauckham (1998: 91–3).

Puech (1994: 247) cites other recently published Aramaic texts from cave 4 which 'testify to hope in the resurrection of the just for the great judgment'.[29] Thus bodily resurrection may not feature centrally in the community's own documents, but seems nevertheless to have been part of their beliefs.

By New Testament times, belief in resurrection was common among Pharisees and many other Jews (Acts 23:8). Resurrection was envisaged as God's restoration of Israel in the present transformed and recreated world, not in an ethereal heavenly realm. However, the Sadducees denied the resurrection (Mark 12:8; Acts 23:8), ostensibly because it is not mentioned in the Torah, alone authoritative for them, but probably also because such belief encouraged insurrection and martyrdom which threatened their political authority.

In later Judaism resurrection became widely accepted. The post-biblical phrase 'resurrection of the dead' (*tᵉḥîyaṯ hammēṯîm*) occurs in both the Mishna and the Talmud, and is the title of the second of the Eighteen Benedictions.[30] Resurrection belief was increasingly read back into many biblical passages in later Jewish (as in Christian) exegesis.[31]

b. Resurrection in the ancient Near East

There is a wealth of scholarly literature on afterlife beliefs throughout the ancient Near East, dealing with post-mortem fate in general and resurrection belief in particular.[32] Here the relevant material can only be summarized, and possible influences on Israel noted. This raises the difficult issue of establishing influence, which in turn often raises the equally difficult issue of the dating of ideas and of the earliest sources to mention them. While these issues cannot be pursued at length, a brief overview may be helpful.

i. Egypt

The Egyptians had extensive views on the afterlife, which gradually evolved over the nearly three millennia of dynastic rule. These are recorded primarily

[29] Notably *Testament of Qahat* and *Visions of Amram*; also *Pseudo-Daniel* and *New Jerusalem*.
[30] Mishna Berakhot v. 2; Mishna (4x) and Talmud (41x), cf. Sawyer (1973: 220).
[31] E.g. for Rashi the two yods in 'formed' in Gen. 2:7 symbolize creation and resurrection, cf. Sawyer (1973: 220).
[32] Besides many works already cited, see e.g. Brandon (1967), Griffiths (1991), Bernstein (1993), Yamauchi (1998) and their further references.

in various related texts: the Pyramid Texts from the Old Kingdom (third millennium BCE), the Coffin Texts from the Middle Kingdom (early second millennium) and the Book of the Dead from the New Kingdom (mid-to-late second millennium), as well as in many other Books of the Netherworld from the New Kingdom and later.[33] These texts are in highly pictorial form, in various combinations of images and hieroglyphics. Many deities were involved in the afterlife, principally the sun god Re (also called Amun-Re), the Lord of the Underworld Osiris, and his son Horus.[34]

In the early Old Kingdom, the king alone was mummified to preserve his body for a positive afterlife. He was divinized as a 'Son of Re', and became a star. But by the end of the Old Kingdom, and more so in the Middle Kingdom, both mummification and a positive afterlife were extended to the elite of nobility and officials. In death each individual (NN) could become identified with Osiris and be known as 'Osiris NN'. And by the New Kingdom this was within the grasp of any commoner who had led a good life and knew the correct responses and actions for the journey through the underworld. This latter was assured through possessing a personalized copy of the Book of the Dead, with its nearly 200 spells against a whole series of dangers.

Various texts record in great detail the progress of the deceased through the underworld, until their eventual arrival in the Great Hall of Judgment, where Osiris presided. Here a dead person's heart was weighed against the feather symbol of Ma'at, the goddess of order, harmony and truth. Those judged worthy proceeded to immortality in the Field of Reeds or Field of Offerings, an Egyptian paradise. The unworthy were devoured by the ferocious creature Ammut, crouching beside the scales.[35]

The enormous literary and artistic endeavour invested in the afterlife implies that it held an important place in Egyptian life, one which elicited fascination, hope and fear. While a positive afterlife was increasingly considered attainable, death itself was an enemy which ushered one into a realm of many demons, great danger and inescapable judgment. Death was no light matter, and was often spoken of with euphemisms, e.g. death was 'going out into the day' and the dead were 'Westerners'.[36]

[33] Approximate dates: Old Kingdom: 2700–2160; Middle Kingdom: 2040–1790; New Kingdom: 1550–1070. For full bibliography, and discussion of the other Netherworld Books, see Hornung (1999).

[34] In this Osiris supplanted Anubis, who was left simply as the Embalmer (Silverman in Shafer 1991: 44). Breasted influentially posited a progression in supremacy from Horus to Re to Osiris, but Lesko (in Shafer 1991: 100) notes that they were honoured contemporaneously, in different respects.

[35] Other texts portray a Place of Destruction/Annihilation with its second death, the Lake of Fire, and a cauldron in which the damned are burned (Hornung 1999: 21, 60, 89 etc.).

[36] Cf. Zandee's study (1960), appropriately entitled *Death as an Enemy*; also Milde (1994).

The Egyptians never envisaged a bodily resurrection. While the dead are pictured in human form and the underworld is portrayed as an extension of this life, there is never any hint of a return to earth in renewed human bodies. One of the few points of contact with the Hebrew Bible is the concept of the dead becoming stars, which is echoed in Daniel 12. But this concept was widespread in the ancient Near East, and so cannot be traced specifically to Egypt. So Egypt had no obvious influence on Israelite resurrection belief.

ii. Mesopotamia

By contrast, as already noted elsewhere in this study, afterlife beliefs in Mesopotamia had significant similarities with those in Israel, notably a dark, gloomy and unwelcoming underworld deep below the earth. Various texts give much more detail of this than in Israelite literature, in diverse and sometimes contradictory presentations: its numerous names, its queen Ereshkigal and her consort Nergal, the subordinate Anunnaki gods, the river Hubur with its boatman Humuf-tabal, the gates through which newcomers pass, and the unpleasant subsistence of the *eṭemmu* (spirits of the dead).

Some texts suggest that the dead undergo some form of judgment on entering the underworld, with various possible judges, and are then allocated their proper place. One text suggests a possible mitigation of conditions, since a man intercedes with several gods so that his father may have pure water to drink.[37]

Two texts mention some form of escape from this 'land of no return'. In *Gilgamesh, Enkidu and the Netherworld*, the primeval hero Gilgamesh makes a hole in the earth so that the spirit of his departed friend Enkidu can rise to speak to him. And in *The Descent of Innana/Ishtar to the Underworld*, the fertility goddess is only released when her lover Dumuzi/Tammuz takes her place. The related *Death of Dumizi* notes that his sister Geshtinanna/Belili later replaced him for half the year.[38] Neither of these is a paradigm for human resurrection: the former concerns simply the occasional resurfacing of a spirit, the latter the cyclical descent and ascent of god and goddess in turn. The shorter Akkadian version of the latter text concludes with Tammuz's return to earth, when 'the dead shall come up and smell the smoke offering'.[39] However, as Penglase notes: 'just what this rise is, the state

37 *The Pushkin Elegy*, cf. Kramer (1960: 62f.), Penglase (1995: 194).

38 Innana, Dumuzi and Geshtinanna are the Sumerian names; Ishtar, Tammuz and Belili their Akkadian equivalents.

39 Dalley (1989: 160).

of the dead in it, where the dead rise from, where they go to, and for what purpose, remain unclear'.[40] At most, this suggests an annual and brief return to earth of the spirits of the departed. In short, the successive Mesopotamian cultures of Sumerians, Assyrians and Babylonians had no belief in resurrection from the dead, and therefore exercised no influence on Israel's emerging resurrection belief.

iii. Ugarit

The Ugarit epics recount how Baal was killed by Mot and later returned to life (KTU 1.5–1.6). Baal was the god of fertility, and while he was dead the land became dry and parched. But then Mot himself is killed, Baal returns and order is restored. Later Mot also returns to life. Various further confrontations occur, until the epic ends with Baal back on his throne. Many scholars interpret Baal's death and restoration as a reflection of the seasons, with his period of death symbolizing the summer heat. Thus Baal is a seasonal dying-and-rising god. A similar motif occurs in the epic of Keret. When the king is ill the land suffers, but when he is restored fertility returns. Keret is the archetypal ancient sacral king, the channel of blessing from the gods to humans. But there is a significant difference: Keret is restored from illness, not death. Human resurrection is not at issue.

In the early twentieth century Baudissin argued that Hosea was influenced by the notion of a dying-and-rising fertility god, despite his opposition to Baal cults. Since the discovery of the Ugaritic texts, others have developed this view, though now in terms of the Ugaritic (and presumably also Canaanite) Baal.[41] In particular, Day suggests that the concept of resurrection was appropriated from Israel's neighbours, stripped of its mythological associations and applied to the nation in Hosea 6 and Isaiah 26. Much later, when local fertility cults were no longer a temptation, the notion was reapplied to the supernatural sphere with individual resurrection in Daniel 12. Thus it was borrowed and demythologized, but later remythologized.[42]

Hosea and his audiences may well have been familiar with dying-and-rising fertility deities, and some of Hosea's imagery may possibly reflect this. But this does not mean that Hosea necessarily derived his imagery of revival (or possibly resurrection) from such a source. His own understanding of the

[40] Penglase (1995:194); cf. also Bottéro (1980; ET 1992 ch. 15).

[41] E.g. Martin-Achard (1960: 81–6). Baudissin cited more distant classical parallels.

[42] Day (1996, 1997) notes many thematic links between these chapters. But the links with Baal mythology are less clear.

power of Yahweh, derived from Israelite tradition, and his reflection on the seemingly contradictory oracles of punishment and blessing, could easily account for his use of the concept of renewal for the nation. As argued above, Hosea may not even have thought in terms of resurrection. And even if he did, he hardly needed to borrow the concept from Baalism.

As discussed earlier (Ch. 6.a.iv), some scholars also posit an annual return of the spirits of the dead with Baal at the autumnal New Year. This would be similar to the possible Akkadian reference noted above. However, the textual basis is at best unclear, and there remains no reference in the Ugaritic texts to human resurrection.

iv. Persia

The main religion of the Persian empire established by Cyrus the Great was Zoroastrianism. Its founder Zoroaster probably lived sometime in the late second millennium BCE in central Asia, though little survives directly from him or about him. His teaching spread southwards with the Iranian people, and gained strength in Media and Persia in the seventh and sixth centuries. 'Zoroaster believed profoundly in the justice of God . . . but the injustices of his own time led him to project its strict, final administration to the hereafter' (Boyce, ABD 6:1170). For Zoroastrians, on the third day after death the soul ascends to the sacred mountain, where its previous thoughts and deeds are weighed. If good dominates, the soul crosses a bridge to heaven. If bad, it plunges into the underworld for punishment. At the end of time, there will be a general bodily resurrection, and the last judgment by fire. Here the good will be divinely protected and proceed to eternal bliss on a restored earth, while the bad will completely perish. Many of the extant sources on Zoroastrianism come from long after the Persian empire,[43] but a developed eschatology is attested by the Greek historian Theopompus in the mid-fourth century BCE.

Lang argues for Zoroastrian influence on Israelites already in the early exilic period, and hence before the Persian empire replaced the Babylonian, for three reasons. First, the exposed dry bones in Ezekiel's vision (Ezek. 37) were typical of a Zoroastrian funeral ground, and Ezekiel's lack of protest at being defiled by these bones betrays Zoroastrian influence.[44] (Verse 2 could be read as 'and he caused me to walk among them' and would therefore

[43] Only the 16 *Gathas* can be attributed to Zoroaster himself. The fuller *Avesta* and *Pahlavi* texts were not written down until the mid-to-late first millennium CE (Yamauchi, ISBE 4: 124).
[44] Lang (1986b: 308–14; summarized in 1988b: 19). Cf. Ezek. 4:12–15 for Ezekiel's revulsion at defilement.

imply physical contact, albeit in a vision.) Thus the reconstitution of bodies applies not just to national revival but also to individual resurrection, as in Zoroastrianism. Secondly, the text betrays resurrectionist editing with the inclusion of vv. 12–13. Their secondary nature is betrayed by the change in imagery from a Zoroastrian funerary field to Israelite tombs, and by the textually and grammatically uncertain 'O my people'.[45] And thirdly, the Isaiah Apocalypse dates from the late sixth century, and shows a similar resurrection belief.

However, these arguments are uncertain. First, Ezekiel's vision comes in a section of the book dated shortly after Jerusalem's fall, at the height of Babylonian power.[46] It is most unlikely that Zoroastrianism had already so penetrated the Babylonian empire that an exiled Jewish prophet fell under its influence. Secondly, while vv. 12–13 may well be secondary, their function could easily be the one explained above (section a.iii), to translate the vision into concepts more easily recognizable to an Israelite audience, without affecting the application of the vision to the nation. Also, apart from the repeated 'O my people',[47] the language of these verses is typically Ezekielian, so they may have been added by the prophet himself, and need not imply a later more developed personal eschatology. And thirdly, a late sixth-century date for the Isaianic Apocalypse gives no support for understanding Ezekiel's early sixth-century vision. Even a pre-exilic date for the former is not determinative for the meaning of the latter, since Ezekiel's application is specifically national and not individual. So Lang's reasoning is not persuasive.

Many other scholars trace the emergence of Israel's resurrection belief to the post-exilic period of the Persian empire. Thus the influence of Zoroastrian afterlife beliefs gradually influenced Jewish writers, first in late sections of Isaiah, then more fully in Daniel, 2 Maccabees and other writings.[48] On the usual dating of these texts, this explanation makes good historical sense. Having experienced national revival under the aegis of a largely tolerant empire, Israel gradually adopted and adapted their belief in personal resurrection, and this belief came to the fore in a later time of severe persecution.

However, there are also weighty reasons to significantly modify this view. First, there are several important differences between the two eschatologies.

[45] It is omitted from v. 12 in LXX and Syriac, and from v. 13 in Syriac; similarly Wevers (1969: 194). 'My people' (*'ammî*) occurs 15 times in Ezekiel (so ES), but only in 37:12–13 in the vocative.

[46] Strictly, ch. 37 need not come under the date of 32:17. But Ezekiel's dating is pervasive and precise.

[47] Allen (1990: 183) proposes it was a gloss on 'for a people' in v. 27, but became attached to the wrong column.

[48] Thus typically Boyce (1982: 193f.), though she also notes possible Greek and Israelite influences (1991: 404).

In Zoroastrianism the experiences of judgment, heaven and hell precede resurrection; in Israel resurrection is an awakening from sleeping in the earth. In the former bodies must be recreated from the elements; in the latter the dead rise directly from the ground. Zoroastrians exposed the bodies of their dead for vultures to consume, while their souls journeyed to Mt Hara; in Israel there was no clear distinction between body and soul, and exposure of corpses was abhorrent. Secondly, most of the details of Zoroastrian eschatology come from a ninth-century CE text (the *Bundahishn*). The earliest reference to resurrection comes from the fourth century BCE, and there is significant doubt as to whether Zoroaster himself believed in it.[49] Thirdly, if the Israelite texts are dated earlier, the opportunity for influence shrinks considerably. And fourthly, there were other impulses towards an Israelite belief in resurrection: faith in Yahweh's unlimited power, national 'resurrection', Ezekiel's vision of this in individual form, and possible Canaanite dying-and-rising deities. Zoroastrianism may have contributed another such impulse. But there was no simple line of development from Persian to Israelite belief.

v. Greece

Greek religion and philosophy had a well developed concept of immortality. Plato expounds his belief in the immortality of the soul in his *Phaedo*. Here Socrates and his friends discuss the various arguments in detail, and Socrates reaffirms his belief in immortality before drinking the fatal hemlock. Plato also gives a summary of post-mortem experience in the *Republic*, Book 10, when the slain Er returns to life on his funerary pyre and recounts what he has seen. After death the soul is judged: the just progress to millennial bliss, the unjust return to earth for a millennium of hardship, and the very wicked are cast into Tartarus, the place of punishment in Hades. Plato also adopts the Pythagorean concept of the Transmigration of Souls, with each soul choosing its own destiny.

The Greek concept of immortality certainly influenced some Jewish writing, notably the second-century BCE Wisdom of Solomon. However, even here it is fused with traditional Jewish eschatology. Thus the well-known section which begins 'The souls of the righteous are in the hands of God' (3:1) and notes that 'their hope is full of immortality' (3:4), continues a few verses later: 'In the time of their visitation they will shine forth . . . They will govern nations . . . and the Lord will reign over them forever' (3:7f.). This reflects a typical prophetic hope in God's visitation and vindication of his

49 Cf. Yamauchi (1998: 47f.).

surviving people, with their subsequent reign over the nations on a renewed earth. The location is not specified here, but Greek immortality is clearly reset in a Jewish framework.

At the same time, the Greeks maintained a strong antipathy towards bodily resurrection. While a few scant references refer to isolated miracles,[50] the reaction to the apostle Paul's preaching in Athens indicates a mocking scepticism regarding resurrection (Acts 17:18, 31f.). So Greek philosophy may have encouraged Jewish expectations of a meaningful afterlife, but they did not contribute to belief in the resurrection.

c. Summary and conclusion

Israel's resurrection belief emerged as distinctively Israelite, whatever outside influences were part of the intellectual world of its writers. Its prophets may have known Canaanite traditions of dying-and-rising gods and of the fleeting annual return of the dead. But these concepts contributed only tangentially, if at all, to their proclamation of the nation's restoration after destruction. This national revival would be so unexpected and unwarranted that it might seem like rising from the dead, but the imagery is not dependent on Canaanite cyclical mythology. Similarly, Israel's apocalyptists may have known of Zoroastrian eschatology with its belief in immediate judgment and ultimate resurrection, and this may have encouraged them to greater faith in Yahweh's ability to raise the dead from the grave. But the resurrection faith they expressed emerged as significantly different to that of Persian belief.

As well as the differences already noted, Old Testament eschatology has no concept of judgment after death.[51] Nor does it comment on the punishment or destruction of the wicked. These issues may be the logical consequence of the differentiated fates noted obliquely in Isaiah 26 and directly in Daniel 12, but they were not developed in the canonical texts. The 'shame and everlasting contempt' (Dan. 12:2) remains unexplained and undeveloped. The non-canonical intertestamental literature testifies to increased interest and speculation concerning the fate of the wicked as well as the righteous,[52] and for Christians the New Testament affirms the validity of some of this extrapolation. But the Old Testament stops short of this.

[50] Brown (NIDNTT 3: 261) cites Plato and Lucian (once each) and accounts of Aesculapis and Apollonius.

[51] Tromp (1969: 22 n. 13) sees post-mortem judgment in Job 31:6, but the context implies present punishment. For weighing, cf. also Prov. 16:2; 21:2; 24:12.

[52] See Bauckham (1990, 1995).

If, then, the influence of other faiths was secondary, what were the primary factors in the emergence of Israelite belief in resurrection? Put simply, it was Israel's God and Israel's experience. Israel's God was proclaimed and increasingly acknowledged as the sole, all-powerful deity. The songs of Moses and Hannah celebrate Yahweh's power to 'kill and make alive'. They may have affirmed this theoretically rather than experientially, but they affirmed it nonetheless. The prophetic tradition recorded two instances of resuscitation following the intercession of Elijah and Elisha, and one due to contact with Elisha's bones. Isolated, rural cases perhaps, but nevertheless food for thought for later writers. Yahweh's initial creative power in breathing life into the first human is invoked in Ezekiel's vision, when he prophesies to the breath and it immediately brings the reconstituted bodies to life (Ezek. 37:9f.; cf. Gen. 2:7).[53] And Yahweh's authority extended even to the realm of the dead.[54] The living could not escape him by fleeing to Sheol itself (Ps. 139:8; Amos 9:2), since Sheol was 'naked' before him (Job 26:6). While the dead for their part remained cut off from God, unable to acknowledge or worship him, Sheol was not beyond his remit. Various psalmists and other writers recoil from the thought of Sheol, but a few express a real if imprecise hope of some form of continued communion with God beyond death. Thus Yahweh's proclaimed power to renew life, its occasional experience in life and in vision, his authority over the underworld, and the desire for unending communion with him all contributed to the development of Israelite belief in resurrection.

Israel's experience was one of judgment and mercy, of destruction and restoration, of exile and return. This forms the backdrop of so much of her prophetic literature, and in particular of the resurrection motif which it occasionally employs. Imminent judgment overshadows Hosea's promise of renewal, its devastating effect on the exiles gives sharp relief to Ezekiel's vision of return, while disappointment at its incompleteness underlies the Isaianic delight in resurrection. Israel as a people experienced death and rebirth. National resurrection was a reality in their experience.

But that rebirth seemed only partial. The nation never regained its former autonomy and confidence ('other lords . . . have ruled over us', Is. 26:13), mighty empires were to control its destiny (Dan. 7–12), and many faithful Jews would perish in the Antiochene persecution (Dan. 11:33). How could the rebirth be complete? Yahweh had resurrected the nation as a

[53] Cf. Ollenburger (1993); the Maccabean martyrs continually invoke this same creative power. Greenspoon (1981) traces resurrection faith back to the motif of the divine warrior, who has power over all nature including death. However, the motif is at best contributory, as Greenspoon implicitly admits (276).

[54] Ollenburger (1993: 35) sees this also in Ps. 22:28f., but this is less likely; see Ch. 5.a.vi.

whole; his power over death was unquestioned; his ability to raise the dead had been recorded. Perhaps then the answer to this unfulfilled post-exilic hope was one further development of belief: an ultimate, physical, individual resurrection from the dead.

However startlingly different it might seem from traditional views, this belief clearly built on elements of Israelite faith and experience. And however much the development may have been helped by non-Israelite resurrection belief (in whatever form), it emerged as distinctly Israelite: Yahweh would truly deliver his people. Those who slept in the dust of the earth would awake, some to everlasting life, and some to shame and contempt (Dan. 12:2).

Here at last was the basis for a resolution of the dilemma of Sheol, with its shadowy insubstantial existence, its shadow cast over human life, and its own deep impenetrable shadows, separated from the presence and light of Yahweh. Here was the response to the yearning for some form of continued communion with God: 'your dead shall live . . . and sing for joy' (Is. 26:19). Here was the breakthrough to maintain faith in traumatic times. The details of how, where and when this resurrection would take place, and with what consequences, are left unexplored – the belief itself was enough to begin with.

Here indeed was a response to death, though its sting would not be drawn until another era, a new revelation of God, and a specific, momentous resurrection. As the New Testament asserts: 'Christ Jesus . . . abolished death and brought life and immortality to light through the gospel' (2 Tim. 1:10).

Bibliography

Abbreviations used in the Bibliography

General

#	date of the original edition which was translated into English
ed(s).	editor(s)
ET	English Translation
Fs.	Festschrift volume
Mem.	Memorial volume
repr.	reprinted

Recurrent journals

AfO	*Archiv für Orientforschung*
BA	*Biblical Archaeologist*
BASOR	*Bulletin of the American Schools of Oriental Research*
Bib	*Biblica*
BN	*Biblische Notizen*
BRev	*Bible Review*
CBQ	*Catholic Biblical Quarterly*
ErIsr	*Eretz Israel*
ETL	*Ephemerides theologicae lovanienses*
ExpTim	*Expository Times*
HAR	*Hebrew Annual Review*
HTR	*Harvard Theological Review*

HUCA	*Hebrew Union College Annual*
IBS	*Irish Biblical Studies*
IEJ	*Israel Exploration Journal*
JANESCU	*Journal of the Ancient Near Eastern Society of Columbia University*
JAOS	*Journal of the American Oriental Society*
JBL	*Journal of Biblical Literature*
JJS	*Journal of Jewish Studies*
JNES	*Journal of Near Eastern Studies*
JNSL	*Journal of Northwest Semitic Languages*
JSOT	*Journal for the Study of the Old Testament*
JSS	*Journal of Semitic Studies*
JTS	*Journal of Theological Studies (New Series)*
OtSt	*Oudtestamentische Studiën*
Or	*Orientalia*
PEQ	*Palestine Exploration Quarterly*
RB	*Revue biblique*
RHA	*Revue hittite et asianique*
ST	*Studia theologica*
TZ	*Theologische Zeitschrift*
TynBul	*Tyndale Bulletin*
UF	*Ugarit-Forschungen*
VT	*Vetus Testamentum*
ZAH	*Zeitschrift für Althebräistik*
ZAW	*Zeitschrift für die alttestamentliche Wissenschaft*

Series and publishers

AB	Anchor Bible
AnOr	Analecta Orientalia
AOAT	Alter Orient und Altes Testament
ATD	Alte Testament Deutsch
BAT	Die Botschaft des Alten Testaments
BibOr	Biblica et Orientalia
BIP	Biblical Institute Press
BKAT	Biblischer Kommentar, Altes Testament
BWAT	Beiträge zur Wissenschaft vom Alten Testament
BZAW	Beiheft zur Zeitschrift für die alttestamentliche Wissenschaft
CBC	Cambridge Bible Commentary
CUP	Cambridge University Press
DLT	Darton, Longman and Todd
FAT	Forschungen zum Alten Testament
HKAT	Handkommentar zum Alten Testament
H & S	Hodder and Stoughton
HSM	Harvard Semitic Monographs

ICC	International Critical Commentary
IES	Israel Exploration Society
IVP	Inter-Varsity Press
JPS	Jewish Publication Society
JSOT	Journal for the Study of the Old Testament Press
JSOTSup	Journal for the Study of the Old Testament Supplement Series
KAT	Kommentar zum Alten Testament
MMS	Marshall, Morgan & Scott
MP	Marshall Pickering
NCB	New Century Bible; originally Century Bible New Edition/ Series
NICOT	New International Commentary on the Old Testament
OTL	Old Testament Library
OUP	Oxford University Press
PBI	Pontifical Biblical Institute
PIB	Pontificum Institutum Biblicum
RKP	Routledge & Kegan Paul
SAP	Sheffield Academic Press
SBL	Society of Biblical Literature
SBLDS	Society of Biblical Literature Dissertation Series
SBT	Studies in Biblical Theology
SCM	Student Christian Movement
SPCK	Society for Promoting Christian Knowledge
SVT	Supplements to Vetus Testamentum
TBC	Torch Bible Commentaries
TOTC	Tyndale Old Testament Commentary
UBL	Ugaritische-biblische Literatur
UP	University Press
V & R	Vandenhoeck & Ruprecht
WBC	Word Biblical Commentary
ZBK	Zürcher Bibelkommentare

Bibliography

Abercrombie, J. R. (1979), 'Palestinian Burial Practices from 2100 to 600 BCE', Ph.D. dissertation, University of Pennsylvania.

———(1984), 'A Short Note on a Siloam Tomb Inscription', *BASOR* 254, 61–2.

Ackerman, S. (1989), 'A *Marzēaḥ* in Ezekiel 8:7–13?', *HTR* 82, 267–81.

———(1992), *Under Every Green Tree: Popular Religion in Sixth-Century Judah* (HSM 46, Atlanta: Scholars).

ACUTE (2000), *The Nature of Hell* (Carlisle: Paternoster/ACUTE).

Ades, J. I. (1990), 'Samuel, Whear 'Ast Tha Been Sin' I Saw Thee?', in V. L. Tollers and J. R. Maier (eds.), *Mappings of the Biblical Terrain: The Bible as Text* (Lewisburg: Bucknell UP), 260–67.

Addinal, P. D. (1981a), 'The Wilderness in Pedersen's *Israel*', *JSOT* 20, 75–83.

———(1981b), 'The Soul in Pedersen's *Israel*', *ExpTim* 92, 299–303.

Aistleitner, J. (1963), *Wörterbuch der ugaritischen Sprache* (Berlin: Akademie).

Albertz, R. (1994), *A History of Israelite Religion in the Old Testament Period*, 2 vols. (London: SCM).

Albright, W. F. (1953), *Archaeology and the Religion of Israel* (Baltimore: Johns Hopkins; ^{3}1953, ^{1}1942).

———(1957), 'The High Place in Ancient Palestine', in *Volume du Congrès Strasbourg 1956* (SVT 4, Leiden: Brill), 242–58.

———(1968), *Yahweh and the Gods of Canaan* (London: Athlone).

Alexander, T. D. (1986), 'The Old Testament View of Life After Death', *Themelios* 11, 41–6.

———(1987), 'The Psalms and the After Life', *IBS* 9, 2–17.

Alfrink, B. (1943), 'L'expression '*šākab ʿim ʾăbōtāw*', *OtSt* 2, 106–18.

———(1948), 'L'expression '*neʾĕsap ʾel ʿammāw*', *OtSt* 5, 118–31.

———(1959), 'L'idée de résurrection d'après Dan., XII, 1.2', *Bib* 40, 355–71.

Allen, L. C. (1976), *The Books of Joel, Obadiah, Jonah and Micah* (NICOT, Grand Rapids: Eerdmans).

———(1983), *Psalms 101–150* (WBC 21, Waco: Word).

———(1987), *Psalms* (Waco: Word).

———(1990), *Ezekiel 20–48* (WBC 29, Dallas: Word).

———(1994), *Ezekiel 1–19* (WBC 28, Dallas: Word).

Andersen, F. I. (1976), *Job* (TOTC, Leicester: IVP).

Andersen, F. I. and D. N. Freedman (1980), *Hosea* (AB 24, Garden City: Doubleday).

———(1989), *Amos* (AB 24A, New York: Doubleday).

Anderson, A. A. (1972a), *Psalms (1–72)* (NCB, London: Oliphants).

———(1972b), *Psalms (73–150)* (NCB, London: Oliphants).

———(1989), *2 Samuel* (WBC 11, Dallas: Word).

Anderson, B. W. (1967), *Creation versus Chaos* (New York: Association; repr. Philadelphia: Fortress, 1987).

Anderson, G. A. (1991), *A Time to Mourn, A Time to Dance* (Pennsylvania: Pennsylvania State University).

Archi, A. (1988), 'The Cult of the Ancestors and the Tutelary God at Ebla', in Y. L. Arbeitman (ed.), *Fucus* (Fs. A. Ehrman, Amsterdam: John Benjamins), 103–12.

Arensburg, B. and Y. Raq (1985), 'Jewish Skeletal Remains from the Period of the Kings of Judaea', *PEQ* 117, 30–34.

Arnaud, D. (1986), *Recherches au pays d'Aštata. Emar VI.3. Texte sumériens et accadiens* (Paris: Editions Recherches sur les Civilisations).

Ashley, T. R. (1993), *The Book of Numbers* (NICOT, Grand Rapids: Eerdmans).

Astour, M. C. (1966), 'Some New Divine Names from Ugarit', *JAOS* 86, 277–84.

———(1968), 'Two Ugaritic Serpent Charms', *JNES* 27, 13–36.
———(1973), 'A North Mesopotamian Locale of the Keret Epic?', *UF* 5, 29–39.
Atkinson, D. (1991), *The Message of Job* (BST, Leicester: IVP).
Auvray, P. (1972), *Isaïe 1–39* (Paris: Gabalda).
Avigad, N. (1953), 'The Epitaph of a Royal Steward from Siloam Village', *IEJ* 3, 137–52.
———(1955), 'The Second Tomb Inscription of the Royal Steward', *IEJ* 5, 163–6.
Avigad, N. and J. Greenfield (1982), 'A Bronze *phialē* with a Phoenician Dedicatory Inscription', *IEJ* 32, 118–28.
Bahat, D. (1972), 'The Date of the Dolmens near Kibbutz Shamir', *IEJ* 22, 44–6.
Bailey, L. R. (1979), *Biblical Perspectives on Death* (Philadelphia: Fortress).
Baldwin, J. G. (1978), *Daniel* (TOTC, Leicester: IVP).
———(1988), *1 and 2 Samuel* (TOTC, Leicester: IVP).
Bar-Deroma, H. (1970), 'Ye Mountains of Gilboa', *PEQ* 102, 116–36.
Barkay, G. (1988), 'Burial Headrests as a Return to the Womb – A Reevaluation', *BAR* 14.2, 48–50.
Barr, J. (1961), *The Semantics of Biblical Language* (London: OUP).
———(1989), *The Variable Spellings of the Hebrew Bible* (Oxford: OUP).
———(1992), *The Garden of Eden and the Hope of Immortality* (London: SCM).
———(1993), 'Scope and Problems in the Semantics of Classical Hebrew', *ZAH* 6, 3–14.
Barrick, W. B. (1975), 'The funerary character of "high-places" in ancient Palestine: a reassessment', *VT* 25, 565–95.
Barstad, H. M. (1984), *The Religious Polemics of Amos* (SVT 34, Leiden: Brill).
Barth, C. F. (1947), *Die Errettung vom Tode in den individuellen Klage – und Dankliedern des Alten Testamentes* (Zollikon: Evangelischer).
———(1991), *God with Us: A Theological Introduction to the Old Testament* (Grand Rapids: Eerdmans).
———(1997), *Die Errettung vom Tode* (3rd edn, ed. B. Janowski; Stuttgart: Kohlhammer).
Bartlett, J. R. (1970), 'Sihon and Og, Kings of the Amorites', *VT* 20, 257–77.
Bauckham, R. J. (1990), 'Early Jewish Visions of Hell', *JTS* 41, 355–85.
———(1995), 'Visiting the Places of the Dead in the Extra-Canonical Apocalypses', *Proceedings of the Irish Biblical Association* 18, 78–93.
———(1998), 'Life, Death and Afterlife in Second Temple Judaism', in R. N. Longenecker (ed.), *Life in the Face of Death* (Grand Rapids: Eerdmans), 80–95.
Baumgartner, W. (1917), *Die Klagegedichte des Jeremia* (BZAW 32, Giessen: A. Töpelmann). ET: *Jeremiah's Poems of Lament* (Sheffield: Almond, 1988).
Bayliss, M. (1973), 'The Cult of the Dead in Assyria and Babylonia', *Iraq* 35, 115–25.

Ben-Arieh, S. (1983), 'A Mould for a Goddess Plaque', *IEJ* 33, 72–7.

Benjamin, D. C. and V. H. Matthews (1999), 'Mourners and the Psalms', in M. P. Graham et al. (eds.), *Worship and the Hebrew Bible* (Fs. J. T. Willis, JSOTSup 284, Sheffield: SAP), 56–77.

Bernstein, A. E. (1993), *The Formation of Hell* (Ithaca: Cornell UP).

Beuken, W. A. M. (1978), 'I Samuel 28: The Prophet as "Hammer of Witches"', *JSOT* 6, 3–17.

———(1980), 'Psalm 16: The Path to Life', *Bijdragen* 41, 368–85.

Blau, J. and J. Geenfield (1970), 'Ugaritic Glosses', *BASOR* 200, 11–17.

Bloch-Smith, E. (1992a), *Judahite Burial Practices and Beliefs about the Dead* (JSOTSup 123, Sheffield: JSOT).

———(1992b), 'The Cult of the Dead in Judah: Interpreting the Material Remains', *JBL* 111, 213–24.

Block, D. I. (1997), *The Book of Ezekiel, Chapters 1–24* (NICOT, Grand Rapids: Eerdmans).

———(1998), *The Book of Ezekiel, Chapters 25–48* (NICOT, Grand Rapids: Eerdmans).

Boda, M. J. (1993), 'Ideal Sonship at Ugarit', *UF* 25, 9–24.

Boling, R. G. (1988), *The Early Biblical Community in Transjordan* (Sheffield: Almond).

Boling, R. G. and G. E. Wright (1982), *Joshua* (AB 6, Garden City: Doubleday).

Bordreuil, P. (1990), 'A propos de Milkou, Milkart et Milk'ashtart', *Maarav* 5–6, 11–21.

Bordreuil, P. and D. Pardee (1982), 'Le rituel funéraire ougaritique RS 34.126', *Syria* 59, 121–8.

———(1989), *La trouvaille épigraphique de l'Ougarit, 1. Concordance* (Paris: Editions Recherches sur les Civilisations).

———(1990), 'Le papyrus du marzeaḥ', *Semitica* 38, 49–68.

Boström, G. (1935), *Proverbiastudien: die Weisheit und das fremde Weib in Spr. 1–9* (Lund: Gleerup).

Bottéro, J. (1980), 'La mythologie de la mort en Mésopotamie ancienne', in B. Alster (ed.), *Death in Mesopotamia* (Copenhagen: Akademisk), 25–52.

———(1992), *Mesopotamia. Writing, Reasoning and the Gods* (Chicago, University of Chicago).

Boyce, M. (1979), *Zoroastrians* (London: RKP).

———(1982), *A History of Zoroastrianism*, Vol. 2 (Leiden: Brill).

———(1991), *A History of Zoroastrianism*, Vol. 3 (Leiden: Brill).

Brandon, S. G. F. (1967), *The Judgment of the Dead* (London: Weidenfeld & Nicolson).

Braulik, G. (1986), *Deuteronomium 1–16, 17* (Stuttgart: Echter).

———(1992), *Deuteronomium 16, 18–34, 12* (Stuttgart: Echter).

Bray, J. S. (1993), 'Genesis 23 – A Priestly paradigm for burial', *JSOT* 60, 69–73.

Brekelmans, C. H. W. (1965), 'The Saints of the Most High and their Kingdom', *OtSt* 14, 305–29.

Brichto, H. C. (1973), 'Kin, Cult, Land and Afterlife – A Biblical Complex', *HUCA* 44, 1–54.

Bright, J. (1965), *Jeremiah* (AB21, Garden City: Doubleday).

Broome, E. C. (1940), 'The Dolmens of Palestine and Transjordania', *JBL* 59, 479–97.

Brown, J. P. (1981), 'The Mediterranean Seer and Shamanism', *ZAW* 93, 374–400.

Brownlee, W. H. (1986), *Ezekiel 1–19* (WBC 28, Waco: Word).

Broyles, C. C. (1989), *The Conflict of Faith and Experience in the Psalms* (JSOTSup 52, Sheffield: JSOT).

Brueggemann, W. (1984), *The Message of the Psalms* (Minneapolis: Augsburg).

———(1991), 'Bounded by Obedience and Praise: The Psalms as Canon', *JSOT* 50, 63–92; reprinted in *The Psalms and the Life of Faith* (Minneapolis: Fortress, 1995), 189–213.

Bryan, D. B. (1973), 'Texts relating to the *Marzēaḥ*' (Ph.D., Johns Hopkins University).

Buber, M. (1983), 'The Heart Determines: Psalm 73', in J. L. Crenshaw (ed.), *Theodicy in the Old Testament* (London: SPCK).

Budd, P. J. (1984), *Numbers* (WBC 5, Waco: Word).

Buis, P. and J. Leclerq (1963), *Le Deutéronome* (Paris: Gabalda).

Burger, J. A. (1992), 'Tombs and burial practices in ancient Palestine', *Old Testament Essays* 5, 103–123.

Burnett, J. S. (2001), *A Reassessment of Biblical Elohim* (SBLDS, Atlanta: Scholars).

Burns, J. B. (1979), 'Necromancy and the Spirit of the Dead in the Old Testament', *Transactions of Glasgow University Oriental Society* 26, 1–14.

———(1987), 'The Identity of Death's Firstborn (Job xviii 13)', *VT* 27, 362–4.

———(1989), 'Some Personifications of Death in the Old Testament', *IBS* 11, 23–34.

Bush, F. W. (1996), *Ruth, Esther* (WBC 9, Dallas: Word).

Butler, T. C. (1983), *Joshua* (WBC 7, Waco: Word).

Butterworth, M. (1998), 'Old Testament Antecedents to Jesus' Resurrection', in P. M. Head (ed.), *Proclaiming the Resurrection* (Carlisle: Paternoster).

Camp, C. (1985), *Wisdom and the Feminine in the Book of Proverbs* (Sheffield: Almond).

Caquot, A. (1969), 'Nouveaux documents ougariticiens', *Syria* 46, 241–65.

Carley, K. W. (1974), *The Book of the Prophet Ezekiel* (CBC, Cambridge: CUP).

Carroll, R. P. (1977), 'The Aniconic God and the Cult of Images', *ST* 33, 51–64.

———(1980), 'Translation and Attribution in Isaiah 8.19f.', *The Bible Translator* 31, 126–34.

———(1986), *Jeremiah* (OTL, London: SCM).

Cassuto, U. (1962), 'Baal and Mot in the Ugaritic Texts', *IEJ* 12, 77–86 (# 1942).

———(1967), *A Commentary on the Book of Exodus* (Jerusalem: Magnes; # 1951).
Cavallin, H. C. C. (1974), *Life After Death* (Lund: Gleerup)
Cazelles, H. (1948), 'Sur un rituel du Deutéronome (*Deut.* xxvi, 14)', *RB* 55, 54–71.
Charlesworth, J. H. (ed.) (1983), *The Old Testament Pseudepigrapha*, 1 (London: DLT).
Childs, B. S. (1974), *Exodus* (OTL, London: SCM).
Christensen, D. L. (1991), *Deuteronomy 1–11* (WBC 6A, Dallas: Word).
Clements, R. E. (1972), *Exodus* (CBC, Cambridge: CUP).
———(1980), *Isaiah 1–39* (NCB, London: MMS).
Clines, D. J. A. (1989), *Job 1–20* (WBC 17, Dallas: Word).
Cogan, M. (1995), 'The Road to En-Dor', in D. P. Wright et al. (eds.), *Pomegranates and Golden Bells* (Fs. J. Milgrom, Winona Lake: Eisenbrauns), 319–26.
Cogan, M. and H. Tadmor (1988), *II Kings* (AB 11, Garden City: Doubleday).
Cohen, H. R. (1978), *Biblical Hapax Legomena in the Light of Akkadian and Ugaritic* (SBLDS 37, Missoula: Scholars).
Cole, R. A. (1973), *Exodus* (TOTC, London: IVP).
Cooley, R. E. (1983), 'Gathered to His People: A Study of a Dothan Family Tomb', in M. Inch and R. Youngblood (eds.), *The Living and Active Word of God* (Fs. S. J. Schultz, Winona Lake: Eisenbrauns), 47–58.
Cooper, A. (1981), 'Divine Names and Epithets in the Ugaritic Texts', in RSP 3, 339–469.
Cowley, A. (ed.) (1923), *Aramaic Papyri of the Fifth Century B. C.* (Oxford: Clarendon).
Craigie, P. C. (1976), *The Book of Deuteronomy* (NICOT, Grand Rapids: Eerdmans).
———(1983), *Psalms 1–50* (WBC 19, Waco: Word).
Crenshaw, J. L. (1984), *A Whirlpool of Torrent* (Philadelphia: Fortress).
———(1988), *Ecclesiastes* (OTL, London: SCM).
Cross, F. M. (1984), 'An Old Canaanite Inscription Recently Found at Lachish', *Tel Aviv* 11, 71–6.
Cross, F. M. and D. N. Freedman (1955), 'The Song of Miriam', *JNES* 14, 237–50.
Cundall, A. E. and L. Morris (1968), *Judges and Ruth* (TOTC, Leicester: IVP).
Curtis, A. H. W. (1978), 'The "Subjugation of the Waters" Motif in the Psalms: Imagery or Polemic?', *JSS* 23, 245–56.
Dahood, M. (1959), 'The Value of Ugaritic for Textual Research', *Bib* 40, 160–70.
———(1960), 'Immortality in Proverbs 12:28', *Bib* 41, 176–81.
———(1962), 'Northwest Semitic Philology and Job', in J. L. McKenzie (ed.), *The Bible in Current Catholic Thought* (Fs. M. J. Gruenthaner; New York: Herder and Herder), 55–74.
———(1963a), *Proverbs and Northwest Semitic Philology* (Rome: PIB).
———(1963b), 'Hebrew-Ugaritic Lexicography I', *Bib* 44, 289–303.

———(1963c), Review of B. Albrektson, *Studies in the Text and Theology of the Book of Lamentations*, *Bib* 44, 547–9.
———(1964), 'Hebrew-Ugaritic Lexicography II', *Bib* 45, 393–412.
———(1966), *Psalms 1–50* (AB 16, Garden City: Doubleday).
———(1968), *Psalms 51–100* (AB 17, Garden City: Doubleday).
———(1969), 'Comparative Philology Yesterday and Today', Review of J. Barr, *Comparative Philology and the Text of the Old Testament*, *Bib* 50, 70–79.
———(1970), *Psalms 101–150* (AB 17A, Garden City: Doubleday).
———(1971), 'Additional Notes on the *Mrzḥ* Text', in L. R. Fisher (ed.), *The Claremont Ras Shamra Tablets* (AnOr 48, Rome: PIB), 51–4.
———(1972), Review of J. C. de Moor, *The Seasonal Pattern in the Ugaritic Myth of Baʿlu*, *Or* 41, 137–8.
———(1977), 'Ebla, Ugarit and the Old Testament', in J. A. Emerton (ed.), *Congress Volume Göttingen* (SVT 6, Leiden: Brill), 81–112.
———(1983), 'The Minor Prophets and Ebla', in C. L. Meyers and M. O'Connor (eds.), *The Word of the Lord Shall Go Forth* (Fs. D. N. Freedman, Winona Lake: Eisenbrauns), 47–67.
———(1987), 'Love and Death at Ebla and their Biblical Reflections', in J. H. Marks and R. M. Good (eds.), *Love and Death in the Ancient Near East* (Fs. M. H. Pope, Connecticut: Four Quarters), 93–9.
Dalley, S. (1986), 'The god ṣalmu and the winged disk', *Iraq* 48, 85–101.
———(1989), *Myths from Mesopotamia* (Oxford: OUP).
Davies, E. W. (1995), *Numbers* (NCB, London: MP).
Davies, G. I. (1992), *Hosea* (NCB, London: HarperCollins).
Day, J. (1980), 'A Case of Inner Scriptural Interpretation', *JTS* 31, 309–19.
———(1985), *God's Conflict with the Dragon and the Sea* (Cambridge: CUP).
———(1989), *Molech: A God of Human Sacrifice in the Old Testament* (Cambridge: CUP).
———(1996), 'The development of belief in life after death in ancient Israel', in J. Barton and D. J. Reimer (eds.), *After the Exile* (Fs. R. Mason, Macon: Mercer UP).
———(1997), 'Resurrection Imagery form Baal to the Book of Daniel', in J. A. Emerton (ed.), *Congress Volume Cambridge* (SVT 61, Brill: Leiden), 125–33.
———(2000), *Yahweh and the Gods and Goddesses of Canaan* (JSOTSup 265, Sheffield: SAP).
Dequeker, L. (1960), 'Daniel VII et les Saints du Très-Haut', *ETL* 36, 353–92.
Dever, W. G. (1999), Review of R. Gonen, *Burial Patterns and Cultural Diversity in Late Bronze Age Canaan*, *IEJ* 45, 299–300.
DeVries, S. J. (1985), *1 Kings* (WBC 12, Waco: Word).
Dhorme, E. (1967), *A Commentary on the Book of Job* (London: Nelson; # 1926).
Dhorme, P. (1907), 'Le séjour des morts chez les Babyloniens et les Hébreux', *RB* 4, 59–78.

Dietrich, M. and O. Loretz (1983), 'Neue Studien zu den Ritualtexten aus Ugarit (II) – Nr. 6 – Epigraphische und inhaltliche Probleme in KTU 1.161', *UF* 15, 17–24.

———(1989), 'Rāpi'u und Milku aus Ugarit', *UF* 21, 123–31.

———(1991), 'Grabbeigaben für den verstorbenen König. Bemerkungen zur Neuausgabe von RS 34.126 = KTU 1.161', *UF* 23, 103–6.

Dietrich, M., O. Loretz and J. Sanmartín (1973), '*Pgr* im Ugaritischen', *UF* 5 (1973), 289–91.

———(1974), 'Ugaritisch *ILIB* und hebräisch *'(W)B* "Totengeist"', *UF* 6, 450–51.

———(1975), 'Der stichometrische Aufbau von RS 24.258 = Ug. 5, S. 545–551 Nr. 1', *UF* 7, 109–14.

Dietrich, W. (1987), *David, Saul und die Propheten* (Stuttgart: W. Kohlhammer).

Dijkstra, M. (1988), 'The Legend of Danel and the Rephaim', *UF* 20, 35–52.

Dijkstra, M. and J. C. de Moor (1975), 'Problematical Passages in the Legend of Aqhâtu', *UF* 7, 171–215.

Dillard, R. B. (1986), *2 Chronicles* (WBC 15, Waco: Word).

Dotan, M. (1981), 'Sanctuaries along the Coast of Canaan in the MB Period: Nahariyah', in A. Biran (ed.), *Temples and High Places in Biblical Times* (Jerusalem: Hebrew Union College – Jewish Institute of Religion), 74–81.

Draffkorn, A. E. (1957), '*Ilāni / Elohim*', *JBL* 76, 216–24.

Driver, G. R. (1950a), 'Problems of the Hebrew Text and Language', in H. Junker and J. Botterweck (eds.), *Alttestamentliche Studien* (Fs. F. Nötscher, Bonn: Peter Hanstein), 46–61.

———(1950b), 'Difficult Words in the Hebrew Prophets', in H. H. Rowley (ed.), *Studies in Old Testament Prophecy* (Fs. T. H. Robinson, Edinburgh: T. & T. Clark), 52–72.

———(1954), 'A Hebrew Burial Custom', *ZAW* 66, 314–15.

———(1956), *Canaanite Myths and Legends* (Edinburgh: T. & T. Clark; 1st edition).

———(1962), 'Plurima Mortis Imago', in M. Ben-Horin et al. (eds.), *Studies and Essays* (Fs. A. A. Neumann, Leiden: Brill), 129–43.

———(1965), Review of M. Dahood, *Proverbs and Northwest Semitic Philology*, *JSS* 10, 112–17.

———(1967), 'Isaianic Problems', in G. Wiessner (ed.), *Festschrift für Wilhelm Eilers* (Wiesbaden: O. Harrassowitz), 19–36.

———(1968), '"Another Little Drink" – Isaiah 28:1–22', in P. R. Ackroyd and B. Lindars (eds.), *Words and Meanings* (Fs. D. W. Thomas, Cambridge: CUP), 47–67.

Driver, G. R. and J. C. Miles (1955), *Babylonian Laws*, 2 (Oxford: Clarendon).

Droge, A. J. and J. D. Tabor (1992), *A Noble Death. Suicide and Martyrdom Among Christians and Jews in Antiquity* (San Francisco: Harper).

Durand, J.-M. (1985), 'Le culte des bétyles en Syrie', in J.-M. Durand and J.-R. Kupper (eds.), *Miscellanea Babylonica* (Fs. M. Birot, Paris: Recherche sur les civilisations), 79–84.

Durham, J. I. (1987), *Exodus* (WBC 3, Waco: Word).

Eaton, M. A. (1983), *Ecclesiastes* (TOTC, Leicester: IVP).

Eaton, J. H. (1967), *Psalms* (TBC, London: SCM).

———(1976), *Kingship and the Psalms* (SBT 32, London: SCM).

Ebach, J. H. (1971), '*PGR* = (Toten-)Opfer? Ein Vorschlag zum Verständnis von Ez. 43,7.9', *UF* 3, 365–8.

Ebach, J. and U. Rüterswörden (1977), 'Unterweltsbeschwörung im Alten Testament I', *UF* 9, 57–70.

Edelman, D. V. (1991), *King Saul in the Historiography of Judah* (JSOTSup 121, Sheffield: JSOT).

Eichrodt, W. (1960), *Der Heilige in Israel. Jesaja 1–12* (BAT 17/I, Stuttgart: Calwer).

———(1967), *Theology of the Old Testament*, 2 (London: SCM; # [5]1964).

———(1970), *Ezekiel* (OTL, London: SCM; # 1966).

Emerton, J. A. (1971), 'The Riddle of Genesis XIV', *VT* 21, 403–39.

———(2001), 'Some difficult words in Isaiah 28.10 and 13', in A. Rapoport-Albert and G. Greenberg (eds.), *Biblical Hebrew, Biblical Texts* (Mem. M. P. Weitzman, JSOTSup 333, Sheffield: SAP), 39–56.

Emmerson, G. I. (1984), *Hosea: an Israelite Prophet in Judean Perspective* (JSOTSup 28, Sheffield: JSOT).

———(1989), 'Women in ancient Israel', in R. E. Clements (ed.), *The World of Ancient Israel* (Cambridge: CUP), 371–94.

Epstein, C. (1972), 'Chronique Archaeologique. Golan: dolmens', *RB* 79, 404–7.

———(1973a), 'Chronique Archaeologique. Golan: dolmens', *RB* 80, 560–63.

———(1973b), 'Notes and News: Golan', *IEJ* 23, 109–10.

Exum, J. C. (1981), 'Of Broken Pots, Fluttering Birds and Visions in the Night: Extended Simile and Poetic Technique in Isaiah', *CBQ* 43, 331–52.

Fenton, T. L. (1977), 'The Claremont "*mrzḥ*" Tablet, its Text and Meaning', *UF* 9, 71–5.

Fishbane, M. A. (1985), *Biblical Interpretation in Ancient Israel* (Oxford: Clarendon).

Fohrer, G. (1966), *Das Buch Jesaja*, 1 (ZBK, Zurich: Zwingli; [2]1966, [1]1960).

———(1967), *Das Buch Jesaja*, 2 (ZBK, Zurich: Zwingli; [2]1967, [1]1962).

———(1973), *History of Israelite Religion* (London; # 1968).

———(1989), *Das Buch Hiob* (KAT XVI, Gütersloh: Gerd Mohn; [2]1989, [1]1963).

Ford, J. N. (1992), 'The "Living Rephaim" of Ugarit: Quick or Defunct?', *UF* 24, 74–101.

Foresti, F. (1984), *The Rejection of Saul in the Perspective of the Deuteronomistic School* (Rome: Teresianum).

Fowler, M. D. (1982), 'The Israelite *bāmâ*: A Question of Interpretation', *ZAW* 94, 203–13.
Fox, M. V. (1989), *Qohelet and his Contradictions* (JSOTSup 71, Sheffield: JSOT).
Franke, C. A. (1993), 'The Function of the Oracles against Babylon in Isaiah 14 and 47', in E. H. Lovering (ed.), *Society of Biblical Literature 1993 Seminar Papers* (Atlanta: Scholars), 250–59.
Frey, H. (1957), *Das Buch des Werbens Gottes um seine Kirche: Der Prophet Hosea* (BAT 23/II; Stuttgart: Calwer).
Friedman, R. E. (1979–80), 'The *Mrzḥ* Tablet from Ugarit', *Maarav* 2, 187–206.
Friedrich, J. and A. Kammenhuber (1975), *Hethitisches Wörterbuch* (Heidelberg: Carl Winter – Universität, ²1975–, ¹1952–66).
Frymer-Kensky, T. (1983), 'Pollution, Purification, and Purgation in Biblical Israel', in C. L. Meyers and M. O'Connor (eds.), *The Word of the Lord Shall Go Forth* (Fs. D. N. Freedman, Winona Lake: Eisenbrauns), 399–414.
Fulco, W. J. (1976), *The Canaanite God Resep* (New Haven: American Oriental Society).
Gadd, G. J. (1948), *Ideas of Divine Rule in the Ancient East* (London: OUP).
Gaster, T. H. (1944), 'Folklore Motifs in Canaanite Myth', *Journal of the Royal Asiatic Society* 1944, 30–51.
———(1961), *Thespis* (New York: Harper & Row; ²1961, ¹1950).
Ginsberg, H. L. (1958), 'An Unrecognized Allusion to Kings Pekah and Hoshea of Israel', *ErIsr* 5, 61*–65*.
Giveon, R. (1986), 'Remarks on the Tel Qarnayim Goddess', *BN* 33, 7–9.
Good, R. M. (1991), 'On RS 24.252', *UF* 23, 155–60.
R. Gonen (1984–5), 'Regional Patterns of Burial Customs in Late Bronze Age Canaan', *Bulletin of the Anglo-Israel Archaeological Society* 45, 70–4.
———(1992), *Burial Patterns and Cultural Diversity in Late Bronze Age Canaan* (Winona Lake: Eisenbrauns).
Gordis, R. (1965), *The Book of God and Man* (Chicago: University of Chicago).
———(1978), *The Book of Job* (New York: Jewish Theological Seminary of America).
Gordon, C. H. (1935), '*'elōhîm* in its Reputed Meaning of *Rulers, Judges*', *JBL* 54, 139–44.
———(1955), *Ugaritic Manual* (AnOr 35, Rome: PBI).
———(1965), *Ugaritic Textbook* (AnOr 38, Rome: PBI).
Gordon, R. P. (1986), *1 & 2 Samuel* (Exeter: Paternoster).
Görg, M. (1993), 'Komplementäres zur etymologischen Deutung von *thwm*', *BN* 67, 5–7.
Goulder, M. D. (1982), *The Psalms of the Sons of Korah* (JSOTSup 20, Sheffield: JSOT).
Gow, M. D. (1992), *The Book of Ruth* (Leicester: Apollos).
Gray, G. B. (1903), *A Critical and Exegetical Commmentary on Numbers* (ICC, Edinburgh: T. & T. Clark).

———(1912), *A Critical and Exegetical Commentary on the Book of Isaiah*, I (ICC; Edinburgh: T. & T. Clark).
Gray, J. (1949), 'The Rephaim', *PEQ* 81, 127–39.
———(1957), *The Legacy of Canaan* (SVT 2, Leiden: Brill).
———(1970), *I & II Kings* (OTL, London: SCM; ^{2}1970, ^{1}1964).
———(1986), *Joshua, Judges, Ruth* (NCB, Basingstoke: MMS; ^{2}1986, ^{1}1967).
Greenberg, M. (1983), *Ezekiel 1–20* (AB 22, Garden City: Doubleday).
Greenfield, J. C. (1971), 'Scripture and Inscription: The Literary and Rhetorical Element in Some Early Phoenician Inscriptions', in H. Goedicke (ed.), *Near Eastern Studies* (Fs. W. F. Albright, Baltimore: Johns Hopkins), 253–68.
———(1973), 'Un rite religieux araméen et ses parallèles', *RB* 80, 46–52.
———(1974), 'The *Marzeaḥ* as a Social Institution', *Acta Antiqua* 22, 451–5.
Greenspoon, L. J. (1981), 'The Origin of the Idea of Resurrection', in B. Halpern and J. D. Levenson (eds.), *Traditions in Transformation* (Winona Lake: Eisenbrauns), 247–321.
Griffiths, J. G. (1991), *The Divine Verdict* (Leiden: Brill).
Grintz, J. M. (1970–71), 'Do not Eat on the Blood', *Annual of the Swedish Theological Institute* 8, 78–105.
Grönbech, V. (1931), *The Culture of the Teutons* (London: OUP; # 1909–12).
Gunkel, H. (1895), *Schöpfung und Chaos in Urzeit und Endzeit* (Göttingen: V & R), 3–120; partial ET by C. A. Muenchow in B. W. Anderson (ed.), *Creation in the Old Testament* (London: SPCK, 1984), 25–52.
———(1904), *Ausgewählte Psalmen* (Göttingen: V & R).
———(1926), *Die Psalmen* (HKAT II.2, Göttingen: V & R).
———(1933), *Einleitung in die Psalmen* (ed. J. Begrich, HKAT, Göttingen: V & R).
———(1998), *Introduction to the Psalms* (trans. J. D. Nogalski, Macon: Mercer UP).
Gunn, D. M. (1980), *The Fate of King Saul* (JSOTSup 14, Sheffield: JSOT).
Gurney, O. R. (1977), *Some Aspects of Hittite Religion* (Oxford: OUP).
Gurney, R. M. (1980), *God in Control* (Worthing: H. E. Walter).
Güterbock, H. G. (1961), 'The god Šuwaliyat reconsidered', *RHA* 19, 1–18.
Haag, E. (1986), 'Psalm 88', in E. Haag, F.-L. Hossfeld (eds), *Freude an der Weisung des Herrn* (Fs. H. Gross, Stuttgart: Katholisches Bibelwerk), 149–70.
Habel, N. C. (1964), *Yahweh versus Baal* (New York: Bookman Associates).
———(1985), *The Book of Job* (OTL, London: SCM).
Hahn, H. F. (1956), *The Old Testament in Modern Research* (London: SCM).
Haldar, A. (1945), *Associations of Cult Prophets among the Ancient Semites* (Uppsala: Almqvist & Wiksell).
Hallo, W. W. (1977), 'New Moons and Sabbaths: A Case Study in the Contrastive Approach', *HUCA* 48, 1–18.

———(1991), 'The Death of Kings: Traditional Historigraphy in Contextual Perspective', in M. Cogan and I. Ephual (eds.), *Ah, Assyria* . . . (Fs. H. Tadmor, Jerusalem: Magnes), 148–65.
———(1992), 'Royal Ancestor Worship in the Biblical World', in M. Fishbane and E. Tov (eds.), *Sha'arei Talmon* (Fs. S. Talmon, Winona Lake: Eisenbrauns), 381–401.
———(1993), 'Disturbing the Dead', in M. Z. Brettler and M. Fishbane (eds.), *Minḥah le-Naḥum* (Fs. N. M. Sarna, JSOTSup 154, Sheffield: JSOT), 183–92.
Halpern, B. (1979–80), 'A Landlord-Tenant Dispute at Ugarit?', *Maarav* 2, 121–40.
———(1986), '"The Excremental Vision": The Doomed Priests of Doom in Isaiah 28', *HAR* 10, 109–21.
Hamilton, V. P. (1990), *The Book of Genesis Chapters 1–17* (NICOT, Grand Rapids: Eerdmans).
Haran, M. (1969), '*Zeb-aḥ hayyamim*', *VT* 19, 11–22.
———(1978), *Temples and Temple-Service in Ancient Israel* (Oxford: Clarendon).
Hartley, J. E. (1988), *The Book of Job* (NICOT, Grand Rapids: Eerdmans).
———(1992), *Leviticus* (WBC, Dallas: Word).
Harris, R. L. (1961), 'The Meaning of the Word Sheol as Shown by Parallels in Poetic Texts', *Bulletin of the Evangelical Theological Society* 4, 129–35.
———(1987), 'Why Hebrew She'ol was translated "Grave"', in K. L. Barker (ed.), *The Making of a Contemporary Translation* (London: H & S), 75–92.
Harrison, R. K. (1973), *Jeremiah* (TOTC, Leicester: IVP).
———(1980), *Leviticus* (TOTC, Leicester: IVP).
Hasel, G. F. (1975), 'The Identity of "The Saints of the Most High" in Daniel 7', *Bib* 56, 173–92.
———(1980), 'Resurrection in the Theology of Old Testament Apocalyptic', *ZAW* 92, 276–84.
Hauer, C. E. (1970), 'Jerusalem, the stronghold and Rephaim', *CBQ* 32, 571–8.
Hayes, J. H. (1988), *Amos* (Nashville: Abingdon).
Healey, J. F. (1978), 'Ritual Text KTU 1.161 – Translation and Notes', *UF* 10, 83–8.
———(1986), 'The Ugaritic Dead: Some Live Issues', *UF* 18, 27–32.
———(1989), 'The Last of the Rephaim', in K. J. Cathcart and J. F. Healey (eds.), *Back to the Sources* (Fs. D. Ryan, Dublin: Glendale), 33–44.
———(1990), Review of J. Day, *Molech: A god of human sacrifice in the Old Testament*, *ExpTim* 102, 54.
Heidel, A. (1949), 'Death and the Afterlife', in *The Gilgamesh Epic and Old Testament Parallels* (Chicago: University of Chicago; ²1949, ¹1946), 137–223.
———(1951), *The Babylonian Genesis* (Chicago: University of Chicago; ²1951, ¹1942).

Heider, G. C. (1985), *The Cult of Molek: A Reassessment* (JSOTSup 43, Sheffield: JSOT).

Heimpel, W. (1986), 'The Sun at Night and the Doors of Heaven in Babylonian Texts', *Journal of Cuneiform Studies* 38, 127–51.

Held, M. (1973), 'Pits and Pitfalls in Akkadian and Biblical Hebrew', *JANESCU* 5, 173–90.

Heltzer, M. (1979), 'The Rabb'um in Mari and the RPI(M) in Ugarit', *Orientalia lovaniensia periodica* 9, 1–20.

Herbert, A. S. (1975), *The Book of the Prophet Isaiah – Chapters 40–66* (Cambridge: CUP).

Hertzberg, H. W. (1964), *1 & 2 Samuel* (OTL, London: SCM; # ^{2}1960).

Hertzberg, H. W. and H. Bardtke (1963), *Der Prediger – Das Buch Esther* (KAT XVII 4–5, Gütersloh: Gerd Mohn).

Hill, G. F. (1904), *Catalogue of the Greek Coins of Cyprus* (London: British Museum).

Hillers, D. R. (1972), *Lamentations* (AB 7A, Garden City: Doubleday).

———(1978), 'A Study of Psalm 148', *CBQ* 40, 323–34.

Hobbs, R. T. (1985), *2 Kings* (WBC 13, Waco: Word).

Hoffner, H. A. (1967), 'Second Millenium Antecedents to the Hebrew *'ÔḆ*', *JBL* 86, 385–401.

———(1969), 'Some Contributions of Hittitology to Old Testament Study', *TynBul* 20, 27–55.

———(1973), 'The Hittites and Hurrians', in D. J. Wiseman (ed.), *Peoples of Old Testament Times* (Oxford: Clarendon), 197–228.

———(1990), *Hittite Myths* (Atlanta: Scholars).

Hoftijzer, J. (1970), 'David and the Tekoite Woman', *VT* 20, 419–44.

Holladay, W. L. (1969), '*'ereṣ* – Underworld. Two More Suggestions', *VT* 19, 123–4.

———(1986), *Jeremiah*, 1 (Hermeneia, Philadelphia: Fortress).

———(1989), *Jeremiah*, 2 (Hermeneia, Philadelphia: Fortress).

Holland, M. (1980), *Der Prophet Hosea* (Wuppertal: R. Brockhaus).

Hoonacker, A. van (1898), 'Divination by the *'Ôḇ* amongst the Ancient Hebrews', *ExpTim* 9, 157–160.

Horn, S. H. (1982), Review of C. E. L'Heureux, *Rank among the Canaanite Gods*, *JNES* 41, 55–6.

Hornung, E. (1983), *Conceptions of God in Ancient Egypt* (London: RKP; # 1971).

———(1999), *The Ancient Egyptian Books of the Afterlife* (Ithaca: Cornell UP; # 1997).

Horowitz, W. (1998), *Mesopotamian Cosmic Geography* (Winona Lake: Eisenbrauns).

Hort, G. (1959), 'The Death of Qorah', *Australian Biblical Review* 7, 2–26.

Horwitz, L. K. (1987), 'Animal Offerings from Two Middle Bronze Age Tombs', *IEJ* 37, 251–5.

Horwitz, W. (1979), 'The Significance of the Rephaim', *JNSL* 7, 37–43.

Hubbard, D. A. (1989a), *Hosea* (TOTC, Leicester: IVP).

———(1989b), *Joel and Amos* (TOTC; Leicester: IVP).

Hubbard, R. L. (1988), *The Book of Ruth* (NICOT, Grand Rapids: Eerdmans).
Hubmann, F. D. (1983), 'Textgraphik und Psalm XVI 2–3', *VT* 33, 101–6.
Huffmon, H. B. (1965), *Amorite Personal Names in the Mari Texts* (Baltimore: Johns Hopkins).
Humbert, P. (1957), 'La rosée tombe en Israel', *TZ* 13, 487–93.
Humphreys, J. W. L. (1980), 'The Rise and Fall of King Saul', *JSOT* 18, 74–90.
Husser, J.-M. (1995), 'Culte des ancêtres ou rites funéraires? A propos du "Catalogue" des devoirs du fils (KTU 1.17:I–II)', *UF* 27, 115–27.
Hutter, M. (1983), 'Religionsgeschichtliche Erwägungen zu *'ĕlōhîm* in 1 Sam. 28,13', *BN* 21, 32–6.
Hyatt, J. P. (1980), *Exodus* (NCB, London: MMS; ²1980, ¹1971).
Irwin, W. H. (1967), '"The Smooth Stones of the Wady"? Isaiah 57,6', *CBQ* 29, 31–40.
———(1977), *Isaiah 28–33. Translation with Philological Notes* (BibOr 30, Rome: BIP).
———(1979), 'Syntax and Style in Isaiah 26', *CBQ* 41, 240–61.
Jacob, E. (1958), *Theology of the Old Testament* (London: H & S; # 1955).
Jacquet, L. (1975), *Les Psaumes et le cœur de l'homme*, 1 (Gembloux: Duculot).
Jastrow, M. (1903), *Dictionary of the Targumim, the Talmud Babli and Yerushalmi, and the Midrashic Literature* (New York: Pardes).
Jeffers, A. (1996), *Magic and Divination in Ancient Palestine and Syria* (Leiden: Brill).
Jeppesen, K. (1982), 'Call and frustration. A new understanding of Isaiah viii 21–22', *VT* 32, 145–57.
Jeremias, A. (1906), *Das Alte Testament im Lichte des Alten Orients* (Leipzig: J. C. Hinrichs; ²1906, ¹1904).
Jeremias, J. (1983), *Der Prophet Hosea* (ATD 24/1, Göttingen: V & R).
Jirku, A. (1965), 'Rapa'u, der Fürst der Rapa'uma-Rephaim', *ZAW* 77, 82–3.
Johnson, A. R. (1949), *The Vitality of the Individual in the Thought of Ancient Israel* (Cardiff: University of Wales).
———(1951), 'The Psalms', in H. H. Rowley (ed.), *The Old Testament and Modern Study* (Oxford: Clarendon), 162–207.
———(1979), *The Cultic Prophet and Israel's Psalmody* (Cardiff: University of Wales).
Johnson, D. G. (1988), *From Chaos to Restoration. An Integrative Reading of Isaiah 24–27* (JSOTSup 61, Sheffield: JSOT).
Johnston, P. S. (1993), 'The Underworld and the Dead in the Old Testament', Ph.D. dissertation, Cambridge University (summary in *TynBul* 45 [1994], 415–19).
———(1994), Review of E. Bloch-Smith, *Judahite Burial Practices and Beliefs about the Dead*, *VT* 44, 419f.
———(1995), '"Left in Hell"? Psalm 16, Sheol and the Holy One', in P. E. Satterthwaite et al. (eds.), *The Lord's Anointed* (Carlisle: Paternoster, 1995), 213–22.

———(1996), Review of B. B. Schmidt, *Israel's Beneficient Dead*, *JTS* 47, 169–72.
———(1997), 'Psalm 49: A Personal Eschatology', in K. E. Brewer and M. W. Elliott (eds.), *The reader must understand* (Leicester: Apollos, 1997), 73–84.
Jones, D. R. (1992), *Jeremiah* (NCB, London: MP).
Jones, G. H. (1984), *1 and 2 Kings*, 1, 2 (NCB, London: MMS).
Kaiser, O. (1959), *Die mythische Bedeutung des Meeres in Ägypten, Ugarit und Israel* (BZAW 78, Berlin: A. Töpelmann).
———(1974), *Isaiah 13–39* (OTL, London: SCM; # 1973).
———(1983), *Isaiah 1–12* (OTL, London: SCM; ²1983, # ⁵1981; ¹1972, # ²1963).
Kapelrud, A. S. (1980), 'The Relationship between El and Baal in the Ras Shamra Texts', in G. Rendsburg et al. (eds.), *The Bible World* (Fs. C. H. Gordon, New York: KTAV), 79–85.
Kaufmann, Y. (1960), *The Religion of Israel* (London: George Allen & Unwin).
Keel, O. (1978), *The Symbolism of the Biblical World* (New York; # 1972).
Keel-Leu, O. (=Keel, O.) (1970), 'Nochmals Psalm 22, 28–32', *Bib* 51, 405–13.
Kempinski, A. (1995), 'From Death to Resurrection: The Early Evidence', *BAR* 21.5, 56–65, 82.
Kennedy, C. A. (1989), 'Isaiah 57:5–6: Tombs in the Rocks', *BASOR* 275, 47–52.
Kidner, D. (1973), *Psalms 1–72* (TOTC, London: IVP).
———(1975), *Psalms 72–150* (TOTC, London: IVP).
King, P. J. (1988), 'The *Marzeaḥ* Amos Denounces', *BAR* 14.4, 34–44.
———(1989), 'The *Marzeaḥ*: Textual and Archaeological Evidence', *ErIsr* 20, 98*–106*.
Kitchen, K. A. (1966), *Ancient Orient and Old Testament* (London: Tyndale).
———(1977), 'The King List of Ugarit', *UF* 9, 131–42.
Kissane, E. J. (1960), *The Book of Isaiah*, 1 (Dublin: Browne & Nolan; ²1960, ¹1941).
Klein, R. W. (1983), *1 Samuel* (WBC 10, Waco: Word).
Knibb, M. A. (1989), 'Life and Death in the Old Testament', in R. E. Clements (ed.), *The World of Ancient Israel* (Cambridge: CUP), 395–415.
Knight, G. A. F. (1960), *Hosea* (TBC, London: SCM).
Knoppers, G. N. (1992), '"The God in His Temple": The Phoenician Text from Pyrgi as a Funerary Inscription', *JNES* 51, 105–20.
Koch, K. (1968), 'Gibt es ein hebräisches Denken?', *Pastoralblätter* 108, 258–76; repr. in *Spüren des hebräischen Denken* (Neukirchen-Vluyn, Neukirchener, 1991), 3–24.
Korpel, M. C. A. (1990), *A Rift in the Clouds* (UBL 8, Münster: Ugarit).
Kramer, S. N. (1960), 'Death and the Nether World according to the Sumerian Literary Texts', *Iraq* 22, 59–68.
Kraus, H. J. (1986), *Theology of the Psalms* (Minneapolis: Augsburg; # 1979).

———(1988), *Psalms 1–59* (Minneapolis: Augsburg; # [5]1978, [2]1961).
———(1989), *Psalms 60–150* (Minneapolis: Augsburg; # [5]1978, [2]1961).
Krieg, M. (1988), *Todesbilder im Alten Testament* (Zurich: Theologischer).
Kuhn, K. G. (1960), *Konkordanz zu den Qumrantexten* (Göttingen: V & R).
Kuhnigk, W. (1974), *Nordwestsemitische Studien zum Hoseabuch* (BibOr 27, Rome: BIP).
Lambert, W. G. (1959–60), 'Three Literary Prayers of the Babylonians', *AfO* 19, 47–56.
———(1981), 'Old Akkadian Ilaba = Ugaritic Ilib?', *UF* 13, 299–301.
Lane, E. W. (1863–93), *An Arabic-English Lexicon* (London: Williams and Norgate).
Lang, B. (1986a), *Wisdom and the Book of Proverbs* (New York: Pilgrim).
———(1986b), 'Street Theater, Raising the Dead, and the Zoroastrian Connection in Ezekiel's Prophecy', in J. Lust (ed.), *Ezekiel and His Book* (Leuven: Leuven UP), 296–316.
———(1988a), 'Life after death in the prophetic promise', in *Congress Volume Jerusalem 1986* (SVT 40, Leiden: Brill), 144–56.
———(1988b), 'Afterlife: Ancient Israel's Changing Vision of the World Beyond', *BRev* 4.1, 12–23.
Laroche, E. (1946–7), 'Recherches sur les noms des dieux hittites', *RHA* 7 *fascicule 46*, 7–139.
———(1968), 'Documents hourrites de Ras Shamra', *Ugaritica 5*, 448–544.
———(1977), 'Glossaire de la langue Hourrite, Deuxième Partie', *RHA* 35, 163–322.
———(1984), 'Les dieux du paysan hittite', *Homo Religionis* 10, 127–33.
Lauha, A. (1978), *Kohelet* (BKAT XIX, Neukirchen-Vluyn: Neukirchener).
Leggett, D. A. (1974), *The Levirate and Goel Institutions in the Old Testament with Special Attention to the Book of Ruth* (Cherry Hill: Mack).
Lemaire, A. (1981), *Les écoles et la formation de la Bible dans l'ancien Israël* (Fribourg: Universitaires).
Leveen, J. (1971), 'Textual problems in the Psalms', *VT* 21, 48–58.
Levine, B. A. (1993), *Numbers 1–20* (AB 4A, New York: Doubleday).
Levine, B. A. and J.-M. de Tarragon (1984), 'Dead Kings and Rephaim. The Patrons of the Ugaritic Dynasty', *JAOS* 104, 649–59.
Levy, J. (1876–89), *Neuhebräisches und chaldäisches Wörterbuch* (Leipzig: F.A. Brockhaus).
Lewis, T. J. (1987), 'Death Cult Imagery in Isaiah 57', *HAR* 11, 267–84.
———(1989), *Cults of the Dead in Ancient Israel and Ugarit* (HSM 39, Atlanta: Scholars).
———(1991), 'The Ancestral Estate (*naḥ^alat ʾ^elōhîm*) in 2 Samuel 14:16', *JBL* 110, 597–612.
———(1994), Review of S. Ackerman, *Under Every Green Tree: Popular Religion in Sixth-Century Judah*, *JBL* 113, 705–8.
———(2001), 'How far can texts take us? . . .', in B. M. Gittlen (ed.), *Sacred Time, Sacred Place* (Winona Lake: Eisenbrauns), 169–217.

L'Heureux, C. E. (1976), 'The *yelidê hārāpā*' – A Cultic Association of Warriors', *BASOR* 221, 83–5.

———(1979), *Rank Among the Canaanite Gods* (HSM 21, Missoula: Scholars).

Liddell, H. G. and R. Scott (1940), *A Greek-English Lexicon* (Oxford: OUP, [9]1940).

Lindblom, J. (1974), 'Erwägungen zu Psalm XVI', *VT* 24, 187–95.

Lipiński, E. (1969a), 'Trois hébraïsmes oubliés ou méconnus', *Rivista degli studi orientali* 44, 83–101.

———(1969b), 'L'hymne au Yahwé Roi au Psaume 22,28–32', *Bib* 50, 153–68.

———(1973), '*skn* et *sgn* dans le sémitique occidental du nord', *UF* 5, 191–207.

Loewenstamm, S. E. (1969), 'Eine lehrhafte ugaritische Trinkburlesque', *UF* 1, 71–7.

Loffreda, S. (1968), 'Typological sequence of Iron Age rock-cut Tombs in Palestine', *Studii biblici franciscani liber annuus* 18, 244–87.

Lohfink, N. (1967), *Die Landverheissung als Eid* (Stuttgart: Katholisches Bibelwerk).

Loretz, O. (1979), *Die Psalmen*, 2 (AOAT 207/2, Neukirchen-Vluyn: Neukirchener).

———(1993), '*Marziḥu* im ugaritischen und biblischen Ahnenkult. Zu Ps 23; 133; Am 6,1–7 und Jer 16,5.8', in M. Dietrich and O. Loretz (eds.), *Mesopotamia–Ugaritica–Biblica* (Fs. K. Bergerhof, AOAT 232, Neukirchen-Vluyn: Neukirchener), 93–144.

———(1994), '"Ugaritic and the Biblical Literature": Das Paradigma des Mythos von den *rpum* – Rephaim', in G. J. Brooke et al. (eds.), *Ugarit and the Bible* (Münster: Ugarit Verlag), 175–224.

Lucas, E. C. (1997), 'Science, Wisdom, Eschatology and the Cosmic Christ', in K. E. Brewer and M. W. Elliott (eds.), *The reader must understand* (Leicester: Apollos, 1997), 279–97.

Lust, J. (1974), 'On wizards and prophets', in *Studies in Prophecy* (SVT 26, Leiden: Brill), 133–42.

Maag, V. (1951), *Text, Wortschatz und Begriffswelt des Buches Amos* (Leiden: Brill).

———(1964), 'Tod und Jenseits nach dem Alten Testament', *Schweizerische Theologische Umschau* 34, 17–37; repr. in *Kultur, Kulturkontact und Religion* (as above), 181–202.

Mackenzie, D. (1912–13), 'Excavations at Ain Shems (Beth Shemesh)', *Palestine Exploration Fund Annual* 2.

Magonet, J. (1994), *A Rabbi Reads the Psalms* (London: SCM).

Malamat, A. (1956), '"Prophecy" in the Mari Documents', *ErIsr* 4, vi-vii, 74–84 (Hebrew).

———(1968), 'King Lists of the Old Babylonian Period and Biblical Genealogies', *JAOS* 88, 163–73.

———(1989), *Mari and the Early Israelite Experience* (Oxford: OUP).

Mannati, M. (1972), 'Remarques sur Ps. XVI 1–3', *VT* 22, 359–61.

Marcus, D. (1972), 'The Verb "To Live" in Ugaritic', *JSS* 17, 76–82.
———(1973), Review of J. C. de Moor, *New Year with Canaanites and Israelites*, *JAOS* 93, 589–91.
Margalit, B. (= Margulis, B.) (1979–80), 'The Ugaritic Tale of the Drunken Gods: Another Look at RS 24.258 (KTU 1.114)', *Maarav* 2, 65–120.
———(1984), 'Ugaritic Lexicography III', *RB* 91, 102–15.
———(1987), 'Ugaritic Contributions to Hebrew Lexicography', *ZAW* 99, 391–404.
———(1989), *The Ugaritic Poem of AQHT* (BZAW 182, Berlin: de Gruyter).
Margalith, O. (1985), 'Dor and En-Dor', *ZAW* 97, 109–11.
Margulis, B. (= Margalit, B.) (1970a), 'A Ugaritic Psalm (RS7 24.252)', *JBL* 89, 292–304.
———(1970b), 'The Canaanite Origin of Psalm 29 Reconsidered', *Bib* 89, 332–48.
Martin-Achard, R. (1960), *From Death to Life* (Edinburgh: Oliver & Boyd; # 1956).
———(1988), *La mort en face selon la Bible hébraïque* (Geneva: Labor et Fides).
Mauchline, J. (1971), *1 and 2 Samuel* (NCB, London: Oliphants).
May, H. G. (1955), 'Some Cosmic Connotations of *Mayim Rabbîm*, "Many Waters"', *JBL* 74, 9–21.
Mayes, A. D. H. (1979), *Deuteronomy* (NCB, London: MMS).
Mays, J. L. (1969a), *Hosea* (OTL, London: SCM).
———(1969b), *Amos* (OTL, London: SCM).
Mazar, A. (1990), *Archaeology of the Land of the Bible* (New York: Doubleday).
McAlpine, T. H. (1987), *Sleep, Divine and Human, in the Old Testament* (JSOTSup 38, Sheffield: JSOT).
McCarter, P. K. (1980), *I Samuel* (AB 8, Garden City: Doubleday).
———(1984), *II Samuel* (AB 9, Garden City: Doubleday).
McCown, C. C. (1947), *Tell en-Naṣbeh*, 1 (Berkeley: Palestine Institute of Pacific School of Religion; New Haven: American Schools of Oriental Research).
McDaniel, T. F. (1968), 'Philological Studies in Lamentations. I', *Bib* 49, 27–53.
McGovern, J. J. (1959), 'The Waters of Death', *CBQ* 21, 350–58.
McKane, W. (1970), *Proverbs* (OTL, London: SCM).
———(1986), *A Critical and Exegetical Commentary on Jeremiah*, 1 (ICC; Edinburgh: T. & T. Clark).
McKay, J. W. (1973), *Religion in Judah under the Assyrians* (SBT 26; London: SCM).
McKeating, H. (1971), *The Books of Amos, Hosea and Micah* (CBC, Cambridge: CUP).
———(1975), 'The development of the law on homicide in Ancient Israel', *VT* 25, 46–68.

———(1993), *Ezekiel* (OT Guide, Sheffield: JSOT).
McKenzie, J. L. (1968), *The Second Isaiah* (AB 20, Garden City: Doubleday).
McLaughlin, J. L. (1991), 'The *marzeaḥ* at Ugarit. A Textual and Contextual Study', *UF* 23, 265–81.
Melugin, R. F. (1974), 'The conventional and the creative in Isaiah's judgment oracles', *CBQ* 36, 301–11.
Mettinger, T. N. D. (1995), *No Graven Image* (Stockholm: Almqvist & Wiksell).
Meyers, E. M. (1970), 'Secondary Burials in Palestine', *BA* 33, 2–29; repr. in E. F. Campbell and D. N. Freedman (eds.), *The Biblical Archaeologist Reader IV* (Sheffield: Almond, 1983), 91–114.
Michel, D. (1989), *Untersuchungen zur Eigenart des Buches Qohelet* (BZAW 183, Berlin: de Gruyter).
Milde, H. (1994), 'Going out into the Day', in J. M. Bremer et al. (eds.), *Hidden Futures* (Amsterdam: Amsterdam UP).
Milgrom, J. (1991), *Leviticus 1–16* (AB 3, New York: Doubleday).
Millar, W. R. (1976), *Isaiah 24–27 and the Origin of Apocalyptic* (HSM 11, Missoula: Scholars).
Millard, A. R. (1988), 'King Og's Bed and Other Ancient Ironmongery', in L. Eslinger and G. Taylor (eds.), *Ascribe to the Lord* (Mem. P. C. Craigie, JSOTSup 67, Sheffield: JSOT), 481–92.
———(1990), 'King Og's Iron Bed – Fact or Fantasy?', *BRev* 6/3, 16–21.
Miller, P. D. (1971), 'The *Mrzḥ* Text', in L. R. Fisher (ed.), *The Claremont Ras Shamra Tablets* (AnOr 48, Rome: PIB), 37–49; repr. in *Israelite Religion and Biblical Theology* (JSOTSup 267, Sheffield: SAP, 2000), 51–68.
Miscall, P. D. (1986), *1 Samuel. A Literary Reading* (Bloomington: Indiana UP).
Mitchell, D. C. (1997), *The Message of the Psalter* (JSOTSup 252, Sheffield: SAP).
Montgomery, J. A. and H. S. Gehman (1951), *A Critical and Exegetical Introduction to the Books of Kings* (ICC, Edinburgh: T. & T. Clark).
Moor, J. C. de (1969), 'Studies in the New Alphabetic Texts from Ras Shamra I', *UF* 1, 167–88.
———(1971), *The Seasonal Pattern in the Ugaritic Myth of Baʿlu* (AOAT 16, Neukirchen-Vluyn: Neukirchener).
———(1975), '*'ar* "Honey-Dew" ', *UF* 7, 590–91.
———(1976), 'Rapi'uma–Rephaim', *ZAW* 88, 325–45.
———(1979), 'Contributions to the Ugaritic Lexicon', *UF* 11, 639–53.
———(1980a), 'El, the Creator', in G. Rendsburg et al. (eds.), *The Bible World* (Fs. C. H. Gordon, New York: KTAV), 171–87.
———(1980b), 'An Incantation against Evil Spirits (Ras Ibn Hani 78/20)', *UF* 12, 429–32.
———(1984), 'Henbane and KTU 1.114', *UF* 16, 355–6.
———(1988), 'East of Eden', *ZAW* 100, 105–11.
———(1990a), *The Rise of Yahwism* (Leuven: Leuven UP).

———(1990b), 'Lovable Death in the Ancient Near East', *UF* 22, 233–45.
———(1995), 'Standing Stones and Ancestor Worship', *UF* 27, 1–20.
Moor, J. C. de, and K. Spronk (1984), 'More on Demons in Ugarit (KTU 1.82)', *UF* 16, 237–50.
Moran, W. L. (1969), 'New Evidence from Mari on the History of Prophecy', *Bib* 50, 15–56.
———(1992), *The Amarna Letters* (Baltimore: John Hopkins).
Motyer, A. (1993), *The Prophecy of Isaiah* (Leicester: IVP).
———(1999), *Isaiah* (TOTC, Leicester: IVP).
Mowinckel, S. (1921–4), *Psalmenstudien* (Kristiania: J. Dybwad; repr. Amsterdam: P. Schippers, 1961).
Mullen, E. T. (1980), *The Assembly of the Gods: The Divine Council in Canaanite and Early Hebrew Literature* (HSM 24, Chico: Scholars).
Müller, H.-P. (1969), 'Magisch-mantische Weisheit und die Gestalt Daniels', *UF* 1, 79–94.
———(1975), 'Das Wort von den Totengeistern Jes. 8,19f.', *Die Welt des Orients* 8, 65–76.
———(1988), 'Hld 4,12–5,1: ein althebräisches Paradigma poetischer Sprache', *ZAH* 1, 191–201.
Murphy, R. E. (1963), 'A Consideration of the Classification "Wisdom Psalms"', in J. A. Emerton et al. (eds.), *Congress Volume, Bonn 1962* (SVT 9, Leiden: Brill), 156–67.
———(1988), 'Wisdom and Eros in Proverbs 1–9', *CBQ* 50, 600–603.
———(1992), *Ecclesiastes* (WBC 23A, Dallas: Word).
———(1998), *Proverbs* (WBC 22, Nashville: Nelson).
———(1999), 'The Testament(s): Continuities and Discontinuities', *Biblical Theology Bulletin* 29, 113–17.
Murray, A. T. (1925), *Homer. The Iliad*, 2 (London: William Heinemann).
Myers, J. M. (1965), *II Chronicles* (AB 13, Garden City: Doubleday).
Naveh, J. (1963), 'Old Hebrew Inscriptions in a Burial Cave', *IEJ* 13, 74–96.
———(1967), 'Some Notes on Nabatean Inscriptions from 'Avdat', *IEJ* 17, 187–9.
———(1985), 'Writings and Scripts in Seventh Century B.C.E. Philistia: The New Evidence from Tell Jemmeh', *IEJ* 35, 8–21.
Neef, H.-D. (1987), *Die Heilstraditionen Israels in der Verkündigung des Propheten Hosea* (BZAW 109, Berlin: de Gruyter).
Negev, A. (1961), 'Nabatean Inscriptions from 'Avdat (Oboda), I', *IEJ* 11, 127–38.
———(1963), 'Nabatean Inscriptions from 'Avdat (Oboda), II', *IEJ* 13, 113–17.
Neiman, D. (1948), '*PGR*: a Canaanite Cult-Object in the Old Testament', *JBL* 67, 55–60.
Nickelsburg, G. W. E. (1972), *Resurrection, Immortality, and Eternal Life in Intertestamental Judaism* (Cambridge: Harvard UP).
Niehr, H. (1991), 'Ein unerkannter Text zur Nekromantie in Israel: Bemerkungen zum religionsgeschichtlichen Hintergrund von 2Sam 12,16a', *UF* 23, 301–6.

Nilsson, N. P. (1940), *Greek Popular Religion* (New York: Columbia UP).
Noth, M. (1928), *Die israelitischen Personennamen im Rahmen der gemeinsemitischen Namengebung* (Stuttgart: W. Kohlhammer).
———(1953), *Das Buch Josua* (HKAT 7, Tübingen: J. C. B. Mohr [Paul Siebeck]; ²1953, ¹1938).
———(1960), *The History of Israel* (London: A. & C. Black; ¹1958).
———(1962), *Exodus* (OTL, London: SCM; # 1959).
———(1965), *Leviticus* (OTL, London: SCM; # 1962).
———(1968a), *Numbers* (OTL, London: SCM).
———(1968b), *Könige*, 1 (BKAT IX/1, Neukirchen-Vluyn: Neukirchener).
Nougayrol, J. (1955), *Le Palais Royal d'Ugarit*, 3 (Paris: Imprimerie Nationale–C. Klinksieck).
———(1956), *Le Palais Royal d'Ugarit*, 4 (Paris: Imprimerie Nationale–C. Klinksieck).
———(1968), 'Textes suméro-accadiens des archives et bibliothèques privées d'Ugarit. Textes religieux § 18 – RS 20.24 ("Panthéon d'Ugarit")', *Ugaritica* 5, 42–64.
O'Connor, M. (1986), 'Northwest Semitic Designations for Elective Social Affinities', *JANESCU* 18, 67–80.
Ogden, G. S. (1988), *Qoheleth* (Sheffield: SAP).
Oldenburg, U. (1969), *The Conflict between El and Ba'al in Canaanite Religion* (Leiden: Brill).
Olivier, J. P. J. (1972), 'Notes on the Ugaritic Month Names II', *JNSL* 2, 53–9.
Ollenburger, B. C. (1993), 'If Mortals Die, Will They Live Again? The Old Testament and Resurrection', *Ex Auditu* 9, 29–44.
Olme Lete, G. del (1986), 'The "Divine" Names of the Ugaritic Kings', *UF* 18, 83–95.
Östborn, G. (1956), *Yahweh and Baal* (Lund: Gleerup).
Oswalt, J. N. (1986), *The Book of Isaiah Chapters 1–39* (NICOT, Grand Rapids: Eerdmans).
Overholt, T. W. (1996), *Cultural Anthropology and the Old Testament* (Minneapolis: Fortress).
Pagolu, A. (1998), *The Religion of the Patriarchs* (JSOTSup 277, Sheffield: SAP).
Pardee, D. (1988), *Les textes para-mythologiques de la 24ᵉ campagne (1961)* (Paris: Editions Recherches sur les Civilisations).
———(1991), Review of B. Margalit, *The Ugaritic Poem of AQHT*, *JBL* 110, 326–7.
Paul, S. M. (1970), *Studies in the Book of the Covenant in the Light of Cuneiform and Biblical Law* (SVT 18, Leiden: Brill).
———(1991), *Amos* (Hermeneia, Minneapolis: Fortress).
Pedersen, J. (1926), *Israel. Its Life and Culture I–II* (London: OUP; # 1920).
———(1940), *Israel. Its Life and Culture III–IV* (London: OUP; # 1934).
Penglase, C. (1995), 'Some Concepts of Afterlife in Mesopotamia and Greece', in S. Cambell and A. Green (eds.), *The Archaeology of Death in the Ancient Near East* (Oxford: Oxbow), 192–5.

Perdue, L. G. (1974), 'The Riddles of Psalm 49', *JBL* 93, 533–42.

Peterson, D. L. (1979), 'Isaiah 28, A Redaction Critical Study', in P. J. Achtmeier (ed.), *SBL 1979 Seminar Papers*, 2 (Missoula: Scholars), 101–22.

Pham, X. H. T. (1999), *Mourning in the Ancient Near East and the Hebrew Bible* (JSOTSup 302; Sheffield: SAP).

Phillips, A. (1973), *Deuteronomy* (CBC, Cambridge: CUP).

Pitard, W. T. (1978), 'The Ugaritic Funerary Text RS 34.126', *BASOR* 232, 91–110.

———(1992), 'A New Edition of the "Rāpi'uma" Texts: *KTU* 1.20–22', *BASOR* 285, 33–77.

Pleins, J. D. (1996), 'Death and Endurance: Reassessing the Literary Structure and Theology of Psalm 49', *JSOT* 69, 19–27.

Podella, T. (1988), 'Grundzüge alttestamentlicher Jenseitsvorstellungen *šᵉʾôl*', *BN* 43, 70–89.

Pope, M. H. (1955), *El in the Ugaritic Texts* (SVT 2, Leiden: Brill).

———(1964), 'The Word *šaḥaṯ* in Job 9:31', *JBL* 83, 269–78.

———(1972), 'A Divine Banquet at Ugarit', in J. M. Efird (ed.), *The Use of the Old Testament in the New and Other Essays* (Fs. W. F. Stinespring, Durham: Duke University), 170–203.

———(1973), *Job* (AB 15, Garden City: Doubleday; ³1973, ²1965).

———(1977a), *Song of Songs* (AB 7C, Garden City: Doubleday).

———(1977b), 'Notes on the Rephaim Texts from Ugarit', in M. J. Ellis (ed.), *Essays on the Ancient Near East* (Mem. J. J. Finkelstein, Connecticut: Archon), 163–82.

———(1978), 'A Little Soul-Searching', *Maarav* 1, 25–31.

———(1981), 'The Cult of the Dead at Ugarit', in G. D. Young (ed.), *Ugarit in Retrospect* (Winona Lake: Eisenbrauns), 159–79.

———(1983), Review of C. E. L'Heureux, *Rank among the Canaanite Gods*, *BASOR* 251, 67–9.

Pope, M. H. and W. Röllig (1965), 'Syrien. Die Mythologie der Ugariter und Phönizier', in H. W. Haussig (ed.), *Wörterbuch der Mythologie*, 1 (Stuttgart: Ernst Klett), 217–312.

Porten, B. (1968), *Archives From Elephantine* (Berkeley: University of California).

Porter, J. R. (1976), *Leviticus* (CBC, Cambridge: CUP).

———(1978), 'Biblical Classics III. Johs. Pedersen: Israel', *ExpTim* 90, 36–40.

Procksch, O. (1930), *Jesaja*, 1 (KAT IX.1, Leipzig: A. Deichert).

Puech, E. (1985), Review of V. Cottini, *La vita futura nel libro dei Proverbi*, *RB* 92, 435–8.

———(1986–7), 'The Canaanite Inscriptions of Lachish and their Religious Background', *Tel Aviv* 13–14, 13–25.

———(1993), *La Croyance des Esséniens en la Vie Future*, 2 vols. (Paris: Gabalda).

Rabin, C. (1963), 'Hittite Words in Hebrew', *Or* 32, 113–39.

———(1967), '*ʿôg* / Og', *ErIsr* 8, 75*–76*, 251–4 (Hebrew).

Rad, G. von (1962), *Old Testament Theology*, 1 (London: Oliver & Boyd; # 1957).

———(1966), *Deuteronomy* (OTL, London: SCM; # 1964).

———(1972), *Genesis* (OTL, London: SCM; ^{3}1972, # ^{9}1972; ^{1}1961, # ^{1}1956).

———(1980), 'Statements of Faith in the Old Testament about Life and Death', in *God at Work in Israel* (Nashville: Abingdon; # 1974; first published 1938), 194–209.

Rahmani, L. Y. (1968), 'Jerusalem's Tomb Monuments on Jewish Ossuaries', *IEJ* 18, 220–25.

———(1981), 'Ancient Jerusalem's Funerary Customs and Tombs, 1, 2', *BA* 44, 171–7, 229–35.

———(1982), 'Ancient Jerusalem's Funerary Customs and Tombs, 3, 4', *BA* 45, 43–53, 109–19.

Reines, C. W. (1951), 'Hosea XII, 1', *JJS* 2, 156–7.

———(1954), 'Koheleth VII, 10', *JJS* 5, 86–7.

Reymond, P. (1958), *L'eau, sa Vie et sa Signification dans l'Ancien Testament* (SVT 6, Leiden: Brill).

Ringgren, H. (1963), *The Faith of the Psalmists* (London: SCM).

———(1966), *Israelite Religion* (London: SPCK; # 1963).

Robert, A. (1940), 'Le Yahwisme de Prov. 10:1 – 22:16; 25 – 29', in L.-H. Vincent (ed.), *Mémorial Lagrange* (Paris: Gabalda), 163–82.

Roberts, J. J. M. (1983), 'Isaiah 33: An Isaianic Elaboration of the Zion Tradition', in C. L. Meyers and M. O'Connor (eds.), *The Word of the Lord Shall Go Forth* (Fs. D. N. Freedman, Winona Lake: Eisenbrauns), 15–25.

Rogerson, J. W. (1978), *Anthropology and the Old Testament* (Oxford: Blackwell).

Rogerson, J. W. and J.W. McKay (1977a), *Psalms 1–50* (CBC, Cambridge: CUP).

———(1977b), *Psalms 51–100* (CBC, Cambridge: CUP).

———(1977c), *Psalms 101–150* (CBC, Cambridge: CUP).

Rosenbaum, J. (1979), 'Hezekiah's Reform and the Deuteronomistic Tradition', *HTR* 72, 23–43.

Rosenberg, R. (1981), 'The Concept of Biblical Sheol within the Context of Ancient Near Eastern Beliefs', Ph.D. dissertation, Harvard University.

Rouillard, H. and J. Tropper (1987), '*trpym*, rituels de guérison et culte des ancêtres d'après 1 Samuel xix 11–17 et les textes parallèles d'Assur et de Nuzi', *VT* 37, 340–61.

Rowley, H. H. (1976), *The Book of Job* (NCB, London: MMS; ^{2}1976, ^{1}1970).

Rudolph, W. (1966), *Hosea* (KAT XIII 1, Gütersloh: Gerd Mohn).

———(1971), *Joel–Amos–Obadja–Jona* (KAT XIII 1, Gütersloh: Gerd Mohn).

Rupprecht, K. (1970), '*ʿlh min hāʾāreṣ* (Ex. 1:10; Hos. 2:2): "sich des Landes bemächtigen"?', *ZAW* 82, 442–7.

Saggs, H. F. W. (1958), 'Some Ancient Semitic Conceptions of the Afterlife', *Faith and Thought* 90, 157–82.

Santos, E. C. dos (1973), *An Expanded Hebrew Index for the Hatch-Redpath Concordance to the Septuagint* (Jerusalem: Dugith, n/d, c. 1973).

Sarna, N. M. (1963), 'The Mythological Background of Job 18', *JBL* 82, 315–18.

———(1989), *Genesis* (JPS Torah Commentary, Phildaelphia: JPS)

Sasson, J. M. (1979), *Ruth* (Baltimore: Johns Hopkins).

Sawyer, J. F. A. (1973), 'Hebrew Words for the Resurrection of the Dead', *VT* 23, 218–34.

Schedl, C. (1964), '"Die Heiligen" und die "Herrlichen" in Psalm 16:1–4', *ZAW* 76, 171–5.

Schmid, H. H. (1971), '"Mein Gott, mein Gott, warum hast du mich verlassen?" Psalm 22 als Beispiel alttestamentlicher Rede von Krankheit und Tod', *Wort und Dienst* 11, 119–40.

Schmidt, B. B. (1994), *Israel's Beneficient Dead. Ancestor Cult and Necromancy in Ancient Israelite Religion and Tradition* (FAT 11, Tübingen: J. C. B. Mohr; repr. Winona Lake: Eisenbrauns, 1996).

———(1995), 'The Witch of En-Dor, 1 Samuel 28, and Ancient Near Eastern Necromancy', in M. Meyer and P. Mirecki (eds.), *Ancient Magic and Ritual Power* (Leiden: Brill), 111–29.

Schmidt, H. (1925), '*'ôḇ*', in K. Buddhe (ed.), *Vom Alten Testament* (Fs. K. Marti, BZAW 41, Giessen: A. Töpelmann), 253–61.

Schmitt, A. (1973), *Entrückung – Aufnahme – Himmelfahrt* (Stuttgart: Katholisches Bibelwerk).

Schmitt, G. (1970), *Du sollst keinen Frieden schliessen mit den Bewohnem des Landes* (Stuttgart: W. Kohlhammer).

Schwarz, G. (1974), '". . . zugunsten der Lebenden an die Toten"?', *ZAW* 86, 218–20.

Scott, R. B. Y. (1965), *Proverbs. Ecclesiastes* (AB 18, Garden City: Doubleday).

Scullion, J. J. (1972), 'Some Difficult Texts in Isaiah cc. 56–66 in the Light of Modern Scholarship', *UF* 4, 105–28.

Selms, A. van (1970), Review of N. J. Tromp, *Primitive Conceptions of Death and the Nether World in the Old Testament*, *UF* 2, 367–8.

———(1973), 'Isaiah 28:9–13: An Attempt to give a New Interpretation', *ZAW* 85, 332–9.

———(1975), 'A Systematic Approach to CTA 5,I,1–8', *UF* 7, 477–82.

Seybold, K. (1990), *Introducing the Psalms* (Edinburgh: T. & T. Clark; # 1986).

Seyrig, H. (1940), 'Les tessères palmyréniennes et le banquet rituel', in L.-H. Vincent (ed.), *Mémorial Lagrange* (Paris: Gabalda), 51–8.

Shafer, B. E. (ed.) (1991), *Religion in Ancient Egypt* (Ithaca: Cornell UP).

Shanks, H. (1996), 'Who – or What – Was Molech?', *BAR* 22.4, 13.

Simon, U. (1988), 'A Balanced Story: The Stern Prophet and the Kind Witch', *Prooftexts* 8, 159–71.

Smelik, K. A. D. (1979), 'The Witch at Endor: 1 Samuel 28 in Rabbinic and Christian Exegesis till 800 A.D.', *Vigiliae christianae* 33, 160–79.

———(1991), *Writings from Ancient Israel* (Edinburgh: T. & T. Clark; # 1984).
Smith, H. P. (1899), *A Critical and Exegetical Commentary on the Books of Samuel* (ICC, Edinburgh: T. & T. Clark).
Smith, M. S. (1990), *The Early History of God* (San Francisco: Harper & Row).
———(1993), 'The Invocation of the Deceased Ancestors in Psalm 49:12c', *JBL* 112, 105–7.
———(1994), *The Ugaritic Baal Cycle, Volume 1* (SVT 55, Leiden: Brill).
———(1996), Review of B. B. Schmidt, *Israel's Beneficient Dead*, *CBQ* 58, 724–5.
Smith, W. R. (1894), *Lectures on the Religion of the Semites* (London: A. & C. Black; [2]1894, [1]1889).
Snaith, N. H. (1964), 'Justice and Immortality', *Scottish Journal of Theology* 17, 309–24.
———(1967), *Leviticus and Numbers* (NCB, London: Nelson).
Soden, W. von (1962), Review of CAD 7/I-J, 21/Z, *Orientalische Literaturzeitung* 57, 483–6.
Soggin, J. A. (1972), *Joshua* (OTL, London: SCM; # 1970).
———(1987), *The Prophet Amos* (London: SCM; # 1982).
Sokoloff, M. (1990), *A Dictionary of Jewish Palestinian Aramaic of the Byzantine Period* (Ramat-Gan: Bar Ilan UP).
Soskice, J. M. (1985), *Metaphor and Religious Language* (Oxford: OUP).
Sparks, H. F. D. (1984), *The Apocryphal Old Testament* (Oxford: Clarendon).
Sperling, S. D. (1991), Review of B. Margalit, *The Ugaritic Poem of AQHT*, *CBQ* 53, 476–9.
Spronk, K. (1986), *Beatific Afterlife in Ancient Israel and in the Ancient Near East* (AOAT 219, Neukirchen-Vluyn: Neukirchener).
Stadelmann, L. I. J. (1970), *The Hebrew Conception of the World* (Rome: BIP).
Stähli, H. P. (1986), 'Tod und Leben in Alten Testament', *Theologie und Glaube* 76, 173–92.
Stamm, J. J. (1939), *Die akkadische Namengebung* (Leipzig; repr. Darmstadt: Wissenschaftliche Buchgesellschaft, 1968).
———(1955), 'Ein Vierteljahrhundert Psalmenforschung', *Theologische Rundschau* 23, 1–68.
Stieglitz, R. R. (1990), 'Ebla and the Gods of Canaan', in C. H. Gordon and G. A. Rendsburg (eds.), *Eblaitica*, 2 (Winona Lake: Eisenbrauns), 79–89.
Stern, E. (1982), *Material Culture of the Land of the Bible in the Persian Period 538–332 B.C.* (Warminster: Aris & Phillips; # 1973).
Stœbe, H. J. (1973), *Das erste Buch Samuelis* (KAT VIII.1, Gütersloh: Gerd Mohn).
Strauss, H. (1989), 'Über die Grenzen? Exegetische Betrachtungen zu 1Sam 28, 3–25', *BN* 50, 17–25.
Stuart, D. (1987), *Hosea–Jonah* (WBC 31, Waco: Word).

Stucky, R. A. (1973), 'Prêtres syriens. I. Palmyre', *Syria* 50, 163–80.

Sukenik, E. L. (1940), 'Arrangements for the Cult of the Dead in Ugarit and Samaria', in L.-H. Vincent (foreword), *Mémorial Lagrange* (Paris: Gabalda), 59–65.

Sutcliffe, E. F. (1946), *The Old Testament and the Future Life* (London: Burns Oates & Washbourne).

Swauger, J. L. (1966), 'Dolmen Studies in Palestine', *BA* 29, 106–14.

Tallqvist, K. (1934), *Sumerisch-akkadische Namen der Totenwelt* (Helsinki: Societas Orientalis Fennica).

Talmon, S. (1983), 'Biblical *rᵉpā'îm* and Ugaritic *rpu/i(m)*', *HAR* 7, 235–49.

Tappy, R. (1995), 'Did the Dead Ever Die in Biblical Judah?', Review of E. Bloch-Smith, *Judahite Burial Practices and Beliefs about the Dead*, *BASOR* 298, 59–68.

Tate, M. E. (1990), *Psalms 51–100* (WBC 20, Dallas: Word).

Taylor, J. B. (1969), *Ezekiel* (TOTC, London: IVP).

Taylor, J. G. (1988), 'A First and Last Thing to do in Mourning: *KTU* 1.161 and Some Parallels', in L. Eslinger and G. Taylor (eds.), *Ascribe to the Lord* (Mem. P. C. Craigie, JSOTSup 67, Sheffield: JSOT), 151–77.

Terrien, S. (1962), 'Amos and Wisdom', in B. W. Anderson and W. Harrelson (eds.), *Israel's Prophetic Heritage* (Fs. J. Muilenburg, London: SCM), 108–15.

———(1963), *Job* (Neuchâtel: Delachaux & Niestlé).

———(1978), *The Elusive Presence* (San Francisco: Harper & Row).

Thomas, D. W. (1933), 'En-Dor: A Sacred Spring?', *Palestine Exploration Fund* 65, 205–6.

———(1953), 'A Consideration of Some Unusual Ways of Expressing the Superlative in Hebrew', *VT* 3, 209–24.

———(1955), 'Textual and Philological Notes on Some Passages in the Book of Proverbs', in M. Noth and D. W. Thomas (eds.), *Wisdom in Israel and in the Ancient Near East* (Fs. H. H. Rowley, Leiden: Brill), 280–92.

Thompson, J. A. (1974), *Deuteronomy* (TOTC, Leicester: IVP).

———(1980), *Jeremiah* (NICOT, Grand Rapids: Eerdmans).

Thureau-Dangin, F. (1919), 'Un acte de donation de Marduk-zâkir-šumi', *Revue d'assyriologie et d'archéologie orientale* 16, 117–56.

Tigay, J. (1986), *You Shall Have No Other Gods* (Atlanta: Scholars).

Toorn, K. van der (1985), *Sin and Sanction in Israel and Mesopotamia* (Assen: Van Gorcum).

———(1988), 'Echoes of Judaean Necromancy in Isaiah 28,7–22', *ZAW* 100, 199–217.

———(1990), 'The Nature of the Biblical Teraphim in the Light of the Cuneiform Evidence', *CBQ* 52, 203–22.

———(1991), 'Funerary Rituals and Beatific Afterlife in Ugaritic and the Bible', *Bibliotheca Orientalis* 48, 40–66.

———(1993), 'Ilib and the "God of the Father"', *UF* 25, 379–87.

———(1994), 'Gods and Ancestors in Emar and Nuzi', *Zeitschrift für Assyriologie* 84, 38–59.

———(1996a), *Family Religion in Babylonia, Syria and Israel* (Brill: Leuven).

———(1996b), 'Ancestors and Anthroponyms: Kinship Terms as Theophoric Elements in Hebrew Names', *ZAW* 108, 1–11.

Tournay, R. (1959), 'Le psaume cxli', *VT* 9, 58–64.

———(1962), 'Relectures bibliques concernant la vie future et l'angélologie', *RB* 69, 481–505.

Tromp, N. J. (1969), *Primitive Conceptions of Death and the Nether World in the Old Testament* (BibOr 21, Rome: PBI).

Tropper, J. (1989), *Nekromantie* (AOAT 223, Neukirchen-Vluyn: Neukirchener).

Tsukimoto, A. (1985), *Untersuchungen zur Totenpflege (*kispum*) im alten Mesopotamien* (AOAT 216, Neukirchen-Vluyn: Neukirchener).

———(1989), 'Emar and the Old Testament – Preliminary Remarks', *Annual of the Japanese Biblical Institute* 15, 3–24.

Tsumura, D. T. (1988), 'A "Hyponymous" Word Pair: *'arṣ* and *thm(t)* in Hebrew and Ugaritic', *Bib* 69, 258–69.

———(1989), *The Earth and the Waters in Genesis 1 and 2* (JSOTSup 83, Sheffield: JSOT).

———(1993), 'The Interpretation of the Ugaritic Funerary Text KTU 1.161', in E. Matsushima (ed.), *Official Cult and Popular Religion in the Ancient Near East* (Heidelberg: C. Winter), 40–55.

Tur-Sinai, N. H. (1967), *The Book of Job* (Jerusalem: Kiryath Sepher; [2]1967, [1]1957).

Tuell, S. S. (1992), *The Law of the Temple in Ezekiel 40–48* (HSM 49, Atlanta: Scholars).

Ungnad, A. (1914), *Babylonische Briefe aus der Zeit der Hammurapi-Dynastie* (Leipzig: J. C. Heinrichs).

Ussishkin, D. (1970), 'The Necropolis from the Time of the Kingdom of Judah at Silwan, Jerusalem', *BA* 33, 34–46.

———(1974), 'Tombs from the Israelite Period at Tel 'Eton', *Tel Aviv* 1, 109–27.

———(1983), 'Excavations at Tel Lachish 1978–1983: Second Preliminary Report', *Tel Aviv* 10, 97–175.

Vannoy, J. R. (1974), 'The use of the word *hā'ᵉlōhîm* in Exodus 21:6 and 22:7,8', in J. H. Skilton (ed.), *The Law and the Prophets* (Fs. O. T. Allis, Philadelphia: Presbyterian and Reformed), 225–41.

Vaughan, P. H. (1974), *The Meaning of 'Bāmâ' in the Old Testament* (Cambridge: CUP).

Vaux, R. de (1961), *Ancient Israel. Its Life and Institutions* (London: DLT; # 1958–60).

———(1973), *Archaeology and the Dead Sea Scrolls* (London: OUP).

———(1978), *The Early History of Israel* (London: DLT; # 1971).

Vermes, G. (1995), *The Dead Sea Scrolls in English* (London: Penguin, [4]1995).

Vermeylen, J. (1974), 'La composition littéraire de l'apocalypse d'Isaie', *ETL* 50, 5–38.

Vieyra, M. (1961), 'Les noms du "mundus" en hittite et en assyrien et la pythonisse d'Endor', *RHA* 19, 47–55.
Virolleaud, C. (1934), 'La mort de Baal', *Syria* 15, 305–36.
———(1940), 'Les Rephaim', *Revue des études sémitiques* 7, 77–83.
———(1951), 'Six textes de Ras Shamra', *Syria* 28, 163–79.
Wächter, L. (1967), *Der Tod im Alten Testament* (Stuttgart: Calwer).
Wakeman, M. K. (1969), 'The Biblical Earth Monster in the Cosmogonic Combat Myth', *JBL* 88, 313–20.
———(1973), *God's Battle with the Monster* (Leiden: Brill).
Wallace, H. N. (1985), *The Eden Narrative* (HSM 32, Atlanta: Scholars).
Ward, E. F. de (1977), 'Superstition and Judgment: Archaic Methods of Finding a Verdict', *ZAW* 89, 1–19.
Waterhouse, S. D. and R. Ibach (1975), 'Heshbon 1973: The Topographical Survey', *Andrews University Seminary Studies* 13, 217–33.
Waterman, L. (1952), 'Note on Job 28:4', *JBL* 71, 167–70.
Watson, W. G. E. (1983), 'Lexical Notes', *Newsletter for Ugaritic Studies* 36, 17–19.
———(1984), 'The Hebrew Word-pair *'sp // qbṣ*', *ZAW* 96, 426–34.
Watts, J. D. W. (1985), *Isaiah 1–33* (WBC 24, Waco: Word).
———(1987), *Isaiah 34–66* (WBC 25, Waco: Word).
Webb, B. (1996), *The Message of Isaiah* (Leicester: IVP).
Weinfeld, M. (1972), *Deuteronomy and the Deuteronomic School* (Oxford: Clarendon).
———(1991a), *Deuteronomy 1–11* (AB 5A, New York: Doubleday).
———(1991b), Review of J. Day, *Molech: A god of human sacrifice in the Old Testament*, *JTS* 42, 827–8.
Weise, M. (1960), 'Jesaja 57:5f.', *ZAW* 72, 25–32.
Weiser, A. (1949), *Das Buch der zwölf kleinen Propheten*, 1 (ATD 24, Göttingen: V & R).
———(1962), *The Psalms* (OTL, London: SCM; # ^{5}1959).
Wenham, G. J. (1979), *Leviticus* (NICOT, Grand Rapids: Eerdmans).
———(1981), *Numbers* (TOTC; Leicester: IVP).
———(1987), *Genesis 1–15* (WBC, Dallas: Word).
Wensinck, A. J. (1918), *The Ocean in the Literature of the Western Semites* (Amsterdam: J. Müller).
Wernberg-Møller, P. (1958), 'Two notes', *VT* 8, 305–8.
Westermann, C. (1960), 'Die Begriffe für Fragen und Suchen im Alten Testament', *Kerygma und Dogma* 6, 2–30; repr. in *Forschung am Alten Testament. Gesammelte Studien II* (Munich: Chr. Kaiser, 1974), 162–90.
———(1969), *Isaiah 40–66* (OTL, London: SCM; # 1966).
———(1984), *Genesis 1–11* (Minneapolis: Augsburg; # 1974).
———(1985), *Genesis 12–36* (Minneapolis: Augsburg; # 1981).
———(1986), *Genesis 37–50* (Minneapolis: Augsburg; # 1982).
Wevers, J. W. (1982), *Ezekiel* (NCB, London: MMS; ^{1}1969).
Whitley, C. F. (1978), 'The Language and Exegesis of Isaiah 8:16–23', *ZAW* 90, 28–43.
Whybray, R. N. (1965), *Wisdom in Proverbs* (SBT 45, London: SCM).

———(1972), *The Book of Proverbs* (CBC, Cambridge: CUP).
———(1974), *Isaiah 40–66* (NCB, London: MMS).
———(1978), *Thanksgiving for a Liberated Prophet* (JSOTSup 4, Sheffield: JSOT).
———(1989), *Ecclesiastes* (NCB, London: MMS).
Widengren, G. (1954), Review of M. Seligson, *The Meaning of* npš mt *in the Old Testament*, *VT* 4, 97–102.
Wigram, G. V. (1890), *Englishman's Hebrew and Chaldee Concordance* (London: Bagster, [1]1843, [5]1890).
Wildberger, H. (1978), *Jesaja 13–27* (BKAT X/2, Neukirchen-Vluyn: Neukirchener).
———(1982), *Jesaja 28–39* (BKAT X/3, Neukirchen-Vluyn: Neukirchener).
———(1991), *Isaiah 1–12* (Minneapolis: Augsburg, # 1972).
Willesen, F. (1958a), 'The Yālid in Hebrew Society', *ST* 12, 192–210.
———(1958b), 'The Philistine Corps of the Scimitar from Gath', *JSS* 3, 327–35.
Williams, R. J. (1967), *Hebrew Syntax: An Outline* (Toronto: University of Toronto).
Williamson, H. G. M. (1982), *1 and 2 Chronicles* (NCB, London: MMS).
Wohlstein, H. (1961), 'Zu den altisraelitischen Vorstellungen von Toten- und Ahnengeistern', *Biblische Zeitschrift* 5, 30–38.
Wilson, R. R. (1979), 'Anthropology and the Study of the Old Testament', *Union Seminary Quarterly Review* 34, 175–81.
Wolff, H. W. (1952–3), 'Der grosse Jesreeltag (Hosea 2,1–3)', *Evangelische Theologie* 12, 78–104; repr. in *Gesammelte Studien zum Alten Testament* (Munich: Chr. Kaiser, 1964), 151–81.
———(1974a), *Anthropology of the Old Testament* (London: SCM; # 1973).
———(1974b), *Hosea* (Hermeneia, Philadelphia: Fortress; # 1965).
———(1977), *Joel and Amos* (Hermeneia, Philadelphia: Fortress; # [2]1975, [1]1969).
———(1986), *Obadiah and Jonah* (Minneapolis: Augsburg; # 1977).
Wood, W. C. (1916), 'The Religion of Canaan', *JBL* 35, 1–133, 167–279.
Woudstra, M. H. (1981), *The Book of Joshua* (NICOT, Grand Rapids: Eerdmans).
Wright, G. E. (1953), 'Deuteronomy', in G. A. Buttrick et al. (eds.), *The Interpreter's Bible*, 2 (New York: Abingdon).
Wyatt, N. (1998), *Religious Texts From Ugarit* (Sheffield: SAP).
Xella, P. (1980), 'Sur la nourriture des morts', in B. Alster (ed.), *Death in Mesopotamia* (Copenhagen: Akademisk), 151–60.
———(1993), 'Le dieu B'L 'Z dans une nouvelle inscription phénicien de Kition (Chypre)', *Studi epigrafici e linguistici* 10, 61–70.
Yamauchi, E. M. (1994), 'Persians', in A. J. Hoerth et al. (eds.), *Peoples of the Old Testament World* (Grand Rapids: Baker).
———(1998), 'Life, Death and the Afterlife in the Ancient Near East', in R. N. Longenecker (ed.), *Life in the Face of Death* (Grand Rapids: Eerdmans), 21–50.

Yassine, K. (1985), 'The Dolmens: Construction and Dating Reconsidered', *BASOR* 259, 63–9.
Yee, G. A. (1987), *Composition and Tradition in the Book of Hosea* (SBLDS 102, Atlanta: Scholars).
Young, E. J. (1965), *The Book of Isaiah*, 1 (NICOT, Grand Rapids: Eerdmans).
———(1969), *The Book of Isaiah*, 2 (NICOT, Grand Rapids: Eerdmans).
———(1972), *The Book of Isaiah*, 3 (NICOT, Grand Rapids: Eerdmans).
Zandee, J. (1960), *Death as an Enemy according to Ancient Egyptian Conceptions* (Leiden: Brill).
Zenger, E. (1986), *Das Buch Ruth* (ZBK AT 8, Zurich: Theologischer).
Zimmerli, W. (1979), *Ezekiel*, 1 (Hermeneia, Philadelphia: Fortress; # 1969).
———(1983), *Ezekiel*, 2 (Hermeneia, Philadelphia: Fortress; # 1969).
Zolli, E. (1950), 'Die "Heiligen" in Psalm 16', *TZ* 6, 149–50.
Zori, N. (1952), 'New Light on Endor', *PEQ* 84, 114–17.
Zwickel, W. (1989), 'Über das angebliche Verbrennen von Räucherwerk bei der Bestattung eines Königs', *ZAW* 101, 266–77.

Author Index

Texts Index

Proverbs